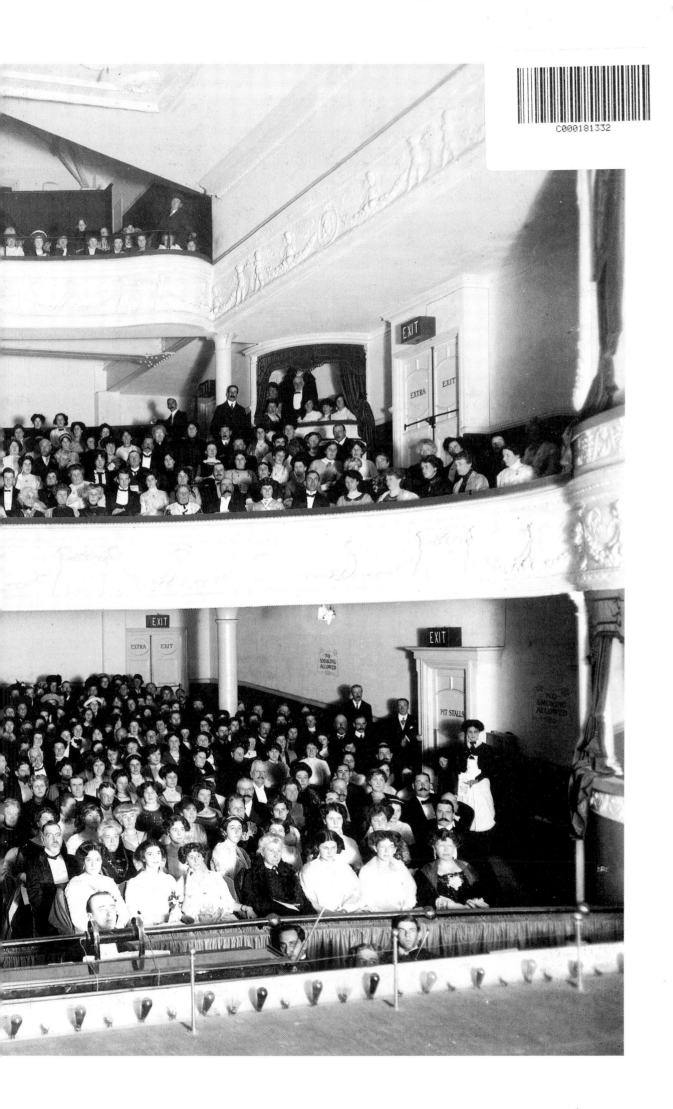

CINEMA WEST SUSSEX

The First Hundred Years

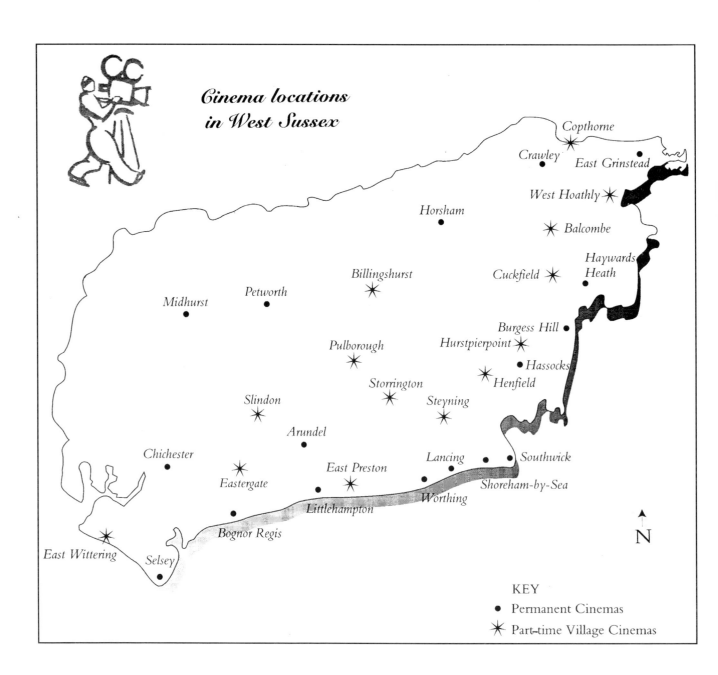

Cinema locations in West Sussex

Copthorne

Crawley

East Grinstead

West Hoathly

Horsham

Balcombe

Haywards Heath

Billingshurst

Cuckfield

Petworth

Midhurst

Burgess Hill

Hurstpierpoint

Pulborough

Hassocks

Storrington

Henfield

Slindon

Steyning

Arundel

Chichester

Lancing

Southwick

East Preston

Eastergate

Shoreham-by-Sea

Littlehampton

Worthing

Bognor Regis

East Wittering

Selsey

N

KEY
● Permanent Cinemas
✳ Part-time Village Cinemas

CINEMA WEST SUSSEX

The First Hundred Years

Allen Eyles • Frank Gray • Alan Readman

Foreword by Lord Attenborough

Phillimore

1996

Published by
PHILLIMORE & CO. LTD.
Shopwyke Manor Barn, Chichester, West Sussex
for
West Sussex County Council

ISBN 1 86077 035 5

WEST SUSSEX PAPERS

◆

present new research into
the county's history and heritage
in a scholarly yet popular format.

It is an occasional series but aims to publish
at least one new title each year.

For details contact:

The County Archivist
West Sussex Record Office
County Hall
Chichester
PO19 1RN

Front cover: main picture: A packed audience at Poole's Picture Palace in Chichester; *small pictures, from top:* Filming at Bosham Regatta in 1911; Joan Morgan, star of the Shoreham film studio; Alma Taylor in Cecil Hepworth's *Tansy*, filmed near Burpham in 1921; Horsham's Central Picture Hall, the county's first purpose-built cinema; The Worthing Odeon as it looked in 1983; Bognor Regis Film Society shooting *Murder at the Theatre Royal* in 1936; The rich splendour of the auditorium of the Ritz in Horsham.

Printed and Bound in Great Britain by
BUTLER AND TANNER LTD.
London and Frome

Contents

List of Illustrations

Acknowledgements

The authors gratefully acknowledge the many people who have kindly permitted reproduction of their photographs in this book.

Sue Beaumont, 18-20, 24; British Film Institute, 1, 3, 4, 8-11, 16, 25, 165; Chichester Institute of Higher Education, 66, 77; Annette and Jeannette Collins, 213, 214, 216; Nora E. Collins, 125-27; Connaught Theatre, Worthing, 234; Cecil Cramp, 64, 65, 67, 68, 71, 72, 98, 110, 122-24, 133, 138, 143, 152, 168, 169, 207, 222, 231, 232; Mervyn Cutten, 59, 60, 62, 70, 95; East Grinstead Town Museum, 135, 139; D. Robert Elleray, 228, 229; Allen Eyles, 57, 58, 79-81, 82, 83, 86, 92, 102-5, 115-19, 128-32, 140, 144, 146-50, 155-63, 171-73, 175, 181-85, 188, 189, 198, 202, 203, 205, 206, 223-25, 237, 238, 242, 243, 246, 247, 250, 251, 255. From the Allen Eyles collection, photographs are reproduced by courtesy of: Sylvia Adams (86); T.J. Braybon & Son and John Fernee (115-19, 146-50, 251); J. Lewis (131); John Maltby and Odeon Theatres (82, 83, 188, 189, 203, 205, 246, 247); Ray Packham and John Fernee (255); Photoview and Granada Theatres (102-105); and Trevor Povey (223-25).

John Fernee, 87-91; George Godden, 26; Ken Green, 93, 96; Owen Gwatkin, 28; Joan and Ron Ham, 233, 257; Leslie Holden, 108, 109, 111; Horsham Arts Centre, 176-79; Horsham Museum, 166, 167; Ron Iden, 30, 33, 36, 37, 41; Peter Jerrome, 212; Alan Lambert, 210; Littlehampton Museum, 197, 199, 201; Joan Morgan, 21-3; Tony Moss, 69, 84, 107, 121, 141, 142, 145, 153, 154, 190, 194, 204, 236, 240, 241, 244, 245, 248, 252. From the Tony Moss collection, photographs are reproduced by courtesy of: Richard Boaste (236); Geoff Jones (248); John Maltby and Odeon Theatres (204); and Kevin S. Wheelan (240, 241).

David Nicholls, 191, 239; Barbara Ovstedal, 76; Malcolm Powell, 136; Lilian Rogers, 164; John Simmons, 211; Keith Smith, 253; South East Film & Video Archive, 5, 6; Jack Tupper, 217-21; West Sussex Library Service, 53, 209, 230; West Sussex Record Office, 2, 12-15, 17, 27, 29, 31, 40, 42-52, 54-6, 61, 63, 73-5, 78, 85, 94, 97, 99-101, 106, 112-14, 120, 134, 137, 151, 170, 174, 180, 186, 187, 192, 193, 195, 196, 200, 208, 215, 226, 227, 235, 249, 254, 256; Valerie Williamson, 7; Vera Worthington, 32, 34, 35, 38, 39.

Foreword

Cinema is, quite simply, *the* art form of the 20th century. Utterly new, utterly revolutionary when it first caught the public's imagination 100 years ago, there is now nothing, in my opinion, that can ever match the compulsive magic of that big screen in a darkened auditorium.

Cinema 100 has provided a platform for a truly nation-wide celebration. Events have reached beyond the cinemas, into schools, galleries and concert halls; and onto radio, television, records and postage stamps.

The UK has made, and continues to make, a major contribution to world cinema and Cinema 100 is an opportunity for all of us to celebrate this unique medium, to foster a more profound knowledge and awareness and, above all, to encourage everyone to experience the joys of the movies.

I am pleased that in West Sussex there should be a tangible legacy of the centenary in the form of this new book on the history of film-making and cinema in the county. It tells a fascinating story of the work of great film

pioneers, of the unique glasshouse studio built on Shoreham Beach and of the often under-praised contribution made by amateur cinematography. The book also describes how the new sensation of moving pictures first arrived in music halls and fairgrounds and chronicles the history of the county's cinemas from the earliest picture palaces to the present day.

Drawing on new research, enhanced by personal recollections, this is a timely contribution to cinema literature and will, I am sure, be of great interest not only to historians but to all who have affection for the cinema.

LORD ATTENBOROUGH CBE
Chairman—Cinema 100 National Council

THEATRE ROYAL
BOGNOR REGIS

Proprietors
W. N. & C. J. TATE

General Manager
W. N. TATE

Resident Manager
BETTY TATE

Visited by all the Leading Touring Companies

Bookings for 1934 Season include

LABURNUM GROVE
THE DESERT SONG
BITTER SWEET
RICHARD OF BORDEAUX
LADIES' NIGHT
THE DUBARRY
TEN MINUTE ALIBI
THE BRONTES
NICE GOINGS ON
THE WIND & THE RAIN
MOTHER OF PEARL
WILD VIOLETS
WALTZES FROM VIENNA
Etc., Etc.

'Phone: BOGNOR REGIS 212

PIER THEATRE & PICTUREDROME

Managing Directors: M. W. SHANLY and S. CARTER

Phone
Picturedrome
138

Continuous 3 p.m. to 10-30

Sundays at 8

Where
Everybody
Goes

Phone
Pier 77

Fully
Licensed
Buffet
Open 6 to 10

Afternoon Teas

Concert Party Daily at
3 and 8 in Pier Hall

Fully
Licensed
Buffet
Open
6 to 10

Dancing in
Sea Pavilion
Nightly 8 to 11
During Season

Diving Exhibitions
from Pier Head

Preface

The Centenary of Cinema offers an opportunity to commemorate for the first time the place of West Sussex in film and cinema history.

It has stimulated research into the associations of the county with the pioneers of the British film industry and into the rôle of the gifted amateurs who stepped into the void left by the collapse of the studios.

It has uncovered the stories of the travelling film showmen who introduced the new wonder of animated photographs to the public halls, pier pavilions and fairgrounds of the late 1890s, and it has brought together the histories of the picture palaces and super cinemas of the county.

The history of cinemas, it has often been said, is an imprecise study, by virtue of the nature of the subject and its source material, and the researcher, even if he were to scour every page of every local newspaper, may still be thwarted in some instances by the absence of recorded evidence. For the early period in particular, it is an area in which much knowledge is still confined to personal memory or to the files of the local historian. Nevertheless, it is trusted that the research inherent in this book will ensure its place as a valuable reference work, and the hope is that it will encourage those who have special knowledge to contribute to the cinema archive which is now being compiled at the County Record Office.

We are fortunate to have brought together here the expertise of two scholars, Frank Gray of the University of Brighton, an authority on the early film industry, and Allen Eyles, a prolific author on cinema history.

We have drawn upon the extensive resources of the County Record Office and the County Library Service in West Sussex, plus the specialist collections at the British Library and British Film Institute, and our thanks are extended to their dedicated and helpful staffs. Much is owed to the County Archivist, Richard Childs, for his support and help in making this book possible, and to Kim Leslie for his advice and guidance throughout the project.

Many people have given generously of their special knowledge in the course of compiling this book, and others have kindly allowed use to be made of their research, documents and photographs. They are referred to in the text and in the source references, but especial thanks must be given here to Sue Beaumont, Annette and Jeannette Collins, Daphne Cox, Cecil Cramp, Mervyn Cutten, Henryetta Edwards, Barbara Ely, John Fernee, Michael Goldsmith, Ken Green, Tony Hounsome, Ron Iden, Peter Jerrome, John Milbank, Joan Morgan, Tony Moss, Martin O'Neill, Barbara Ovstedal, Roland Puttock, Sir Sydney Samuelson, Bill Stamp, Jack and Mollie Tupper, Dennis E. Williams, Valerie Williamson, John Willmer, Fred Windsor and Vera Worthington.

On the production side many thanks are owed to photographer David Nicholls for copying photographs and documents and to Morwenna Wells, Gillian Fowler and Karen Orkibi of the Graphic Design section of the County Secretariat at County Hall for their meticulous work in scanning and enhancing all the illustrations for this book. Grateful thanks are also extended to Ann Hudson for indexing and to the publishers, especially Noel Osborne, the Managing Director, Nicola Willmot, Production Manager, and Christine Hanson, Production Assistant, for all their help and advice.

Finally, may we dedicate this book to the memory of all those film-makers, travelling showmen and picture palace managers who brought the wonder of the silver screen to West Sussex a hundred years ago.

ALAN READMAN

West Sussex Record Office

I

IN THE BEGINNING

Few inventions have affected our 20th-century civilisation more profoundly than the cinema. It is now a major economic, political and cultural force but it began as a mere novelty one hundred years ago, and owed its beginning to the amalgamation of a series of existing technologies and to the inspiration of a handful of pioneers in France, Britain and America.

1 Robert William Paul—the first film-maker in Sussex.

THE BIRTH OF CINEMA

On 28 December 1895 thirty-three people gathered in the Indian Room at the Grand Café on the Boulevard des Capucines in Paris and paid to watch an exhibition of moving pictures projected by the Lumière brothers on their Cinématographe. Without knowing so, they were making history, for this was the first public film show before a paying audience. They were witnessing, in other words, the birth of cinema.

Within ten weeks the Cinématographe had arrived in London, with the first cinema screening at the old Empire Music Hall in Leicester Square on 7 March 1896, and later that month, on 25 March, it made its first appearance in the provinces, at the Pandora Gallery opposite the West Pier in Brighton.

It was to be a matter of some months before, at the Pier Pavilion, Worthing, audiences in West Sussex were introduced to the 'new wonder of the age'. Here it was, on Monday 31 August 1896, that Lieutenant Walter Cole presented a programme of 'Electric Animated Photographs' which the local press anticipated would prove 'the greatest sensation of the Worthing entertainment season'.[1]

It is these events, the hundredth anniversary of the first paying film audiences, which are commemorated in 1996 in this country as Cinema 100, the Centenary of Cinema.

2 Early film-making at Bosham.

ORIGINS OF MOVING PICTURES

Of course the history of film itself goes back earlier. It drew upon three existing concepts: the magic lantern, optical toys and photography.

The magic lantern introduced the phenomenon of projected pictures. It dated back to 1665 and, in its improved form in the late 19th century, with photographic images replacing hand-drawn slides, it enabled itinerant show-men and local clergymen to entertain audiences with illustrated lectures and views of foreign lands.

Optical toys, such as Plateau's Phénakistiscope and Horner's Zoëtrope developed in the 1830s, explored the concept of moving pictures. They exploited the principle of persistence of vision, whereby images shown in rapid succession appear to the human eye as one continuous moving picture. Sold for amusement, by giving the impression of movement and the sensation of life, their principle was to form the basis of film-making.

The technical advances in photography since its inception in the 1820s, notably the work of Eadweard Muybridge and Etienne Marey, and the commercial provision of celluloid roll film by George Eastman, were such that by the late 1880s the technical pre-conditions for the existence of cinema—the camera apparatus, high-speed photography, and film capable of projection—were all in place.

THE PIONEERS

Moving pictures began their viable commercial life with the film camera and viewer invented by William Kennedy Laurie Dickson, 'the father of film-making', at Thomas Edison's research laboratory in the United States. However, the Kinetoscope, the viewing equipment, was basically a peep-show machine, capable of use by one person at a time, and it was the Lumière brothers, Auguste and Louis, who in France in 1895 developed their Cinématographe for projecting films onto a screen. At the same time in England Robert William Paul, a scientific instrument maker from London and Britain's first film-maker, produced his Theatrograph, subsequently renamed the Animatograph.[2]

It was this equipment which the Lumières and Paul took to Leicester Square in March 1896, to the Empire and the Alhambra respectively, the first venues in England to present films on a regular nightly basis to paying audiences. By the end of the year the new animated photographs had been shown in public halls, assembly rooms, corn exchanges, pier pavilions and fairgrounds throughout the country.

There, audiences would marvel at the flickering images projected before them, and although it would take a while to take root as part of the local entertainment scene and would be some years before the emergence of the first full-time purpose-built picture palaces, the age of the silver screen had dawned.

Early Film-makers in West Sussex

Throughout the country there now emerged a number of pioneers inspired by the Lumières and Paul to make their own films. There was a concentration along the South Coast taking advantage of the favourable weather, good light, attractive scenery and convenient communications with London.

Commercial film-making began in Sussex in 1896 and for the next 25 years first Hove and then Shoreham were significant centres of film production. The first film to be made in Sussex was the one-minute view of Brighton beach shot by Robert Paul in June 1896. He was followed by Esme Collings, the first Sussex film-maker, who produced a number of 'animated photographs' of seaside scenes during the rest of that year. They were followed by the most important Sussex pioneers of the new medium: G.A. Smith and James Williamson. They both acquired cameras and projectors in 1896 and each would build his own film studio in Hove. From 1899 to 1914, film audiences in Sussex and across the world viewed comedies and dramas made for their kinematograph companies. For the purposes of this history, Smith will provide the focus as he lived for many years in Southwick.

G.A. Smith—Sussex Film Pioneer

George Albert Smith (1864-1959) was a founder of the British film industry. He began as a popular entertainer and magic lanternist. In 1892 he acquired the lease to St Ann's Well Garden in Hove. This was only a short distance from Brighton and the seafront. He cultivated this site so that it became a popular pleasure garden. A Hove newspaper described it as, 'This delightful retreat ... presided over by the genial Mr. G. Albert Smith, is now open ... In the hot weather the refreshing foliage of the wooded retreat is simply perfect, while one can enjoy a cup of Pekoe in the shade.' Lawn tennis, 'ferns, flowers, grapes and cucumbers for sale in the glass houses', a gypsy fortune-teller, a monkey house, lantern exhibitions given by Smith of 'dissolving views' and the occasional 'thrilling parachute descent' provided it with a distinctive character. The garden would also become the location for his 'film factory'.

Smith saw and appreciated the Lumière programme in Leicester Square in March 1896 and must have been impressed by R.W. Paul's great success with the new medium during that year. Paul's films had been presented in Brighton and Worthing. At the end of 1896 he acquired his first camera. Barnes lists 31 films made by Smith in 1897. The few which have survived still display a remarkable charm and fascination and show how quickly he had acquired an understanding of how to work within the confines of 75 feet of film.[1]

3 George Albert Smith of Hove and Southwick—an innovative figure in the early film industry.

4 James Williamson—another Sussex film pioneer.

By 1898, with *Santa Claus*, he was using superimposition to effect the arrival of Santa. As a magic lanternist, he understood the cutting techniques perfected with biunial and triunial (two-lensed and three-lensed) lanterns and brought this consciousness to his film-making. Smith made only the studio shot of the train carriage in *The Kiss in the Tunnel* (1899) but when he inserted it into Hepworth's phantom ride, *View From an Engine Front—Train Leaving Tunnel*, he created an edited film which demonstrated a new sense of continuity and simultaneity across three shots. This filmic imagination was radical for the time and it continued to develop in the next year. *As Seen Through a Telescope, Grandma's Reading Glass, The House That Jack Built* and *Let Me Dream Again*, all of 1900, were remarkable for the interpolative use of close-ups, subjective and objective point-of-view shots, the creation of dream-time and the use of reversing. Smith was instrumental in the development of continuity editing. He taught his contemporaries how to create a filmed sequence.

By the late 1890s, Smith had developed a successful commercial film production and processing business. His clients included David Devant, Charles Goodwin Norton and John Benett-Stanford. Chemicals were purchased from the Hove chemist and fellow Sussex film pioneer—James Williamson. At 'St Ann's Well and Wild Garden' in 1897 he turned the pump house into a space for developing and printing and in the grounds from 1899 he built a 'glasshouse' film studio. His largest customer became the Warwick Trading Company. Through this relationship, Smith became part of the Company and developed a long partnership with its then managing director, Charles Urban. By 1902 Smith was referred to by Warwick as the manager of its 'Brighton Studio & Film Works'. The two-colour additive process known as Kinemacolor would dominate the rest of his career in film. Urban acquired the Lee and Turner process in 1902 and financed Smith to develop it. Probably as a result, he would produce no significant films after *Dorothy's Dream* and *Mary Jane's Mishap* in 1903. In that year he gave up the lease on St Ann's Well.

By this time he had built a new home at Roman Crescent, Southwick, and erected behind it what he called 'Laboratory Lodge'. This is where Kinemacolor was developed. The first demonstration of Kinemacolor took place on 1 May 1908, with the first public demonstration following in early 1909. Special presentations of this new colour system also took place in Paris and New York. For this work, Smith was awarded a Silver Medal by the Royal Society of Arts. Urban turned Kinemacolor into a new enterprise—the Natural Colour Kinemacolor Company. It had success in the period 1910 to 1913, producing over 100 short features at its studios in Hove and Nice. A patent suit brought against Kinemacolor by William Friese-Greene in 1914 would lead to its collapse and end Smith's life in the film business. Hove Museum & Art Gallery with the South East Film & Video Archive are engaged in a major research project on the work of Smith and Williamson.

DICKSON AT WORTHING

DIRECTOR

In 1898 'the father of film-making' arrived in the county. William Kennedy Laurie Dickson (1860-1935) in the early 1890s had invented the first viable 35mm film camera (the Kinetograph), shot the first films on strips of 35mm Eastman cellulose nitrate and designed the film viewer (the Kinetoscope). This work was conducted at the Edison research laboratory at West Orange, New Jersey. The films, cameras and projectors of A. & L. Lumière and R.W. Paul were all indebted to Dickson's achievements.

By 1895, Dickson realised the significance of this new medium. He conceived of a grand vision for the future of moving pictures.

> The invalid, the isolated country recluse, and the harassed business man can indulge in needed recreation, without undue expenditure, without fear of weather, and without the sacrifice of health or important engagements. Not only our own resources but those of the entire world will be at our command. The advantages to students and historians will be immeasurable. Instead of dry and misleading accounts, tinged with the exaggerations of the chroniclers' minds, our archives will be enriched by the vitalised pictures of great national scenes, instinct with all the glowing personalities which characterised them.[2]

Dickson left Edison in 1895 and helped to establish the American Mutoscope and Biograph Company and later its British division. The American Biograph arrived at the Palace Theatre of Varieties, London, in 1897 and began to delight audiences for many years with a programme of topical films of very good photographic quality. The Company's unique use of 70mm film, as devised by Dickson, produced a sharp, large image which filled the theatre's proscenium arch. Dickson took the responsibility for directing most of the films produced by the Company outside the United States. To capture typical scenes of the English seaside, Dickson arrived in Worthing in early April 1898.

On 6-7 April, Dickson made at least seven films in the town, but most are connected to two specific events. The first three were shot on the 6th and relate to the launch of the Worthing lifeboat: *Emerging from the Boathouse*, *Entering the Water* and *Coming Ashore*. The other works were made on the following day: a water polo match at West Worthing Baths, views of the steamboat 'Brighton Queen' approaching Worthing Pier, the disembarking of her passengers and a view of promenaders on the Worthing seafront. The *Optical Magic Lantern Journal* in its issue of May 1898 produced a full report on Dickson on the beach.

> On the 6th April the inhabitants of Worthing were suddenly startled by the report of a cannon, which meant to those 'not in the know', a ship in distress. Consequently crowds gathered quickly on the seafront, hastening westwards along the Marine Parade as far as the flagstaff opposite the coastguard station, where the lifeboat was ominously emerging from its shelter. Great excitement prevailed; four horses were connected, the crew donning their coats of cork and mounting with all the speed their pet-life saving apparatus—one of the many monuments of England's bene-ficence. Soon the command was give, 'Let her go!' On this occasion, however, that command had a double meaning, and many in the crowd were greatly puzzled as to the meaning of all they saw. Close to the esplanade stood a horse with a heavy cart behind it, laden with what connoisseurs called electric batteries, which send their mysterious powers through a red double cord up to a huge camera mounted on a rigid iron tripod, and inside of this instrument there was a reel holding a sensitised

CINEMA

film about 200 feet long. This, too, was 'let go', to run its entire length down behind a lens, recording many impressions per second of the interesting procession rushing by towards the scene of action. As soon as the first performance was completed, the whole machinery was erected on the pier to take the launching and departure of the lifeboat. When this had been accomplished the mutograph [the Company's film camera], was loaded for the third time to photograph also the landing of the corky crew. For this event the spectators had to wait nearly two hours, during which time many of them dispersed. As the boat was nearing the shore and surmounting the last few breakers, Mr. Dickson shouted once more, 'Let her go!' When the lifeboat struck the beach many rushed forward to assist in pulling her up, while some of the crew jumped hastily out of the boat into the foaming waves, and quick as lightning, yet most carefully, laid upon the sand the body of a man drowned (?) for the purpose of pleasing sightseers and in the interests of science. Medical aid was, however, at hand, and by means of proper restoratives and a most scientific manipulation of breathing apparatus, the drowned mariner was soon able to return to his home and friends. And thus ended the noble work of life-saving and animated photography. The sun was shining all the time, there was a good breeze blowing and plenty of sea—all very favourable circumstances, so that the pictures taken (about 4,000) ought to be very effective when finished and projected upon the screen. The following day (the 7th inst.) the Worthing Swimming Club played some games of water polo, etc., in the big baths at West Worthing, while the mutograph was again actively looking on and taking it all in.[3]

By the end of 1898, Dickson's films of the launch and return of the Worthing lifeboat were being incorporated into the Biograph film programme at the Palace to music composed by Alfred Plumpton. The other Biograph films exhibited included scenes from the coronation of the Queen of Holland, panoramic views of Conway

5 A still from the earliest surviving film made in West Sussex. The *Henry Harris*, comes ashore with a rescued mariner on 6 April 1898.

Castle and pelicans at the zoo. The half-hour Biograph show was a major feature of the near three-hour entertainment at the Palace. On 13 December, it would also feature such live acts as Marie Lloyd, Sam Lockhart's Elephants and the music of Wagner. Dickson's superior animated pictures, which also now included the first films made of Pope Leo XIII, brought distinction to the Company and a new confidence to the medium. The Worthing scenes formed part of the Biograph's (and Dickson's) ambitious attempt to produce a moving image portrait of the contemporary world.

Three of the Dickson films have survived and they are in the collection of the National Film and Television Archive: *Emerging from the Boathouse*, *Coming Ashore*, and *Water Polo Match*.

The Worthing lifeboat figures prominently in the early history of film-making in West Sussex and one reference pre-dates the Dickson visit in April 1898. The Snewin Year Books in Worthing Reference Library note the lifeboat crew performing evolutions for an unspecified film-maker on 31 March 1897. Later, on 15 January 1904, the Gaumont Company filmed a 750ft. drama, *Man the Lifeboat*, at Worthing. An eight-scene story, listed in Denis Gifford's *British Film Catalogue*, it showed the launch of the *Richard Coleman* and the recovery of a body from the sea.

THE HEPWORTH COMPANY IN BOGNOR

For a brief period, in the early years of the century, Bognor was the temporary home of Cecil Hepworth, a pioneer of film-making in Britain, and one of the most innovative figures in the early film industry.

He had begun making fifty-foot outdoor films in 1899, railway scenes such as *Express Trains in a Railway Cutting* and comics, notably *The Explosion of a Motor-car*, before building a daylight set in his garden at Walton-on-Thames for longer stories.

A year after registering The Hepworth Manufacturing Company in 1904 he achieved a major success with *Rescued by Rover*, written by his wife and starring the entire family, with their eight-month-old daughter playing the heroine and their pet dog the hero. Produced at a cost of £10 13s. 6d., including fees for the employment, for the first time, of professional actors, it told a coherent, properly edited story and was Hepworth's most polished film to date.

Suitably encouraged, he built an indoor studio at Walton, only for it to be consumed in 1907 by a disastrous fire, which claimed the life of a young technician. Whilst the studio was being rebuilt, it would seem that his repertory group, now known as the Hepworth Stock Company, spent at least two seasons, possibly three, at Bognor. There is no explicit reference to this episode in his autobiography, *Came the Dawn*, perhaps because, as he explains, his diary at this time of hiatus was a mixture of jumbled entries and blank pages.[4]

6 William Kennedy Laurie Dickson photographed at New York in 1895.

7 A First World War portrait of Cecil Hepworth. He filmed in West Sussex and sailed from Chichester Harbour.

8   A still from *A Seaside Girl*, with a bathing machine helping May Clark escape the attentions of her unwanted suitors.

At least fifteen Hepworth films were shot at Bognor between August 1907 and October 1908 according to Denis Gifford's *British Film Catalogue* (1986). All were directed by Lewin Fitzhamon, who had joined the Company in 1904, bringing with him fresh ideas and a puck-like humour. They tended to be short chases and comedies, 200-450 feet in length, with the seaside, Pier and bathing machines all featuring strongly. Dolly Lupone and Gertie Potter played the girls, and Thurston Harris filled the various rôles of father, suitor or villain.

A sad reflection on the poor survival of our early film heritage is the fact that only two of these 15 films appear to have survived. *A Seaside Girl* (325ft.), released in August 1907, has May Clark desperately trying to evade the attentions of three suitors, via the Pier, a carriage and a bicycle, before taking a bathing machine out to sea. *Dumb Sagacity* (450ft.), shot a month later, stars a pet dog and a horse, combining to rescue Gertie Potter stranded by the tide. Animal pictures loom large in the Company's prolific output, Hepworth with his dogs and Fitzhamon his horses and, occasionally, elephants!

Hepworth may not have recalled his visits to Bognor, but they left their mark on local people, and a number of recollections were recorded in Morton Swinburne's column, *Leaves from my Notebook*, in the *Bognor Post* during the late 1940s and '50s.

An old Bognor resident informs me that, some 40 years ago, such a thing as a film studio, the Hepworth Company, 'on location', produced a number of films in and around Bognor. They were chiefly short 'slapstick' comedies and thrillers. One of the former category was entitled 'Painting the Pier'. Among the latter was an animal story ... in which an extremely intelligent pony discovers the body of his murdered master on the Bognor-Pagham Road. This was followed by a man-hunt in which a number of Bognor residents (including a well-known local fisherman) were more or less 'bludgeoned' into taking part, and in which the murderer was chased around the Rock Gardens![5]

CINEMA

David Fellick served as agent for the Company while it was in Bognor, and also was one of a number of local men who acted as 'extras' during the film-making. His reminiscences were first quoted by Swinburne on 20 January 1951 when he was in his early seventies:

> The company used the old skittle alley in the *Ship Inn*, Aldwick, as stores, and one of my jobs was to go around to get concessions from various owners for permission to use suitable premises as background for the taking of the films. A pony and dog were housed at the Royal Norfolk stables, and these, I may say, were the principal stars of one short film called 'Animal Sagacity'. One of the films I best remember was 'Fire at Sea'. For the purpose of this film we bought the hull of an old ship that used to lie at the end of Barrack Lane, and put 25 trusses of straw on it. This was set light to, and at the appropriate time a dozen men had to jump out into the sea. The incident was photographed from the beach, and everything went according to plan, the film later being shown, together with the others taken in Bognor, at the first cinema at the end of the Pier in 1910. In addition to myself, 'locals' who acted as 'supers' in the films included Tom Pipson, John Walls, G. Fellick (my father), Alan Lee, 'Rocker' Ide and Albert Perry.[6]

Writing eight years later, his daughter, Mrs. E. Still of Runcton, recalled his stories of the Hepworth stars, including Chrissie White, who joined the Company as a 12-year-old in 1907 and was later to team up with Alma Taylor in the successful *Tilly Girl* series.

> He has many rich tales to tell of the mishaps and laughs that arose during production, and particularly remembers the famous actress of those silent days, Chrissie White, whom he supplied with fresh fish during her stay in Bognor as she had not been too well prior to filming.

She too remembered watching the films when they were shown at the Pier Pavilion: 'I was only three at the time ... and when I saw my father and grand-mother on the screen, I shouted out: 'Look, there's my daddy!'[7]

9 A pet dog and a horse combine to rescue Gertie Potter in Cecil Hepworth's *Dumb Sagacity*.

10 Gertie Potter relates her adventure to a relieved father in another still from *Dumb Sagacity*.

Another whose parents and grandparents took part in the films as extras was Miss Ouida Webber of Shripney Road, and she remembered the Pavilion being packed for the subsequent shows. Her mother, Mrs. Alice E. Webber, was Bognor's first riding mistress, and appeared in one of the films riding down the High Street with her pupils.

Miss Annie Taylor of Richmond Road North acted in two of the films:

I was awarded first prize for the carnival scene on the Pier. I was also taken to Felpham, in company of two Great Danes, riding round the Upper Bognor Road, in a trap to play the part of the maid in a film called 'Her Pony's Love'[8]

The drama, *Fire at Sea*, to which David Fellick referred, was also recalled by Leonard Rogers, whose father was at the time Bognor's piermaster, and apparently made use of a Brixham ketch, *The Foundling*, which had run aground at Aldwick in 1906.[9]

The evidence of the film catalogues is that Hepworth and Fitzhamon were filming in Bognor in 1907 and 1908, whilst the recollections of local residents also refer to a six-month stay in 1909.

The local newspapers of those years are silent on the subject, barring cryptic references in the Bognor Visitors Lists published by the *Bognor Observer* to visits in July-August of each of those three years by a Mr. and Mrs. Hepworth, family and nurse, staying in the Steyne, at Salisbury House in the first year and at Lynn Cottage thereafter.[10]

It is quite probable that the number of films made at Bognor during this period was far higher than the 15 quoted. Personal recollections, for example, refer to additional titles not listed in the film catalogues. Moreover, in the catalogues themselves there are many other films credited in these years to the Hepworth-Fitzhamon Company for which no specific locations are recorded, and which may well have been shot in Bognor.[11]

What would appear certain is that the association between Bognor and Cecil Hepworth was brief. By 1910 the new studio at Walton was in operation, and Lulworth Cove in Dorset had replaced Bognor as the venue for the annual migration of the Company to the South Coast. Hepworth was to return to West Sussex in 1921 to direct a film version of *Tansy*, the romantic novel by Tickner Edwardes, shot on the Downs around Burpham near Arundel and starring Alma Taylor as the shepherdess. Within three years Walton had become a victim of the post-war crisis in the British film industry, and the studio was declared bankrupt.

Although it was of brief duration, this little-known association between Bognor and one of the film industry's most prominent and well respected

11 Alma Taylor on the Downs near Burpham. The publicity poster for *Tansy* proclaimed 'a picture that embodies the fresh vigour and ripe beauty of the English countryside'.

pioneers is an important element in the film history of Sussex. It is estimated that out of the 2,000 films made by Hepworth only five per cent remains, and it is a great shame that so little is available today as evidence of his work at Bognor. However, his love of photography and films was to live on in the town, and in the next decade his mantle would be assumed by a remarkable group of gifted amateur film-makers.

Indeed, Bognor's place in the film history of the county might have been enhanced further in the early 1960s had plans been fulfilled for the construction by Sweethill Studios of a three-million-pound film and television studio complex on the Rookery Farm Estate at North Bersted.[12]

See Appendix 1 for catalogued list of films made at Bognor by Cecil Hepworth in 1907-8.

THE PICTURE PALACE FILM-MAKERS

Such was the competition amongst the first generation of full-time Picture Palaces and Electric Theatres that their managers adopted a range of marketing strategies to attract audiences. The shooting of newsreels of local events, using their own hand-cranked 35mm cameras, was one such ploy, inducing people to visit the cinema in the hope of seeing themselves on the silver screen.

Desmond Holderness at the Littlehampton Electric   An early proponent of the art was Desmond Sidney Holderness, managing partner, engineer and chief projectionist at the Electric Picture Palace in Littlehampton, opened on 11 May 1911. Before the end of the month, patrons were watching the first local interest film, footage of the Duchess of Norfolk laying the foundation stone for the local Cottage Hospital on 22 May. A year later, over the Whitsun weekend, Holderness was out and about filming *Littlehampton Holiday Scenes*, which were immediately screened at the Electric and subsequently loaned for publicity purposes to the town's advertising committee.

> The Littlehampton holiday pictures were a source of great interest, and especially to those patrons who had the pleasure of seeing either themselves or their friends depicted upon the screen. These pictures, which are very clear, reflect great credit upon the enterprise of the Management who, not for the first time, have sought to advertise the town.[13]

The challenge to Holderness was to screen a film as soon as he could after the actual shooting, and on the evening of Friday 7 June 1912 he succeeded in showing a film of the Corpus Christi procession at Arundel which he had taken only the previous afternoon. This film, depicting the Duke of Norfolk carrying the canopy over the Sacred Host, was screened all week, and drew large numbers of Arundel folk to the Electric. Described as 'beautifully clear', it became a nationwide hit, and was distributed all over the country by a major film agency.[14]

The value of such films in advertising a town, particularly a seaside resort, was not lost on local councillors, and the local newspaper was able to report in July that *A Day at Littlehampton*, taken by Holderness, had been greatly admired at the Clapham Pavilion, and was about to woo potential holiday-makers in the Midlands.[15]

Holderness and his camera appear to have been inseparable. In August they were on the spot to film a lifeboat rescue off the coast, the children's sports on the Green, the Friendly Society Hospital Parade, the British Motor Boat Club races, and the Arundel Regatta. These were immediately screened at Littlehampton and at the partnership's new cinema at Arundel.[16]

This was not in itself particularly exceptional for other cinemas were by now doing much the same thing—the ever-enterprising Poole's Pictures at the Corn Exchange in Chichester began showing local interest films in September 1911 as did the Olympia at Northgate in April 1912—but Holderness was to go one step further and extend his film-making into the realms of feature films.

Amateur acting talent was employed in the making of a comedy filmed by Holderness in the town and neighbourhood of Littlehampton, and shown at the Electric for a week in October 1912. It took its place in a programme which included *Dick Turpin and the Gunpowder Plot* and Pathé Gazette's birthday celebrations of Lord Roberts, and earned high praise in the local press as a major innovation in West Sussex cinema.

CINEMA NOVELTY.

LITTLEHAMPTON AMATEUR ACTORS IN CINEMATOGRAPH COMEDY.

There was a crowded attendance at the Picture Palace on Monday evening, when the comedy performed by local amateurs and specially taken by Mr. Holderness, had an enthusiastic reception. The scenes are laid in Littlehampton and the immediate neighbourhood, the plot is well thought out, and the acting is clever and reflects great credit on all who took part.

12 *Top.* Corpus Christi procession at Arundel filmed by Desmond Holderness in June 1912.

13 *Above.* A review of the Holderness comedy, *Following in Father's Footsteps.*

As Mr. Smith, the manager of a light and power company with a great weakness for the fair sex, Mr. Frank Flavin specially scored a great success, his facial expressions being both realistic and clever. He also duplicated the part of Farmer Torney most admirably. He was well supported by Miss Charlcraft as the jealous wife, and Miss Samuels, the typist. Miss K. Harris and Miss D. Shepherd were admirable as the two daughters, and their elopement scene with the two clerks (Mr. A. King and Mr. G.H. Thompson) whose facial expressions were also very clever, was very funny. Mr. A. Cowles was funny and deserves special mention for his rendering of the difficult part of the comic policeman, and the other parts were well sustained by Miss E. Wallis, Messrs. B. Floyd, H. Deane, Guile and Field.

Judging by the roars of laughter and tremendous applause with which the film was greeted it may safely be asserted that Mr. Holderness has scored another great success with his new venture, one which is quite a new departure in cinema circles in this county.[17]

The film, entitled *Following in Father's Footsteps*, was to appear later at a number of cinemas, including the Clapham Pavilion, one of the finest of the South London Picture Palaces. One of its minor stars, George Herbert Thompson of York Road, was himself an amateur film-maker of some note, his series of films of Devonshire having been shown at the Electric in May 1912.[18]

Holderness was to continue with his filming of local events and he had a happy knack of choosing subjects that appealed to his audiences. Thus, the Christmas programme at the Electric in 1912 included specially taken film showing the principal shops of the town bearing their seasonal window displays. Occasionally his films were adopted by Pathé for inclusion in their national newsreels—an intriguing example being his picture of 'Mr. W. Robinson's brick-carrying effort to Worthing and back' filmed in June 1914.[19]

Sadly, there is no known evidence of the survival of the films made by Desmond Sidney Holderness. It is said that overall some 80 per cent of pre-1929 films has been lost, and one may assume that these Littlehampton films fall into this category. It would be good to be proved wrong, for without doubt they would constitute a marvellous record, not only of the work of an early film-maker, but also of the local history of the town.

14 & **15** Filming the Bosham Regatta for Poole's Picture Palace in Chichester on 14 September 1911.

Frederick Maplesden at the Whitehall, East Grinstead   Elsewhere, the situation regarding survival of local newsreel is brighter, for example at East Grinstead, where the manager of the Whitehall, Frederick C. Maplesden, and later the chief projectionist, George W. Bax, shot local films for the cinema between 1916-28. Their footage included soldiers marching through the town during the First World War, parades and processions, horse shows and hunt meetings, and fêtes and sporting events on the old West Street Cricket Ground.

As Tony Hounsome notes in *Three Pennyworth of Dark*, the appearance of the cinema's cameraman caused great excitement at local events and people did their best to include themselves in the shot. It was all good box office for the following week as they would all rush to the cinema to see themselves on screen.[20]

Fortunately, the films were kept at the Whitehall and, although some reels disintegrated beyond redemption, approximately 2,000 ft. survived, and is now preserved in the Huntley Film Archives in London. In 1995 a very much smaller quantity came to the South East Film & Video Archive, where it has now been copied, a precious sample of the quality and historic fascination of these early cinema newsreels.

Pathé and Scott at the Central Hall, Horsham   The Electric Picture Palace at Littlehampton and the Whitehall Cinema at East Grinstead were by no means the only cinemas in the county which shot their own local newsreels to attract patrons, but it was more common, perhaps, for the major newsreel companies to hire out their camera crews to cover local events on behalf of a cinema.

16   A still showing the Carnival decorations in West Street, Horsham, filmed by Pathé in July 1913.

Thus, the Pathé Company came to Horsham on Thursday 24 July 1913 to film Cricket Week and the Grand Carnival for the Central Picture Hall, finishing as was often the case with shots of the cinema itself. Happily, in this instance, the film survives in the care of the National Film Archive in London.

Later other news films were made for the cinema in Horsham by Harold Scott, a projectionist employed by the Central Hall and then by the Capitol, including the annual Horsham and Crawley Point to Point Races. He was still filming in 1933 but, without the luxury of a spoken commentary, such local newsreels began to lose their appeal to cinema audiences once the talkies had arrived.[21]

FILM-MAKING ON SHOREHAM BEACH, 1914-23

The county's first, and only, film studio complex was erected on Shoreham Beach. It operated primarily from 1919 to 1923. Film production began at the Old Fort and then moved to a site near to the Church of the Good Shepherd. At the latter a 'glasshouse studio' was erected as well as various workshops and residences. The Progress Film Company dominates the history of this studio complex. From 1919 to 1922 it made 17 features at Shoreham for the British market. Financial difficulties and the general uncertainties of the British film industry led to the closure of the Shoreham studio at the end of 1923.

The origins of the studio, and film-making at Shoreham, began in 1914 with the creation of the Sunny South Film Company. Francis Leonard Lyndhurst, an established scenic artist for London theatres and the owner of a bungalow on Shoreham Beach, formed the Company with the comedians Will Evans, Arthur Conquest and George Graves. Evans was a well-known music hall entertainer with significant work at Drury Lane and a resident of Shoreham Beach. It appears that he was the only member of the Company to have had a close connection with film before 1914. As early as 1899 he had featured in three films for the Warwick Trading Company: *They Do Such Things at Brighton, Let 'Em All Come—Will Evans' Cornet Solo* and *Will Evans, the Musical Eccentric.* This last work was described as, 'Introducing Will Evans, one of the favourites of the London music halls, in his speciality act. He enters the scene by a series of somersaults and proceeds with acrobatic feats, into which he introduces much action and humour. Once scene [sic] never to be forgotten.'[22]

17 A typical road in Bungalow Town, New Shoreham, home for stars of stage and screen, pictured in 1916.

The Sunny South Film Company produced four films in 1914: *Building a Chicken House, The Jockey, Harnessing a Horse* and *The Showman's Dream.* All the productions made use of an open-air studio, consisting of a platform stage and painted backdrops, erected on the open Parade Ground of the Old Fort, Shoreham Beach. Shooting also took place at locations on the Beach and in the town of Shoreham. These outside productions were all made during that summer. The films have not survived but we know that they were all based on Evans' comic sketches and each was a 'one reeler'— no more than 15 minutes in length. *The Bioscope,* the film trade weekly, welcomed the arrival of these 'British comedy subjects' but the films were never reviewed.[23]

From contemporary accounts and reminiscences, N.E.B. Wolters was able to construct a description of one of the films.

> *The Showman's Dream* was quite simple. 'Professor Evanso' [Will Evans] dreamt that his circus caught fire and the tiger, played by Arthur Conquest, escaped. Then followed a chase, next taken up in Old Shoreham at the thatched Post Office near to the junction of Connaught Avenue and Upper Shoreham Road. The tiger ran into one of the cottages and jumped into bed with an old lady, played by one of the younger comedians, probably Joe Evans. The old lady rushed out in nightgown and nightcap, running towards the 'Red Lion' closely followed by the tiger. But the day was so hot and perspiration and a slipping facial mask obscured Conquest's vision and he lost sight of his quarry at the very moment that a not too sober man stepped out of the pub. He took one look at the tiger rushing towards him, turned white and fled up the Steyning Road closely followed by the tiger. The scene was so funny it was kept in—in any case, film was not wasted in those days.[24]

CINEMA

No commercial information exists on these films but they must have provided Lyndhurst with enough confidence to abandon his first collaborators and initiate a grander project in the next year. He launched the Sealight Film Producing Company, the successor to his Sunny South Film Company. In July 1915 *The Bioscope* announced its arrival. 'This company was registered on June 15th, with a capital of £10,000 in £1 shares to carry on the business of manufacturers, hirers and renters of and dealers in cinematograph films, apparatus, posters and literature, etc., and to adopt an agreement with F.L. Lyndhurst. Private company. The number of directors is not to be less then two nor more than five. F.L. Lyndhurst, Lyndora, Shoreham-by-Sea, is sole managing director. Qualification 100 shares.'[25]

The land deeds, in the possession of John Payne, tell us that the site for the new studio was acquired from the Easter family of Old Salts, Lancing, for £200. The indenture, dated 8 September 1915, permitted Lyndhurst to erect, 'a private dwelling house or private dwelling houses or a building or buildings for the purpose of Cinematograph performances and manufacture and production of Cinematograph films including the provision of housing and accommodation for artists and others engaged thereon.' The plot was located immediately north-west of the Church of the Good Shepherd on Shoreham Beach. Here Lyndhurst built the 'glass-house' film studio from 1915-16. (Nothing of the studio complex remains today. Industrial units now occupy the site.) The studio measured 75 x 45 feet with about 30 feet of head room. It was designed by a firm from South London who specialised in the construction of greenhouses.[26]

18 *The Showman's Dream* being filmed on the Parade Ground of the Old Fort on Shoreham Beach, with Will Evans in top hat.

At least one film was made in the new production facility before Lyndhurst's new Company ran into problems, caused in part by the difficulties of war-time film production. It defaulted on its mortgage of £1,500 in 1916 and the studio and the property was sold to the Olympic Kine Trading Company. There is no evidence that the new owners used the studio until the arrival of the Progress Film Company. It is this Company which dominates the history of the Shoreham film studio. The Progress Film Company was founded in 1914 in Manchester by Frank Spring. Having made a number of feature films, with Sidney Morgan as its principal producer, and with the imminent

19 The all-glass studio built on Shoreham Beach took full advantage of the good light on the coast.

end of the war, the Company announced in October 1918 its intention to 'build and complete a modern studio, either outside London or in the States.'[27]

Shoreham Beach became the site for this development. Progress started its first production at the Shoreham studio, as founded by Lyndhurst, in 1919 and purchased the property in April 1920. Progress would use Shoreham as its home until 1922. The Progress Film Company, with the original Lyndhurst 'glasshouse' studio in place, used the next three years to purchase more land and develop a complete film production complex. This included a joiner's shop, darkroom facilities, a preview theatre and accommodation for cast and crew. The studio, initially, was without electricity. It therefore had to rely on natural, and not artificial, light. The glass was probably either of a muranese or morocco type for diffusing the sunlight and reducing the shadow effects of the sun. Blinds, calico diffusers and reflectors (either mirrors or metal surfaces or painted canvas) were also used to control the natural light. The absence of artificial light meant that the Shoreham studio could only be used from late spring to early autumn.

Wolters in his study described the lighting process in the glasshouse.

> He [Stanley Mumford, the cameraman] 'lit' the scene first by placing the actors in the most favourable natural light—allowing, of course, for the set and requirements of the action. The light was diffused by means of muslin curtains strung at either side on stretched wires under the glass roof. Even then strong shadows could be thrown on both set and actors, so ingenious use was made of mirrors [reflectors] to reflect a strong light, and painted squares of canvas, either blue or white, stretched on wooden frames to reflect a softer light—for example under an artiste's chin to produce a more natural and pleasing appearance ... [28]

Of the 33 film studios in the country around 1918, Shoreham was one of only two which did not possess artificial lighting. Electric generators for studio lighting were not introduced at Shoreham until 1922. There was no ventilation other than the sliding doors of the main entrance. The intense heat of this glasshouse often caused the artists' make-up to run.

Most studios in this period possessed their own laboratories for the developing and printing of film stock. Before the arrival of mains water on the Beach, Progress'

negatives were taken to Thames Ditton for processing. Darkroom facilities came to the studio lot in around 1921 or 1922 as well as a preview theatre. It was used in order to view the 'rushes'—the newly printed film from a current production. Before its construction, the Bijou Cinema in Shoreham played this rôle.

Stanley Mumford believed that Shoreham was the only studio,

> in the country where the artists and key staff lived on the job. They had the time of their lives at this seaside studio, apart from hard work they made a regular holiday of it, so much so that when the picture was finished, the Director could not get rid of them. They always wanted to stay a few days longer, what with parties, and sometimes a little gambling in the evening, apart from moonlight bathing—the sea being only 200 yards from the studio. You can guess they were not anxious to leave. Sidney Morgan and his daughter Joan were a delightful couple to work for, in fact the whole studio unit was a very happy crowd. We worked seven days a week and all through the holidays, from eight in the morning till seven in the evening, then dinner in the bungalow, afterwards talking about the days work, or see the rushes of the previous days takes.

'Studio Rest' was the name of the 22-bedroom bungalow built by Progress for its acting company. Next to it was found 'Blink Bonny', the home built for Frank Spring, the managing director. By the summer of 1922,

20 *Top.* Frank Spring, managing director (front row, second left) and Stanley Mumford, cameraman (wearing the bow tie), with the Progress Board, *c.*1922.

21 *Above.* Sidney Morgan and his daughter, Joan, director of production and main star of the Progress studio at Shoreham.

the modernisation and improvements of the studio enabled Progress to carry out all aspects of film production on the Beach.[29]

Wolters has described Progress' pattern of work at Shoreham.

> The policy was to film every day of the week when the light was sufficiently good—after all no artificial light was available there at the time—and this went on for about six months of the year [May to October]. During the rest of the year the basic stock company of actors dispersed and the films were edited and prepared for trade shows, then a feature of the industry ... Trade shows were important as the cinema managers would then make their bookings and the production company could arrange to make a suitable number of prints for distribution.[30]

As director of production, Morgan produced more than 20 films for Progress. This included at least 15 titles at the Shoreham studio from 1919 to 1922. The

Company's aim was to make from five to six features each year. 'Sidney Morgan was very much in charge, from the choice of story, preparation of the script, casting, directing, dressing the set and players—in fact every detail contributing to the final result on screen ... .' Joan Morgan became the star of the Shoreham studio, featuring in most of the films made by her father, Sidney. She was described by Progress as 'the beautiful British star'. Born in 1905, she was in her teens throughout Progress' years at Shoreham. After the critical success of *Little Dorrit* in 1920, she was offered a five-year Hollywood contract. Speaking in 1976, Joan Morgan said, 'I was the right type for Hollywood—a soft little blond'. Her father rejected this American offer. The Morgans left Progress after the 1922 season.

Film adaptations of classic novels were central to Progress' identity as a film production company. As such, they were working within an ethos shared by many of their British rivals. Hepworth, in particular, had established this interest in what we would now call heritage drama. The Progress film, *Little Dorrit*, was shot in 1919 and released in the late summer of 1920. It was Sidney Morgan's ambitious adaptation of the novel by Dickens and it was a significant critical success. This film of 6,800 feet [about 68 minutes] is 'missing, presumed lost' but a 12-minute 9.5mm version has survived. The film starred Lady Tree as Mrs. Clennam, Langhorne Burton as Arthur Clennam and Joan Morgan, at age 14, as Little Dorrit. *The Bioscope* gave it unqualified praise:

22 *Below left.* Joan Morgan as *Little Dorrit* in 1920.

23 *Below right.* The classical beauty of Joan Morgan, aged 15, at the height of her fame in 1920.

A worthy production of a beautiful story by a great master. The acting is artistically restrained throughout; the photography and setting alike excellent ... The producers have achieved a great artistic triumph and one which will delight Dickensians in all parts of the world. Watching this photoplay as it appears upon the screen, we live, as it were in the old haunts so loved by the great master-novelist; we see again the characters his incomparable imagination conceived, characters which his marvellous skill as a word-painter enable the reader to also see in imagination.[31]

The film's design was inspired by Phiz's illustrations for the 1857 edition of Dickens' novel. Particular care was given to the design of the set of the Marshalsea Debtors Prison within the Shoreham studio. Nathans of London provided the costumes and Nymans Gardens in Sussex was used as one of the locations. Joan Morgan, in the BBC programme *Bioscope Days*, of 1976, remembered the film with particular affection.

The best thing I ever did was 'Little Dorrit'. It had such integrity—a wonderful part in a wonderful film. The public reaction was just right from the start. The Dickens Society was delighted. They said it was done in the true spirit of the master. The press was wonderful. We got nine-and-a-half marks from one of the reviewers. It was much the best thing we ever did.

The Mayor of Casterbridge, of 1921, was another film by Progress which received great acclaim. This was the first film version of the novel. Some of the location work took place in Sussex. A postcard, acquired by N.E.B. Wolters, depicts Stanley Mumford with his film camera at work in Steyning High Street. The *White Horse* public house in Steyning was 'dressed' in order to represent the home of Michael Henchard, the Mayor of Casterbridge. The film received its trade show at the end of 1921 and was described as a 'beautiful' production by *The Bioscope*. It wrote:

It is an ambitious task to attempt to condense within the limits of a five reel film any work of Thomas Hardy's, but Sidney Morgan, who is responsible for the scenario as well as the production of this version of *The Mayor of Casterbridge*, has succeeded beyond expectation. This partly due to a concise and well constructed story, in which most of the main features have been retained, partly due to the very sympathetic appreciation shown for the story and its settings, and partly to the valuable assistance rendered by an excellent company ... Fred Groves [as Michael Henchard] gives one of the finest performances he has yet contributed to the screen.[32]

N.E.B. Wolters offered a remarkable anecdote connected to the making of the film. 'Before work started on this picture, its famous author, Thomas Hardy, came to talk things over with the producer. He was then about 80 years of age and was taken around the studio in a wheelchair.'[33] Unfortunately, this has proved to be apocryphal. Dennis Bird, a member of the Thomas Hardy Society, has drawn attention to Hardy's autobiography. In it Hardy states that in July 1921 he met the cast and crew from Progress in Dorchester, while they were making parts of the film in Dorset, and drove members of the Company to Maiden Castle. Hardy was not in his wheelchair in 1921! This information however does expand our appreciation of the work of Sidney Morgan for here was a considered production which used exteriors in Sussex and Dorset and constructed the interiors in the Shoreham studio. Morgan decided not to fake 'Wessex' but to travel to the Hardy landscape in order to give his film the appropriate verisimilitude. Like *Little Dorrit*, so far we have only found the 9.5mm version of *The Mayor of Casterbridge*.[34]

During the winter of 1922/3, a fire destroyed many of the studio buildings but not the 'glasshouse studio'. Progress' nitrate negatives survived but, tragically, many were later lost in a laboratory fire. With the departure of Sidney Morgan after the 1922 season and the fire damage, Progress did not mount a 1923 production programme. However film-making continued in that year at Shoreham under Walter West. Two films were produced, both starring the 'Vitagraph Girl'—Florence Turner. The titles were *Hornet's Nest* and *Was She Justified*. These were the last features to be made at the Shoreham studio. In 1927 the Progress Film Company was wound up and a liquidator was appointed and in 1929 the major portion of the property was sold to Mrs. A.C.J. Easter for £250. This was only £50 more than the original purchase price agreed by Lyndhurst and the Easter family in 1915. The clearance of most structures from Shoreham Beach at the start of the Second World War removed all evidence of the existence of the Shoreham studio.

The late N.E.B. Wolters was responsible for bringing this story to the present. His papers, photographs, articles, radio programme and book of 1985—*Bungalow Town - Theatre and Film Colony*—chronicled the history of Shoreham Beach and the Shoreham studio. He had lived in Shoreham during the Progress period, knew many of the studio's employees and was an extra in *Little Dorrit*. All subsequent histories, including this one, are indebted to his work. This was particularly true of the 1995 exhibition, 'The Showman's Dream: Film-Making on Shoreham Beach, 1914-1923'. It was the product of the combined efforts of Marlipins Museum (part of the Sussex Archaeological Society), Adur District Council, Brightrose Productions

24 'Kinematographing at Steyning.' Stanley Mumford films the *White Horse* in the High Street for *The Mayor of Casterbridge*.

25 *Right*. Still from *Hornet's Nest*, filmed at Washington, near Storrington, and featuring local people.

26 *Below*. Joan Morgan today, star of the Cinema 100 celebrations in West Sussex.

and the South East Film & Video Archive. Of special interest was the display, on video, of *A Lowland Cinderella*, *The Mayor of Casterbridge* and *Little Dorrit*. The discovery of these films by the Archive brought a new and essential ingredient to this historical work, for here were surviving examples of films made on the Beach. These moving images had not been seen in Sussex since the 1920s. The exhibition toured across Sussex and formed part of the 1996 Centenary of Cinema exhibition mounted by the West Sussex Record Office and the South East Film & Video Archive.

All of these activities in the 1990s were enhanced through the active presence of Joan Morgan. As Britain's oldest film actress, she brought rich memories and a palpable charisma to our work on Shoreham. She placed us in direct contact with silent cinema and the beginnings of the cinema in Sussex. The centenary year of 1996 saw the unveiling by Miss Morgan of a Centenary of Cinema plaque dedicated to the studio and her attendance at a 'live' screening of *A Lowland Cinderella*. It was also fitting that she unveiled the plaque in Brighton to mark the Pandora Gallery—the location of the first film screening outside London (25 March 1896).

See Appendix 2 for list of feature films made at the Shoreham studio, 1919-23, and Appendix 3 for a general list of feature films made in West Sussex, 1913-95.

III

AMATEUR FILM-MAKING

Even in the very early days of film-making, amateurs were making their own moving pictures, but generally the standard 35mm gauge was too expensive, too difficult to manipulate and, being made of celluloid, too dangerous for the average layman.

The real growth of amateur cinematography began with the development of a cheaper and more convenient film than 35mm, and with the consequent introduction of camera and projection equipment within the price range and technical competence of the home movie-maker.

Experiments with various sizes of film were tried by manufacturers on both sides of the Atlantic, but it was the production by Pathéscope of 9.5mm in 1921, closely followed a year later by the American 16mm, which provided the breakthrough. At the same time the perfecting of the Direct Reversal Process meant that amateurs' films could be developed more quickly and cheaply than hitherto.

Of the two 'sub-standard' sizes, 9.5mm made maximum possible use of film width by means of central perforations, and, being cheaper than 16mm, immediately proved more popular in Britain.

The amateur film-maker was soon able to equip himself with a complete movie-making out-fit for £9 1s. 0d. The hand-cranked 'Baby Ciné', Pathéscope's first 9.5mm camera, was superseded by the motor-driven Motocamera in 1925, the cheapest model of which cost £6 6s. 0d. Although the later electrically powered projectors, capable of a 10ft. screen size, were priced at £15, the basic hand-operated 'Kid' projector cost only £2 15s. 0d.

The editor of *Pathéscope Monthly* pointed out in 1931 that film-making was cheaper than photography—a good roll film camera then costing more than the combined cost of cine camera and projector.[1]

Amateur Cinematography
Living Records of Travel and Pleasure

A new era in photography has begun with the introduction of the PATHÉSCOPE CAMERA, by means of which the old lifeless pictures have been replaced by animated records depicting with absolutely life-like effect holiday and travel incidents—scenes from the hunting field—amusing and exciting incidents in every-day life—children at play—your friends—family gatherings, such as christenings, weddings, &c.

THE
PATHÉSCOPE CAMERA

is a compact, portable, and beautifully finished instrument, and is the most perfect Camera of its kind ever produced.
There is no difficulty in working it. Every owner of the Pathéscope can become an expert cinematographer.

THIS INSTRUMENT IS INDISPENSABLE TO THE TRAVELLER AND TOURIST WHO DESIRES TO POSSESS A PERMANENT *LIVING* RECORD OF HIS JOURNEY.
The Pathéscope Camera is provided with a Voightlaender lens, diaphragm, view-finder, sun-shield, spirit level, exposure and speed indicators, and tripod.

THE PATHÉSCOPE
is a really scientific instrument of a simple design, permitting the realisation of what has hitherto appeared impossible:—

THE CINEMATOGRAPH AT HOME
If you own a Pathéscope Camera you can make your own films, thus recalling to the eye and mind the enjoyable moments of the past.
By subscribing to the Pathéscope Library you can obtain an endless variety of films depicting every kind of subject suitable for the home.
In addition to the ordinary hand-driven Pathéscope, which is absolutely self-contained, and generates its own electricity, there is a power-driven model specially constructed to connect with the ordinary house current.

Write or call for Free Illustrated Book and List of Films.

THE PATHÉSCOPE Ltd., Dept. P.M.P. 64, REGENT STREET, LONDON. W.

27 Advertisement for the Pathéscope camera.

THE GIFTED ENTHUSIASTS

One whose interest in films has lasted a lifetime is Cecil Cramp of Horsham whose passion for film-making began in 1929 when, as a 14-15-year-old pupil at Collyers School, he watched a film of Sports Day shot by a friend.

His father was a jeweller and antique dealer, and one day came home with a second-hand Pathéscope 9.5mm camera. Cecil read the articles in the free *Pathéscope Monthly*, learnt from his friend how to keep the camera steady and pan very slowly, and gradually taught himself the art of film-making.

He remembers that the films lasted a minute and cost six shillings with processing. They were reversal films and it was important to have the exposure just right. When the film was returned from the processors, the laboratory report was quickly scanned to see whether it had been under or over exposed. He still has his first film—of the masters at Collyers School in 1929.

His first projector—given by his father as a Christmas present—was a 55-shilling Pathé 'Kid'. It was hand-turned and only showed one- or two-minute films, but he built an improvised adaptor from Meccano to take seven-inch spools for longer films. As well as his own films, he hired or bought films from the Pathéscope Library, having a particular fondness for Harold Lloyd comedies.

Film-making, particularly for a schoolboy, could become a costly hobby, and he decided that if he wished to continue he must decide between films and cigarettes. Happily, he chose the former, and although on occasions he used other gauges, he remained loyal to 9.5. It was cheaper than 16mm, and its frame size, because of the central perforations, was barely smaller. Its advocates felt that its clarity was just as good as 16mm, although it was susceptible to scratching on either side, depending on the gate of the projector, and the central sprocket holes could be a source of weakness if the film became brittle.

He remembers that 9.5 became very popular in the 1930s and, even when 8mm came along in 1934, many amateurs remained with 9.5, believing it produced better results, partly because the perforations on the new gauge occupied a third of the frame and limited the screen size. Its popularity was enhanced in 1938, with the introduction to 9.5 of Dufaycolor and sound-on-film, enabling the enthusiast to film in colour and project 'talkies'.

Cecil took films of his family, shot footage of meetings of the International Friendship League to which he belonged, experimented with animation and trick films, but was not inspired to make feature films. His local films include the excellent *Horsham Magazine*, a 30-minute view of the changing face of the town over a 20-year period beginning in 1935, famous for a sequence shot in West Street from a bicycle-mounted camera.

28 Cecil Cramp today at his home in Horsham.

He was a lone enthusiast, for there was no cine club to join in the Horsham District, and, without a car, visits to film societies at Bognor and Shoreham were impractical. After the Second World War, however, he did attend meetings of the Haywards Heath and District Amateur Cine Society.

Today, surrounded in his home by films and tapes gathered over a lifetime, he still presents film and slide shows, lectures on his other passion, musical boxes, and remains a member of the national Group 9.5. A charming man, ever willing to share his knowledge and his enthusiasm, he is a fine example of the gifted enthusiasts who turned to amateur film-making in the inter-war era.[2]

FILM SOCIETIES AND CINE CLUBS

It was an inevitable consequence of the growth of interest in amateur cinematography that like-minded enthusiasts should come together at the local level to form amateur film societies or cine clubs. The trend gathered momentum as a result of encouragement given by the first National Convention of Amateur Cinematograph Societies on 22-26 October 1929.

In some cases, as at Cambridge and Leicester, they emerged as separate sections of existing photographic societies, while in others, at Brighton and Northampton for example, they were offshoots of local branches of the British Film Institute. In the main, however, it was at the motivation of a lone enthusiast, or small group of individuals, that a society was formed.

On occasions, film societies were set up as venues for the presentation of films in areas where no cinema existed, or for the screening of documentary, educational and continental films which might not normally play in a commercial cinema. Generally, however, the societies and clubs which emerged in the first few years of the 1930s were created to produce films, to organise lectures and social events, and to raise the profile and standard of amateur cinematography in the local area.

Their activities are reported in the pages of *Pathéscope Monthly*, which from 1929 specifically recorded the proceedings of clubs using 9.5mm, and *Amateur Cine World*, another monthly which commenced publication in April 1934. Both periodicals actively encouraged the setting up of amateur groups, the former detailing the procedure for *Forming A Cine Society* in its edition of December 1933, and the latter in its first issue publishing Mary Glynne's thesis that the amateur cine society should be a training ground for the film studio just as the drama school was for the theatre.

The acting and film-making aspirations of the new societies were critically reviewed in *Amateur Cine World*. A work of particular merit would be awarded a 'leader' which might then be spliced on to the beginning of the film for public presentations. Both periodicals introduced annual competitions for amateur film-makers in 1934, and other similar contests were organised by the Institute of Amateur Cinematographers, *The Sunday Referee*, and *The Era*.

Judging by the evidence of the club news in the two monthlies, it would seem that there were at least 75 societies in the country by the beginning of 1934. They were particularly numerous in the North, Midlands, and London, fewer in the South, and, at that stage, there was none at all in West Sussex.

THE BOGNOR REGIS FILM SOCIETY

Amateur film societies did not consist simply of members armed with cine cameras, but drew on the whole range of expertise required to produce a film. This point was made in the letter to the editor which appeared in the *Bognor Post* on 3 February 1934, announcing the intention to form an amateur film society in the town, and inviting contact from any reader interested in acting for films, writing scenarios, building scenery and sets, and undertaking electrical work.

This first intimation of the proposed formation of a film society in Bognor was the work of Alfred Cecil McDonald of The Chalet in Aldwick Road. He had previously been a member of the Bournemouth Amateur Film Society, formed in 1930, a flourishing group which had already produced a number of films.

Ironically, showing at the Pier Theatre a week later was *Up to the Neck*, a comedy written by Ben Travers, which had been partly shot in Bognor the previous summer. It featured Ralph Lynn, star of the Aldwych farces, he of the famous monocle and inane grin, who had a seaside home at Bonnie Lodge on Victoria Road, and in 1937 was to become patron of the Bognor Regis Film Society.[3]

The inaugural meeting of the new Bognor Regis Film Society was held on Friday 16 February 1934 in a room in the High Street lent by Edward John Cleeves, who owned three chemists and photographic shops in the town. The chair was taken by Alfred McDonald who explained that the Society aimed to produce motion pictures of entertainment and interest value, on 16mm, 9.5mm and 8mm, and sought to attract all who were interested in film acting or technique.

Co-founder of the new Society was Harry Guermonprez, son of Henry Leopold Foster Guermonprez, himself the elder son of a Belgian emigré and well-known in Bognor as a distinguished natural historian and collector of flora and fauna of West Sussex. Harry, known to everyone as 'Gomey', was a photographer, who managed one of the Cleeves shops, and was elected the Society's first cameraman. Whilst he was responsible for the news films, the feature films were shot by Barry Hart, and it was as producer and director that Harry Guermonprez became the inspiration behind the film-making activities of the Society.[4]

Following the guidance of *Amateur Cine World*, the first move, designed to bring the Society to the notice of the public, was to put on a film presentation. This was held at a packed Pavilion Annexe at 8 p.m. on Monday 5 March, with a varied programme starring *The Metropolis*, one of the classic productions of the silent days, and local newsreels including the legendary convalescence of George V in Bognor in 1929. Guermonprez was the projectionist, and so successful were the accompaniment and effects, superintended by H.W. Blythe, that according to the report in *Pathéscope Monthly* some of the audience had the impression that a sound film was being shown. The evening produced new recruits, paying a subscription of 10s. 6d. for full membership, and soon there were 36 members.[5]

One of the founder members was Vera Bateman, now Mrs. Vera Worthington, whose experience in local dancing schools and the Amateur Operatic and Dramatic Society was shared by others who joined the Film Society in those first few months. She was interested in films and stage work, and her job in a beauty parlour in London led her to seek advice from Leichners on stage make-up, which she put to good use with the Film Society.

Most of the original members were attracted by the idea of acting in films, or interested in the technical aspects of film production, and as time went by some were to reveal exceptional talent. Daphne Heale, now Mrs. Daphne Cox, she remembers as 'a natural', while Robin ('Robert') Ayres was to make the transition to the professional stage, appearing in a number of 'B' movies.

Now aged 82, Vera Worthington remembers her association with the Film Society with affection, and describes it as a close-knit family group. Work commitments meant that filming sessions were mostly confined to Sundays, and she recalls the actors and actresses piling into cars for their days 'on location'.[6]

First Feature Films   The July 1934 issue of *Amateur Cine World* reproduced a still from the rushes of the first film, a farce provisionally entitled *The Lion Hunt*, and quoted an extract from a local newspaper:

> Great excitement was caused to villagers and passers-by in the vicinity of Pagham on Sunday morning when this newly-formed society went on 'location' in close proximity to the Bear Inn, where a portion of their first film was shot. Several well-known local residents were recognised and it is with interest we await their first public appearance on the screen.

The 14-minute film was ultimately titled *What a Hunt* and was derived from the story of Rex, Bognor's immortal lion, which had stolen the headlines the previous summer. A bogus publicity stunt timed for the opening of Billy Butlin's new zoo on the Esplanade, the story of the lion lost en route from Skegness had reporters and photographers dashing from Fleet Street, appetites whetted by numerous sightings and the discovery of a mauled sheep's carcase on a Pagham farm.

With some good local photography, largely at Pagham but also at Felpham, Aldwick and Bognor itself, the film told the tale of a rector's garden party interrupted by a cross-country hunt for the missing beast. It achieved its primary object of

29   Still from *What a Hunt* issued as publicity material by the Bognor Regis Film Society.

making people laugh when screened at the Society's first public show, and although technical weaknesses were noted, it was favourably reviewed by the local press:

> ... Mary Parfrement certainly ran away with the acting honours and filmed remarkably well, while Betty Masters had to throw several faints and did this very naturally.[7]

When the first Annual Meeting was held at the Pavilion in November 1934, the chairman was able to report a most successful first year, and work progressing on the second production, an altogether more ambitious project than the first.[8]

A newspaper cutting from the *Daily Mail* in Vera Worthington's scrapbook suggests that the storyline may well have been based on a real-life case of drug smuggling in the Black Sea, but *Cross Currents* was written by members of the

30 A dramatic scene from *Cross Currents*, one of the Society's most widely distributed films.

Society as a tale of cocaine smuggling in Chichester Harbour. The plot begins with the discovery of a phial of drugs in a fish bought from a local fisherman by summer holiday-makers, suspicion falling on a customs officer posing as an angler, who ultimately emerges as the hero in a dramatic offshore confrontation with the smugglers.

The production commenced in September 1934, but owing to bad weather continued through Christmas, with actresses shivering in their flimsy summer dresses. Shooting took place at Bosham and Itchenor, haunts of the Sussex smugglers of old, and Chichester Yacht Club granted the use of a barque, the *Frances and Jane*, for some of the final scenes. Vera Worthington recalls an amusing scene of Gomey directing operations from a small boat, drifting in circles around the barque, moored off Itchenor.

Reports of the local film-makers' progress were published in the local press, and the *Bognor Observer* reproduced a still photograph from the rushes in its issue of 30 January 1935. Meanwhile, members were enjoying their winter programme of dances, lectures and acting competitions, interspersed with screenings of amateur films loaned by a dozen other societies, including Brondesbury, Doncaster, Lincoln, Stockport and Wimbledon.[9]

The major event was the first annual show of the Society's own films which was held at the Pier Hall (seating 480) on the evenings of 11, 12 and 13 February 1935. *Amateur Cine World* commented on the professional way in which the show was advertised, with posters and display boards, and heavy advanced bookings ensured full houses.[10] The souvenir programme, too, was professionally composed, illustrated with stills from the two main features, *What a Hunt* and *Cross Currents*.

With the exception of the first two pictures, contributed by the Lincoln and Derby Film Societies, all the films selected had been shot on 9.5 by the Bognor Film Society. Barry Hart presented *The Silver Sea*, his expressive and artistic study of light on the sea in wind and calm, which had won an award in a Pathéscope National Competition. Then there was *Moko the Monkey*, the first of a series of animated cartoons drawn by Alan Fraser and filmed by Guermonprez and Hart. Costing only £2 in materials, this involved the filming of 6,000 pictures, and was to attract the attention of national film companies. Cartoons were then looked upon as an American monopoly so *Moko* broke new ground for an amateur film society in Britain, and was to be awarded a leader by *Amateur Cine World* in January 1936 for its originality and animation. Finally *Regis Review*, a newsreel of the year's local events, gave townsfolk the chance of seeing themselves on screen, and this too was to become a regular feature of future programmes.[11]

31 Advertising for the Society's first annual show on Bognor Pier in February 1935.

The first public show received an enthusiastic reception, and its success established the Film Society as part of the local entertainment scene in Bognor, and enhanced its status and reputation amongst the country's amateur cine societies. The star feature, *Cross Currents*, three reels and 40 minutes in length, had cost only £30 to make, but its production was seen as a mark of the Society's ambition and progress, and a measure of the expertise of its producer and director, Harry Guermonprez. It was awarded a leader by *Amateur Cine World* in its review published in September 1935:

32 Programme for the 1935 show.

The acting of the girls is expressive and pleasing; that of the men, with the exception of Batchelor, the detective, can only be regarded as fair. Nearly all of the characters are good, well differentiated types. There is frequent change of angle, the cutting is good and there are more worth-while close-ups—close-ups that really help the development of the film—than we can remember seeing in any other amateur film of the same length. And this from a new society! ... Camera work and quality are alike first rate. This film is the result of good team work and imaginative direction and we look forward with interest to the society's future productions.[12]

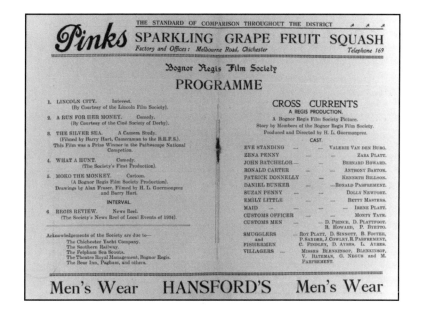

Rising Ambitions Encouraged by the reception afforded *Cross Currents*, the Film Society began work on Production No.3, and in April 1935 the local newspaper reported crowds gathered on the promenade to watch the shooting of scenes for another comedy. Again progress was protracted, continuing into the following January before *Where was George?* was finally completed.[13]

A half-hour film, it stars Kenneth Billson as George Trott, a hen-pecked husband whose efforts to enjoy an illicit holiday at the seaside meet with the attentions of two private detectives hired by his domineering wife, and includes good views of the Seafront, Pavilion Gardens, High Street and *Royal Hotel*.

Described as 'a sparkling comedy of the finest vintage' in the *Bognor Observer*, it was the continuity and local scenes which earned the praise in reviews, though technically it was less advanced than the fourth film, a thriller, *Murder at the Theatre Royal*.[14]

Production No. 4 was intended to be a romantic drama, *Her Name was Mary*, filmed against the background of Goodwood Races, but this had to be shelved owing to the indisposition of one of the leads. A report in *Amateur Cine World* for August 1935 noted that the Society's electricians had assembled a portable lighting system, and this may account for the choice of the replacement murder mystery, which was shot entirely by artificial light.[15]

A dramatic story, again written by members of the Society, *Murder at the Theatre Royal* was set behind the scenes of a theatre, and revolved around the murder of two actors. A 16mm camera had now been acquired, and for the first time 9.5 was abandoned in favour of the larger gauge. Filming commenced on 14 January 1936 and was this time completed within ten weeks. Starring Robin Ayres and Mary Parfrement, it was regarded by critics as the most polished film yet produced by the Society, both in acting and production, and as one of the most ambitious made by any amateur film society.

Audiences had the added attraction of seeing the film in the very building in which it was shot when the Society put on its second annual show, attended by nearly 2,000 people, at the Theatre Royal on 23-25 March 1936. Particularly

33 Still from *Where was George?* with Kenneth Billson being led astray on his seaside holiday.

34 Harry Guermonprez directs, Barry Hart films and Robin Ayres performs in *Murder at the Theatre Royal*.

impressive were the speciality dancing scenes filmed from above by Barry Hart in the true style of Busby Berkeley. Reviews show that this intense picture gripped the audience with its illusion of jealousy, love and death.

The show was advertised as 'three hours of 100% local entertainment' and apart from the two new feature films included a more elaborate Moko the Monkey cartoon, showing his adventures in a *Haunted House*, and the annual *Regis Review*, a longer newsreel this year, with footage of the Silver Jubilee celebrations in May, the opening of the Marine Park Gardens, the Hospital Fête in August, and the Great September Storm.

Significant in the 1935 newsreel was the use, for the first time, of colour in filming the Jubilee carnival procession. 'Must be seen to be believed' advised the correspondent in the *Bognor Observer* (11 March 1936), but not all reviews were yet convinced by the ability of colour film to catch the tones of nature.[16]

Murder at the Theatre Royal, 'Specially Commended' by *Amateur Cine World*, confirmed the Bognor Regis Film Society as one of the leading cine societies in the country, with a reputation for the versatility and excellence of its productions.

Imaginative direction, good camera work, and growing competence in acting were backed by tremendous ambition and enthusiasm, and an awareness of the exciting new films which were emerging. A number of shots in *Murder at the Theatre Royal* reflect the German expressionism in the films coming from Berlin in the 1920s—films which used shadow and spots of light, films about doubt, pessimism, intrigue and criminality. It had a kinship to the work of Alfred Hitchcock whose films from the late 1920s brought ideas about mood and style from Germany to the popular British cinema.

The marked advance made by the Society was highlighted by the *Bognor Observer* which had for some time campaigned for the films to be used as advertising material for the town—just as the Information Bureau was doing in Bournemouth. It was pointed out that within a year *Cross Currents* had been shown to 60 film societies across the country and in so doing had helped to put Bognor on the map.[17]

35 Shades of Busby Berkeley in Bognor.

36 The Horsham Silver Band parades down the High Street during Bognor's celebration of the Silver Jubilee of George V in May 1935.

37 The Film Society's winning tableau for the 1936 carnival, modernistic dress, sky-scrapers, and air flight, inspired by *Things to Come*.

Carnivals and Colour Standards may have been rising but film-making was still fun, and there was a family spirit about the Society. Dances were held regularly at the Masonic Hall in Canada Grove, and were often attended by over a hundred people. Competitions were organised—for the 'Best Film Face' (April 1936) or for the best imitation of the 'Stars of the Screen' (May 1936). Miss Swain as Mae West won the latter, with Gomey as The Invisible Man in second place.[18]

A month later the Society was honoured when one of its leading members, Barbara Morrison, an 18-year-old hairdresser, was elected Carnival Queen. The town's first ever carnival, ruined though it was by poor weather, was filmed for the *Regis Review*, and footage survives of the arrival of Miss Morrison at a wind-swept gala ground in an aircraft piloted by Sir Alan Cobham. The profile of the Society was raised further when its float, based on the H.G. Wells film *Things to Come*, won first prize in the carnival procession later in the week.[19]

The carnival was filmed in Kodachrome, and was well received when screened at a local cinema.[20] Barry Hart continued to experiment with colour, and during 1936 produced his *pièce de résistance*, the all-colour *Symphony of the Seasons* (300ft. 16mm), which was to steal the show at the Society's third annual presentation.

Depicting nature through the changing seasons, most of the views were taken locally, including haymaking against the background of the rolling Downs, but shooting also took place in Cornwall, in order to bring in studies of waves breaking over a rocky coast. The scenes were introduced by lines from well-known poems— 'I must down to the seas again' (John Masefield)—and the poetic beauty of the photography at every stage captured the imagination of critic and audience alike:

> Spring, Summer, Autumn and Winter were all depicted in their varying but colourful moods. So many films, produced by large and professional companies, which have supposed to be taken in natural colour, have been artificial and gaudy looking, simply because of over-colouring. But no such criticism can be levelled at the Bognor Society. It was one of the most natural colour films I have seen. The natural studies, flowers, fields, trees, etc., and studies from life were all realistic and excellently filmed.[21]

Thrillers, Comedies and Cartoons The principal feature film made in 1936 was a thriller, *Room 17* (720ft. 16mm), which starred Robin Ayres and Barbara Morrison in the lead rôles. Again shot indoors, this time in the *Clarehaven Hotel*, the story hinged on the theft of a necklace, and included a memorable cabaret scene with Stanley Burgess and his band. It is perhaps a measure of the Society's growing stature that it now came in for a degree of objective criticism in the local press which commented on an unconvincing plot and occasionally indecipherable captions.

Nevertheless, the attendances at the third annual show held at the Pier Roof Garden Theatre on 10-13 March 1937, surpassed all previous years, and the general impression was that the Society had continued to make great progress, particularly with colour and cartoons. The souvenir programme pointed out that Bognor was the only amateur film society making and exhibiting animated cartoons, and the third in the series of Alan Fraser's Moko the Monkey films, entitled *Continental Cafe*, reflected the growing competence in this exacting and painstaking area of film-making.[22]

By now the Society had a second cameraman, which provided the potential for more elaborate productions, and in the summer of 1937 both were working on a new comedy. Written by Martin Jordan, it was a story of the endeavours of two local reporters to obtain an exclusive interview with a visiting film star, and the exterior shots included an air chase sequence filmed at Ford Aero Club. Originally called *Chase a Star*, it was completed in January 1938 and re-titled *News from Hollywood* (1,050ft. 16mm), starring Harry and Mary Parfrement in the leading rôles.[23]

38 A cabaret scene from *Room 17* has 18-year-old Barbara Morrison singing with the Band.

39 Moko the Monkey, Bognor's award-winning cartoon character.

The second film produced in 1937-38 was the thriller *Death Let Loose* (1,120ft. 16mm), a story written by Jordan about the theft of a War Office secret, with Robin Ayres as the villain and Donald Vinten as the scientist in an action-packed plot involving murder, kidnap and romance, and including frantic car chases through the night and a revolver fight in Arundel Park.

Both films were presented in the fourth annual show, held again at the Roof Garden Theatre, on four nights between 16-19 March 1938, with a Saturday matinee. By request, *Symphony of the Seasons* opened the programme, and a second all-colour film was shown, *Furs*, depicting the work of the Spinney Fur Farm at Aldingbourne, near Chichester. Again filmed by Barry Hart, this was the first of a proposed series of films of industries which the Society had been commissioned to make for the Guild of Handicrafts, but there is no evidence of the production of further titles. Colour was also represented in the newsreels of the 1937 Coronation celebrations in Bognor and Chichester which featured in the new *Regis Review*.

The three-hour programme was once more ecstatically received—'Previous Efforts Surpassed' ran the headline in the *Bognor Observer*—and the reviewer in the *West Sussex Gazette* considered that this was by far the best of the shows to date:

> The Society is only four years old, and each year's show marks a steady advance in technique ... Photography, story-telling, and acting, all show a competence rare among amateur efforts to entertain, and under the lead of the director, Mr. H.L. Guermonprez, the team-work is sound and good ... The Society, with a capable story-writer in Martin Jordan and first-rate camera work by Barry Hart, has shown itself capable of producing films of genuine interest, and its reputation is spreading every year.[24]

Technical Excellence and Experiments with Sound Bognor's prominent status in the world of amateur film societies was a product of the dedication of its members to raise standards in all aspects of the making and presentation of films.

This extended to its publicity and advertising campaigns. The quality of its stills, the responsibility of the second cameraman, K. Brooker, was such that they were regularly reproduced in *Amateur Cine World*, much more so than those of other societies, and in January 1937 the high standard was singled out by Howard Cricks in *The Photographic Journal* following an exhibition at the Royal Photographic Society. It was now producing a monthly publication of its own, called *News Reel*, in which details of the Society's activities and dates of shooting were recorded.[25]

Nowhere was the commitment to professionalism more pronounced than in the technical department. Headed by Guermonprez, this consisted of Vi Sinnott, the assistant director, Barry Hart and K. Brooker, the two cameramen, Vera Bateman (Worthington) in cosmetics, Dora Vinten and C. Start in the sound section, and L. Timms and C. Start as electricians.

Vera Worthington remembers that when feature films were screened in the small hall on the Pier she was responsible for providing the accompaniment, sitting in the little projection box with Gomey, and cueing in classical records from two turntables. Newsreels were presented with a background of recorded music and an occasional commentary provided by Robin Ayres. There was no live musical accompaniment.

In the year before the outbreak of war she recalls that the Society had begun experimenting with sound films, and voice tests were carried out in the Committee Room of the Pavilion. There are no reports of a fifth annual show in March 1939,

but a month later *Amateur Cine World* announced that work was proceeding on a three-reel comedy, entitled *The Green Card*, with Harry Parfrement playing the lead. Interior shots were to be completed by Easter after which Vera Worthington remembers shooting a nightmare scene in Arundel Park including a comic dance by wood nymphs.[26]

War Intervenes There is a note in the report of April 1939 that 'owing to several members being occupied with ARP matters the Society is behind schedule with this production', and preparations for war meant that the last film of the Society was not completed.[27]

The membership disbanded, in common with other film societies at this time, and the momentum which had built up since 1934 was lost. An attempt was made to revive the Film Society at a meeting at the Magnet Restaurant on 21 November 1946, when two films were screened, *Symphony of the Seasons*, inevitably, and *Death Takes a Holiday*, about which little is known. The aims of the Society were explained to a 'surprisingly good' audience, and plans were made for fortnightly meetings, but no further reports appear over the next few months.[28]

The Guermonprez Legacy Harry Guermonprez, the inspiration behind the Film Society, latterly ran Chichester Photographic Service in Whyke Lane, and when he died in December 1973, the films were left in the attic of his home in Westmead Road, Fishbourne. Five years later, in October 1978, at the instigation of Daphne Cox, *News from Hollywood* and a selection from *Regis Review* were shown again, 40 years after the last public show, at the old Esplanade Theatre. There were other presentations over the next ten years, to packed houses at the Esplanade and the Regis Centre, providing a new generation of audiences with a nostalgic look back to the Bognor of the 1930s.

40 Harry Guermonprez captured the moment when Canon Sacre, the Chairman of Bognor UDC, bade farewell to George V after his convalescence in 1929.

Whilst the thrillers and comedies reflect the growing competence of the Society in producing good feature films, and *Symphony of the Seasons* illustrates the excellence of the camera work and the willingness to experiment with innovations such as colour, it is the newsreels which inevitably appeal most to the audiences of today. Some of the news films pre-date the Society, with footage most probably shot by Guermonprez in the late 1920s and early '30s, showing the early Bognor 'Birdmen' plummeting from the end of the pier, the famous visit of George V and Queen Mary in 1929, and the less well-chronicled appearance of Mahatma Gandhi in October 1931. Regenerated by the good fortune of the royal visit, Bognor enjoyed a golden decade in the 1930s, and the newsreels capture the atmosphere of the times, with the crowded beaches, wing-walking air shows, carnivals and fêtes, and seafront improvements in a way which no other archive source can emulate.

The manner in which the films have survived is remarkable in itself. The chance that they remained undisturbed in an attic for 40 years, were then brought again to public notice by people who knew of their background and their importance, and finally were 're-discovered' now 250 miles from Bognor by a Film Archive dedicated to preservation. It is a story which, in its own small way, illustrates the fine line which exists between the survival and the loss of heritage.

The films had stood the test of time well, but the natural ageing process had caused them to dry out and become brittle, and now they have been properly copied in a conservation programme organised by the South East Film & Video Archive and sponsored by the West Sussex Arts Working Party. Their preservation assured, they provide a rare and remarkable record of amateur film-making in the 1930s and a fitting tribute to the enthusiasm and expertise of one of the country's premier film societies.

41 The annual summer fête in the grounds of the War Memorial Hospital — a feature of the newsreels shot by the Bognor Film Society.

OTHER FILM SOCIETIES EMERGE

The evidence of the cine periodicals tends to confirm the view that there were no other amateur film societies in existence in West Sussex at the time of the formation of the Bognor Regis Film Society in February 1934. Little over a year later, partly at least as a result of the example and encouragement of Bognor, cine societies were established at both Chichester and Shoreham, to be followed soon afterwards by new clubs at Ferring and Littlehampton.

Chichester Amateur Cine Club   The British Film Institute had been created in 1933 'to encourage the use and development of the cinematograph as a means of entertainment and instruction', and its quarterly journal, *Sight and Sound*, indicates the setting up of a number of local branches in its early years, including Brighton and Hove in March 1934.

On Friday evening 1 February 1935 a meeting was called at the Girl Guides Hall in Whyke Lane to consider the formation of a branch of the B.F.I. in Chichester, and through the columns of the local *Observer* newspaper the acting secretary, G.A. Wilkins of 57 Orchard Avenue, offered an invitation to all interested in promoting the greater use of 'this powerful recreative and educational force'.

The idea had some impressive local support. The meeting was chaired by the Dean of Chichester, the Very Rev. A.S. Duncan-Jones, with West Sussex County Council's Secretary for Education, Evan T. Davis, in attendance, and the wife of the Division's Conservative M.P., Major J.S. Courtauld of Burton Park, elected as President. One of the first members was the Bishop of Chichester, Dr. George Bell, signalling an intriguing liaison between church and cinema in the diocese, and a firm belief on the part of the former that films could be of great value in spreading the gospel. Indeed, three years later, on Sunday 9 January 1938, Chichester Cathedral would attract a congregation of 2,000 for an evening service using talkie films, projected on a huge screen suspended between the nave and the choir, the first cathedral in England to take such a bold step in the name of evangelism.[29]

Known as the Chichester Film Institute Society, the local branch organised lectures and debates, and worked with the managers of local cinemas, with the object of encouraging quality and decency in film-making, and educating public discrimination in film-watching.

Within a month of its formation, the branch decided to set up a Cine Camera Club, run on similar lines to the Bognor Regis Film Society, and invited to join anyone interested in photography, acting, scene writing, stage management, stage lighting, or producing.[30] Originally a Sub-Committee of the branch, its first work was a 600ft. news film, on 16mm, of the celebrations in Chichester to commemorate the Silver Jubilee of George V and Queen Mary on 6 May 1935, capturing the scenes of that joyful occasion as the city expressed its patriotic feelings in a carnival day of processions, sports, children's entertainments and fireworks. The film was well captioned and partly shot in Dufaycolor, with initial production costs being met by Major and Mrs. Courtauld. It received 'prolonged and enthusiastic applause' when first shown to members and friends at a branch meeting at the Girl Guides Hall on 18 October 1935. Fortunately this superb film survives and has been copied as part of the conservation programme of the South East Film & Video Archive.[31]

42 The Spanish galleon, manned by Shippam's Social Club, one of the prize-winning tableaux featured in Chichester's 1935 Jubilee film.

Meanwhile, the Sub-Committee had been succeeded by an independent society, the Chichester Cine Club. At its inaugural meeting, on 16 July 1935, a committee was elected and subscriptions fixed, in the first year, at 12s. 6d. of which 2s. 6d. would go to the B.F.I. The aims were to produce feature films of artistic quality with local actors and actresses, and news films concerning Chichester. Members were given clear advice at the branch meeting in October when Miss R. Matson, speaking on the objectives of the B.F.I., urged higher standards of film-making, claiming that films were being produced simply as a means of entertaining the poor, with little or no intellectual direction or story merit.[32]

A public show was arranged on three successive evenings in early November, at which a number of the Club's news films were presented, including Jubilee Day, school sports and a local pageant. As an exercise in raising profile and stimulating recruiting it was evidently a success, with 37 new members joining at the first AGM on 14 January 1936. Here the chairman, Leslie Evershed-Martin, known later as the inspiration behind the Chichester Festival Theatre, emphasised the liaison with the Bognor Film Society by screening its first two films, *What a Hunt* and *Cross Currents*.[33]

There is intimation in the *Chichester Observer* that the Cine Club intended to produce a short comedy during its first year, but there is no further evidence of this, and the early emphasis seems to have been on newsreel, mostly the work of its honorary secretary, F.J. Chapman. On 28 February 1936 there was a showing at St Bartholomew's Hall of the scenes in the city in January following the announcement of the death of George V, the royal memorial service in Chichester Cathedral and the proclamation at the Cross of the accession of Edward VIII.

> Many prominent figures in the City came to life on the screen ... when a projector took us back over those never-to-be-forgotten days ... when huge crowds paid homage to their late ruler.

The local newspaper praised the high standard of the photography and declared the films to be 'another unique and valuable contribution to the records of Chichester'. Today, sadly, their whereabouts, if they have survived, is unknown.[34]

In March 1936 came news of a feature film, an ambitious project involving between 30-40 characters in costume, in a story of King Arthur and the Knights of the Round Table. Directed by Chapman, it was to have the beautiful scenery of Goodwood and Chichester Harbour as its backcloth, with shooting beginning in May. Its progress was reported in the summer issue of *Sight and Sound*, but there is no reference to its completion, and at the annual public show in the Guides Hall in November it is again the newsreels which dominate contemporary accounts of the proceedings.[35]

Projected by Charles Howard and accompanied by a running commentary from Mr. Chapman, the films captured familiar faces and scenes at the local carnival, the sports meetings at the two high schools, and the commemoration in the city of Remembrance Sunday and Armistice Day. Further afield, the Cine Club had filmed the crash of the aviator Miss Jean Batten at Bepton, near Midhurst, and the Empire Air Display Day at Tangmere airfield. Their efforts were rewarded with four packed and enthusiastic houses.[36]

Although its impact was far less pronounced than its more illustrious counterpart at Bognor, particularly in the realm of feature films, the Cine Club at Chichester made its mark during the short period of its existence, and the quality of its newsreels of local events was consistently praised. It is a matter of regret that, with the notable exception of the Jubilee film, the legacy of its work does not survive amongst the city archives.

Adur and District Cine Society Another amateur film society formed in the county in 1935 in the wake of Bognor's growing reputation was the Adur and District Cine Society which met for the first time at the Shoreham Club in West Street, Shoreham-by-Sea, on 18 June 1935. A programme of professional and amateur films was presented, using projection apparatus and films loaned by Messrs. Foster and Paulin, and plans were made for film production to commence in the near future. Full membership was 10s. 6d. per annum, and the catchment area extended to Hove, Shoreham, Lancing and Worthing.[37]

The Society's first film was a newsreel of local events, entitled the *Adur Cine News*, and was well received when it was screened at the Shoreham Club on 22 October 1935. The correspondent of the *Lancing and Shoreham Times*, suitably impressed by the production, believed that the Society would become a telling force in the local entertainment world:

> The *Adur Cine News*, the Society's first and so far only production, was remarkably good. Shoreham regatta provided some exceptionally good and clear shots. The cameraman's picture of the senior fours rowing race was particularly good; and there was one scene, embracing the whole portion of river, with Shoreham Church upflung above the waterside sheds and dwellings, which makes me entertain very high hopes for the Society's future.
>
> There were also some very good scenes at Ferring village fair, while the Duke of Norfolk figures in a film which was taken at Worthing World's Fair in the summer. The camera has caught the Duke in some very natural poses, following him from the turnstiles, where he pays his modest entrance fee, to the platform where, before a huge crowd, he performed the opening ceremony.[38]

A week later, the chairman, George Alfred Browne, revealed that Adur was to start shooting a feature film, a comedy, mostly around Shoreham but also in the surrounding district as far afield as Henfield. There was to be a novel approach to the production: 'The plot is to be kept secret until the film is projected. The cast taking part will enact their own parts without knowing the story. This should give an interesting result.'[39]

The film, entitled *Lunatics at Large*, was still shooting, though nearing completion, in May 1936, according to *Amateur Cine World*, and by then a second feature was in production, but no evidence can be found to confirm that either of these films was finished and screened.[40]

The Society seems to have become well established with a programme of regular meetings. These were held at the Shoreham Club at 8 p.m. on the second and fourth Mondays in each month, and at every meeting there were exhibitions of films by members of this and other amateur societies. A presentation of its own films, including the *Adur Cine News*, was given on three separate evenings early in December 1935 at the Lido Centre in Hove. There were dances, script readings and film competitions, and, on 6 January 1936, a demonstration of talkie equipment.

This latter meeting was conducted by George Henry Gardener of Harrington Villas in Brighton, a member of the Adur Society, and an amateur film-maker well known on the South Coast, who had recently displayed his work in Somerset. A number of 16mm sound films were shown, illustrating the comparison between synchronised sound and sound-on-film, and he also showed several hundred feet of 16mm Dufaycolor including pictures of the Brighton Jubilee procession and some shots of Worthing.[41]

As at Chichester, so too at Shoreham, the stimulus provided by the Bognor Regis Film Society was apparent. The rules of the Adur Cine Society were based on those at Bognor, and members of the two Societies visited each other's meetings, with Harry Guermonprez lending his support at Shoreham. The first two Bognor films, *What a Hunt* and *Cross Currents*, were shown to Adur members to encourage their involvement in the production of feature films, and in March 1936 a party from Shoreham attended the second annual public show at Bognor to watch *Murder at the Theatre Royal*.[42]

The Adur Society held its AGM in June 1936, announcing plans to hold a public show at the end of September, but whilst it was certainly active in that month, organising an elaborate 'Film Face' competition using special studios at Worthing, Shoreham and Brighton, there is no report of such a show in the local press.[43]

The evidence suggests that, in common with the Chichester Cine Club, the Adur Cine Society was of short-lived duration, and was not destined to emulate the Bognor Regis Film Society in terms of reputation or legacy as a corporate film-making organisation. The present whereabouts of its work, if it has survived, is unknown.

Film Societies at Ferring and Littlehampton Francis Reginald Claridge of Ocean Drive, Ferring, was the original honorary secretary of the Adur and District Cine Society when it was formed in June 1935. Six months later, most probably at the meeting on 6 January 1936, he is reported as resigning to form a new film society at Ferring. No information about future progress was found until a chance meeting with the founder's son, at a Chichester film presentation by the South East Film & Video Archive in July 1996, revealed that the Ferring group had produced both news and feature films on 9.5mm and had given shows at the Village Hall.

Happily, the surviving films are to be copied for preservation by the Archive. The Ferring Cine Club disbanded before the outbreak of war in 1939, but today there is a successor, the Southdown Film and Video Society, which continues the tradition of amateur film-making in the area.[44]

In May 1938 *Amateur Cine World* announced that a meeting had been held at the *Norfolk Hotel* in Surrey Street, Littlehampton, on 25 March, at which a number of persons interested in amateur cinematography in Littlehampton and District had decided to form a film society. A second meeting was arranged on 4 April to consider draft rules, and a short programme of 16mm films was presented, including some colour shots of the area.[45]

The prime mover was Bernard Philip Vincent Elsden, a local solicitor, and meetings were held at his premises in Beach Road. The correspondent of the *Littlehampton Post*, doubtless influenced by the success enjoyed by the Film Society at neighbouring Bognor, had no reservations about the potential value to the town of this new initiative:

> These societies are certainly a benefit to a town, for not only do they provide amusement to residents, but through the medium of their news reels they do keep a permanent record of important happenings in the town.[46]

The society was formally constituted as Arun Film Productions, with Elsden as the honorary secretary, and had a membership of about twenty. A meeting on 11 April resolved to shoot a newsreel of events of local interest during the course of the year, and invited members to submit scripts for a feature film. A director was chosen—Mr. P.E. Davison—and plans were made to commence shooting in the summer.[47]

There are however no reports in the *Littlehampton Post* of the progress of filming during the summer months, and its hopes for the new society may not have been fulfilled, thwarted perhaps by the preparations for war which eventually undermined the existence of the Bognor Film Society.

FILM SOCIETIES TODAY

After the War a number of film-viewing and film-making societies were set up in the county, and some have become established elements of the local entertainment scene.

Film-viewing societies   The Sussex Film Society was formed in 1948 and became a member of the Federation of Film Societies. A film-viewing society, it established venues at the Town Hall in Worthing and Trinity Hall in Hove, and its members became free Associates of the British Film Institute, enabling them to obtain tickets for the National Film Theatre. The policy was to show popular mainstream films, as well as specialist scientific films and minority films for the connoisseur, plus *Amateur Cine World*'s ten best prize-winning amateur films of the year.

Amongst the film-viewing societies set up in specific towns in the late 1940s and early '50s was the Crawley Film Society. Michael Goldsmith, author of *Around Crawley in Old Photographs* (Alan Sutton, 1990), was a member in the 1960s and remembers 80 to 100 people attending its monthly shows at Hazlewick School in Three Bridges.[48]

The value of film-viewing societies was enhanced as cinemas began to close down in the 1970s and 1980s, and in some towns they came to offer the only venue

for cinema audiences. A case in point is Chichester, once the home of three cinemas, but reduced to none on the closure of the Granada in 1980.

At this time Roger Gibson, a lecturer at the local College of Technology, set up the Chichester College Film Society, partly to replace the cinema but also to foster an interest in films in the community. Open to both the general public and students, it offered the best of world cinema releases, introducing audiences to lesser known movies and foreign films, as well as showing more popular titles. For an annual subscription of £15, members had access to a 30-week programme on Wednesdays and Thursdays between September and May. In 1985 he received a Film Society of the Year Award from the British Federation of Film Societies for his work in building up the College Society.[49]

Running parallel to the College Film Society was the Chichester City Film Society which initially showed films on Fridays at the New Park Community Centre in New Park Road. Here the programme, again arranged by Roger Gibson, tended to concentrate on the popular box-office hits, but there was also room for more specialist films and for themes such as British Film Year. As at the College, films were shown during the September-May season, but in 1985-86 this was extended to include the summer. For a time, a Junior Film Club was run at the Centre, for seven- to 15-year-olds, meeting on Saturday mornings, with membership for the season costing £6. Walt Disney was well represented in the programmes, but the Club was forced to close in 1984 through lack of interest, with the blame being placed on the growing popularity of domestic videos.

During this period, Chichester also had a Film Theatre, meeting during the season at the Newell Centre in St Pancras, and so was able to offer a wide range of films, in pleasant and intimate surroundings, a contrast perhaps to the anonymity of mainline cinemas.

The Chichester City Film Society has gone from strength to strength since the mid-1980s, and its New Park Film Centre (125 seats) continues to offer members and non-members a well balanced programme of specialist films and Hollywood blockbusters. From 1986 it was providing an all-year-round programme, with screenings every Thursday and Friday evening (extended to Saturdays in 1990), and in the 1992 summer season it began operating seven days a week for the first time, with three performances daily, a practice which has been maintained in holiday periods. Also in this latter year it introduced a summer film festival, initially as part of the Chichester Festivities programme, and this has become an annual event. In 1995, with Roger Gibson as artistic director, the fourth Chichester Film Festival, spread over 17 days in August, included previews of unreleased UK and international films, a retrospective of the work of director Ken Loach, and a series of early Hitchcock films as part of a Cinema 100 celebration.

The New Park Film Centre, with its large screen and Dolby Stereo sound, continues to fulfil a vital rôle in Chichester, a testimony to the value of film societies, generating interest in film and filling the void left by the closure of the city's cinemas.

Film-making societies The tradition of cine enthusiasts combining as film societies and cine clubs to produce films, both newsreels and features, which had emerged in the 1930s, re-surfaced once the problems and restrictions of the war years were over.

Such a society was founded at Haywards Heath on 16 February 1949, and continues today as the Haywards Heath Cine and Video Society. Films were made by individual members for inclusion in a film library from which others could draw for screening in their own homes. Public shows were organised—the first being held on 13 December 1949. Members also combined to make club films, with actors and actresses drawn from the Society, and Richard Mercer remembers the first one, shot in 1952 and titled *TV Thief*, about a family burgled while watching television.[50]

A collection of the Society's work, mostly silent news and documentary films on Standard 8, Super 8 and 9.5mm, is now preserved by the South East Film & Video Archive. Covering the period 1959-87, the films range in length from 2-40 minutes, and include such titles as *Bluebell Railway*, *Cuckfield Donkey Derby*, *Ditchling Fair*, *Haywards Heath Market Place*, and *South Downs Way*.[51]

Richard Mercer remembers that the advent of television led to a decline in what had been a good membership roll, but the Society still meets every fortnight at Clair Hall in Perrymount Road. Members continue to make films, either individually or as a club, entering them in competitions with other societies, and although much work is now done on video, they have this year produced a four minute black-and-white comedy on cinefilm, *The Celebration*, in commemoration of Cinema 100.

Although it was of only short duration, the Crawley Film Unit was another active film-making society, and produced at least one film a year between 1954-63. According to local historian, Michael Goldsmith, there was no film society in Crawley before the Second World War, although there was a tradition of amateur film-making in the town. Moses Nightingale and his son-in-law produced marvellous 9.5 footage of local events in the inter-war era, some of which is now preserved by SEFVA, including a memorable sequence of Sunday traffic in the Brighton Road in 1929.[52]

The Crawley Film Unit, however, was formed by a small group of people led by George Howe and his wife, Lindey. They started a film production section of the Crawley Film Society, and their film of the De Maupassant story, *Two Friends*, was nominated as one of the ten best amateur films of the year in 1954. The Film Unit came into existence as an independent club, and met initially at the Community Hut in Northgate. Later it met for a time at 'The Beeches', the home of Sir Norman Longley, as Lady Longley was a keen member.

Shot as they were during the early days of the New Town, the films made by the club now constitute an interesting record of buildings and views no longer in existence. The majority were fiction films, but a notable exception was a ten-minute record of the Queen's visit to Crawley in June 1958.

The Film Unit disbanded in *c.*1963, but amateur film-making in the town resumed in 1968, with the birth of a new group, the Crawley Cine Club, inspired by Michael Goldsmith and Jim Slater, with George Howe as its first chairman. The name was changed to the more fashionable Crawley Film Makers after three or four years, and at its peak it had 40 to 50 members meeting in the YWCA Hall in Bank Lane. A number of films were produced, but membership dwindled, and the club was disbanded in 1983, so ending sixty years of amateur film-making in Crawley.[53]

The Bognor Regis Film Society and the Chichester Cine Club have a worthy successor in the Chichester Film and Video Makers which began life as the Southern Sound and Cine Club in autumn 1960.

Originally it had a strong Bognor emphasis, meeting at the Picturedrome Cinema, but by 1964 it had moved to the Camera Shop in East Street, Chichester, of which its chairman, John Davis, was proprietor. Its focal point today is still Chichester, meeting fortnightly for lectures, competitions and social events at St Pancras Church Hall, but the membership is drawn from further afield, generally south of the Downs, and along the coast, from Rustington to Fareham.[54]

Over the years its emphasis has changed, beginning with sound recording and cinefilm, and now, as is generally the case, geared more to video, in deference to the popularity of video cameras and camcorders. Some members remain loyal to cine, however, and the club's archive includes film on Standard 8, Super 8 and 16mm. Its title was changed from the Southern Sound Film and Video Club to the Chichester Film and Video Makers in 1996 to emphasise its association with the city.

The club is a member of the South East Region of the Institute of Amateur Cinematographers, and inter-club competitions are an important element in its life. In 1986 it won an award at the annual Shoreham Challenge, held at their Lancing club room, with *Where are the Clowns?*, a film based on the annual Clowns Convention at Bognor. Such films would be shown publicly at Bognor's Alexandra Theatre. This year (1996) the club has produced *Time to Go*, a 7½-minute feature film on video, with acting parts played by the members, as its contribution to the annual Albany competition, in which it will be challenging 16 other societies from the region, from Portsdown to Haywards Heath.[55]

This flourishing club has now inaugurated its own video competition, open to societies nationally, in memory of Bill Glue, a long-standing member who died in 1991 and is remembered as one of the finest amateur film-makers in the area.

Another very active group of cine enthusiasts was the East Grinstead and District Cine Society founded in 1961 by Bill Scragg. It had a membership of around forty, and produced a number of films, with sound, on Standard 8 and Super 8, both documentaries and dramas. Founder member Malcolm Powell remembers that members of local dramatic and operatic societies took part in the films. The club disbanded in the early 1970s but happily some of the films have been preserved by Mr. Powell.[56]

Returning to the 9.5mm gauge used by the Bognor Regis Film Society in its early days, it is perhaps appropriate that one of the six regional branches of the national society, Group 9.5, should be based in Bognor, where it was formed in September 1981 by Hugh Hale, who had begun producing his own movies in 1947. This gauge was very popular before the war, and still continues to have its loyal adherents in this country and on the continent. The national society meets annually at Chiswick and Pimlico, and members contribute film each year to their own International Film Festival.[57]

The West Sussex group, which began in Bognor with 16 members, still meets monthly, and continues to make films on 9.5. Significantly, it was two founder members, Hugh Hale and Ron Middleton, who, with John Davis of Southern Sound, re-spliced and projected the old films of the Bognor Regis Film Society when they were re-shown in the town in the late 1970s and early 1980s.

It is gratifying that there are still such enthusiasts with the devotion and expertise to carry on the traditions of amateur film-making in the county. Our hope is that their example will continue to be followed in the future, and our duty is to ensure that their work is preserved as part of the film heritage of the region.

IV

THE TRAVELLING FILM SHOWMEN

Before the emergence of the permanent or purpose-built cinema, a variety of existing buildings were pressed into use to meet the new demand, and to provide occasional venues for the travelling showmen who brought with them the apparatus which Edison, the Lumières and Paul had developed. Across the county of West Sussex the advent of the new sensation of moving pictures, or animated photographs, was reported in enthusiastic style by the correspondents of local newspapers. A selection of experiences from within the county may best illustrate the manner in which the cinematograph was received in those first few years of cinema history.

FIRST SCREENING ON WORTHING PIER

It is perhaps appropriate that in the seaside county of West Sussex the first known venue for the showing of films should have been a pier pavilion.

Lieutenant Walter Cole was one of several entertainers who, with a touring company, made periodic visits to towns in the county during the latter years of the

43 The Pavilion at the sea end of Worthing Pier—where animated photographs made their first appearance in West Sussex.

The Pier, Worthing.

45

19th century. His Operetta and Concert Company of London artistes gave annual shows during the summer season at the Pier Pavilion in Worthing, to which he contributed his own ventriloquial act. In 1896, however, the *Worthing Gazette* promised there would be special significance to his week-long engagement beginning on Monday 31 August, with evening performances and three matinees:

> ... he will introduce to local audiences a distinct novelty in the form of a series of animated photographs. This latest electric invention has created the greatest enthusiasm amongst London audiences, and if it is produced here with anything like the success attended at the Empire or the Alhambra, we are sure that it will prove the greatest sensation of the Worthing entertainment season.[1]

The Pier Pavilion was soon to be the scene of another early display of films when, on Easter Monday, 19 April 1897, the Meier family's touring troupe of Tyrolean Minstrels gave a concert which included an 'Exhibition of the Scenomatograph or perfected animated photographs'.[2]

In between these two performances on the Pier, there were to be two other presentations elsewhere in the town, at the Theatre Royal.

As was often the case at this early stage, in the first of these displays, a demonstration of Robert William Paul's Theatrograph, the films were shown as an additional item in a programme of live entertainment.

> Mr. Sydney Grundy's charming comedy, *A Pair of Spectacles*, is to be produced by Mr. Edward Graham Falcon's Company at the Theatre Royal ... and the attractiveness of the entertainment is to be increased by the production by Mr. John D. Ablett of Mr. R.W. Paul's marvellous invention, the Theatrograph. The comedy alone is at any time splendid value for money, but with the marvellous animated photographs thrown in, patrons of the Theatre will find abundance of entertainment.[3]

The show was presented at 8 p.m. on Friday 27 and Saturday 28 November 1896—'front seats 3s.' and 'carriages 10.15' suggesting a refined audience—and the films were projected by Ablett at the end of the play.

> The pictures, as exhibited, were somewhat wanting in distinctness, but several of them—and notably the representation of a railway station—were received with considerable enthusiasm by the audiences.[4]

A fortnight later, regular patrons of the Theatre Royal were to see a demonstration of the Cinematoscope by E. Baruch Blaker, who was already known in the town as a lantern slide lecturer. It was an event eagerly anticipated by the correspondent of the *Worthing Gazette*:

> Prior to an engagement at the Crystal Palace, Mr. E. Baruch Blaker will give ... an entertainment by means of his Cinematoscope, being photographs which accomplish nothing less marvellous than the presentation of accurate records of real living scenes of everyday life. One special scene is Brighton Front on a Bank Holiday, described by the London Press to be a 'triumph of scientific mechanism and art.' The Cinematoscope is a scientific machine, and up to the present the most perfect obtainable. No description can adequately convey an idea of the realistic presentations; life, movement, detail and animation being faithfully reproduced.[5]

There were three short shows at 6.30, 7.30 and 8.30 on Friday 11 and Saturday 12 December 1896, and admission was 1s. 3d. and 1s. 6d. ('schools half-price').

Unfortunately, there was a mechanical breakdown in the first performance but thereafter the programme progressed without mishap.

> Among the more interesting and amusing of the pictures were a reproduction of a game of leap frog by a group of boys and a skirt dance by Miss Loie Fuller.[6]

For local interest, the films were accompanied by still photographs of a recent wreck off Lancing, and the return of the Worthing lifeboat to the Pier. It is perhaps not surprising that the lifeboat at Worthing was to figure prominently in the early history of film-making in the county.[7]

GRAND CARNIVAL IN HORSHAM

Assembly Rooms were often the venues for the earliest film performances in a town, and this may well have been the case at Horsham, where John D. Ablett was booked to bring his Theatrograph for two evening performances on Wednesday 25 and Thursday 26 November 1896, before moving on to Worthing. Again promoted in conjunction with the comedy, *A Pair of Spectacles*, which had played before the Queen at the Garrick Theatre in London, the Theatrograph was expected to draw large audiences to the King's Head Assembly Rooms.[8]

There is no subsequent report, unfortunately, to confirm that this was the case, but a year later the Assembly Rooms was again advertised as the venue for another show of moving pictures, this time as part of a variety bill, and featuring shots of Queen Victoria's Diamond Jubilee celebrations in London.

> Pringle and Kirk's celebrated Pierrot's Minstrels and Grand Variety Confederation, in conjunction with Professor Sear's Latest Improved Cinematograph, 50 magnificent Animated Pictures, including Her Majesty's Jubilee Procession, the most gorgeous pageant in the History of the nations of the World. These magnificent living pictures are portrayed in a manner so real and truthful, that it is easy to imagine that you are present at that memorable occasion.

There were to be two 8 p.m. performances on Friday 8 and Saturday 9 October 1897, with a grand Saturday morning performance, and seats were 6d., 1s. and 2s.[9]

Between these two shows at the Assembly Rooms, there was a display of animated photographs as part of the Horsham Grand Carnival commencing at 6.30 p.m. on Bank Holiday Monday, 2 August 1897, on Springfield Meadow. This was the biggest Bank Holiday attraction for a wide area, with people arriving by train, carriage and cycle.

> Soon after the fancy dress parade in the lower portion of the meadow, and when twilight set in, preparation was made for the display of animated photographs. When the performance began the hill-side was covered with thousands of people, who now and then applauded the particularly animated photographs. The pictures were not always distinct, but the invention appeared to receive considerable appreciation. At 9.30 was commenced the display of fireworks ...[10]

The publicity for the Grand Carnival described this as the 'first appearance' in Horsham of animated photographs, so either it overlooked Ablett's advertised visit the previous November or that visit failed to take place. Excellent sources though they are, local newspapers can leave frustrating queries and, in the absence of other sources, these cannot always be resolved.[11]

The films which had been seen at the Carnival had earlier been shown in London, and in these early years provincial towns such as Worthing and Horsham received only very occasional visits from touring companies such as Ablett and Cole. Only three shows are advertised for Horsham in 1896-97. The next took a different form, a combined film and lantern slide entertainment, *A Tour round the World*, presented by Mr. Horace Banks to the Horsham Mutual Improvement Society at the Albion Hall on 18 January 1898.[12]

CINEMATOGRAPH AT THE CORN EXCHANGE

Another of the travelling companies operating in the county at this time was owned by Miss Maggie Morton, who began bringing her Christmas pantomime to the Corn Exchange in Chichester in the early 1890s, and she it was who introduced the Cinematograph to the city at 8 p.m. on Boxing Day, Saturday 26 December 1896.

The pantomime, for which she had a troupe of 40 artistes and a string band, was entitled *Blue Beard*, and the new attraction was presented in scene six:

> In Scene 6 (Blue Beard's Palace Gardens) will be introduced the greatest sensation and most wonderful invention of the age, The Cinematograph (Animated Pictures) as now being exhibited at the Empire, Alhambra, Crystal Palace, etc., showing the same pictures projected by the same instrument as exhibited before HM the Queen and Royal Family.[13]

The Boxing Day performance was followed by two performances on Monday 28 December, at 2.30 and 8 p.m., before the company moved on to Midhurst (29-30 December) and Petersfield (31 December-1 January). Luckily the advertisement in the *Chichester Observer* on 23 December includes a list of 'Irving Boscot's Pictures' from which a selection would be made for the audience at the Corn Exchange.

44 *Chichester Observer* heralds the arrival of the Cinematograph in the city.

GRAND ILLUMINATED MORNING PERFORMANCE
On Monday, Doors Open at 2 for 2.30.
Plan and Tickets now ready at Mr. Pillow's.

MISS MAGGIE MORTON'S original, farcical, comical, funny, gorgeous Christmas PANTOMIME entitled:—
BLUE BEARD
Or the BLUE ROOM and the TRAGIC KEY.

Company of 40 artistes. String band. New and magnificent scenery, up-to-date music, the charming and costly costumes, intricate scenery, wonderful mechanical effects, limelight, armour, comic scene, new and popular songs. Harlequinade. In Scene 6 (Blue Beard's Palace Gardens) will be introduced the greatest sensation and most wonderful invention of the age—The CINEMATOGRAPH (Irving Boscots) animated pictures, as now being exhibited at the Empire, Alhambra, Crystal Palace, &c. Pictures from the following selection shown by the Most Perfect Instrument Made:—Arrival of the Czar in Paris. Bathing in the baths at Brighton. Infantry on the march. Gardeners burning weeds. Going for a row from Margate. Fight between a man and a bear. Spanish cattle market in Madrid. Arrival of a train at Portsmouth station. Sea breaking over the rocks. Cavalry crossing a bridge. Reaping at harvest time. Glove boxing contest. At the photographer's studio. The Boulevards at Paris.

Prices at 7 p.m.—3s., 2s., 1s. 6d., 1s.
Performance commencing at 8.

Arrival of the Czar in Paris. Bathing in the baths at Brighton. Infantry on the March. Gardeners burning weeds. Going for a row from Margate. Fight between a man and a bear. Spanish cattle market in Madrid. Arrival of a train at Portsmouth station. Sea breaking over the rocks. Cavalry crossing a bridge. Reaping at harvest time. Glove boxing contest. At the photographer's studio. The Boulevards at Paris.

For people in Chichester this would have been their first experience of watching moving films, and it is not difficult to imagine the impact they would have made. These early pictures were mostly short single reelers, of 50 feet or a minute in length, and were usually single shot productions with one camera in a fixed position. They were silent, of course, and whatever the subject matter they invariably portrayed movement of one form or another: waves breaking against a sea wall as in Birt Acres' *Rough Sea at Dover* (1895), a train arriving at a station in the Lumière's *L'arrivée d'un train en gare de la Ciotat* (1895) or, nearer home, in George Albert Smith's *Train Entering Hove Station* (1897), or people walking on a beach in Robert William Paul's *Scene on Brighton Beach* (1896).

It is easy to allow ourselves to be amused by the innocent naivety of those early cinema audiences as they took fright at the Lumière's train as it steamed straight towards them, but such accounts were reported in West Sussex as the new wonder of the age made its initial impression on local people. In Bognor, for example, patrons at the Assembly Rooms watching *The Fire Brigade Call* in December 1897 found themselves diving for cover as the galloping horses approached the screen.[14]

BIOSCOPE SHOWS AT SLOE FAIR

The Corn Exchange was used only occasionally for films over the next few years, but Cicestrians could also look forward to the bioscope shows which came with the travelling fairs that periodically visited the district. These were in fact mobile cinemas, and some, initially at least, were fairly crude in conception and design. A canvas booth, a row of wooden platforms for the penny seats with a raised dais for the twopenny patrons, and a three-sided screen behind which the operator and a hand-cranked projector were housed. Outside, next to a gaudily painted caravan, a barker would give his spiel through a megaphone to his prospective audience. Later, drawn by steam traction engines, the travelling bioscope shows became quite ornate affairs, with hand-painted panel facades, strings of coloured lamps, canvas marquee, decorated proscenium arch, and Gavioli steam organ. They may not have had the appearance of a palace, but for many, especially children of course, they were rare palaces of delight, dark places into which they could escape and allow their imaginations to be captured by the mesmeric flickering images on the silver screen.[15]

Russell Burstow has identified W. and S. Hancock as the largest of the travelling bioscope operators in the south, visiting Chichester and Bognor, but also venturing as far afield as Devon and Cornwall.[16]

One of the fairs patronised by these travelling cinemas was Sloe Fair, held every autumn in Chichester at Northgate, and one of the most eagerly awaited events in the city's year, drawing thousands with its switchbacks, roundabouts, shooting galleries, boxing booths, coconut shies and innumerable side shows. Sadly, substantial reports are few and far between, but one was published in the *Chichester Observer* on 26 October 1904, albeit it seems because this ancient institution was then under threat. A reference to the bioscope conjures up the sights and sounds that attended such shows with the dancing girls doing their best to entice the customers inside.

> The cinematograph exhibitors did a roaring trade. On the platform outside the booth a young girl, clad in the cheap and tawdry finery that makes so brave a show under the glare of naphtha lamps, was dancing to the tune of a popular song, blared from the pipes of a mechanical organ, the strident melody (?) being punctuated by groans of a hooter near by, while the babel was increased by other alleged musical instruments voicing a conglomeration of all too popular tunes, the sights and sounds reminding one of a page from Dickens' or 'A peep behind the scenes', and one naturally wondered if under the glare and glitter there was an aching heart and if the tiny feet that moved so nimbly were aching and sore. Still there was a large crowd watching the dancing with evident enjoyment and one was bound to admit that there was no more harm here than in the innocent ball patronised by the aristocracy.

The show would last on average for fifteen minutes, with 'topical' scenes such as trains arriving at a station and 'actualities' of stormy seas, plus comedy shorts such as Smith's *The Miller and the Sweep* (1897), showing those age-old adversaries of music hall and popular song exchanging their flour and soot. Later there would be newsreels and dramas, for the bioscope shows were to survive until the First World War. Indeed, Russell Burstow has suggested that between 1908-14 the standard of projection, presentation and comfort of the 'Bio' exceeded that of many of the Electric Theatres and Picture Palaces which were then emerging as permanent cinemas.

MOVIE THERAPY AT THE COUNTY ASYLUM

Although for most people in the city at the turn of the century it was the Corn Exchange or the travelling bioscope show which gave them their first introduction to the magic of the silver screen, these were not the only venues showing moving pictures in Chichester in the very early years of cinema history.

45 *Above*. The West Sussex County Asylum at Chichester pictured soon after its opening in 1897.

46 The Recreation Hall at Graylingwell as it looked in 1901.

Graylingwell Mental Hospital was situated in extensive grounds to the north of the city and, under the management of a Committee appointed by West Sussex County Council, it cared for all classes of the mentally ill. It opened in July 1897 and had a capacity for 600 patients. It possessed its own spacious Recreation Hall, with a stage at one end and an upper gallery at the other, and seating accommodation for 600.[17]

The first Annual Report of the Medical Superintendent, in May 1898, stated that recreation was regarded as 'a most valuable agent in the treatment of the insane', and that during the winter months the Hall had been used for dances, theatrical performances, presentations by local clubs, and concerts by the hospital's own String and Brass Bands. From the beginning, film shows were also to be a regular feature in the programme of entertainment therapy arranged for the patients.[18]

There were 368 patients in residence when the first film presentation was made at 7.30 p.m. on Saturday 27 November 1897. This was described in the beautifully printed souvenir brochure as a 'Programme of Mr. David Devant's Animated Photographs. Direct from Maskelyne and Cooke's, Egyptian Hall, under the direction of Mr. R.A. Roberts'. Part One, introduced and concluded by the Band, consisted of a number of short films including *The Fire Brigade Call*, *Mr. David Devant Conjuring with Rabbits*, *The Spanish Bull-Fight*, *The Twins Tea Party*, and *Changing Guard at St James' Palace*. Songs from a Mr. R.M. Steere preceded another selection of shorts in Part Two including *Brighton Beach*. Finally, after some incidental music, came the star turn, *The Queen's Diamond Jubilee Procession*, 'Reproduced upon the Screen with all the actual movements of real life'.

With no public admittance, there was no reference in the local press, nor was there for the second presentation which had to wait until Friday 10 March 1899. This was again from the Egyptian Hall, with Roberts showing a selection of 21 films from the London Photographic Association, with the usual musical interludes.

The County Asylum kept the programmes of its various entertainments in a series of scrapbooks covering the period 1897-1912, and another superb brochure survives for the third film show, at 7.30 p.m. on Friday 3 November 1899. This was a display by Mr. R.P. Goodacre of Lumière and other films, each from 55 to 170 feet in length, using the Bio-Cinematograph, producing an image 15ft. 6in. by 10ft. 6in.

The institution presented its own show on 2 March 1900, the living pictures interspersed with dances, but it was the norm to hire outside exhibitors, and in 1901 John L. Dyer of Emsworth put on two mixed evenings of animated photographs, lantern slides and shadowgraphy, being paid three guineas on each occasion. His second show, on 1 November, had a distinctly

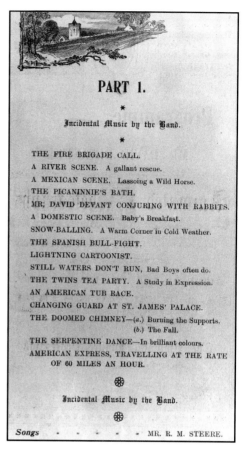

47 Souvenir brochure for the first film show at Graylingwell.

48 Programme of short films presented at the Asylum by David Devant in November 1897.

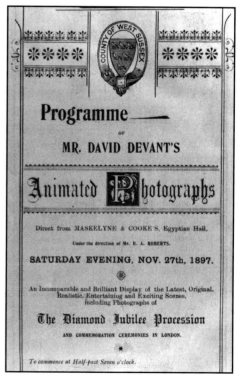

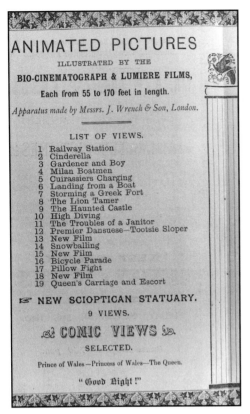

49 Brochure for the third exhibition of animated pictures.

50 Programme for Goodacre's visit to Graylingwell in November 1899.

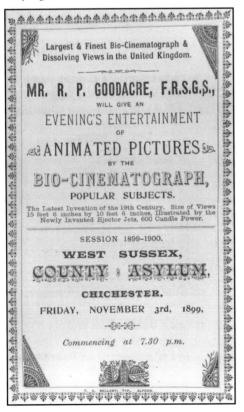

military beginning, with films of the British Army at home and in South Africa, but finished with a local emphasis, including *Emsworth Regatta* and footage of gymnastics, sack racing, motor cycle racing, and bun eating in Priory Park, Chichester.

Dances and entertainments followed each other weekly throughout the autumn and winter months, on Friday evenings, between October and March, and by 1901 films were being shown twice during the season. There are some well-known early films represented in the programmes. On 26 October 1906 E.H. Mason of Seven Kings, Ilford, came with his Vitascope, a refinement by Thomas Armat of the Edison and Lumière machines, and showed, amongst 15 films, George Albert Smith's comedy *Mary Jane's Mishap or Don't Fool with the Paraffin* (1903) and Cecil Hepworth's *Rescued by Rover* (1905), the inclusion of the latter a clear indication that mere 'cinematograph views' were giving way to real story films.

An annotation in the scrapbook notes that this latter exhibition, hired for four guineas, was 'very good', and Mason's visit became an annual fixture. On 22 November 1907 he was back with eight films, now longer of course, of which top billing was accorded Hepworth's *Dumb Sagacity*, one of his animal rescue stories, shot at Bognor earlier that same year.[19]

The London Bioscope Company was another visitor, on 6 March 1908, and one of the final entries in the scrapbooks is the appearance of Messrs. Poole and Co., with The Biograph, on 19 October 1911. A year earlier they had commenced running the Corn Exchange as a regular cinema, and now, at the County Asylum, they put on a programme including a 'local film' and a Pathé Gazette newsreel.[20]

The notion that films were regarded as an integral part of the therapy and entertainment offered to patients is confirmed by the installation of the hospital's own bioscope in 1912-13. The annual report for that year mentions, amongst the new building works, the 'alteration to roof of corridor for Bioscope' and a year later there is reference to 'the Bioscope being found a most useful adjunct to the entertainments'. No longer dependent on travelling companies, the Asylum now increased the frequency of its film shows, and in February 1913 put on three consecutive weekly performances, two of them in conjunction with a concert and a dance.[21]

Graylingwell was to function as a Military War Hospital during the First World War, its regular cinematograph shows proving popular with the wounded, and thereafter returned to its original rôle as a mental hospital. Films continued to be included as part of the entertainments given in the Recreation Hall, and today vestiges still remain of its use as a cinema, a reminder of former days when it was one of the first venues in the county for the screening of moving pictures.

VICTORIA HALL AND ASSEMBLY ROOMS IN BOGNOR

As was the case in Chichester, so too in Bognor, the first displays of living pictures or animated photographs to paying audiences were presented by travelling showmen visiting public halls and fairgrounds.

The Victoria Hall, opposite St John's Church in London Road, was built in 1826 as the town's first Congregational Chapel, but in the summer of 1897 was converted by Alfred Adlington into a theatre. With seating, including a balcony, for 350, it put on melodramas and comedies by travelling artistes, and on Thursday 9 and Friday 10 December 1897 provided the venue for Mr. R.A. Williams to show animated pictures on his Cinématographe. A year later, beginning on 14 November 1898, Messrs. Braide and Wyndham's Comedy Opera and Pepper's Ghost Company fulfilled a week's engagement at the Hall, their variety entertainment concluding with an exhibition of moving pictures projected on the Eventographe, which impressed the reviewer in the local newspaper.

> One of the Animated Photographs shown on Monday night, that of releasing horses from a burning stable during the recent great fire in London, was of itself a good return for the amount charged for admission to this most comprehensive entertainment.[22]

Such visits were few and far between, and films appear to have played only a minor part in the entertainment offered at Victoria Hall. Even so, the following year there was a variation when, on 1 February 1899, it was the venue for a musical concert, gramophone recital and display of animated photographs, put on by the Bognor Lodge of the Royal Antediluvian Order of Buffaloes for 400 of the poorer inhabitants of Bognor, Bersted, Pagham and Felpham.[23]

The New Assembly Rooms, situated opposite the railway station, was another public hall in Bognor used by the early travelling film showmen, and on 14-16 December 1897 it played host to David Devant's pictures, no doubt a programme similar to that exhibited at Graylingwell a few weeks earlier.

> The manager of the Assembly Rooms has waited until the animated photographs from the Egyptian Hall could be engaged in order to give Bognor audiences a realistic idea of the real animatographe .... Mr. Devant is the talk of London, and is re-engaged wherever he goes.[24]

Later, there would be annual visits by the Poole brothers, with variety and pictures, and by Alfred John West, with his patriotic films. A marine photographer from Gosport, West turned to cinefilm in 1897, producing films of the Royal Navy and British Army which were shown throughout the Empire, a handful of which now survives with the Wessex Film and Sound Archive.

However, as will be described more fully in Chapter 5, usually there would be only two or three such shows a year in Bognor in the early days of film. The Assembly Rooms, though, like the Corn Exchange in Chichester, was destined to graduate to full-time cinema status once films had become recognised as a long-term feature of popular entertainment.

Another venue in Bognor which began by hosting occasional travelling film shows before eventually turning to full-time cinema was the Pier Pavilion. Concerts were performed there during the season and Lieutenant Walter Cole visited annually. He was there with his company of 'Merry Folks' at 8 p.m. on Saturday 19 August 1899,

Poole's Annual Visit. The best of them all.

ASSEMBLY ROOMS, BOGNOR.

Positively for One Week Only!

Commencing Monday, Nov. 9th, 1908,

Nightly at 7.45.

Doors open at 7.30. Early Doors at 7, 3d. extra to all parts.

Grand Select MATINEES on WEDNESDAY and SATURDAY at 3.

Doors open at 2.30. (Equal to Night.)
Poole's popular prices—2/-, 1/6, 1/-, and 6d.
Children Half-price. Seats may be booked at the usual places.

THE "JOSEPH"

POOLE'S No. 1 Colossal MYRIORAMA.

Everything entirely new for this visit! Just added—A Splendid Series of Tableaux, OUR COLONIES, the mighty British Empire, on which the sun never sets. JOSEPH POOLE'S MYRIOGRAPH, the very best Animated Photos ever seen, Always something new at Poole's. At every performance will be shown a Splendid Animated Picture of THE MARATHON RACE from Windsor to the Stadium. His Majesty the King and President Fallieres at THE WHITE CITY, etc. JOSEPH POOLE'S ENTERTAINERS. Twelve star artistes, including LOUDON CAMERON and MAUD DUNHAM, the Celebrated Mystifiers, in their artistic speciality, THE PALACE OF FANTASTIC SURPRISES, must be seen to be believed. Important engagement of Miss Fredrica's Wonderful PERFORMING TERRIERS, and celebrated CAKE-WALKING PONY, "DOT." "The Last Word in Animal Training.—Vide Press.

The whole enlivened and accompanied by Joseph Poole's FAMOUS ORCHESTRAL BAND! Conductor, Mr. W. A. Abbey.

Enormous Attraction!!
ASSEMBLY ROOMS, BOGNOR.

For one week only!
COMMENCING MONDAY, NOVEMBER 7th.
Each Evening at 8.
Matinees, Wednesday and Saturday at 3.
Doors open at 2.30 and 7.30.
WEST'S GRAND NAVAL AND MILITARY CINEMATOGRAPH ENTERTAINMENT
From the Polytechnic,
"OUR NAVY AND ARMY."
Entirely New Programme.
Cruise on a Battleship. Naval Manœuvres.
Our latest Dreadnoughts. Battle Practice.
How our Bluejackets Fight on Land.
Grand Military Tournament.
Humorous Scenes Afloat and Ashore.
Other Pictures of extraordinary interest.
Prices—Reserved, 2s.; Unreserved, 1s. and 6d. Children half-price to 2s. and 1s. seats.
Early doors open at 7, 3d. extra to all parts.
Seats booked at Lawrence Wood's, High Street, Bognor.

51 *Above left.* At the end of the century there were five Poole brothers touring the country with their myrioramas—panoramic pictures drawn across the stage on rollers—but in Bognor from 1901 they added films shown on their myriograph. (*Bognor Observer.*)

52 *Above right.* Alfred West's visit to the Assembly Rooms in 1910 is announced in the *Bognor Observer.*

but that their show included animated photographs, as it did elsewhere in the county, is not specifically confirmed by newspaper reports.[25]

In the summer of 1906 the season of promenade concerts on the Pier included, in the week commencing 3 September, 'an exhibition of animated pictures from the Egyptian Hall', supplied by Maskelyne and Devant 'the world-renowned entertainers'. This would appear to be the only performance of films on the Pier during that season, but two years later, under new management, the Pier Pavilion would become Bognor's first regular cinema.[26]

Bognor can provide yet another example of the travelling shows which gave local people their first experience of animated photographs in the days before the advent of permanent cinemas. On a piece of waste land, now St Clair Terrace, near the junction of Longford and Linden Roads, on a site where marionette shows were occasionally given, a Church Army mission van brought a film show in 1904-05 which was recalled by Mr. R.F. Rose in a letter published in the *Bognor Post* in 1951.

> In the utter darkness, to which we were accustomed to in those days, the crowd consisting of 90 per cent children watched with fear and bated breath, figures coming to life on this huge sheet, and I remember running with other children to witness it from the rear of the screen.[27]

TEE THE SHOWMAN

We are fortunate that we have a rare insight into the travelling film exhibitor at the turn of the century in the form of three scrapbooks compiled by Archibald Tee and now in the collection of Brighton Reference Library. One of the earliest items is a handbill from 1899. It advertises Archibald and his brother Charles and their exhibition of animated photographs and dissolving views of the 'Transvaal War' to be presented to the Young Men's Christian Institute in Hove. We can assume, with some confidence, that this film programme was seen across Sussex. The scrapbooks reveal that A. Tee specialised in Christian visual entertainments and that in 1903 he acquired the lease to St Ann's Well Garden to provide him with a base for this work. G.A. Smith, his predecessor at St Ann's, had moved to Southwick to pursue Kinemacolor.

From 1903 to 1906, Tee developed the attractions at his garden. Tee's advertisements for the Garden drew attention to the fact that it was run on 'temperance principles', the entertainments were 'strictly refined and humorous' and that 'the place is always free from the objectionable element one finds sometimes at similar places of amusement'. He was particularly interested, as his publicity materials stated, in welcoming choirs, schools, Guilds, Mothers' Meetings and the Band of Hope Union to this 'veritable utopia'. At this 'arcadia in miniature', the prospective visitor was informed that, 'In the evening the grounds will be prettily illuminated, and a novelty will be the open-air display of animated pictures, and the whole will conclude with a grand ascent of fire balloons at ten o'clock.'

An issue of the Christ Church Parochial Calendar is found towards the end of Volume 3. Dating from one of the summers from 1904-6, it describes an 'annual treat' organised by this Worthing church for the children of the Sunday Schools. A party of 200 children and 70 adults took the train to Hove for the purpose of visiting St Ann's. They attended the pictorial lecture, given by the manager (Mr. Tee) on the Legend of St Ann's Well. 'At four o'clock tea was provided under the trees, which was not the least important part of the day. After tea a very good display of Cinematograph Animated Photographs was given in a large concert hall which was much appreciated.'

Tee, with the skills mastered at St Ann's Well, organised outside entertainment in towns across Sussex in 1905-6. The *East Grinstead Observer*, on Saturday 26 August 1905, gave a glowing report on the imminent arrival of the Hove showman. 'Mr. A.H. Tee, who so well manages the popular St Ann's Well at Brighton, is going to wake up East Grinstead on Wednesday week. He is arranging a grand illuminated evening fete and carnival to take place on the cricket ground, which is to be adorned with thousands of lamps and for the time being turned into a veritable fairyland. There will be music and dancing, animated pictures, ascents of fire balloons, a display of fireworks and a continuous round of entertainment for some hours.' The accompanying advertisement announced 'grand open-air-display of A.H. Tee's celebrated Bioscope, Animated Pictures'.

In July 1906 he staged a 'Grand Illuminated Fete and Fancy Dress Carnival' in Worthing at Beach House Park. It included the 'ascent of fire balloons', a procession of fancy dresses and decorated bicycles, fireworks and dancing. In the next month something similar was mounted at Burgess Hill with an added attraction—a 'battle of confetti'! In that decade before the arrival of the first purpose-built cinemas, Tee brought to Sussex a magic of spectacle and make-believe. He recognised the importance of moving pictures to such outside entertainments.

Maggie Morton and Walter Cole at Midhurst

It was not only the more sizeable towns which were visited by the travelling showmen. Midhurst, with a population of 1,674 in 1891, was one of the first in the county to see the Cinematograph when Maggie Morton brought her pantomime *Blue Beard* to a crowded Public Hall on 29-30 December 1896, showing no doubt the programme presented earlier in the week at the Corn Exchange in Chichester.[28] Again the Hall was packed to overflowing on Wednesday evening, 25 August 1897, when Mr. P.M. Short demonstrated his Kinematographe in a show designed to advertise Sunlight soap and Nestle's milk. During the afternoon he had filmed scenes from the annual show of the Midhurst Horticultural Society in the grounds of Cowdray Ruins and had taken a panoramic shot of the railway station from a moving train. These he intended to show at the Queen's Hall in London.[29]

A fortnight later, at 8 p.m. on Tuesday 7 September 1897, patrons at the Public Hall were promised 'Two hours refined mirth with Lieutenant Walter Cole, the highly gifted and popular Ventriloquist'. He brought with him his company of London artistes and 'at a great expense the latest and cleverest scientific novelty, the animatograph'. With this he showed views of the Queen's Jubilee Procession in London and a selection from fifty short films.[30]

Whilst there were packed audiences for these first presentations, there was no immediate upsurge in the number of visits to Midhurst by these travelling companies over the next few years, and theatricals, musical concerts and variety shows remained the staple diet of patrons of the Public Hall.

Elsewhere, too, the evidence suggests that animated photographs made only occasional and irregular contributions to the programme of entertainments held at halls, pavilions and fairgrounds in the county. One or two of the travelling showmen, Lieutenant Walter Cole for example, became annual visitors, but even so it was uncommon for any town to have more than two or three film shows per annum during the first decade of cinema history.

53 The Public Hall in North Street, Midhurst, with its distinctive spirelet and clock, a venue for film shows from the very early days of cinema.

It has to be remembered, of course, that many regarded the cinematograph merely as a novelty, and there were those, the Lumières amongst them, who doubted that the new wonder of the age would become a lasting phenomenon. For some, of course, the appeal of the short 'cinematograph views' would soon pall, and the sustained interest of a more sophisticated audience would await the technical advances which permitted longer films with a real story line.

DRILL HALL FIRE IN LITTLEHAMPTON

A more practical deterrent to the speedier development of the cinema may have been the well-publicised blazes which were not uncommon in the early days of the picture shows. The inflammable cellulose-nitrate base with which 35mm films were manufactured readily enabled them to ignite, occasionally with an explosive force, particularly if stored in damp or otherwise unsatisfactory conditions. Although there are no reports of fatalities, nevertheless the panic attendant upon such fires made them frightening experiences, and doubtless left an impression on the public mind.

One such incident was recalled in 1964 by Mrs. Matilda Peacock who remembered, as an eight-year-old living in Littlehampton, a free tea and picture show given to the children of the town at the Drill Hall, Pier Road, in what must have been 1896 or 1897.

> We had a very nice tea, then we all settled down to see a Cinematograph. My sister and I was sitting close to the machine and they were showing a Children's Tea Party, with nurses handing around cakes to the children. It was most amazing to see people moving about on the Picture. But suddenly the machine caught fire and the Hall was in complete darkness. P.C. Carpenter had been standing near. He took his cape off and put out the flames. We were all struggling in the darkness to get to the door. Someone lit a Oil Lamp and we were just able to get out. It was very frightening, but I am glad to say no one was hurt ... I remember my mother being so relieved to see us safe.[31]

Accidents at cinematograph exhibitions convinced the Urban District Council at Bognor to improve the 'very insufficient' fire precautions at the Assembly Rooms in October 1907, and it was concern for safety which was paramount in ensuring a place on the statute book for the Cinematograph Act of 1909. From the beginning of the following year, premises holding cinematograph exhibitions, in which inflammable films were used, required a licence, unless such use was for no more than six days a year. The Act insisted upon the provision of a separate fire-resistant projection box, and the availability of fire-fighting equipment within the auditorium.[32]

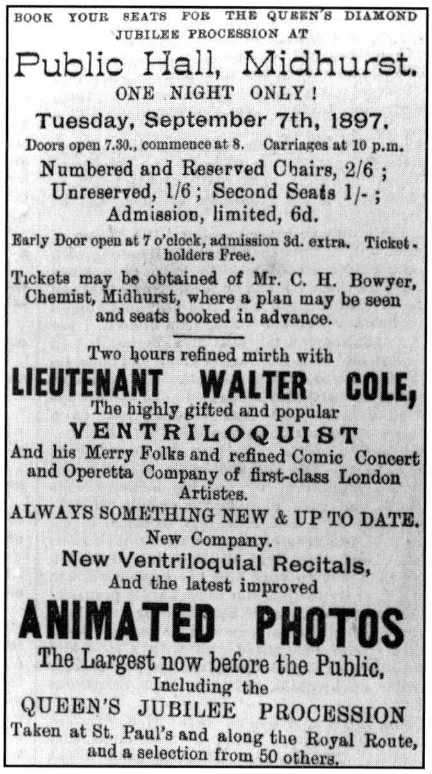

54 Advertisement from the *Midhurst Times* for the visit of Walter Cole in 1897.

55 The Walford family from Redhill were popular visitors to Midhurst with their vocal and instrumental concerts. The *Midhurst Times* shows they added films in 1902, the year of the postponed coronation of Edward VII.

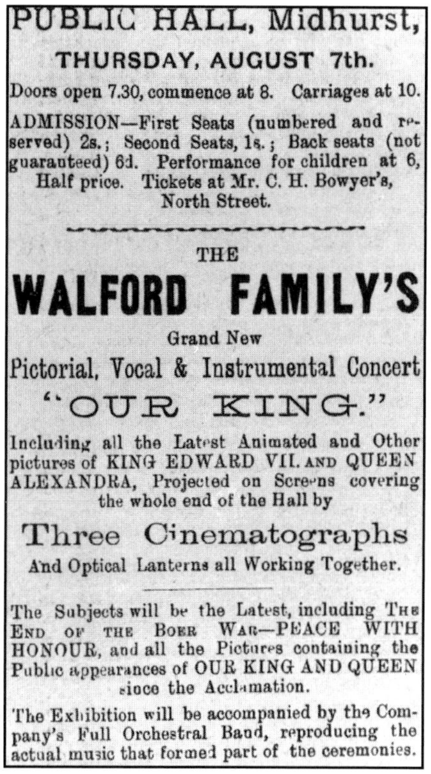

In West Sussex the County Council delegated its powers under the Act to the Justices of the Peace sitting in Petty Sessions who were responsible for keeping the Licensing Registers. The survival rate of these documents is poor, but where they are available, usually now at the County Record Office, they are an excellent source of information on the history of cinemas.

A more practical consequence of the Act was that cinema owners had to improve their buildings, and there was now an incentive to erect new purpose-built cinemas which could be advertised as complying with the new safety regulations.

56 The Old Barn Theatre, High Street, Littlehampton, a venue for theatricals and very early films, displaying a poster advertising 'Animated Pictures', sometime before its demolition in about 1897.

PICTURE PALACES EMERGE

Trying to identify the first purpose-built cinema is a fascinating field of research, and much has already been done at the national level to discover those built before the Cinematograph Act. The earliest appear in 1901—two in Portsmouth and one in London, the Mohawk Hall, Islington—but although a few others emerged later, not many were built before the Act became operational in 1910.[33]

There was change, of course, in the period leading up to the Act. Before the First World War and American competition intervened, the British film industry was expanding and prospering, with Cecil Hepworth leading the way with his story-films and film 'stars'. As interest in the movies took root, so many halls turned to regular film performances where before they had only occasionally hired the travelling film showmen. The latter in their turn, in many cases, found a profitable pitch and settled down to run their permanent picture palaces.

In the years before the 1909 Act, the typical venues in West Sussex would still have been the hired public halls, corn exchanges and assembly rooms, where occasional shows of moving pictures would have taken their place alongside live theatre and variety. However, during this period permanent cinemas were to emerge in existing halls or converted buildings. Michael W. Shanly, who was later to develop cinema interests in Bognor and Littlehampton, opened the first full-time cinema in Worthing in a converted chapel in Montague Street in about 1906. Two years later another former chapel in Worthing was adapted for the same purpose, and permanent cinemas were established in Bognor (Pier Pavilion) and Horsham (Gem Picture Theatre).

Once the new Act was in place the level of activity in the county increased. In 1910 existing halls were turned over to regular cinema use in Bognor, Chichester, East Grinstead, Midhurst and Shoreham. Moreover, in the initial two years of the Act the first purpose-built cinemas exclusively devoted to films appeared in West Sussex: in 1910, the Central Picture Hall in Horsham, and in 1911 the Pier Picture Palace in Bognor, the Olympia Electric Theatre in Chichester, the Imperial Picture Theatre in Crawley, the Carfax Electric Theatre in Horsham, and the Kursaal Electric Theatre in Worthing.

It is to the history of these buildings, the permanent picture theatres and the purpose-built cinemas, that we turn in the next section of the book.

V

The Cinemas of West Sussex

This chapter chronicles the history of the permanent picture palaces and purpose-built cinemas of the county. It is arranged alphabetically by place-name, and the cinemas of each town are described chronologically according to the date of their opening. A check-list can be found in Appendix 4.

INTRODUCTION

In the early years of the 20th century, cinema took over from the music hall and the live theatre to become the leading form of mass entertainment until it was, in its turn, eclipsed by television.

Once past the novelty stage when short films and newsreels were shown as part of a music hall bill or in halls hired by the night, cinema warranted investment in specially designed and specially constructed buildings, or lavish adaptations of existing large properties as happened in the creation of the Dome Cinema at Worthing. Feature-length films and three-hour shows required comfortable, well ventilated buildings with good sightlines. Soon every town had at least one picture house—and West Sussex was no exception. The arrival of talking pictures at the end of the 1920s was another milestone in the evolution of the medium, initially not welcomed by all but soon accepted.

The cost of converting old halls to sound films, plus the effect of changes in the legislation regulating film exhibition, now tended to concentrate the cinema business into a few large circuits. In the depressed 1930s, cinemas were one of the few booming sectors of the building industry, as the Odeon, Gaumont and Granada chains developed the distinctive styles of their new 'super cinemas'. Specialist architects, many of them very young, came along and created cinemas that were often at the forefront of modern design. The Odeon Worthing was a landmark in cinema design when it appeared in 1934. The Gaumont Chichester, Ritz and Odeon at Horsham, and Embassy Crawley were other pleasing buildings that unmistakably dated from the 1930s (as did the Rex Haslemere and Savoy Petersfield just over the border). Often there were cafés, sometimes cinema organs, sometimes adjacent dance halls to add to the enjoyment. There were also, of course, Saturday morning pictures to develop the cinema-going habit from an early age.

More and more films were made in colour, partly to combat the black-and-white television screen. And then wide screens arrived and extended runs of epic pictures.

But, with the steady decline in attendances, cinemas began to close down from the late 1950s onwards to become bingo halls, supermarkets, office buildings and the like. While they were open, they were taken for granted; but once they had gone, they were often sorely missed, having provided so many fondly remembered hours of enjoyment and escape from a harsh reality, especially during the years of austerity and war. (Of course, there were also the queues, the duff films, the technical breakdowns, the smoky atmosphere, the restricted view of the screen past the head in front ... but all that now seems to have been part of the fun.)

Chichester, which had three cinemas run by major circuits, has lost them all. Worthing has also lost all three of its big cinemas, leaving only the Dome, a colourful survivor which has become a *cause célèbre* as it soldiers on under threat of becoming a nightclub rather than a cause for celebration in the Centenary year.

But there is better news. In Horsham, the Ritz has become a splendid arts centre. In East Grinstead, two new cinemas have emerged, though not without delay, on the site of the former Radio Centre. And, in Burgess Hill, against all the odds, the formerly decrepit Orion cinema has survived—more than survived, as it has been smartly twinned—seeing off competitors at Haywards Heath and Hassocks that once had all the advantages.

At one time, the arrival of video and satellite television brought predictions of a virtual end to picture-going, but doomsayers ignored the advantages the cinema still retains: an escape from home, somewhere for couples to sit in privacy in the dark, a communal experience, entertainment on a big screen, and the only place to see films when they are new. The old barriers, by which a film played in London and perhaps Brighton months before it could be seen locally, have broken down. But by the early 1980s many cinemas had become uncomfortable and behind the times, far too expensive, often awkwardly sub-divided in a cheap attempt to improve choice.

The successful introduction of the American multiplex cinema with as many as twelve or fourteen screens transformed the situation, making a night out at the pictures fashionable again so that traditional cinemas also benefited and could be smartened up. The doubling of attendances nationally since the nadir of 1984 has helped West Sussex's cinemas to survive, although the multiplex has yet to make an appearance within the county. The Crawley area has been examined for sites, while Worthing has been spared so far as its ageing population profile makes it less attractive than other places with a younger, more mobile headcount.

It is clear that, as the medium of cinema celebrates its centenary, the history of the cinema building has a long way to go. In the following account of the story so far, complete to the end of June 1996, it will be noticed that some cinemas receive more space than others. This is simply because more information and illustrations were available. Undoubtedly there is more to say about all of these cinemas—particularly about the people who worked in them—but it is hoped that overall a good idea of the history and operation of West Sussex cinemas will emerge. It is also hoped that the publication of this book will encourage readers to come forward with more details and more photographs for inclusion in later editions and for recording by the West Sussex Record Office.

ARUNDEL

On 26 June 1912, readers of the *Littlehampton Observer* were informed that Charles Letchford Shepherd of Maxwell Road, Littlehampton, was planning to open a picture palace in the Borough of Arundel. This would be his third venture in the cinema business, as he had opened the Electric Picture Palace in Littlehampton in May 1911, followed by another picture house in Bridport, Dorset, in February 1912. In each case, he was supported by his managing partner and neighbour, Desmond Sidney Holderness, an engineer whose practical contribution extended not only to installing and maintaining the plant but also to filming local events to boost the popularity of their picture programmes.

Doubtless, the 'large number of Arundel folk' who had travelled to Littlehampton earlier in the month to watch Holderness's film of the Corpus Christi procession to Arundel Castle welcomed the news that they were soon to have their own picture palace.[1]

On 8 July 1912 C.L. Shepherd applied for a cinematograph licence. The property in Queen Street was described in the Licensing Minute Book as 'the Parish Church Club Room' but more simply in the *Littlehampton Observer* (10 July 1912) as the 'Church Hall'. It was located directly opposite where the later Arun Cinema stood and a new Texaco petrol station is to be found today.

The licence was granted for 12 months, at the usual fee of £1, subject to various conditions, notably that emergency bars be fitted to both exits and the outer doors at the town end be padlocked back.[2]

The Electric Palace opened on Monday 22 July. According to the *Littlehampton Observer* two days later, 'The attendance at the Arundel Picture Palace when it was opened on Monday was large and enthusiastic, and with good series of pictures shewing there is every indication that the latest enterprise of Mr. Shepherd will be greatly appreciated.' Indeed, it was felt that Shepherd, with his growing empire, would be able to command a better selection of pictures from the film distributors. During the summer months, patrons at both Arundel and Littlehampton were treated to films of local events shot by Holderness, including the annual Regatta held on the River Arun in August.

Roland Puttock of the Arundel Society has kindly gathered information about the cinema from the memories of local residents John Bull, Philip Taylor and Jack Ayling.

It was in a building once owned by Henty and Constable and known as the Swallow Brewery. It was the malthouse (the oast house still stands behind it but is now a private house). The entrance to the Arundel cinema was immediately adjacent to what was the *Abercrombie* public house. The screen was basically a sheet hanging from the wall and the projector was situated on a platform at the other end of the building, completely open to the audience. The cost of admission was tuppence ha'penny and it was a real treat for the children if they could sit on the platform.

The piano was played alternately by a Miss Tranah, daughter of the station master at Arundel railway station, and Miss Agnes Budd who later married Dick Blackman, a very well-known Arundel man who worked at the *West Sussex Gazette* for sixty years and had a dance band. It is also thought that Mrs. Shepherd played the piano as well. It has to be remembered that they had two cinemas and the pianists must have been swapped around as I am told that Agnes Blackman also played at the Littlehampton cinema. The cinema was not open every day and the piano had to be taken to pieces before each performance and dried out in front of the boiler because the building was so damp.

The stars remembered are Mary Pickford, Douglas Fairbanks senior, Janet Gaynor, Charlie Chaplin, Lupino Lane and Fatty Arbuckle. The films themselves seem to be rather obscure but cowboy films are remembered and the performance always ended with a Pearl White cliffhanger!

Shepherd renewed his licence for the Arundel Electric Palace annually—a condition being imposed on 6 July 1915 that the cinema remained closed on Sundays, Christmas Day, Good Friday and any special Thanksgiving days. Thereafter, its progress is much more difficult to trace, and it may well have succumbed to the problems encountered within the cinematograph trade during the First World War.[3]

In the first months of war, Shepherd's comments on the difficulty of obtaining films were reported in the *Littlehampton Observer*, together with his fears that he might no longer be able to guarantee his programmes. Inevitably, the serious fire at his Littlehampton hall on 14 August 1914 added to his troubles.[4]

Certainly the Arundel Electric Palace is not listed in the County Directory for 1918, and nor is it included in the Register of Cinematographic Licences granted by the Arundel magistrates between 1921 and 1928.

In this later period only one cinema was registered in Arundel. The Blue Flash Cinema Company, formed at Horsham by a Royal Sussex officer, Captain R.C.G. Middleton, M.C., took out a 12-month licence on 13 November 1922 for the Drill Hall (with a seating capacity of 200) in London Road. The *Kinematograph Year Book* for 1923 states that there were showings only on Wednesdays and clearly this was a shortlived enterprise for the licence was not renewed. In 1924, Arundel was without a cinema.[5]

9 JANUARY 1939
ARUN
QUEEN STREET

After so many years without a picture house, the arrival of the Arun cinema could be accurately described at the opening as a 'long needed amenity'.

Plans for a cinema to be built on the site of a riding school in Queen Street were first submitted in July 1938 by architect E. Norman-Bailey of Maidenhead on behalf

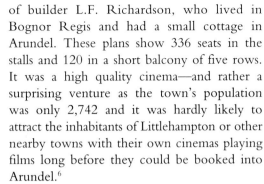

of builder L.F. Richardson, who lived in Bognor Regis and had a small cottage in Arundel. These plans show 336 seats in the stalls and 120 in a short balcony of five rows. It was a high quality cinema—and rather a surprising venture as the town's population was only 2,742 and it was hardly likely to attract the inhabitants of Littlehampton or other nearby towns with their own cinemas playing films long before they could be booked into Arundel.[6]

When the plans were passed by the Borough Council at their meeting on 11 August 1938, Councillor William John Jones nevertheless suggested that the proposed cinema was a proper size for the town, and felt that it would do Arundel a great deal of good. In practice, local inhabitants were probably content enough to wait for films to arrive at what was the most modern cinema in the area, with much better sound and more comfortable seating than much of the competition.[7]

In fact, at the opening ceremony, Herbert A. Yapp, the chairman of the company behind the venture, declared that many people in the film trade had told him he was 'risking his shirt' and he drew laughter when he said that he was not in the least perturbed. Yapp had been behind the creation of the three Forum super cinemas at Fulham Road, Ealing and Kentish Town in London, which he had sold to the nationwide ABC circuit in 1935. The company that built and opened the Arun cinema was called Rickenya, after parts of the surnames of its three partners: 'Ric' for L.F. Richardson; 'ken' for A.N. Kendal, who was a cinema proprietor already operating the Garrison Theatres at Bulford and Larkhill as well as the Hippodrome Tidworth; and, of course, 'ya' for Yapp.

This was the first of an intended circuit. Yapp and his colleagues opened the second Rickenya cinema this same month, the Palace at Gorleston-on-Sea, Norfolk (also designed by E. Norman-Bailey), followed by the Regal Banbury in October 1940. The company had another planned for Strood, Kent, but this was never built because of the Second World War.

The Arun was set well back with a forecourt and a car park to one side for 40 vehicles. Queens Lane was directly behind. The front elevation was faced entirely in brick without stone dressings. The foyer was tiled

with a central door to the auditorium and carpeted stairs to the right leading up to the balcony.

The Duke of Norfolk declared the cinema open on the Monday evening and the feature shown was *A Yank at Oxford* with a supporting programme that included a Donald Duck cartoon.[8] Lorna Puttock was an usherette and ice-cream girl, dressed in green with braid and polished buttons, for the first three years until called up for war service. She recalled (*West Sussex Gazette*, 16 September 1993):

> Seats were sixpence and one shilling down-stairs, one shilling-and-threepence and one shilling-and-ninepence upstairs, covered with green plush and very comfortable. It was a popular place and business was pretty good in the first years. During the war it was a boon for Arundel, and there were queues as British soldiers, Canadian troops and later American troops came into town for enter-tainment.

The cinema changed programmes on Sunday and mid-week. By the end of the 1940s, Rickenya had been absorbed into the company of one of the original partners, A.N. Kendal. Around 1954, it passed to H.J. and M.E. Trenchard who were its last proprietors. Attendances were badly hit by television and the increasing comfort of staying at home as living standards improved.

57 The Arun in its opening year, 1939.

58 Auditorium of the Arun in 1939.

The Arun seems to have closed during a newspaper dispute in July 1959, although one source has suggested it went out of business in August. The last advertised programme that was seen in the *Littlehampton Gazette* runs to 28 June, and the cinema was no longer appearing in the paper when it resumed publication after missing two issues (perhaps the loss of newspaper advertising was the last straw).

The front part of the cinema was demolished in April 1962. The site became a petrol station and the auditorium was turned into a garage which stood until 1993, although disused for some time prior to that after a decision was taken, but not immediately implemented, to construct a new Texaco service station on the site. Demolition was completed in early September 1993 and the new petrol station was built before the end of the year.

BOGNOR REGIS

1 AUGUST 1908
PIER PAVILION
BOGNOR PIER

An attractive little Pier Pavilion was opened in July 1900 by Bognor Urban District Council at the seaward end of the 1865 Pier for band concerts in the summer and for roller skating in the winter. The Pier was forced to close in 1908, in need of extensive repairs, and in July the Council sold it for the nominal sum of 10s. 6d. to Michael W. Shanly and Alfred Carter who formed the Bognor Pier Company and agreed to carry out the repairs. Known as 'The Chair King', Shanly had made a fortune supplying chairs for London parks, royal occasions, bandstands and seaside resorts. Based in West Hampstead, London, and with a house

at Felpham, he also ran concerts, firework displays and put on film shows at Weston-Super-Mare and Worthing. In Bognor, he already had the deckchair concession. Carter was the local manager.

Claude H. Flude, who was employed at Shanly's Worthing cinema, recalled receiving instructions from Mr. Shanly: 'Pop over to Bognor and start 'em off.' Except for service in the First World War from 1915 to 1918, Flude would spend the rest of his working life on the Pier, managing various entertainments, finally retiring at 81 years of age in 1964.[9]

It is clear that films were to be a major part of the new company's policy and on Saturday 1 August 1908, the evening following the formal transfer of the Pier, the first film show was presented in the Pavilion, the local

59 A charming Edwardian scene as holiday-makers stroll down the Pier at Bognor for films in the Pavilion or a trip on a paddle steamer.

Pier Pavilion, Bognor

press marvelling at the speed with which Shanly and Carter had worked. *The Bognor Observer* (5 August 1908) declared:

'It says much for the enterprise of the new proprietors that by noon on Saturday arrangements were made for a cinematograph entertainment in the evening, and for two sacred concerts on Sunday, in which the season band took part ... Judging by the remarks one heard on all sides, the entertainments have been highly appreciated.

The initial show did not go entirely to plan, however, as Claude Flude later recalled. On his arrival, he found that the windows had been whitewashed under the impression that this would make the hall dark enough. With no curtains available, he had to wait until the light faded before operating the hand-turned projector, while his wife kept the audience happy with selections on the piano.[10]

The ledgers and cash books of the Pier Company suggest that films were being hired weekly through the remainder of that first summer season until 31 October 1908. Shanly was renting films from the Walturdaw Company of Shaftesbury Avenue, London, and the cost of film hire seems to have been quite substantial—Walturdaw received £51 for four

weeks' cinematograph shows to 28 August 1908.[11]

The film shows in the first year do not appear to have been advertised in the Bognor newspapers but the local High Street stationers, Webster and Webb, were paid for printing work and undoubtedly posters and handbills were issued.

Contractors moved in during October 1908 to begin repairs on the Pier. Their activities formed the basis of a slapstick comedy, *Painting the Pier*, shot by Cecil Hepworth's company— and the work was finally completed, at a cost of £2,565, the following spring.[12]

The Pier Pavilion re-opened for films on Wednesday 7 April 1909, in time for the Easter Bank Holiday and the summer season. The first advertisements and posters announced 'Shanly's High-Class Animated Pictures', and reassured patrons that the 'latest Automatic Fire Prevention' had been installed.

There were performances daily at 3 p.m. and 8 p.m., except on Wednesdays and Saturdays, when there were three houses at 3 p.m., 6.30 p.m. and 8.30 p.m., and on Sundays when 'special pictures' were presented at 8.15 p.m. Admission was 2d., 4d. and 6d., plus presumably the Pier toll of 2d. There were changes of programme on Wednesdays and Saturdays.[13]

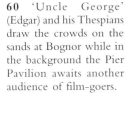

60 'Uncle George' (Edgar) and his Thespians draw the crowds on the sands at Bognor while in the background the Pier Pavilion awaits another audience of film-goers.

Claude Flude continued as projectionist but Miss May Petitt, L.A.M., was now the accompanist on a piano hired from Webster and Webb. The films were now listed in the press, the programme commencing with an overture on the piano and comprising a mixture of up to a dozen short comedies, dramas, romances and travelogues, interrupted by an interval midway and enlivened by the occasional local film and a newsreel.

In May 1909, patrons saw *A Fascinating Game*, shot in Bognor, a specially coloured picture called *Samson and Delilah*, and, over Whitsuntide, their first 'singing pictures'. On 23 June they watched a newsreel of the 1909 Derby and in August footage of the Naval Review on the Thames and the earthquake in San Francisco.[14]

'Singing pictures' were a particular novelty and in July a 'Cinephone' was purchased from the Warwick Trading Company to better present synchronised films. The results were less than perfect, as intimated by the recollections of Leonard Rogers, whose father was piermaster from 1899 to 1910: 'I remember them advertising Singing Pictures, with a concealed gramophone that rarely played in synchronisation with the movements of the singer's lips on the screen.'[15]

Pictures continued on the Pier daily up to the end of October, but thereafter on only three nights a week, including Sundays, because of falling attendances. They ceased on 21 November 1909 with *Aviation Week at Rheims*, the last of a number shown illustrating the exploits of pioneer aviators of the day.[16]

When films recommenced on 23 July 1910, prices had been increased to 3d., 6d. and 1s., but in return patrons were further reassured of their safety: 'One of the latest improvements in cinematograph exhibitions is the invention of a non-inflammable film. With these pictures the possibility of explosion leading to a fire is completely removed. The films may be placed in a flame, but will not ignite. The Pier Company at Bognor have secured these films for their exhibitions during the season.'[17]

Audiences were very aware of the dangers of attending a film show. As Leonard Rogers recalled: 'The seats were threepence front, sixpence back and I heard a father say "We'll sit in the threepennies in case the machine explodes." The resourceful Mr. Flude kept a

blanket soaked in water by the side of the projection box.' The introduction of non-inflammable film stock did not last, as it was not until the early 1950s that it replaced nitrate in cinemas.[18]

The season of films was due to end on Monday 3 October 1910 to make way for the highly popular roller skating, but Shanly was persuaded by patrons to screen some pictures every night in the intervals between the skating with a special show at 9 p.m. The *Observer* (12 October 1910) noted: 'The machine has been fitted behind the stage and the curtain is suspended at the entrance end of the pavilion, so that it can be lowered and raised out of the way of the skaters.'

In January 1911, film shows were seemingly limited to evening performances at the weekends, but by March there were again evening shows on Wednesdays, Thursdays and Fridays with matinees on Wednesdays and Saturdays.

One item which was particularly remembered from this period is the Pathé Gazette newsreel of the police siege of Russian anarchists in London. The story is told in the *Bognor Post* (7 November 1964): 'When, in 1911, cameramen filmed the Battle of Sidney Street, a copy of the film was rushed to Bognor next day. The audience crammed the hall, even climbing on top of the projection cabin and nearly toppling it. "And it was not much of

61 A close-up view of the Pier Pavilion, Bognor's first regular cinema, taken in June 1911.

a film", says Mr. Flude. "Just a lot of smoke in an East End street, but you could see the Home Secretary, Winston Churchill, with his cigar".'

Films continued at the Pavilion, playing to packed houses over Easter, but work was now nearing completion on a new and larger picture hall, purpose-built at the shore end of the Pier. The Pier Company had by now invested almost £25,000 on their improvements to the Pier, widening the shore end and building there a complex comprising a theatre and an arcade of 12 shops with the cinema, to be known as the Pier Picture Palace, over the arcade.[19]

The new cinema was officially opened on Whit Saturday, 3 June 1911, and thereafter a visit to the moving pictures no longer entailed a struggle across the stormy deck of the Pier. The Pavilion reverted to live entertainment for the next fifty years with a gap during the Second World War when the Pier was taken over by the Navy. (The Pier Pavilion, by the way, should not be confused with another Pavilion—a huge, Council-owned entertainment centre in Waterloo Square which functioned from 1922 to 1948.)

The Pier Pavilion was operated after the war by the Buxton circuit which arranged such attractions as aqua-shows. It was a popular venue, too, for children's entertainments, but any use ceased in November 1964 when it was severed from the main deck as a result of structural weakness, after which it was finally swept away in gales and high seas on the night of 3-4 March 1965—a dramatic and sad end to Bognor's first regular picture hall.

14 NOVEMBER 1910
ELECTRIC THEATRE
OLYMPIAN GARDENS, ESPLANADE

The Olympian Gardens was Bognor's principal concert party hall from 1900 to 1930. It had originally been a coal yard at the foot of Lennox Street and here in the 1890s, using a coal cart for a stage, early pierrot shows had entertained holiday-makers. In 1900 the yard was fenced in, given a canvas roof, and christened the Olympian Gardens by impresario Wallis Arthur whose Summer Entertainment Syndicate also presented shows at Lowestoft, Cromer, Westcliff-on-Sea, Hastings, Eastbourne and Weston-super-Mare.

'Al Fresco Concerts' was the billing. If it rained, those at the back were soaked, as the roof did not extend that far until a more permanent covering was installed.

Major improvements were carried out in readiness for the 1910 season—a sloping floor was introduced, the building was redecorated, and a new lighting and heating system installed.[20]

In order to capitalise on the growing interest in the cinematograph, and to extend business into the winter months, Wallis Arthur, in partnership wth Edward Lawrence Wood of High Street, Bognor, opened the Gardens as an electric theatre on 14 November 1910. The licence register gives the floor space as 50ft. by 40ft. and the seating capacity as 400.[21]

Performances were given at 8 p.m. every evening, at 'popular' prices of 4d., 6d. and 1s. The *Bognor Observer* (23 November 1910) reported:

62 A postcard, postmarked 1914, shows the Pier Pavilion now dwarfed by the new Picture Hall.

The Olympian Gardens ... has been made into a warm and cosy electric theatre, where some of the best animated pictures are being shown nightly on the screen. Two modern radiators give heat to the building ... so that the patrons of these popular entertainments can sit in comfort and enjoy the pictures. The pictures are both clear and steady, and as the alterations to the place become better known, we are sure that the enterprise ... will meet with the success it deserves.

Within months, however, there was to be serious competition from two new purpose-built cinemas in Bognor—the Pier Picture Palace and the Kursaal—and the early expectations of the Electric Theatre's owners were not fulfilled. There is no indication in the licence register that the licence for the Olympian Gardens was renewed in November 1911.

Wallis Arthur continued to present his concerts at the Olympian Gardens until September 1930. The following year Billy Butlin erected a fun fair on the site, and today there are flats and an amusement centre.

3 JUNE 1911
PIER PICTURE PALACE/
PIER ELECTRIC THEATRE

The Pier Picture Palace was opened on Whit Saturday evening at the shore end of the Pier by Shanly and Carter's Bognor Pier Company, replacing the Pier Pavilion as a cinema. It was part of a new complex of buildings with a stuccoed exterior that included an arcade of shops and the Pier Theatre. The architect was G.E. Smith of Southsea.

The cinema was built into the area that had been the former entrance to the Pier, located above the 80ft. long arcade, with roof-top tea gardens adjoining. It was reached by stairs just inside the arcade to the left. The auditorium was 30ft. wide and, according to company records, the seating capacity was 528, comprising 33 rows of 16 chairs.[22] The cinematograph chamber, or projection room, declared to be 'absolutely fireproof', was hidden away at the west end of the hall above the heads of the audience, the only sign being the two projection holes in the wall. The Boyle system of ventilation was adopted, consisting of an iron ventilator passing through the roof, keeping the hall cool and free from stuffiness.[23]

ELECTRIC THEATRE.

OLYMPIAN GARDENS, BOGNOR.

ANIMATED PICTURES

Every Evening at 8 p.m.

Latest and best Pictures. Popular Prices—
4d., 6d., and 1s. (reserved).

Seats booked at Wood's, High Street.

Commencing MONDAY, NOVEMBER 14th.

Shows were initially at 3 p.m. and 8 p.m., with a change of films twice a week and 'special pictures' at 8.15 p.m. on Sunday. The prices previously charged at the Pier Pavilion of 3d., 6d. and 1s. remained unchanged—here, the threepenny seats were of the form type but covered, the sixpenny ones tip-ups and covered, while the shilling ones, which could be booked in advance, were properly padded tip-up seats. There were just three rows of 1s. seats, 20 rows at 6d., and 10 rows at 3d. Mr. and Mrs. Flude transferred from the Pier Pavilion to run the new Picture Palace.[24]

Such was the demand that by August a second performance had been added each night. New projection equipment was introduced in June, and electric lighting was used for the first time in July, the Pier now having its own plant which greatly improved the standard of film presentation.[25]

The Picture Palace was sometimes referred to as the Minor Hall to distinguish it from the larger Pier Theatre which, according to the licence register, had a seating capacity of 1,180. So popular were the 'star pictures' on Sunday evenings that by 10 September it had proved necessary to transfer these shows from the Minor Hall to the larger theatre, where music was provided by the full theatre orchestra.[26]

Further evidence of the success of Shanly and Carter's new venture is provided by the *Bognor Observer* (30 August 1911):

The animated pictures at the comfortable Picture Theatre on the Pier are as well nigh perfect as anyone could wish for, and for its size there is no more popular place of amusement in the town. There are crowded audiences at every performance, and the fine selection of scenic, dramatic and humorous films delight everyone. The pictures are splendidly shown and are clear and flickerless.

63 The Olympian Gardens advertise in the *Bognor Observer* in 1910.

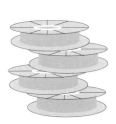

64 *Above.* The Pier Picture Palace, Bognor's first purpose-built cinema, opened in 1911.

65 *Left.* A Donald Massey postcard showing the relationship between the Minor (Picture) Hall and the Pier Theatre.

In October, the management announced that it would be presenting a complete change of programme five times a week, and would be doing so throughout the winter. A more frequent change was necessary to obtain a greater number of attendances from the smaller number of patrons out of season.[27]

In April the following year, weekly news-reels from Pathé were introduced. Local pictures screened in October carried a prize for the person specially marked on the film. Saturday afternoon children's matinees were presented with over 500 youngsters packing the hall, paying a penny and receiving a free bag of sweets.[28]

Competition between picture houses to obtain the more popular topical and dramatic films was now intense. Films of the war in the Balkans would be screened as soon as they arrived from London. Blockbusters such as Pathé Frères' *The Queen's Necklace*, a hand-coloured historical drama, and Cecil Hepworth's version of *Oliver Twist* were lavishly promoted. When the epic *The Charge of the Light Brigade* was shown in October 1912, it was accompanied by special effects supplied by the local Territorials.[29]

The practice of showing films in the Minor Hall during the week and in the Pier Theatre on Sundays continued until August 1914 when the latter became the regular daily venue for films.

However, the Minor Hall continued to be licensed for cinematograph shows and by 1916 it had become the pattern to show films in this smaller hall, now known as the Pier Electric Theatre, in the summer months to allow the larger theatre to concentrate on stage shows during the season before returning to films in the winter.

Even after the First World War, the smaller hall, renamed the Pier Concert Hall or Pier Hall, continued to be used occasionally for films. But for the most part it was the home of live shows and dances. The main venue for cinemagoers was now the larger theatre which, from July 1919, was known as the Pier Picture Theatre.

By the time Claude Flude retired in 1964 after 55 years of running entertainment on the Pier, the smaller hall which he had opened in 1911 as a picture house had resorted to bingo and the theatre which had succeeded it as a cinema had been transformed into an amusement arcade.

June 1911
Kursaal Theatre/Theatre Royal/
Theatre Royal Cinema
Belmont Street

In 1902 an Edwardian arcade opened in Belmont Street with a commissionaire 'to assist passengers alighting from carriages'. This was built by William Tate who, in 1910, added the large complex between the arcade and the sea front called the Kursaal. In his *A History of Bognor Regis*, Gerard Young refers to the Kursaal as

a large complex building resplendent with copper domes and white woodwork. One part of it housed an excellent theatre, to whose main entrance the Arcade provided a convenient covered approach; while the seaward half, presenting a highly decorative façade to the Esplanade, housed a roller-skating rink, a balconied tea room and an entertainment hall called Pierrotland. The whole edifice, designed by Mr. W. Tillot Barlow, was given the fashionable German name of the Kursaal ...

(Worthing also had its Kursaal.)[30]

66 A rare photograph, again by Massey, showing the interiors of the Pier Theatre (left) and the Minor (Picture) Hall.

Arcade Bognor

67 *Top.* The arcade, pictured in a postcard postmarked July 1913, with bicycle partly obscuring a poster advertising 'Electric Pictures' at the Kursaal Theatre.

68 *Above.* Beach entertainers perform alongside the new Kursaal leisure complex with its theatre at the rear and skating rink at the front.

The theatre was opened on Whit Sunday, 4 June 1911, the day after the debut of the Pier Picture Palace. Beautifully carpeted and comfortably seated, it was reputedly superior to many West End theatres, and was one of the first to boast electric lighting, with no fewer than thirty frosted globes hanging from the carved ceiling.

A cinematograph chamber was incorporated at the rear of the dress circle, fitted with 'one of the best and most expensive machines on the market'. Although the main emphasis was to be on live shows—plays, musicals and concerts—a cinematograph licence was immediately taken out by the manager, Harold Reading, and in its opening month films of the coronation of King George V were shown.[31]

The licence register gives the dimensions of the theatre as 54ft. by 51ft. and the seating capacity as 850.[32] It would seem, from newspaper reports, that initially films were shown on Sunday evenings during the summer season but in winter were screened nightly, with musical accompaniment from the Kursaal Band.[33]

There was an innovation in 1913 when the Kursaal presented a special six-night run of the latest pictures in 'natural colours'. The Hove pioneer George Albert Smith had developed Kinemacolor, a commercial colour film process, in 1906 and complete programmes of films in the system had been presented for the first time in London and Brighton in 1911. When the Kursaal Theatre announced its arrival in April 1913, Kinemacolor was described in the *Bognor Observer* as 'the World's Greatest Wonder'.[34]

The Kursaal was renamed the Theatre Royal in April 1919. Jack Hylton was the pit pianist at this time while the comedian Tommy Handley made an early appearance here. Films seem to have played little or no part in the life of the Theatre Royal over the following two decades. The opening of the Picturedrome in June 1919 seems to have forced the Theatre Royal to concentrate on live entertainment.

In 1939, John Gielgud was directing plays here but live shows ceased on the outbreak of the Second World War. After the Pier Cinema was forced to shut down, the small Philpot circuit of Coventry decided to lease the Theatre Royal and show films. William Tate, the proprietor, transferred the music and dancing licence to Harold Thomas Austin Philpot on 13 September 1941. (Another Coventry firm called Godiva Cinemas soon became the lessee, but this was probably a Philpot subsidiary.) New projectors and Western Electric sound equipment were installed and stage and screen comedian Sydney Howard performed the re-opening ceremony on Monday 3 November 1941 at 2 p.m. when the first film attraction was the Bob Hope and Bing Crosby comedy *Road to Zanzibar*.[35]

Now known as the Theatre Royal Cinema, it claimed 850 seats and styled itself 'Bognor's Intimate Cinema' while also claiming that it was 'Always First with the War News'. In 1947, Philpot, who owned a house at Felpham, acquired the remainder of the Kursaal complex, which was extensively refurbished and re-opened as the Rex Entertainment Centre comprising restaurant, ballroom and theatre.[36]

However, the Coventry operators of the Theatre Royal Cinema were succeeded by a local company called Theatre (Bognor) Ltd.

by 1948. In 1950, the number of seats was given as 718.

As a local independent cinema, the Theatre Royal competed with the town's Picturedrome for all the films that the Odeon didn't show. The Theatre Royal was close to the sea front while the other two cinemas were near each other in the centre of town close to the railway station.

In the 1960s the Theatre Royal found it difficult to obtain attractive regular releases and played extended runs of special attractions for the holiday season. In 1960, *South Pacific* opened on 17 July and ran for several months. On Wednesday 28 June 1961, an invited audience of 250 gathered at 11 p.m. to watch a gala presentation of the MGM epic *Ben-Hur* which ended at 3 a.m. The film then played at the Theatre Royal for three months, completing its run at the end of September.[37] A year after *My Fair Lady* had an extended run at the Astoria Brighton, it became the 1966 summer attraction at the Theatre Royal, opening on 26 June. In 1967, *The Sound of Music* reigned from 18 June to 30 September.

Out of season, the Theatre Royal turned to nights of wrestling and bingo to improve business, while still playing films on the other nights of the week. In 1963, wrestling matches took place on Fridays and then some Wednesdays after which bingo was introduced from mid-September on Thursdays and Fridays. In 1966, bingo continued even while *My Fair Lady* was playing, on Sunday afternoons and after the film on Thursdays. By late 1967, bingo had spread to three nights of the week: Tuesdays, Thursdays and Saturdays.

The days would change but bingo continued to occupy three nights a week. This weakened the Theatre Royal's ability to book good new films as it could not offer a complete week or even all the best nights of the week. In 1971 the decision was taken to go over to full-time bingo. The last film booking was a three-day revival of the James Bond picture *On Her Majesty's Secret Service* which finished on Friday 16 July.

At the end of 1974, the Theatre Royal was faced with closure and demolition to make way for part of a £2 million sea-front redevelopment scheme that was to include a new three-screen cinema (the largest auditorium to have theatre facilities as well). Anxious to keep the bingo club open, the lessees trans-ferred it to the Regal (ex-Odeon) and stopped all films there.

A big campaign was mounted for the Theatre Royal to be retained permanently as a live theatre. However, when the new sea-front scheme was delayed, the Theatre Royal re-opened as a full-time cinema under the control of Victor Freeman. Now called the Royal Movie Centre, its first advertised attraction, which opened on Sunday 29 December 1974 for a week, was the Gary Glitter film *Remember Me This Way* plus the outdoors picture *Brother of the Wind*. There were special Saturday late night shows.

The return of cinema was shortlived as the Royal (which had been refused a preservation order as a theatre building after a public inquiry) was forced to close on Saturday 30 August 1975 at the end of a ten-day run of an X certificate comedy *Confessions of a Pop Performer*, shown on a 'World Première Concurrency', i.e. simultaneously with many other cinemas.

Bulldozers moved in and the building was quickly demolished at the very moment when the redevelopment scheme (now costed at £2.5 million) was savagely revised by Arun District Council (which had inherited it from Bognor Regis Council) to exclude the three-screen cinema and the associated car park. There was such a huge uproar that the Council was forced to provide some more modest entertainment facilities. When the new, grim-looking Bognor Regis Centre opened on 11 March 1980 at a cost of £1.2 million, it did include a multi-purpose hall called the Alexandra Theatre at which some films were shown along with live events.

69 The stage tower and roof girders of the Theatre Royal can be seen on the left during demolition in 1975 while the domed frontage of the Rex, on the right, awaits the inevitable.

10 SEPTEMBER 1911
PIER THEATRE/PIER PICTURE THEATRE/
PIER ELECTRIC THEATRE/PIER CINEMA

The Pier Theatre was opened on Sunday 6 August 1911 by Shanly and Carter. Part of their grand programme of Pier improvements, it was designed by G.E. Smith of Southsea and built by W.H. Archer and Son of Gravesend. It was an imposing structure with two turrets at the northern end, a central dome, and lofty stage accommodation at the seaward end.

It had a ground floor and dress circle, with exits from the latter onto an open-air promenade which encircled the building. Although intended primarily for live stage and music hall shows, it was immediately licensed for the cinematograph and its greater seating capacity (1,180 according to the Licence Register) meant that it was soon utilised for this purpose, taking the Sunday 'star pictures' from the Minor Hall (Pier Picture Palace) from 10 September 1911.[38]

The building was almost full for its opening film show and the *Bognor Post* in its 15 November 1911 issue reported a record-sized audience for the two 'star films': Edison's *Battle of Trafalgar* and Pathé Frères' *Notre Dame de Paris*, a coloured production of Victor Hugo's novel.

Two performances were given on Sundays, at 3 p.m. and 8.15 p.m., but their growing popularity soon attracted opposition. In July 1912, the local Baptist minister, the Rev. F.G. Wheeler, opposed the renewal of the Sunday licence, complaining that the shows 'depreciated the moral life of the town and tended to popularise the Lord's Day as a day of holiday and pleasure instead of a day of rest and worship'. The County Bench, chaired by the Duke of Richmond, nonetheless renewed the licence.[39]

Every evening performance now included a 'singing picture' but it was the special pictures which continued to attract the biggest crowds. On 3 November 1912, over 1,000 people flocked to see *The Mysteries of Paris*, an adaptation of a novel by Eugene Sue shown in five parts. The following Sunday another packed house watched *The Relief of Lucknow*, an Edison drama on the Indian Mutiny of 1857.[40]

The huge Sunday audiences seem to have encouraged the management to go over mainly to films during the rest of the week, leaving live entertainment primarily in the hands of the nearby Kursaal Theatre. From August 1914, the Pier Theatre took over from the Minor Hall (Pier Picture Palace) as the principal cinema on the Pier.

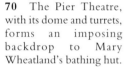

70 The Pier Theatre, with its dome and turrets, forms an imposing backdrop to Mary Wheatland's bathing hut.

Mr. and Mrs. Flude again transferred. Mrs. Flude played the piano accompaniment to the films and one youthful patron recalled lobbing small conkers from the circle at her while she played.[41] A big attraction of 1915 was all 26 rounds of the Jess Willard–Jack Johnson boxing match.

By 1916, the Pier Theatre had reverted to being a live theatre in the summer season but went back to films for the rest of the year.

The Pier was occupied for a time by 200 soldiers, but it remained open to the public and the Pier Theatre regularly presented war films including the official film, *The Battle of the Somme*, shown at the end of October 1916.[42] The presence of war was directly felt during one matinee in 1917. German aircraft were thought to be planning a raid and the film was speeded up in an attempt to finish the show quickly, then it was stopped and Mr. Flude asked the audience to leave. It was, of course, a false alarm.[43]

Films soon became the sole attraction, in recognition of which the building was renamed the Pier Picture Theatre in July 1919. By 1922, Shanly and Carter were also operating the Picturedrome, both cinemas being managed by Claude Flude. The Pier Picture Theatre seems to have been regarded as the more

important of the two, taking top place in press advertising, no doubt due to a combination of factors: its sea-front location was better for attracting holiday visitors, it had more seats, and it meant more to its owners as they had built it.

Among the big films that played at the Pier Picture Theatre were the Rudolph Valentino epic *The Four Horsemen of the Apocalypse* in 1924 and *Ben-Hur* with its famous chariot race in 1926. Regarding the latter, Mr. Flude recalled in the *Bognor Post* (7 November 1964):

We opened on a Boxing Day, with a snow-storm raging. Backstage, a few of us provided the sound effects listed on a cue-sheet, and my wife had an orchestra of four out front. I was pounding away with coconut shells for hooves. There were only a few children in the house, so we regarded it all as a dress-rehearsal.

On Wednesday 18 September 1929, the new rage of talking pictures arrived in Bognor at the Pier Theatre, as it was once again called. The management had invested in one of the best sound systems available. According to the *Bognor Post* (3 June 1972), drawing on Flude's memories, 'Western Electric, who supplied the sound system, said the theatre's acoustics were

71 A postcard, post-marked August 1915, showing the two cinemas on the Pier, the Pier Theatre and the smaller Picture Hall.

the best along the south coast and sent their clients there to hear it. The theatre's dome in the ceiling and lath-and-plaster construction instead of brick was said to be the secret.'

The first talkie to be screened in Bognor was *The Perfect Alibi*, a '100% Talking, Singing, Dancing and Dramatic Thriller' starring Chester Morris. Unlike earlier attempts to provide sound, the latest system worked but not all cinemagoers were immediately impressed or convinced of its long-term future. The writer of the 'Out and About' column of the *Bognor Observer* declared:

All cinema enthusiasts in Bognor—and there are many—will, I suppose, be visiting the Pier Theatre this week to get their introduction to the 'talkies.' I myself went on Monday, and found that great interest was being taken in the new style of pictures. Like most other people, I came to the conclusion that the 'talkies' are really marvellous and have come to stay, although there is room yet for improvement. Quite a different technique is required and this the cinema 'fan' accustomed to the rapid action of silent films has got to get used to. My colleagues at Chichester, who have seen several 'talkies,' tell me that one becomes

used to this new technique very quickly. At first they were not sure that they really liked 'talkies,' but they are now confirmed 'talkie' fans and would not like to go back to silent pictures. I therefore suggest that if there are any people who imagine at the first performance that they do not like the new methods, they should withhold their verdict until they have seen several films.[44]

The first talkie was immediately followed by another, *The Leatherneck*, starring William Boyd, as the management sought to cash in on the interest in talkies and recover some of their substantial investment.

However, by 1936 the Pier Theatre had fallen behind the times. The renewal of the cinematograph licence was opposed on safety grounds and work was required both in the stage area and to improve the isolation of the projection box in case of fire.

After having been known as the Pier Theatre, the building advertised itself as the Pier Cinema from 1 July 1936. It still took precedence over the Picturedrome, charging higher prices, and is recorded as having 924 seats. Although films had been shown here throughout the First World War, the cinema

72 Entrance to the cinema in 1936 advertising the Universal film, *The Bride of Frankenstein*, starring Boris Karloff.

Childhood Memories of the Pier Theatre

Of the two cinemas, the Pier was our favourite, a choice not so much swayed by the sweep of its handsome, wrap-around balcony, as from the sense of adventure that came from watching a film from a seat — really, a kind of a red velveteen tourniquet — only a few feet above a demented sea, sloshing around the frail-looking supports. Given enough on the Beaufort scale, it could be quite exciting; the whole place shook, the emergency doors banged open, curtains ballooned, broken glass tinkled and Mr. Flude, the manager, came out looking slightly anxious. Often it was better than the film itself!

At the end of the performance we emerged from the protective gloom of the auditorium into blinding daylight, to be greeted with the roar of a blustering sou'-wester, an angry sea, rattling signs and the complaining calls of herring gulls poised motionless over the silent slot machines. It was as if Æolus and Poseidon were trying to upstage the silver screen — and only bettered by the bit where Oliver Hardy's trousers had fallen down in the last reel! Then our Joan made us link arms as we bent to the boisterous wind and struggled towards the bus-stop by the Western Bandstand.

Michael Alford [45]

was compelled to close for most of the Second World War: the Pier as a whole was taken over by the Navy and renamed H.M.S. *Barbara*. Films ended on 1 June 1940 after a three-day run of *Sons of the Sea*.

The Pier Cinema re-opened at 7 p.m. on Saturday 22 June 1946 with the provincial première of a minor western, *Renegades*. Then, or by the following year, it was operated by the Buxton Theatre Circuit of Manchester which also ran the Picturedrome and Roof Garden Theatre and for a while grouped the sites as 'The Three Aces' in advertising, with a background design of playing cards. The Pier Cinema had a café in the vestibule known as the Silver Screen.

Then films were dropped from time to time when variety shows, Christmas panto-mimes and other live entertainment took over. Its name changed in advertising from week to week from Pier Theatre to Pier Cinema according to use.

As late as 1950, advertising still claimed 'The Best Sound in the District' but, even if this remained true, it was by now the choice of films that counted, and the Pier Cinema no longer had access to the best of them. After

making way for a variety season which started on 3 July that year, pictures ceased, returning briefly in March-June 1951, before finally giving way to live shows.

As a theatre, the venue lasted until the late 1950s. The competition of television was blamed for the small houses and meagre box-office returns when in November 1959 it was announced that the Pier Theatre would close. Variety, summer shows and concerts were to make way for slot machines.

Ten years later, now shorn of its seaward end, the hundred-year-old Pier was feeling its age. Early in 1976, the Pier Theatre, with its distinctive tower, was partially demolished. In May of that year, the Pier was taken over by John Harrison, who ran seaside amusements in Bognor and Littlehampton, with plans for gradual renovation. In 1996, it houses an amusement arcade, children's play-area, café and shop, with a nightclub above. In recent times there has been concern expressed over the future of the Pier, but on 27 June 1996 the *Bognor Observer* announced a new owner, John Ayres, an Eastbourne amusement arcade proprietor, pledged to a programme of restoration.

5 JUNE 1919
PICTUREDROME/CLASSIC/CANNON/ABC
CANADA GROVE

Located opposite the station, this was originally the New Assembly Rooms, designed by local architect Arthur Smith and opened in May 1886 at a cost of £4,500. It was used for a variety of purposes, including stage shows, dancing, roller skating, badminton, and community functions. There was a main hall and a 'minor' upstairs hall.

The most prominent feature of the building was an octagonal lantern tower which at one time housed a revolving light, operated by a boy pedalling a bicycle-type mechanism, that advertised its presence for miles around.[46]

Films were first presented in 1897 when David Devant brought his Animatograph to Bognor on 14-16 December. Reputedly, such was the impact of *The Fire Brigade Call* that it had patrons ducking for cover beneath the chairs in front of them for fear that the galloping horses would descend from the screen and crash down amongst them.[47]

Among the regular touring entertainers who used the Assembly Rooms, the Poole brothers were eagerly awaited on their annual visits, and they were among the first to bring films to Bognor as part of their all-round variety programmes.

Patrons were already familiar with their myriorama, presenting panoramic pictures on a screen 27ft. long and nearly 14ft. high which was drawn across the stage on rollers. On this were shown, with the aid of a running commentary, famous places, battle scenes, trains leaving stations, and ships at sea. Then, in September 1901, the Poole brothers introduced their myriograph, displaying 'most amusing and up-to-date cinematograph pictures'.[48]

In the *Bognor Post* (28 November 1959), Jesse Holden recalled those first moving pictures at the Assembly Rooms. Children were given a half-holiday to see them. Admission was one penny, and the films included a ship sailing very slowly across the screen and a car blowing up with a policeman collecting the pieces.

Another annual visitor to the Assembly Rooms was Alfred West with his patriotic selection *Our Navy, Army and Colonies*.[49]

Films were frequently included in variety performances, as when in November 1909 a cinematographic record of Shackleton's voyage to the South Pole was shown as part of Lloyd's Grand Illustrated Concert.[50]

The Assembly Rooms were hired out two or three times a year to the travelling film showmen in the first decade of the century. Poole's would stay for a whole week, giving one evening performance each day and two

73 Section from Peter Stonham's plans for the new Picturedrome in Bognor.

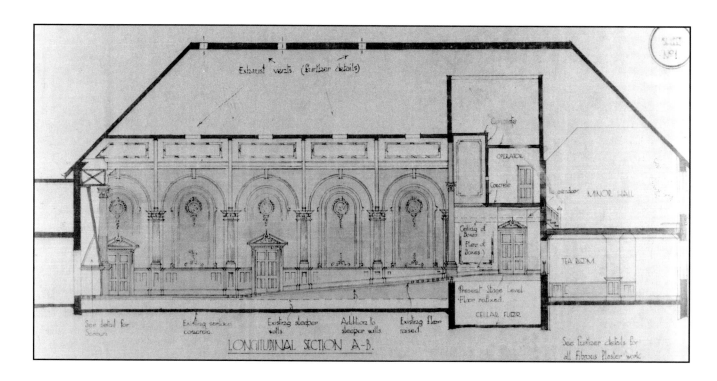

LONGITUDINAL SECTION A-B.

matinees, usually arriving in the last quarter of the year.

Concern was being expressed as early as 1907 over safety while films were being shown but it was not until 1911 that major improvements were made as part of structural alterations carried out by the proprietors, W.H. Lorden and Son. The major problem of the hall—bad acoustics—was remedied by lowering the ceiling, and a special room was constructed for the projection equipment outside the main hall with an external entrance. This gave rise to speculation that the hall was to be let as a permanent cinema.[51]

It was in August 1911, to commemorate the coronation of George V and Queen Mary, that the building was renamed the Queen's Hall.[52] The licensee was Hubert Alexander Hay, and the register shows that the hall was 86ft. long by 45ft. wide and capable of seating 700 people.[53]

The popularity of the new venues which had opened on the Pier seems to have inhibited much cinema use—in 1912, for example, apart from a cinematograph lecture on Port Sunlight in February, live entertainment seems to have reigned.[54]

During the First World War, the Queen's Hall was used as a barracks and occupied by the Services, but afterwards it was taken over by a company called The Picturedrome (Bognor) Ltd., which was headed by Eastbourne architect and businessman Peter D. Stonham and backed by two local businessmen, builder and bathing machine owner Frederick Jenkins and chemist C.T. Cooper.

In February 1919, Stonham submitted his plans for the conversion of the Queen's Hall into a full-time cinema to be called the Picturedrome. Stonham had earlier been associated, as an architect and principal shareholder, in the successful launching of the Picturedrome Worthing, and this was a follow-up venture. The plans were approved by the District Council on 11 April and the premises re-opened on Thursday 5 June 1919 as the Picturedrome.[55]

Outside, there was a glass canopy supported by columns with elaborate grillework around the entrance with the new name of the cinema set on the front in coloured glass lettering against a sunburst pattern.

The position of the projection box and the screen were reversed. The former operator's box dating from 1911 was now concealed behind a new 'picture board' (or screen) and became the orchestra room with a new opening knocked into the back wall, while an orchestra pit with a curved rail in front was built to accommodate the pianist who accompanied the silent films.

A new side entrance with its own pay box was created in the front left-hand corner of the auditorium. The main entrance to the auditorium was now located halfway down the left-hand side, leading directly from the foyer. The flat floor was raised in a gradual upward slope in the half furthest from the screen. Ventilation was improved and 660 comfortable seats in blue were fixed into place on the single floor (there was no balcony).

Four boxes were introduced at the rear of the auditorium: two in each corner, to each side of the old proscenium arch which was retained. A passage leading off to the right from the foyer took patrons to the back of the auditorium for the boxes, which were entered from the rear, and to the back rows of seating which extended onto the old stage area between the boxes. A new projection box was built inside the original arch above the boxes and rear seats. A tea room was created directly behind the auditorium on the ground floor below the secondary or 'minor' hall which was at first floor level separated from the new projection box by a thick wall. This hall was hired out for various functions including whist drives and dances.

The re-opening ceremony was performed by James Fleming, benefactor of the town's new War Memorial Hospital, to which the day's takings were donated. The first programme included the British feature *Boundary House*, starring Alma Taylor and Gerald Ames, plus footage of the Victory Derby just run at Epsom, and the Pathé Gazette. The musical accompaniment came from the Picturedrome Orchestra, directed by Miss Beatrice Travers.

Admission prices were 5d., 9d., 1s. 3d. and 1s. 10d., with children half price at matinees. There were continuous performances daily from 3 p.m. to 10.30 p.m.[56]

A Sunday licence was opposed in a petition signed by 1,046 local residents, claiming that Sunday performances were 'very injurious to the religious life of the community'. However, a seven-day licence was granted and the local

QUEUE HERE

FORTHCOMING CINEMA ATTRACTIONS

74 *Right.* The opening of the Picturedrome announced in the *Bognor Observer* in 1919.

75 *Far right.* Alma Taylor, star of the opening feature, photographed in 1919.

76 *Below.* John Douglas Geils, the Picturedrome's first manager.

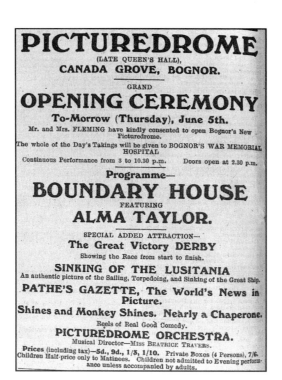

PICTUREDROME
(LATE QUEEN'S HALL),
CANADA GROVE, BOGNOR.
GRAND
OPENING CEREMONY
To-Morrow (Thursday), June 5th.
Mr. and Mrs. FLEMING have kindly consented to open Bognor's New Picturedrome.
The whole of the Day's Takings will be given to BOGNOR'S WAR MEMORIAL HOSPITAL
Continuous Performance from 3 to 10.30 p.m.   Doors open at 2.30 p.m.
Programme—
BOUNDARY HOUSE
FEATURING
ALMA TAYLOR.
SPECIAL ADDED ATTRACTION—
The Great Victory DERBY
Showing the Race from start to finish.
SINKING OF THE LUSITANIA
An authentic picture of the Sailing, Torpedoing, and Sinking of the Great Ship.
PATHE'S GAZETTE, The World's News in Picture.
Shines and Monkey Shines. Nearly a Chaperone.
Reels of Real Good Comedy.
PICTUREDROME ORCHESTRA.
Musical Director—MISS BEATRICE TRAVERS.
Prices (including tax)—5d., 9d., 1/3, 1/10. Private Boxes (4 Persons), 7/6.
Children Half-price only to Matinees. Children not admitted to Evening performance unless accompanied by adults.

A "PICTURED" BEAUTY.

police later welcomed the decision as, in their experience, Sunday films had 'the effect of taking young people off the streets, who would otherwise be at a dead end, and ... a source of annoyance'.[57]

The manager from opening to 1923 was John Douglas Geils, who had learned about the cinema business in Winnipeg, Canada, and who had seen war-time service with the Canadian Expeditionary Force. He was the son-in-law of Frederick Jenkins and his daughter, Barbara Ovstedal, relates that he was dissuaded from returning to Canada with his new bride by the offer of the manager's job at Bognor.

She remembers him standing in white tie and tails to welcome audiences to the new picture house. He had a magnificent baritone voice and would sing for the audience during the intervals. When the film *My Old Dutch* played at the Picturedrome, he sang the famous song, synchronising his voice with the lip movements of Albert Chevalier on the screen, and there wasn't a dry eye in the house.

In a letter written by John Geils shortly after the opening and retained by his daughter, he hints at the competition with the Pier for booking feature films. The Pier had secured a number of Charlie Chaplin films but he remained optimistic, having managed to obtain a few Chaplin subjects himself as well as films starring Mary Pickford and Margarita Fischer.

Rowdyism sometimes erupted in the cheaper seats but Geils summarily ejected troublemakers onto the street. Sadly, he was to die at the early age of 32 in 1925.[58]

By 1922, the problem of competition with the Pier Theatre had been resolved by the Picturedrome coming under the same ownership, having been taken over by M.W. Shanly and A. Carter through the Bognor Pier Company. With a lower price range and fewer seats, the Picturedrome was secondary to the Pier Theatre, although film historian John Montgomery, then an Aldwick schoolboy, preferred the former as, in his recollection, it 'showed better films and was more comfortable'. At this time there were no other cinemas operating in the town.[59]

The musical accompaniment was a key factor in operating a cinema in the so-called silent period. There was a whisper of excitement as the pianist took his or her seat, indicating that the film show was about to commence. The pianist at the Picturedrome was Mrs. Eve White, who had become Claude Flude's relief pianist at the Pier Theatre in 1920 before moving over to the newer cinema. In the orchestra pit, she had to have her wits about her, alternately peering at the music in a green piano light and glancing up at the screen to cue herself in. If it was an important picture, a special score arrived with the film, including sound effects provided by extra staff using bells, thunder sheets and drums, but as the music would arrive on the day of showing there would be little or no time to rehearse. At other times, the choice of music was left to the pianist and quick-witted improvisation was required.[60] Barbara Ovstedal recalled her childhood memories in an article for *Country Life* (5 December 1968):

At the piano Eve White thundered out dramatic chords, and the audience stamped, hissing and booing the villain. Then with a change of tempo on the keys the hero arrived in the nick of time. I sat with my paper-bag of dolly mixtures forgotten, dazed and delighted as the lights went up.

Eve White relied on the trains from Portsmouth to get her to work, not without worry when a train broke down. In her 12 years as a cinema pianist at Bognor, she had only one break and that was because of a fire. Barbara Ovstedal has described the occasion:

When the picture vanished from the screen Eve White played on, thinking that the film had broken, and knowing that it was a lengthy procedure for the operator to mend it again. But glancing up over her shoulder she caught the blaze in the operator's box before the shutter was closed. The audience left without panic, money was refunded, and in the orchestra pit Eve White played on until the last person had departed.

That was the only evening off she ever had. Even when she married the violinist, who with a 'cellist later formed a trio with her for film accompaniment, the wedding ceremony was held early in the day, and the bride and groom went back in the afternoon to play for a cowboy picture.[61]

By 1930, both the Picturedrome and the Pier Cinema had been equipped with Western Electric sound and were operating with the same ticket prices. Mrs. Beatrice Louisa Young was the Picturedrome's well-known manageress of this period, having started at the Picturedrome in 1919 as a cashier and been placed in charge a few years later. She gave up the job in 1938 through ill health. After she died in 1969, it was recalled in the *Bognor Post* (17 October 1970) that she would cycle down London Road with the cinema takings in a shopping bag and the policeman on point duty in the High Street would halt the traffic for her. On her return, the fishmonger and butcher would be waiting with her order and put it in her shopping bag as she passed ...

77 The Picturedrome, Bognor, seen here in the 1920s promoting Mary Pickford in *Cinderella*.

78 A Picturedrome publicity campaign in 1937 to advertise the musical, *Glamorous Night*.

Shortly after the Second World War, control of the Picturedrome passed from the Bognor Pier Co. to the small Manchester-based Buxton Theatre Circuit (which also ran the venues on the Pier) but around 1949 it was leased by a Mrs. S. Leigh.

On the night of Tuesday 27 April 1954, a fire seriously damaged the interior of the Picturedrome and it remained closed for more than four months. This was the era of the new wide screen and it was decided to widen the proscenium arch to take a large CinemaScope screen. At 30ft. across, it was almost double the width of the old screen. The auditorium was completely redecorated and refurbished with 700 new seats and new carpets. It is likely that the braces which still support the ceiling were introduced at this time.[62]

Although the cinema lost a valuable holiday season's takings, it was able to boast of the earliest CinemaScope installation in the area. There was a gala re-opening by the chairman of Bognor Regis U.D.C. on Tuesday 14 September 1954 with the first British-made CinemaScope feature, MGM's *Knights of the Round Table*, which played for nine days, followed by a week's run of *Beneath the Twelve Mile Reef* (evenings) and *Flight of the White Heron* (royal documentary, afternoons), both CinemaScope productions from 20th Century-

Fox which had launched the new wide screen system. This was more than two months ahead of CinemaScope arriving in Chichester, and more than three months before it appeared at the Bognor Odeon. The Picturedrome competed with the Theatre Royal for all the films not committed to the Odeon and generally gained the better attractions.

In 1959, the Picturedrome was taken over by Drummer Theatres (Bognor Regis) Ltd., whose managing director Basil Fortesque had been behind the opening of the Luxor Lancing. Unfortunately, ill health compelled him to sell the property and in April 1962 it passed into the hands of John Robertson, a cinema owner from Welwyn Garden City, Hertfordshire.[63]

The cinema now had 553 seats. Bingo was established in the Small Hall upstairs which had been used for whist drives and dances in earlier years. When the cinema celebrated its jubilee in June 1969, telegrams of good wishes were received from two British luminaries of the silent screen: Alma Taylor, star of the opening film, and Chrissie White, whose film *Toward the Light* had been shown at the Picturedrome later in its opening year.[64]

John Robertson died in 1975 and the lease was inherited by his son James who ran it for several years from his home in Devon, together with three other cinemas in Bideford, Barnstaple and Launceston. By 1980, down to 522 seats, the Picturedrome was the only full-time cinema left in Bognor.

In 1983, Robertson sold the Picturedrome (now seating 472) for more than £60,000 to the Cannon Classic circuit which took over on 1 July 1983. The cinema continued to be known as the Picturedrome for a while before being renamed Classic from Thursday 25 August 1983.[65]

The new owners modernised the cinema and added a second screen in place of bingo in the upstairs hall. Attractively designed with a new false ceiling meeting arches on the side walls, the 96-seat Classic 2 made its debut on Friday 17 August 1984 with the move-over of *Star Trek II* from the main auditorium, which opened *Indiana Jones and the Temple of Doom*.[66]

Then the cinemas were renamed Cannon from Friday 6 December 1985. There are currently 391 seats in the original auditorium and 99 in the upstairs addition. The tower, which had been boarded up, has been restored

79-80 The auditorium as the Classic, Bognor Regis, in 1983. In the view to rear note the old proscenium arch plus boxes to each side and ceiling braces.

81 The Cannon, Bognor Regis, in 1993, since renamed the ABC.

and turned into the living room of an upstairs flat. Dolby stereo has recently been installed and it is planned to re-open the long closed boxes at the rear of the auditorium, with one box to each side seating four or five people.

The Cannon name was displayed in an illuminated sign on the side wall while the old Picturedrome name is pleasingly still to be found set in the coloured glass on the front of the canopy over the entrance. Like the Dome Worthing, this is a surprising and appealing survivor from the boom years of cinema-going, both having seen off 1930s Odeons and other competitors. The cinema was recently acquired by Virgin, along with the rest of the Cannon/MGM circuit. However, on 2 May 1996 it was sold to ABC Cinemas and on 14 June it was renamed ABC. One hopes that the new operator will highlight the historic atmosphere of the building as part of its appeal.

14 JULY 1934
ODEON/REGAL
64 LONDON ROAD

This was the 16th new Odeon cinema to open in a period of a little over a year, following in Sussex those at Lancing, Kemp Town, Worthing, Portslade (the Rothbury) and Lewes. It was constructed in the centre of town on a site once occupied by Albany Lodge, a music school run by the Carter family.

The gala opening at 8 p.m. on Saturday 14 July 1934 included an orchestra on stage, a Laurel and Hardy short, a cartoon called *Opening Night*, Movietone News, and a preview of the British comedy *Radio Pirates*. The ceremony was conducted by Captain Herbert C. Pocock, O.B.E., R.N., the chairman of Bognor Urban District Council, supported by Oscar Deutsch, chairman of Odeon Theatres, and by three of the stars of the big feature. All were eclipsed, however, by Fred Perry, accompanying one of the film stars, who was mobbed by autograph hunters following his recent triumph in the lawn tennis championships.[67]

The first regular attraction was *It's a Cop*, a comedy starring Sydney Howard. The first manager of the Odeon was Harry Yorke, who came to Bognor after running cinemas in Birmingham.

The freehold of the site had cost £5,000 and the Odeon was built at a contract figure of £14,000 by William F. Blay Ltd. of London. The total for furnishing and equipping was £3,346 8s. 9d. This latter sum represented the cost of floor covering (£570 0s. 9d.), seating (£1,145 9s. 3d.), curtains (£201 18s. 0d.), sound equipment (£879 4s. 0d.), operating box equipment (£374 15s. 2d.), screen (£26 17s. 11d.) and sundries (£148 3s. 8d.).

The architects—Whinney, Son and Austen Hall—had previously designed the impressive Odeon at Worthing but this one at Bognor was a much less ambitious undertaking, costing under half as much to build. Its frontage lacked a landmark tower like that at Worthing but was still very modern in treatment. The auditorium was built behind the long, low front of the cinema, at right angles to the narrow entrance. This entrance was centrally placed, between two low wings of ground-floor shops and flats above. The cinema was opened before these wings were anywhere near completed.

The cinema entrance section gained prominence because it was recessed and the back wall above the canopy protruded well above the height of the wings, being capped by a flagpole. Also above the canopy, the surface was covered in the biscuit-coloured faience tilework characteristic of the circuit in contrast to the exposed brickwork of the flats. The Odeon name was set up high on the back wall, mounted above a ledge supported by four vertical black piers. Narrow horizontal bands in colour (probably green) were set between the piers. There were two small, identical, circular decorative plaques mid-way along each wing in white against a green background, depicting Pan playing his pipes on a donkey. Overall, the cinema entrance had a vertical thrust separating it from the extended horizontality of the side sections.

The foyer was streamlined with a broadly curved far wall and a curve-ended flat ceiling feature with cove lighting. The 920-seat auditorium was of the stadium type without a balcony overlapping the rear stalls. As at the Picturedrome, there was an entrance door to the auditorium halfway down the left-hand side. This provided access to the 592 seats of the front section or stalls, with a gangway extending across. Behind this gangway were a further 328 seats in the separate, raised rear section: these were reached by a side passage from the foyer, outside the auditorium but within the main building, which brought patrons in at the back on the left-hand side. The passage was built out slightly into the auditorium and matched by an exit on the other side.

The auditorium was extremely plain, relieved mainly by a recessed panel running down the centre of the ceiling which was lit by concealed lighting, and by more concealed lighting around the very wide proscenium arch. In later years at least, with its curved ceiling and wide floor, it felt like sitting in a large aircraft hangar.[68]

As the only modern cinema in Bognor and with access to the generally strong releases of the Odeon circuit, it performed satisfactorily for many years. In the 1950s, it sometimes used its clout and higher seating capacity to take films that would normally have appeared at the Picturedrome or Theatre Royal. Rather than play a poor Odeon release for a full week, it would often show a programme booked nationally by the Gaumont circuit for half the week. Occasionally it grabbed a hit film like *The Quiet Man* (1952), released to the other national circuit, Associated British Cinemas.

A new wide screen was introduced on 12 September 1954 (two days ahead of CinemaScope arriving at the Picturedrome) but the Odeon's first presentation in the much wider CinemaScope process was *The Black Shield of Falworth*, another Gaumont circuit release, shown from 20 December.[69]

Modernisation plans were announced by the Odeon's owners, the Rank Organisation, in November 1963. These included redecoration and new equipment. The old gold-flecked walls and green and silver of the 1934 decor were to give way to warmer colours, of flamingo and bronze rose, with pendant lights of the chandelier style replacing the indirect lighting in the auditorium.[70]

As an Odeon, the cinema outlasted the other nearby Odeons at Chichester and Littlehampton. But when attendances continued to decline, a small-town outlet like this one was no longer of great importance to Rank and, like the Littlehampton Odeon before it, the cinema was disposed of as a going concern.

From 23 January 1971 the Odeon was leased by the independent operator of the Theatre Royal and renamed the Regal. The freehold was subsequently acquired from Rank for £42,500. At this time or before (perhaps

82   The Odeon, Bognor, in 1934.

83   The auditorium, Bognor Odeon, 1934.

as part of the 1963 overhaul), the tiles and black piers were removed from the back of the cinema frontage above the canopy, exposing the brickwork underneath, while the protruding top was reduced so that it barely exceeded the sides of the frontage. Only the tilework on the sides of the recess remained.

The Theatre Royal went over to bingo in the summer of 1971 and, when it faced closure in 1974, the bingo operation was transferred to the Regal which stopped showing films as they were clearly less profitable.

Planning permission for bingo was granted on Wednesday 13 November 1974 and on the following Saturday, 16 November, the Regal promptly ended its days as a cinema on a squalid note, concluding a week's run of a sex and horror double X certificate programme, *House of Whipcord* and *Hotel of Free Love*. Matinees had by this time been restricted to Mondays, Thursdays and Saturdays outside school holidays.

And so the Regal, ex-Odeon, became a bingo club in place of the Theatre Royal. The Regal name was retained until December 1987, since when it has been known as the Crown bingo club. The cream-coloured bands along the windows and tiles above the shops on one side of the entrance have been insensitively painted green.

Many original Odeon features survive in 1996, from the double set of entrance doors to cove lighting in the streamlined ceiling of the foyer. The auditorium was substantially altered in work started in May 1995 and completed in January 1996. The stage and lower part of the proscenium arch have been removed to open up space underneath for book sales and game machines while the former gents' toilets to one side have been turned into offices. The bingo caller's stand and numbers screen have been set high up within the top half of the proscenium arch where the decorative detail has been carefully highlighted in purple with the curved inner edge of the arch and fillets above it picked out in gold. Seven grilles over the proscenium have also been picked out. On the right-hand side of the front half of the auditorium, the lower part of the wall has been knocked out and a bar and café built outside the area of the former cinema. The rear section of the auditorium has been raised and platformed. The cove lighting in the ceiling has been discontinued while the line of down lights is still in use. With a little imagination and study of the original auditorium photograph, one can still gain a feel for what the place must have been like as the Odeon cinema.

26 APRIL 1994
ODEON 1 & 2
BUTLIN'S SOUTHCOAST WORLD

Two new cinemas, each seating 240, were opened as part of the leisure attractions. They came into full operation on the date shown above and have been screening a selection of the latest releases. They are not part of the main Odeon chain of cinemas but use the Odeon name as Butlin's, like Odeon, is part of the Rank Organisation.

The cinemas were opened to the general public in late May or early June through a £5 ticket of admission to the entire Southcoast World centre from 5p.m. to 11p.m., the price including the two cinemas among the other attractions. In February 1996, the purchase of a cinema ticket at £3 gave admission to the whole complex after 5 p.m.

Addenda: Bognor Regis

In the 1930s, Bognor almost received a second modern cinema. In June 1936 the fast expanding Union circuit applied to erect a 980-seat cinema in Waterloo Square. It was thwarted—partly on police objections to the site, and partly on grounds of lack of need. The Odeon (seating 920), Picturedrome (662) and Pier Theatre (924) were thought to provide sufficient accommodation for a population of 18,440.[71]

The Esplanade Theatre showed some films on Sundays in the 1970s. A scheme for the Esplanade unveiled in October 1993 proposed a six-screen cinema within a £12 million leisure centre on a site provided by Arun District Council that would also include a theatre, ten-pin bowling centre, nightclub, two theme pubs, a laser action game centre, health and fitness centre and snooker club. Bognor is still waiting.[72]

(John Milbank, formerly manager of the Cannon Bognor Regis, is warmly thanked for contributing to research on the history of his cinema.)[73]

BURGESS HILL

c.1913
THE CINEMA/SCALA
CYPRUS ROAD

The Cinema was erected on waste ground locally nicknamed 'The Clamp' as it had been used in the early 1900s by brickmakers as a dump for their clay. It was a single storey building of wood and brick with a capacity of 200. The proprietors were John Hampton and his wife.

It is not clear precisely when the building was erected, but the cinema was certainly functioning in 1914 as the Rate Book of Burgess Hill U.D.C. for April of that year lists John Hampton as owner/occupier of the Electric Theatre in Cyprus Road. The *County Directory* for 1918 describes it as the Picture Theatre, again with John Hampton as proprietor.[74]

The front elevation was flat and followed the contours of the roof, tapering to a point. Double doors were set in the front wall facing the road, and the right-hand doors led to a small lobby where tickets were sold. The left-hand doors led to another lobby from which a ladder went up to the projection box. The sloping eaves of the roof made space very restricted and it housed only one projector. Every few minutes the show had to stop so that the projectionist could change reels.

In the hall, seats were set to either side of a centre aisle. At the front, behind a low velvet curtain, was a barrel organ which provided music. This organ had a range of ten tunes and had to be wound up by hand every 30 minutes. Fire exits were on either side of the screen. Outside, a shed housed a gas engine complete with a rotating flywheel—this machine generated the electricity for the lights and projector arcs, but in those days the

projector was hand-cranked by the operator. One door led to a rather primitive outside toilet, and this door was often used by youngsters to sneak in without paying. Seat prices were 2d., 4d., 6d. and 9d.

In 1922, Harold Swire, a man who had worked in the cinema world in Manchester, Buxton and London, purchased the cinema and had it redecorated and reseated while the operating box was enlarged and two Gaumont projectors installed. He re-opened it on 9 November as the Scala. The first attraction was Mary Pickford in *Daddy Long Legs* supported by Ray Hughes in *A Long-Stalled Romance*, a Graphic newsreel and a *Movie Chat* short. The musical accompaniment was provided by a piano and 'jazz set'. For the first three days, there was a matinee each afternoon at 2.30 p.m., but generally performances were twice nightly at 6 p.m. and 8.15 p.m.

84 The original Burgess Hill Cinema in Cyprus Road, replaced by the new Scala on the same site. The adjacent building still stands.

For unknown reasons, the Scala closed for a while as the *Mid-Sussex Times* reported that Harold Swire had re-opened it on 31 July 1923. *Kelly's Directory of Trades* for the following year names Percy Reynolds as the proprietor (he later operated cinemas at Portslade and Southwick). Reynolds was succeeded by Frederick J. Freeman in the 1927 edition (Freeman operated the cinema in Southwick at this time). Admission prices at Burgess Hill were restructured to include tickets at 1s. Regular performances continued until early in 1928 when Freeman closed the cinema and had it demolished to make way for a new Scala on the site.

3 DECEMBER 1928
SCALA/ORION/CINEMA/
ROBINS TAKE TWO/ROBINS/ORION
CYPRUS ROAD

The new Scala opened on the site of the old cinema with a seating capacity of 511 in a semi-stadium layout, a stage 17ft. deep, a dressing room to each side, and a policy of 'pictures and variety'.

85 Frontage of the Scala from Ernest Shennan's plans of 1928.

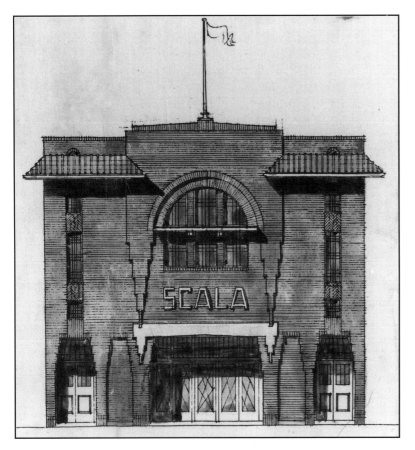

The original idea had been to enlarge the old Scala. Designs and estimates had been drawn up by a Major J.J. Jacobs, an architect and engineer who lived at Holmsleigh, Burgess Hill. Then the owner, Frederick J. Freeman, in partnership with H.H.D. Sawdy, decided to spend more money and build an entirely new cinema on up-to-date lines. They sought an experienced cinema architect and the Keymer Brick and Tile Works at Burgess Hill suggested A. Ernest Shennan, a specialist in building cinemas in the Liverpool area who regularly purchased the company's bricks. Shennan accepted the assignment but insisted on retaining Jacobs as the resident architect. He also encouraged Liverpool builders F. & T. Chappell to submit a tender which was accepted.

The cinema was substantially built of brick and reinforced concrete with steel girders. 225,000 locally-made bricks were used in the construction. The basement rooms were entirely enveloped in inch-thick solid asphalt, preventing any possibility of damp; the boiler was in the basement and pipes carried hot water round the building to radiators in suitable positions. Two systems of lighting—electricity and gas—were used.[75]

The Scala's opening attraction was Charlie Chaplin's latest picture, *The Circus*, and music was provided by a Celebritone instrument (an acoustic gramophone that played larger-than-usual records).

Mrs. G.A. ('Topsy') Goldsmith has recalled applying for a job as an usherette at the age of 16 in 1929.

> I was accepted and very proud of my green and gold uniform. Wages were then ten shillings a week, and hours 5 p.m. to 9 p.m. one week and 5 p.m. to 10.30 p.m. the next. A Saturday afternoon matinee and one Sunday evening was included every two weeks. There was only one house on Sundays, starting at 7 p.m., because of people going to church. During the interval I was also the chocolate girl, going round with a tray. For this I received one penny in every shilling commission on the sales. Sixpence was the price of a quarter-pound box of chocolates, and two shillings would buy a really lovely box!

The Scala faced unwelcome competition from November 1938 with the opening of the Studio cinema at Hassocks, which was part of a chain able to obtain new films at a much earlier date. The cinemas at Haywards Heath, by now part of a major national chain, also showed films long before the Scala, which was placed in a thoroughly inferior position. This may explain why the cinema was put up for sale. The new owner from 1939 was Philip C. Bingham, followed after his death in 1941 by his son, also named Philip Bingham. The son died in 1945 and the cinema was again on the market.

The next proprietor was E.F. Lyons, joint managing director of G.B.-Kalee, a leading cinema equipment manufacturer. Lyons, who lived in Hove, was looking for a suitable business within the entertainment field for his daughter and her husband, J.C. Knowland, a Canadian ex-serviceman. He purchased several Sussex cinemas, including the Scala Burgess Hill, and grouped them as Cranfield Cinemas with his son-in-law and daughter as directors and booking managers and himself as a director.

Lyons decided to improve the Scala and it closed after the Sunday performance on 11 August 1946, to re-open on Monday 23 September as the Orion, the name by which all but one of the Cranfield properties were to be known. The auditorium had been completely redecorated to give an impression of lightness and freshness. The main surfaces had been treated in peach with a fine green speckle, and the light fittings on the walls were surrounded by abstract floral patterns. There were new seats of green crushed velvet and new red and beige piled carpeting, the latest G.B.-Kalee sound and projection equipment, and a new screen and new main curtains—an appliqué in satins comprising a mass of flowers in different settings—which was placed to the rear of the stage close to the screen. The manager was L. Hunt, a director of Cranfield Cinemas. Soon after, the Studio Hassocks became part of the small circuit and, renamed Orion, served as its headquarters.

Knowland tired of running the chain and returned to Canada with his wife, but Cranfield Cinemas continued with a new booking manager. The Burgess Hill Orion closed on 19 December 1953 for a week to allow the installation of a new panoramic screen further forward on the stage. A short while later, it was fitted out to show films in CinemaScope, although the limited proscenium opening unfortunately required the masking to be lowered, resulting in a smaller picture. There were 402 seats with prices in 1955 ranging

from 1s. 6d. to 3s. 2d. Burgess Hill was beginning to expand rapidly and during 1955 thought was given to purchasing the property adjacent to the Orion (now Rooney & Co., estate agents) to provide a completely new entrance to the cinema so that the auditorium could be rebuilt with stalls seating extended further back across the old foyer and a proper balcony placed overhead.

The name 'Orion' was very close to that of 'Odeon' and the Orion cinemas had the temerity to imitate the current Odeon style of lettering and display heading in advertising to suggest an affinity with the prestigious national circuit.

By 1962, the cinema was once more up for sale and from Sunday 2 July it came under the ownership of Myles Byrne, who had operated a cinema in Kemp Town, Brighton, and wanted to move back into the area after running cinemas in Hereford. Byrne introduced a Walt Disney season right away in August and it did exceptional business, becoming an annual feature of the summer school holiday period for several years. Byrne hammered away at a barring clause in film bookings which prevented the Orion from

86 The new Kalee projector on display in the foyer of the Orion in 1958, prior to installation, with the projectionist Graham Head.

87 *Left.* The Orion, Burgess Hill, in 1973.

88 & **89** *Below.* The foyer and auditorium of the Orion in 1973.

90 & **91** *Bottom.* The auditorium of the Orion, looking to the front and the rear, 1973.

showing new releases at the same time as Haywards Heath and Hassocks, and won an allocation from the Trade Dispute Committee by which every sixth new film could be played in Burgess Hill before the other two towns. As it happened, the Orion Hassocks closed in 1964 (Byrne wanted to buy it, but would not meet the asking price) and the Perrymount Haywards Heath also shut down shortly after the Orion Burgess Hill had been granted a complete concurrency with it by which both cinemas could show films at the same time.

As the only cinema in the area, and under faster release patterns, the Orion found itself able to show some films at the same time as the Odeon Brighton. Byrne explored the possibility of subdividing the cinema into two so that he could show more films but decided this was not a viable proposition. In 1970, he refused to sell waste ground behind the cinema to the local Urban District Council which wanted to extend the adjacent car park but a few years later the space was used for the construction of a bingo club which, after several changes of name and ownership, is still operating in 1996. (Had not bingo been established here, it is possible that the cinema would have been taken over for the purpose.)

In 1982, because of personal problems, Byrne gave up his cinema interests and leased the Orion to a small independent chain run by Tim Partner and Peter Dobson. In November 1983, the manageress, Mrs. M. Stevens and her husband Malcolm took over the lease for £23,000. In June 1985, when the video boom had severely dented cinema attendances, the lease was acquired by a consortium headed by Jeff Grieves.

The Orion then closed for five weeks to have its second revamp. It was redecorated and the lighting changed from wall brackets to recessed downlights in the ceiling. The auditorium was reseated with old seats from the Warner Leicester Square and every other row of the stepped rear section was left vacant to provide enormous amounts of leg room. Only one projector was now used, together with a Philips 'cakestand' with horizontal platters on which an entire programme could be stored. A new screen was installed but, like its predecessor, had to be masked down for CinemaScope instead of widening out. In the entrance foyer, a combined paybox and confectionery counter was set up at right angles

to the old one, blocking one of two passages to the middle of the auditorium.

Re-opening took place on 19 July 1985 with the Orion name being discarded. It was now the Burgess Hill Cinema. The first film shown was the James Bond feature, *A View to a Kill*.

When Jeff Grieves became the manager of a new multiplex at High Wycombe, he offered the remaining ten years of his lease for sale at £36,000. Myles Byrne died around this time, in the summer of 1986, and his widow put the freehold of the cinema up for auction. In April 1987, Mid-Sussex District Council acquired the property for £92,500 but insisted there were no plans to redevelop the site and, if this did happen, another home for a cinema would be provided. On 12 February 1988, Jeff Grieves sold the lease to Stephen Wischhusen, who also operated the Dome Worthing.

Then, in 1990, the cinema was taken over by the Robins chain, a company headed by veteran showman Bill Freedman and his son, Ben. They put in hand the most drastic alterations that had happened to the property since it opened—carrying out at a stated cost of £200,000 the twinning that Myles Byrne had contemplated. The cinema closed on 21 May 1990. When it re-opened five weeks later, on 6 July, a half-height wall had been erected across the auditorium and the rear stepped section had been enclosed by a new lower ceiling to become a smaller second cinema, seating 121. The front stalls section became a separate auditorium seating 144, using the existing screen with the image being projected from the old operating box over the ceiling of the second cinema.

In the second cinema, the film reaches the screen by a system of mirrors from a projector facing downwards that sends the picture through a hole in the floor of the old projection box. The results are excellent. There was not enough space to install speakers behind the new screen and they were placed to either side. Motorised masking of the screen was also ruled out and the screen has to be widened manually in front of the audience for a 'scope film after the advertisements and trailers have been shown.

Soundproofing between the two cinemas has proved effective but the sound and smell of the oil-fired central heating was noticeable in the front auditorium.

92 The Burgess Hill Orion Cinema in June 1996.

New seats were installed throughout. In the back rows of each cinema were to be found a Robins speciality—double seats known as lovers' couches. Modern Tivoli lighting strips were used to mark out the aisles. The foyer was completely remodelled with a central sales counter. The passage to the left now led to the rear cinema, the one to the right to the front cinema. A new canopy was put up and the exterior brickwork was painted a cream colour.

A competition was held to find a new name for the cinema and the winning suggestion was 'Take Two'. This was only half-heartedly adopted, being combined with the circuit name to give Robins Take Two, then dropped in favour of the Robins name on its own. No name was displayed on the front of the cinema, although some time later the circuit symbol of a red robin was painted on the ends of the canopy. After a while, the paybox was moved from the centre to one side of the entrance doors. Some splendid old curtains had been retained in the front auditorium but these became too dirty and worn and were taken down, since when the screen has remained bare except for some coloured lighting effects from below.

In June 1995, the cinema was taken over by Lee Allwood, a newcomer to the film business who arranged for Robins to continue handling film bookings. As a change of name was required, the building became known once again as the Orion from Friday 16 June. The Orion name appears on the ends of the canopy in place of the robin symbol. In December, the cinema was repainted in white and blue.

The Orion remains open in 1996, a rare survivor in mid-Sussex despite many changes of ownership. Few would have guessed in the boom years of cinema-going that it would out-last its rivals in Haywards Heath and Hassocks. But it is now attractively adapted to meet current cinema standards, playing the biggest hits concurrently with Brighton and catching up with other films some weeks later.

(*This section is based on published research by John Fernee.*)[76]

CHICHESTER

MAY 1910
CORN EXCHANGE/
POOLE'S ELECTRIC PICTURES/
POOLE'S PICTURE PALACE/EXCHANGE/
GRANADA EXCHANGE/GRANADA
EAST STREET (CORNER OF BAFFINS LANE)

How many customers of McDonald's realise the extraordinarily rich history of the building? Once it was the town's Corn Exchange and archive sources suggest that it was the first venue in Chichester both to present animated photographs to a paying audience and to serve as a regular cinema building. It is fortunate that Minute Books have survived in the County Record Office for the period 1877–1921.[77]

The Corn Exchange, with its magnificent colonnaded portico, was erected in 1832 as a market place for local farmers, corn merchants and millers, but in 1883 the Committee in charge decided to hire out the Sample Room for occasional drama productions and other live entertainments. In February 1884 the Chichester Minstrels were using the building, but seats had to be brought in and many in the audience sat on corn bins ranged around the hall.

In August 1889, a Mr. Poole hired the hall, paying £18 for the first week and £12 for the second. On 26-27 December 1892, Maggie Morton brought her pantomime company. These represent early visits by two figures who would become pioneers of the cinematograph in Chichester.

93 The Corn Exchange in Chichester, venue for the city's first screening in December 1896 and for its earliest permanent cinema, Poole's Pictures, in 1910.

CORN EXCHANGE, CHICHESTER.

Positively for one week only.

COMMENCING MONDAY, OCTOBER 30th

Nightly at 7.45, Doors open at 7.15. Early Doors open at 7 o'clock, 3d. extra to all parts.

GRAND SPECIAL DAY PERFORMANCES
(same as at night)

On Thursday and Saturday at 3, Doors open at 2.30

Prices of Admission—2s., 1s. 6d., 1s., and 6d.
Children under 10 half-price to all parts except 6d. places. Tickets and Plan at Messrs. Pillow and Son's, East Street.

JOSEPH POOLE'S

NEW MYRIORAMA!

GREATER BRITAIN AND SAVAGE SOUTH AFRICA.

THE TRANSVAAL.   JOHANNESBURG.

England versus America. Sir Thomas Lipton's new Yacht "Shamrock," the Race for the American Cup.

THE SOUDAN WAR.

BATTLE OF OMDURMAN.

The Grand Charge of the 21st Lancers.

AMERICA AND SPAIN.

Poole's Perfect Vaudeville Organization.

Poole's Kinematograph of Animated Photography

Joseph Poole's Admired Orchestral Band.

94 October 1899, the Boer War has begun, and Joseph Poole has brought his Kinematograph to the Corn Exchange. (*Chichester Observer.*)

It was on Boxing Day, Saturday 26 December 1896, at 8 p.m. that Miss Morton introduced 'the greatest sensation and most wonderful invention of the age' in scene six of her pantomime *Blue Beard*, screening in the Sample Room a number of Irving Boscot's short pictures, ranging from *Arrival of the Czar in Paris* to *Gardeners Burning Weeds*.[78]

Charles W. Poole brought in his 'Royal Myriorama' for a week in November 1897. Huge pictures of Victoria's Diamond Jubilee celebrations were presented on a long white sheet drawn across rollers and attracted crowded houses.[79]

When Joseph Poole booked the Corn Exchange a year later, the reference in the Minutes to his liability for 'any extra fire insurance' suggests that he had added films to the packed programme of variety and myriorama, and certainly his visit in 1899, commencing on 30 October, included 'Poole's Kinematograph of Animated Photography'.[80]

Regular bookings of the Corn Exchange were made by the local flower shows, badminton club, musical society and others. There were occasional charity, political and civic events, plus bazaars, concerts and plays— sufficient usage to persuade the Committee to

purchase its own chairs, 250 of them, in April 1899.

Moving pictures featured only occasionally. Charles W. Poole was back with his 'Royal Myriorama' in February 1901, augmented this time with the Edison-Poole Eventograph, showing war films 'just arrived from South Africa' and footage of Victoria's funeral and the State Opening of Parliament shot only days previously. On Easter Monday 1901, West's 'Grand Naval Entertainment', *Our Navy*, began a week's visit, to be repeated in future years, demonstrating in pictures and variety how Britannia ruled the waves.[81]

The Corn Exchange continued to be regularly used for corn and wool sales, but the range of leisure activities was increasing, with Saturday afternoon roller skating from 1901 and evening table tennis a year later.

The number of performances of animated pictures gradually rose—at least five were recorded in the *Chichester Observer* in 1907. The National Animated Picture Company paid its first visit in July, to coincide with Goodwood Race Week. Its repertoire of sporting, travel, humorous and dramatic films included pictures of the King's visit to the races. The compère was Charles Waterfield, described in the *Observer* (24 July 1907) as 'the Naval Jester, who is an expert on the musical walking stick and the champion with the piccolo'. Variety invariably accompanied the films, as in September when W.F. Jury's Imperial Picture Company visited the Corn Exchange, its topical and comic pictures including its 'latest screamer', *The Short-Sighted Cyclist*.[82]

In February 1908, Luther Dyer contributed to the annual variety show in aid of the Chichester Infirmary, showing comic pictures loaned by the proprietors of the Brighton Hippodrome and two locally shot films, one of the Chichester Gymnastic Club and the other called *Scenes from Priory Park*.[83]

Three months later came 'Stewart's Colossal Animated Pictures and Refined Entertainers', the latter including Alvan-Tee ('King of the Slanting Wire') and Kitty Woodford's Dogs.[84] Perhaps this was the occasion in 1908 that Jack Tupper remembered when as a six-year-old he was taken to a matinee at the Corn Exchange. The projector was enclosed in a black box on trestles midway down the hall and the children created mayhem during the changing of the reels.[85]

By 1910, the Corn Exchange was listed as being available for hire at the rate of four guineas for an evening or 15 guineas for a week, offering a capacity of 800.

The Minutes confirm that 1910 was a crucial year in the cinema history of the Corn Exchange, for it was then that the hall was first hired by Poole's for the regular screening of films. At a meeting on 2 March, the secretary drew the attention of the directors to the requirements of the new Cinemato-graph Act, and pointed out the difficulties in complying with the new rules and regulations. It was decided to make the necessary expensive alterations for the building to continue presenting films and a cinematograph licence for the Corn Exchange, taken out in the name of the clerk, John William Jacobs of Cawley Road, was issued on 23 April 1910.[86] The projection box was moved to a platform high up outside the hall, accessed by a ladder, and the equipment modified to provide a steady image—'a result rarely attained at any picture show', noted the local paper. Inside, electric lights and an electric ventilation fan were installed, tip-up seats were provided at the front, and by the New Year the hall had, in the words of the *Observer*, 'assumed quite a theatre-like appearance'.[87]

On 25 May 1910 it was reported that an agreement had been signed with J.W. Poole for the hire of the hall for cinematograph entertainments for three months during the summer, a term which on 20 July was extended by a further three months. The use of the Corn Exchange as a regular cinema had begun—and very successfully, to judge from local press reports and the fact that the hire was extended. In October, shows were being held nightly at 7.45 p.m. with matinees on Thursdays and Saturdays.

Poole was still at the hall at the end of the year. The *Chichester Observer* commented in its 21 December edition:

> Messrs. Poole's continue to attract large crowds to the Corn Exchange where they are well maintaining their reputation as the leading exhibitors of electric pictures. Their films are carefully selected, and they have a happy knack of providing pictures exactly to the taste of the Chichester public. This is undoubtedly the most popular entertainment that has ever been presented to Cicestrians. An hour and a half at Poole's is an hour and a half enjoyably spent.

Poole's were busy with innovations to appeal to audiences. They had been quick to acquire 3,000ft. of film of Edward VII's funeral in June 1910, and six months later were

95 A packed house at Poole's, ever popular despite the hard wooden seats and the obstructions posed by the ladies' hats.

On Monday 15 May 1911 a gala night was held to celebrate the first anniversary of Poole's establishment in Chichester and this included, for the first time, a singing competition for local amateurs with cash prizes. Two shows took place, the second so full that hundreds had to be turned away.[90]

Another popular initiative, in September 1911, was the screening of recently shot local films, showing a cricket match, police versus tradesmen, at Priory Park, a garden fête at East Pallant House, scenes outside the Corn Exchange, and the Regatta at Bosham. The following month pictures of Sloe Fair were shown only 24 hours after they had been filmed.[91]

Poole's rapidly acquired a reputation in Chichester for the variety and high standard of their cinematograph performances, combining dramatic and humorous shorts with newsreels and local footage and a 'star picture'. On 1 March 1911 the *Observer* commented:

> There has probably been nothing as remarkable in recent years as the way in which picture palaces in all parts have come so much to the front as a form of popular entertainment. The reason is not far to seek, for with such diversified programmes, varying so quickly from grave to gay, and between instruction and amusement, it would be difficult to find a patron who goes away dissatisfied. That is exactly why Poole's Electric Pictures are so popular and continue to draw such crowded houses.

96 The Corn Exchange decorated by Poole's Electric Picture Company for the coronation of George V and Queen Mary on 22 June 1911.

showing Pathé Gazette newsreel.[88] In February 1911, 'singing pictures' were introduced with Miss Florrie Norris synchronising her voice to the lip movements on the screen, much to the delight of the audience. On 8 February the *Observer* reported:

> The film was a pathetic convict subject in which an escaped convict is arrested at the moment he is about to murder the judge who sentenced him, by the voice of the judge's daughter singing, 'Lead, kindly light.' He is so impressed with the hymn that he releases the judge, asks his pardon, and goes quietly back to prison. The piece brought down the house every evening.

The pianist at this time is remembered as an elderly man who wore a large black hat and a dramatic black cloak with red lining. When he was unwell, young Jack Tupper would deputise for 2s. 6d. a performance, becoming very accomplished at improvising 'hurry music' or 'hearts and flowers'.[89]

On 25 December 1911 a new three-year agreement was authorised between the directors of the Corn Exchange and Poole's Pictures, enabling the latter to use the hall, at 15 shillings a night, whenever it was not required for other purposes. The seating capacity was now said to be 1,000. The general managers of Poole's Picture Palace, otherwise known as Poole's Electric Pictures, were by now Fred Mayer, who was Joseph Poole's brother-in-law, and Felix Somers. Fred's son, Bernard, was the projectionist, responsible for that well-remembered announcement: 'Pause while the operator changes the spools'. Another name associated with Poole's was Natt Abatt, who had been the raconteur with the travelling myriorama before taking up residence hosting the shows at Chichester.[92]

In December 1912 it was agreed that Mayer and Somers should be permitted to put on theatrical performances, up to a maximum of twenty a year, in addition to the film shows.

In 1914-15, Mayer and Somers briefly extended their activities to run the town's other cinema, the Olympia, as well.

Barbara Ely records Jack Tupper's memories of the Corn Exchange at this period. By now films were longer, with good stories and stars such as Fatty Arbuckle and the Keystone Kops, but he could recall no British films, an indication of the growing strength of the American film industry. He could remember, though, the lame woman who sold sweets in the intervals and was popularly known as 'Chocolate' because that was her cry.[93]

The building was partly occupied for the first few months of the First World War, but the entertainment hall escaped and the shows continued. Late in April 1915 the star attraction was *Little Lord Fauntleroy* and on 25 October 1916 crowds flocked to see the official war film, *The Battle of the Somme*.[94]

However, the war did affect business and in May 1917 Mayer and Somers asked for their lease to be cancelled, eventually settling for a reduction of £100 on their £300 rental, an abatement which continued until July 1919.

Doris Mainwaring was a schoolgirl at the High School around this time and remembers that the Corn Exchange was the favourite cinema of her four sisters and herself:

My sisters and I always sat in the ninepennies (half-price, of course) about six rows from the front of the stage. We longed to sit on the corn bins for tuppence which lined the hall

but we were not allowed to do so as it would not have been ladylike! The pictures shown were in black-and-white and silent, and were very flickery. The dialogue was flashed on the screen. Before each film commenced a man named Natt Abatt came onto the stage wearing a greenish-black frock coat and top hat, and he explained what the film was all about. (I imagine this was because some of the audience were unable to read.) There was usually a news story, a drama or comedy (Charlie Chaplin, Buster Keaton or Harold Lloyd) and then a serial. I remember Pearl White being gagged and placed on the railway line—when the train was almost upon her, that instalment ended until the next week! Halfway through the programme there was an interval—probably to allow the projector to cool down—and this period of about fifteen minutes was filled with a very third-rate live show.[95]

97 *Below.* Filming the Regatta at Bosham, with Natt Abatt (half-hidden, on the extreme right) and Bernard Mayer (standing next to him), 14 September 1911.

98 *Bottom.* The frontage of the Corn Exchange prevented the easy and effective advertising of films.

99 A mobile hoarding for Poole's Picture Palace outside the Assembly Rooms in North Street. Pubs would be plastered with posters and free passes distributed.

100 Special reduced prices for the unemployed were offered at the Corn Exchange for the new Chaplin film in 1922. (*Chichester Observer.*)

The opening in July 1920 of the Picturedrome, which had better facilities and which engaged the services of both Natt Abatt and Poole's chief projectionist, must have damaged business here and may have brought about a change of proprietors—for in the early 1920s Stanley James took over and reverted to the Corn Exchange name. On the afternoon of Christmas Day 1921, Mr. James provided a free show for the unemployed and the inmates of the Infirmary consisting of a film, concert and tea.

In an attempt to improve business, the building no longer operated exclusively as a cinema. It combined boxing, whist drives, 'select' dances, variety shows and films—with Chaplin's *The Idle Class* and Betty Blythe's *The Queen of Sheba* both receiving well-advertised three-day runs. (One problem that faced all the film operators of the Corn Exchange was the difficulty of making an effective display of the cinema name or the titles of the films showing because of the line of massive columns along the front of the building.)

Then, from 6 November 1922, the Corn Exchange went over to films entirely with continuous performances (rather than separate shows as previously) from 5.45p.m. to 10.30p.m. with a matinee on Saturday at 2.45.

Archie Greenshields remembers that a special children's film show was put on for the underprivileged on Boxing Day mornings. An invitation would be included to the children of poorer families who were recipients of a food and coal gift from the Lord Mayor's Fund at Christmas time. The cinema treat was eagerly anticipated and children would pester their mothers to see if the gift had yet arrived. As well as the film—and the last one Archie remembers had prehistoric monsters (probably *The Lost World*)—each child would be given a bag of goodies containing sweets and an orange.[96]

In 1927 the building was taken over by the London-based Wainwright circuit and closed in early August for four months of major alterations that turned it into a proper cinema with stage facilities. The architects who designed the changes were G.S. Hall and G. de Wild. New lamps were hung in the colonnade and the entrance had new white marble steps with inlaid mosaic work. There was a handsome new vestibule with much oak panelling.

101 The Exchange, Chichester, during a run of Samuel Goldwyn's musical comedy, *Strike Me Pink*, in 1935.

In the auditorium a raked floor replaced the old flat one. There were new seats and a new proscenium. Along each side wall, eight windows were retained with curtains and pelmets. Those nearest the proscenium arch were filled in and illuminated. A new lower ceiling may well have appeared at this time.

The stage was slightly enlarged and sloped forward to give a better view of the performers. Several dressing rooms were provided behind. In front of the stage in the ceiling there was a wide blue dome with three large floodlights installed at the back to shine down and illuminate the stage. The walls of the auditorium had a chocolate brown base, then lighter colours from orange to gold to yellow next to a frieze at the top. The yellow matched the colour of eight pagoda-style light fittings which were suspended from the ceiling and gave a sunset effect. A dimmer system brought on a delicate sequence of light changes as the auditorium darkened and the curtains opened at the start of a film.

There were some 800 seats in all. The most expensive were the 52 seats in the loges of a new balcony, costing 2s. 4d. These seats were arranged in two sets of four loges to either side of the operating box which completely occupied the centre of the balcony. Three of the loges on each side held six orange wicker-style chairs with green cushions, while two larger ones held eight. The seats were staggered on three levels to provide better sightlines.

Now known as just the Exchange, the cinema seems to have re-opened on 8 December 1927 with the Harold Lloyd comedy *The Kid Brother* shown for three days at 6.05 p.m. and 8.20 p.m. In 1929, it claimed to be the first to show talking pictures in West Sussex, screening *Fox Movietone Follies of 1929* from Monday 19 August for six days, three times daily, with continuous performances from 2.30 p.m. to 10.15 p.m. The main feature was supported by the 'first all-talking comedy', *At the Dentist*. As elsewhere, this first showing of talkies drew huge crowds. By this time, the Exchange was one of five cinemas in the circuit operated by John G. and Richard B. Wainwright.[97]

During the early 1930s the Exchange gave occasional spot prizes during the Saturday evening performance. A spotlight was directed at patrons from the screen area and swung at random—whoever the light picked out when it stopped received a prize. Archie Greenshields

itself 'The Family House' in 1941. It became the home of the national ABC circuit release, as the Plaza (later Odeon) and Gaumont played the weekly programmes of the other two major circuits.

Michael Rowe recalled going to the Exchange in the Cinema Theatre Association's *Bulletin* (March/April 1987):

> It was a very rectangular building with a small 'upstairs'—you could hardly call it a circle. To me, as a youth, the most interesting architectural feature was the paybox (the cashier sat in front of the wall that separated her from the back row of the stalls) which had a small hole, about the size of a brick, through which she could, if she turned around, see the screen. I remember seeing much of *Scarface* when it was shown as a reissue in the 1940s by standing in front of the peep-hole.

The larger Granada circuit took over London and District's chain from 24 November 1946. On 28 February 1948, Granada started a Saturday morning children's club called the Exchange Rangers with the usual western, cartoon and serial.

The Exchange closed after the one-day Sunday show on 6 June 1948 for interior alterations. These involved increasing the seating capacity from 740 to 900, partly by raising and moving the projection box to the rear of the balcony to make space for more seats so that the upstairs could accommodate 130. In addition, new sound, carpets and heating were installed and the auditorium was redecorated in powder blue and peach.

Re-opening took place at 7.30 p.m. on Monday 22 November with a fanfare from the trumpeters of the Royal Sussex Regiment and a special showing of the new British film *The Guinea Pig* with one of its stars, Sheila Sim, making a personal appearance. The cinema was now called the Granada Exchange with the latter word receiving the greater emphasis. Because of the additional seats in the balcony, some were now priced at 2s. 9d. while the rest remained at the old price of 3s. 6d.[99]

The Exchange name was dropped and the cinema became simply the Granada with effect from Sunday 15 January 1950, also styling itself 'The Service-with-a-Smile Theatre'.

Programming featured some of Granada's own choices as well as those of the ABC circuit. The former included the European première of *Stromboli* on 15 May 1951.

102 & 103 The Granada and its foyer, pictured on 18 October 1961.

remembers his mother's amazement when she won a prize of a free flight with Sir Alan Cobham's Flying Circus, whose team was operating in the Hunston area (but the prospect of a five-minute ride in an open cockpit bi-plane rather alarmed her and she gave the prize to her sister).[98]

The Wainwright chain totalled six properties in 1935 but by the end of the decade it had doubled in size by taking over other picture houses and had become London and District Cinemas Ltd. Its provincial cinemas besides the Exchange were two at Aylesbury and one at Leatherhead. The Exchange styled

However, this was a mass event, the film also opening simultaneously at the Theatre Royal Bognor and many other cinemas.

In 1954, Granada's cinemas became part of a new circuit showing 20th Century-Fox's releases in the new CinemaScope process. The Chichester Granada was one of the last on the circuit to be outfitted with the new wide screen and accompanying magnetic stereophonic sound. Earlier 'scope films like *Knights of the Round Table* that were taken as ABC circuit releases appeared at Chichester in non-'scope alternative versions. Then from Monday 22 November 1954 the Granada played the first CinemaScope film, 20th Century-Fox's *The Robe*, for a week, together with a CinemaScope short, *Vesuvius Express*. To fit in the widest possible screen, a festoon curtain which rose and fell was installed in place of the old side-opening tabs. A season of Fox CinemaScope films followed: *Three Coins in the Fountain, Beneath the Twelve Mile Reef, Hell and High Water, King of the Khyber Rifles, How to Marry a Millionaire, Prince Valiant ...* Attendance figures are not available, but it is likely that the Granada streaked ahead of the Odeon and Gaumont at this period.

Despite being in an older building, the Granada outlived both its rivals and from 1960 became the only cinema in town for nearly twenty years, playing the pick of all the releases. By 1977, as a single-screen cinema seating 820 and serving an immediate population of 21,000, it had become an anomaly. As it was in a listed building, it could not be readily subdivided into smaller cinemas. Quite apart from this, its shape would have made conversion expensive. In fact, Granada had enthusiastically switched most of its cinemas over to bingo and by February 1978 had the same fate in mind for Chichester, proposing to spend £120,000 on conversion and claiming that film shows had an average audience of only 123.

When planning permission was refused, Granada appealed and a public inquiry was held in 1979. The Inspector upheld the refusal, referring in his report to 'the remarkable volume of public protest ... mainly voiced through a petition organised and heavily supported by young people', noting the lack of other public entertainment including alternative cinemas, and deciding that it was 'very desirable to retain the existing use for social reasons'. In December, the Environment Secretary confirmed the Inspector's decision. A Councillor and former Mayor prominent in the campaign hailed the verdict as a triumph for democracy. However, Granada did not see it that way and carried out its threat to close the cinema regardless of the outcome, although the last show did not take place until Saturday 9 August 1980.

Mrs. Pam Jones, the last manageress (who had worked 19 years at the Granada, preceded by five at the Gaumont), declared that attendances (with three shows a day) had averaged 300-400 per day, so it appeared that all those petition signatories had failed to support the cinema.

104 & 105 The auditorium of the Granada, Chichester, 1961.

The last attraction was a four-week run of *The Empire Strikes Back*, the sequel to *Star Wars*. The long runs demanded by distributors for hit pictures made life difficult for single screen cinemas. There were only 300 patrons on the last day, 100 at the last performance, although on the preceding Monday (with the help of rain) 1,160 had paid to see the film.[100]

So ended the building's 84-year association with moving pictures. It remained empty and unused for more than six years, although in March 1983 London and Manchester Securities proposed a £1.6 million conversion into two shop units with offices overhead, a scheme which received listed building consent after another public inquiry.

However, the entire building has now become a McDonald's fast food establishment with a trademark 'M' on the top of the frontage which is floodlit at night. No trace of the cinema auditorium remains on public view.

1 MAY 1911
OLYMPIA ELECTRIC THEATRE
NORTHGATE

The Olympia Electric Theatre was owned by a local company, Chichester Olympia Ltd., the secretary of which was David Henry Falconer of 12 North Pallant, in whose name the licence was granted on 22 April 1911.[101] The year was a busy one for cinema openings in this part of the county.

106 Advertisement in the *Chichester Observer* announcing the opening of the Olympia.

Adjacent to the cinema on its south side was the Olympia Skating Rink which had opened on 23 May 1910 and was operated by the same company, serving the passion for roller skating which lasted until the First World War.

The licence register shows that the dimensions of the hall were a modest 35ft. by 38ft. and that the seating capacity was 374. It was built by Messrs. Vick and Sons of Tower Street. Externally the cinema had an imposing white stone-like façade with plaster relief scrolls over the entrance. Inside, the floor was sloped and fitted with tip-up seats, and two staircases led from the vestibule to a roomy balcony. Decorated in white and dark red, the hall boasted electric lighting and had ventilators, electric fans and heating apparatus. The operator's box was enclosed in fire-proof walling with a separate entrance, and was isolated from the rest of the cinema.[102]

The Olympia was opened on the Monday afternoon of 1 May 1911 by the Mayor of Chichester, Alderman George Michael Turnbull who was accompanied on stage by the directors of the owning company: T.S. Adcock, E.E. Caffin, D.V. Noble, G.K. Smith, and H.C.F. Smith. While declaring the cinema to be a great ornament to the town, the Mayor wished it had been sited further up North Street, nearer the centre of the town.

The first show included a coloured travelogue (*Across the Passes of New Zealand*), a historical drama (*Judas Maccabaeus*), some comics, and news footage of the Newcastle versus Bradford City Cup Final at Crystal Palace.[103] The pictures—'very clear and with the minimum of vibration'—were shown on a plaster screen measuring 18ft. by 16ft., placed above the stage. (Within a year a canvas screen had taken over from the plaster one.)[104] Shows were held twice nightly at 7 p.m. and 9 p.m. plus matinees on Thursdays and Saturdays at 3 p.m., but there was no Sunday licence. Prices of admission to the ground floor or 'pit' were 3d. (front seats) and 4d. (back seats) with children charged a penny less and balcony seats cost 6d. and 1s. with children paying 4d. and 6d. respectively. The films were changed twice weekly.[105]

Professional variety acts were engaged to accompany the films. The first performer to appear was Miss Phoebe Lyndhurst, a vocalist from the London stage, followed by Gordon Meagor, a young baritone, who both played

---

OLYMPIA ELECTRIC THEATRE
(NORTHGATE, CHICHESTER).
The most comfortable and up-to-date Electric Palace in the neighbourhood.

Open Monday next, May 1st,
Twice nightly—7 and 9.

Balcony, 1s. and 6d. (Children 6d. and 4d. Pit, 4d. and 3d. (Children 3d. and 2d.)

MATINEES—Thursdays and Saturdays at 3.

No expense spared to secure all the latest and most up-to-date pictures.

the Olympia, for a week at a time, in its first month of operation. They were succeeded by the Sisters Clancy, dancers and comediennes, and then by Kloof and Waylet, described as 'eccentric musical entertainers'.

Taking a lead from Poole's at the Corn Exchange, the Olympia introduced local talent competitions, weekday heats culminating in a Saturday final, offering as a prize a sovereign and a week's engagement at the cinema. The first winner, with a comedy act, was L.R. Mead who worked for Lewis and Co., house furnishers, in Southgate.

Local tradesmen—Mr. F. Chitty (mineral water) and Messrs. Woolgar and Son (fruit and sweets)—were persuaded to donate their wares when 50 inmates of Chichester Workhouse were treated to a mid-week film matinee on 17 May 1911.[106]

The inclusion of locally shot films was another well-known ploy to attract patrons with the prospect of seeing themselves on the screen. In April 1912 these included footage of children coming out of the Lancastrian schools, employees of Henty's brewery leaving work, and a football match at the Barracks between the county regiment and a village team from Bosham.[107]

There is an interesting revelation that the Olympia got off to a poor start, with the first manager, H.H. Nichols, being replaced within a few months by Will Wright. The *Chichester Observer* (6 March 1912) noted:

Under the experienced management of Mr. Will Wright, the Chichester Olympia Electric Theatre is week by week becoming increasingly popular, and the scanty houses which characterised this up-to-date place of entertainment originally, are now quite things of the past. The secret of the success of the Olympia is undoubtedly the ability of the management to exactly appreciate the requirements of the public in the way of amusement, and both in the matter of variety artistes and pictures, they have now succeeded in gauging the public taste.

On 9 May 1912, Wright was quick to stage a special benefit to aid the fund for those left destitute by the sinking of the *Titanic*, and the Olympia was among cinemas to screen the first authentic film, taken aboard the *Carpathia*, of the rescue of the survivors and their arrival in New York.[108]

There was rivalry between the city's cinemas to secure the best of the new films.

At the beginning of June 1912, the Olympia gained the exclusive right to show the Selig production of *Christopher Columbus*, a big budget film of the period that had been a hit in London and drew fulsome reviews from the local press which must have boosted attendances for its Chichester engagement.[109]

At the beginning of 1914, there was a change of management, the Olympia re-opening on Monday 12 January with an improved stage and lighting system and now under the control of Messrs. Mayer and Somers, managers of Poole's Electric Pictures at the Corn Exchange. They seem to have run the Olympia under the banner of South of England Amusements Ltd., as this is the name shown in the *Kinematograph Year Book*. In January 1915, Mayer and Somers withdrew and control of the cinema reverted to the original proprietors, Chichester Olympia Ltd. The general manager by now was Ern Miles.[110]

107 Chichester's first purpose-built cinema was the Olympia, known locally as 'The Electric', which opened in May 1911, a year after the adjacent roller-skating rink.

108 *Above left.* A pre-Christmas programme at the Olympia in 1911—with free parking of bicycles.

109 *Above right.* The programme for January 1912 announced another amateur carnival at the Olympia—a proven means of boosting audiences for films.

By 1922, H.E. Terry had become the resident manager. Prices then ranged from 5d. to 1s. 3d.

In a series of letters to the *Daily Mirror* in 1991 about gaining admission to cinemas with jam jars rather than cash, it was suggested that one reader paid for entry to the Olympia with a rabbit skin! If true, this hints at the lowly status of the cinema. One Chichester resident, Violet Adams, has recalled shopkeepers distributing complimentary tickets for the Olympia when customers bought bags of flour.[111]

Undoubtedly, the location of the Olympia on the northern edge of town was not ideal and from July 1920 it suffered from the competition of the new Picturedrome as well as the Exchange. Both these venues were more centrally located and much larger.

However, its end came suddenly and dramatically after the normal film performances on Monday 6 February 1922. Shortly after 5 a.m. the following morning the building was observed to be on fire. The blaze had apparently started on the right-hand side of the balcony and the flames were breaking through the asbestos roofing. The auditorium was gutted along with the stage and dressing rooms, but it was possible to rescue the piano while £500 worth of films stored in the fire-proof projection box were found to be intact after the blaze had been extinguished. The lack of wind and the 14 in. thick walls stopped the flames from spreading to the builders' premises adjacent, where earlier the skating rink had been. The cause of the fire was thought to have been a burning cigarette discarded by a patron the previous evening.[112]

In later years the building became the Southdown bus garage and more recently it has served as a warehouse with glass panels in the roof. It still stands on an island site that includes the fire station, its frontage shorn of the original embellishments, looking wistfully over to the Festival Theatre, a sad reminder of its own distant days as a place of entertainment.

26 JULY 1920
PICTUREDROME/PLAZA/ODEON
55 SOUTH STREET

The Picturedrome was opened on the Monday afternoon of 26 July 1920 by the Mayor and Mayoress, Alderman and Mrs. George Michael Turnbull, with the usual charity show, the proceeds of which went to the Royal West Sussex Hospital. The opening happily coincided with crowds flocking into town for the horse racing at Goodwood.

The Picturedrome was the third venture headed by architect Peter Stonham and followed the Picturedromes at Worthing and Bognor. A fourth and last Picturedrome opened later in the year at Eastbourne (now the Curzon cinema).

The new cinema normally offered two changes of programme weekly and tickets were priced from 4d. to 1s. 6d. There were two projectors, all the seats were 'tip-up', and the gangways were noted as being wide. Musical arrangements were under the direction of Percy Lewis of East Street but, for the opening,

Monsieur Phillite R. Mering was engaged to provide the orchestra and perform a violin solo. The manager was Natt Abatt, who for a number of years had been associated with Poole's Pictures at the Corn Exchange, and the chief projectionist was Bernard Mayer, who also transferred from Poole's.[113]

Archie Greenshields recalls as a small boy being taken to the Picturedrome by his grandmother in the 1920s. The entrance they used was in the West Pallant and his child's ticket cost 2½d.

> Granny always pointed to the lights in the auditorium ceiling in the form of stars and, probably noting my impatience for the film to start, told me that it would when the stars went out. There were adverts either before or between a cartoon featuring Felix the Cat or Tugboat Bill. I remember clearly one that advertised Storey's Music Shop in North Street. Their advert showed a trumpet from which a jumble of letters were blown to make words of what one could purchase there.[114]

Special attractions like *Beau Geste* in 1927 came with their own score which was played by an augmented orchestra.

The Picturedrome was acquired by County Cinemas, a small chain which expanded into a circuit of some national significance, and in August 1929 the cinema was renamed the Plaza. The Western Electric sound system was installed here and talking pictures arrived three weeks after the Exchange, with the Al Jolson smash hit *The Singing Fool* opening on 9 September 1929. Huge crowds were reported for the following week's talkie, *On Trial*.[115]

A new manager, Cyril Chalk, arrived from County's Alexandra at Aldershot, and introduced a new policy of three performances daily at 2.30 p.m., 6 p.m. and 8.15 p.m. Tickets ranged from 6d. to 1s. 6d. (children half-price).

According to Russell Burstow, one of the great successes at the Plaza in the early 1930s was the Gaumont-British musical *Evergreen* with Jessie Matthews.[116]

When it became known that Chichester was to have a brand-new Gaumont cinema, County responded by closing the Plaza rather abruptly on 27 June 1936, following a three-day run of the Errol Flynn swashbuckler *Captain Blood* plus the B western *Song of the Saddle*, to enable 'complete reconstruction'. Over a period of nearly six months it was totally reconstructed within the old side walls

110 The Band of the Royal Sussex Regiment photographed outside the Chichester Picturedrome, Alexandra Day, 22 June 1927.

111 The new auditorium of the Chichester Plaza reproduced from the souvenir programme of its re-opening in December 1936.

to the plans of a prominent cinema architect, Andrew Mather (whose practice also designed the Odeon Littlehampton), gaining a balcony and an increased total of 1,063 seats (the original seating figure has proved elusive). The very narrow single-storey entrance and adjoining shops were demolished and replaced by a new, unobtrusive Georgian-style frontage set further back with a wide entrance covered by a canopy and one shop alongside. There was a café-restaurant on the first floor behind tall windows. The new but still narrow auditorium with a modern decorative scheme appeared behind. Advertisements accurately proclaimed: 'Only the name remains the same'.

The gala charity re-opening, in aid of the Royal West Sussex Hospital (like the original opening), took place at 8.15 p.m. on the cold, rainy evening of Friday 18 December 1936 when all seats were 1s. The new Plaza was opened by the Mayor, Councillor W.H.G. Napper, with the Trumpeters and Band of H.M. The Queen's Bays (2nd Dragoon Guards) playing, while the film shown was *Rembrandt*, starring Charles Laughton, being given its first screening outside London for the one night only. From Saturday and for the ensuing week, the attraction was *Rhodes of Africa*, followed by Shirley Temple in *Poor Little Rich Girl*.[117]

Tickets to the balcony were now 1s. 6d. and 2s., while admission to the stalls cost 6d., 1s. and 1s. 6d. Performances were continuous daily from 2 p.m. to 10.15 p.m. When House Full signs were displayed, Archie Greenshields remembers that a commissionaire in full uniform would usher in queueing patrons with calls of 'A single one-and-six' or 'Balcony only'. During a full house, it was not unknown for the manager in evening dress or the uniformed commissionaire to pass down each aisle freshening the air with a special appliance.[118]

The County circuit was absorbed by Odeon, which took full control from the beginning of the Second World War in September 1939. As a young relief manager, Dennis Williams spent 10 days in charge of the Plaza in 1941.

> Now Chichester had far too many seats for the size of the town. One of the biggest money losers Odeon had was the Plaza at Chichester. The film showing was Carole Lombard in *Mr. and Mrs. Smith*, which was an absolute stinker. It was one of Odeon's 'punishment' shows. If you upset anybody at head office, they used to send you for a relief to Chichester because it was a place that didn't do any business. You'd go there at two o'clock to open the show and there'd be nobody waiting. You'd put out a notice 'Open at 3.30' and come back and find two people waiting. The first seven days I was there the total takings were £85. The wage bill was £109, so about Tuesday you sent a chit to head office that you hadn't taken enough money to pay the wages. That applied to quite a number of theatres.

The Plaza was renamed the Odeon from Sunday 13 May 1945. To overcome the limited visibility of its recessed frontage, the Odeon sign was perched on the top of the building where it could be seen from a distance.

The war years were exceptionally difficult along the South Coast with the widespread evacuation and restrictions on movement, but Odeons as a matter of policy remained open regardless of trading conditions. When hostilities ceased, cinema attendances nationally shot to an all-time high. The Odeon's trading performance must have improved as it survived the 1950s when a substantial number of other Odeons were closed. The restaurant remained open long after that at the Gaumont had been sold off, and afternoon performances were not cut back as an economy measure.

CINEMA

112 'Let's Go To The Pictures.' The Odeon, Chichester, showing Darryl Zanuck's *David and Bathsheba*, a Technicolor Bible-in-pictures, in 1951.

113 & 114 Queueing for Walt Disney's *Living Desert* at the Chichester Odeon, 18 August 1954. His first full-length true-life adventure film, it was given the usual six-day run.

FORTHCOMING CINEMA ATTRACTIONS

From January 1959, a shortage of films forced the Odeon and Gaumont circuits to abandon separate weekly release programmes: the best cinemas on the two chains now played what was called the Rank release with the others playing left-overs as part of what was euphemistically named the National release. The owner of the two circuits, the Rank Organisation, stated that many National release outlets would be sold off when opportunities arose. In Chichester the Gaumont was allocated the Rank release and the Odeon took the National release.

Given the poor programmes that the Odeon now had to play, it was no surprise when in January 1960 Rank announced that the cinema had been sold and would close on 6 February. Some of its 24 staff (many part-timers) were found jobs at other sites, including the manager for the past seven and a half years, Frederick Gompertz.

The last presentation, from 31 January for seven days, was a British X-certificate crime thriller *The Shakedown*, starring Terence Morgan, supported by a dubbed Russian war picture, *Heart of a Man*. Daily matinees were retained to the end.[119]

The Odeon then sat mysteriously dark and unused until December when work started on conversion into a Fine Fare supermarket. The ground floor was levelled and a new floor built out from the balcony front to provide storage space, offices and a staff room above. The balcony itself, with the seats removed, provided a further storage area.

The supermarket opened a year later. In recent times it has become an Iceland store. Externally, above the ground floor it looks much the same as when it was a cinema. The tall, steeply descending roof of the auditorium is clearly visible. Inside there is no trace of the original cinema building in the ground-floor selling area open to the public, but above (as recently revealed in an inspection kindly arranged by Iceland manager Colin Parrott) a surprising amount of the old cinema remains. The first-floor café space stands empty, still with its 1936 decorative ceiling. Stairs still lead up into the centre of the balcony which retains its steppings but not any seats. A new wall has been built across the front of the circle and in front of that there is no trace of the auditorium or the proscenium arch. But overhead in what was the circle there remains untouched the

QUEUE HERE

ceiling introduced in 1936 with its two slanting troughs (which once contained concealed lighting) extending straight forward above each side wall. The garish colours of the last redecoration are still visible. 1930s light fittings on the side walls have gone but their backplates remain. On the rear wall, the projection portholes, decorative grillework over vents at each side, and vestiges of a central exit sign can still be seen. Further back, various empty rooms still have signs painted on the doors identifying the former plenum room, manager's office, staff room... And, most amazing of all, various loose sections of a specially painted display, clearly made to be mounted on the front of the cinema, are lying on the floor nearly half a century after they were needed, like pieces of a giant jigsaw puzzle. Partially assembled, they prove to advertise a 20th Century-Fox Technicolor musical with Dan Dailey and Anne Baxter, *You're My Everything*, shown here in 1950.

20 SEPTEMBER 1937
GAUMONT
EASTGATE SQUARE
(CORNER OF EAST STREET/ST PANCRAS)

The Gaumont was constructed on a site at the eastern edge of the town centre, conspicuous to visitors arriving from that direction but otherwise slightly out of the way, rather as the Olympia had been on the northern extremity. As happened in many other cases, a sufficiently large, reasonably priced site was only available on the fringe of the town centre and it was felt with some justification that a modern cinema would be a strong enough draw to overcome a less than perfect location. The site also provided space for a substantial car park which the city's other cinemas lacked.

The architect of the cinema was Harry Weston, who had earlier designed the Majestic Rochester and the Gaumont Rose Hill (Carshalton) which had opened as part of the Gaumont circuit. Weston had a financial interest in many of his cinemas, and the Gaumont Chichester was owned by a special subsidiary, the Chichester Regional Theatre Co., which was controlled by the Gaumont-British Picture Corporation. This was the only Gaumont cinema ever to operate in West Sussex. Its design did not conform to the general circuit style and it even had a distinctive carpet pattern of its own rather than the standard circuit one.

115 The Gaumont, Chichester, as it looked on opening in 1937.

116 Interior view of the Gaumont in 1937.

117 Entrance foyer and paybox of the Gaumont, 1937.

118 Auditorium of the Chichester Gaumont with its underwater decorative effect, 1937.

The Gaumont was built on part of a site totalling one and three quarter acres. It was said that 'the remainder will form a spacious car park with ample space for the construction of a swimming pool and pavilions. The site enjoys the distinction of having as its boundary a portion of the City Wall which ... was built during the Roman period.' The notion of a swimming pool remained alive until the outbreak of war.

The foundation stone of the Gaumont was laid on Thursday 31 September 1936 by the Mayor of Chichester, Councillor W.H.G. Napper, being tapped into place with a silver trowel after it was lowered into position. Harry Weston was there along with F.G. Talbut Butler, a director of GBPC. The cinema was said to be costing £30,000 with building work to commence immediately for an opening at the end of January 1937. This date may have been issued to disconcert the owners of the rival Plaza cinema, which was undergoing urgent reconstruction to meet the impending challenge of a brand-new Gaumont. It was not until the autumn that the Gaumont opened its doors.[120]

The debut of a cinema in the 1930s was a major event. The gala opening took place at 7.45 p.m. on Monday 20 September 1937. The ceremony was performed by the Mayor of Chichester, Councillor W.H.G. Napper, who had officiated at the foundation ceremony almost a year earlier. He was supported by six

Gaumont-British starlets and the Band of H.M. Royal Marines. The house was full and hundreds who queued outside had to be turned away. The big picture was the Gaumont-British production of *King Solomon's Mines* and there were 30 minutes of the Farr-Louis big fight as well. Proceeds went to the often-favoured Royal West Sussex Hospital in Chichester.[121]

In design, the Gaumont combined the traditional with the modern, having a Georgian exterior faced with red bricks and stone that curved in a streamlined fashion around the corner to terminate abruptly at the boundary of the site. The Gaumont sign and the top edge of the frontage were lit by neon. A café occupied first-floor space, reached by a separate entrance on the extreme left. There was a ground-floor waiting lounge behind the curving corner of the frontage. The entrance was not on the main street but just past the corner on the side street. The auditorium extended back down this side street which led to the car park.

A paybox was placed immediately facing the entrance. Stairs off to the left curved round behind the paybox, leading up to what was called the circle. To the right, steps led down to an inner foyer and the stalls. A particular detail of the foyer stuck in the mind of local cinemagoer Michael Rowe as a young patron:

> Though there was a free-standing paybox in the foyer, when there was a sudden demand a second was brought into action just inside the main doors. I was puzzled that this second one seemed to disappear completely when not in use—and then I discovered how. A quad poster frame covered the opening completely when it was not needed!

The auditorium was arranged in the stadium style, like the Odeon Bognor Regis. It had a stepped rear section of nine rows of seats rather than a separate balcony or circle. This design had the advantage of reducing the ceiling height and cutting building costs but it did not pack in as many seats as the more widespread arrangement of a circle overhanging the rear stalls. It did provide excellent sightlines and a near level throw from the projection box, just five degrees from the horizontal, resulting in a better picture. The space below the so-called circle was mainly occupied by an inner foyer, 70ft. long and 18ft. wide, with entrances at each end to the front part of the auditorium or stalls.

The rear section seated 404 while the front part seated 874, giving a total of 1,278. Although on the modest side for a new cinema in this period, this was more than enough to meet demand and to make the Gaumont the largest of Chichester's three picture houses.

The decorative scheme in the auditorium suggested an underwater setting. The walls were in shades of blue with painted bubbles, seaweed and ripples. There were two large painted canvas panels, 40ft. long and 6ft. 6ins. high, painted by French artist Henri Hague and placed high on each of the side walls. Floodlit from below, these depicted underwater plants and fishes. A lighting trough down the middle of the ceiling (painted in blue) was the main source of interval lighting. Seats in the stalls area were upholstered in red with grey arms, while those in the raised section were the reverse—grey with red arms.

The proscenium opening measured 34ft. by 24ft. and the screen 25ft. by 18ft. In front was an orchestra well. Three large dressing rooms were available to support live presentations on the 20ft. deep stage.

The Gaumont offered continuous performances from 2.30 p.m. to 10.30 p.m. 'Not just another Cinema *but* something different' was the message to Cicestrians and press advertisements made much of the Gaumont's café and free car park.

The Gaumont played its own circuit releases and carried on, apparently uneventfully, until its café was closed on 15 December 1951, having clearly become less successful than the one at the Odeon which continued. However, after two years the café area with its own separate entrance was leased out and re-opened as the Marsham Restaurant. A Saturday morning show for children was established here rather than at the Odeon.

From the middle 1950s the Gaumont suffered from the weak choice of pictures on its circuit release until the Rank Organisation, owning both Odeon and Gaumont circuits, allocated it the new, superior 'Rank release'. Strong films like *The League of Gentlemen*, *Suddenly Last Summer* and *Doctor in Love* were shown for a week, others for three or four days only.

With a population of 17,890, Chichester was absurdly well-off for cinema seats, even allowing for the influx of visitors, its three halls offering over 3,000 places in total. The closure of the Odeon seemed to solve the problem, at least for a while, and it was a surprise when only six months later it was announced that the Gaumont would shut down too—on 15 October 1960. Its departure was part of an unpublicised arrangement between Rank and the Granada circuit, covering certain towns in which they were in damaging competition, whereby one cinema was closed to aid the survival of the other. On the same day as the Gaumont went in Chichester, leaving only the Granada, the Granada circuit shut its cinema in Epsom, Surrey, in favour of Rank's Odeon. Because of the deal, Rank stated that there was 'no possibility' of another company running the Gaumont as a cinema, even though there was no buyer for the property. 'We are simply closing it down,' the company said. The restaurant, however, remained open in outside hands.

The final attraction at the Gaumont was a U certificate Disney double-bill, *Toby Tyler* and *Zorro the Avenger*, which had begun a three-day run on Thursday 13 October. The first half of the week had been occupied by a Jerry Lewis comedy *The Bellboy* plus *Tarzan the Magnificent*. The cinema had 21 members of staff (including part-timers), besides manager Jack Turner (who had moved to the Gaumont two years previously after 18 years at the Odeon Woking) and a black and white cat

119 The café area of the Gaumont on opening, 1937.

120 Eastgate Square, Chichester, with St Pancras Church, the war memorial and Gaumont Cinema, showing a re-release of Frank Capra's *Lost Horizon*.

called Whisky who had wandered in full-grown 12 years before and stayed. Whisky was given a new home by the head cleaner.[122]

At the time, there were two competing appeals to provide Chichester with a theatre and a swimming pool. It seemed only appropriate, given the earlier plans for a pool in the vicinity and the cinema's own watery decorative motifs, that the closed property should be acquired by the Council on 29 December 1961 after six months of negotiations and subsequently turned into swimming baths. The main foyer remained virtually unaltered as the entrance hall.[123]

In 1996, the building stands closed but the three sets of double entrance doors and the foyer itself remain in place. The canopy has gone and an Indian restaurant occupies the old café with a false ceiling and Asian trimmings placed in the Georgian-shaped windows that look out onto Eastgate Square.

1982
NEW PARK FILM CENTRE
NEW PARK ROAD

After the closure of the Granada in 1980, Chichester returned to part-time venues for its film entertainment, firstly through the Chichester College Film Society which met at the College of Technology in the Avenue de Chartres and the Chichester Film Theatre at the Newell Centre in St Pancras. Both offered weekly performances during the winter season in the early 1980s. However, by 1982 a film club had also been established at the Community Centre in New Park Road, meeting on Friday evenings during the season. This was to be the beginning of the New Park Film Centre which subsequently developed into a prestigious film venue under the direction of the Chichester City Film Society.[124]

The New Park Film Centre is located in a school building dating from 1888 in which a wide range of activities takes place in various rooms, including dance classes, yoga, judo, gymnastics, painting, and meetings of various societies. Film shows are presented in a hall entered by a door just to the right of the screen. The 125 seats are in well stepped rows with a centre aisle and projection is on 35mm from a box at the back. The roof and its supporting beams are exposed so that there is no proper ceiling, giving a church hall atmosphere. Despite its small size, the New Park Film Centre has an ambitious annual film festival and deftly combines specialised pictures with mainstream attractions. Stage productions by the Chichester Players are also performed here.

Addenda: Chichester

Before the First World War, films were also shown in the Concert Hall at the Chichester Institute (capacity: 300) which was booked by the Royal Canadian Life-Motion Picture Co. Screenings also took place in the Recreation Hall of the West Sussex County Asylum at Graylingwell (capacity: 600) although these were intended for patients only.[125]

In more recent years, films have been extensively presented not only at the New Park Centre but also at the 212-seat Minerva Studio Theatre which opened on 22 April 1989 as an extension of the Chichester Festival Theatre. This space is, like the main auditorium, primarily designed for theatrical performances and has no cinema atmosphere, while much of the side seating cannot be used for film shows.

CRAWLEY

PRE-1911
'THE TIN HUT'
EAST PARK

Crawley's first cinema is remembered as 'The Tin Hut'—its real name is lost in obscurity. Sited in East Park, some 200 yards from the Imperial Picture Theatre on the Brighton Road, it had hard wooden benches for seats and access to the projection box was via an outside staircase. Film of the coronation of King George V is said to have been shown here in June 1911, but business declined once the Imperial opened, and roller skating took over.[126]

1911
IMPERIAL PICTURE THEATRE
BRIGHTON ROAD

The Imperial Picture Theatre was newly constructed and opened in 1911 by Charles Gadsdon on a site just south of the railway line in what was then the centre of Crawley. Gadsdon was one of the town's most enterprising businessmen and six years earlier had built his own garage and motor car showroom on an adjacent site in Brighton Road. Initially he leased the Imperial to W. Howard Flint, then in 1912 the lease passed to H.W. Hire. By 1918, according to *Kelly's Directory*, G.S. Hire, presumably a relative, was leasing the cinema, but in 1919 Gadsdon took over the running himself.

A photograph of the Imperial taken in or about 1911 reveals a programme of seven shorts accompanied by 'Mr. Syd Raymond's Songs'. The cinema is often in the background of photographs and postcards of the marches and parades which took place in the main street during the first quarter of the century.[127]

121   An early view of Brighton Road, Crawley, and Charles Gadsdon's Imperial Picture Theatre built in 1911.

122   The Imperial in 1923, photographed as the background to a parade along the main street in Crawley.

PRE-1914
VICTORIA
HIGH STREET

The short-lived Victoria Picture Theatre on the east side of the High Street became the premises of the Bell Precision Company before the First World War. It is possible that the Victoria Hall (opened in 1920, see Addenda) was an adaptation of this building.

20 JULY 1929
IMPERIAL
BRIGHTON ROAD

Replacing the old Imperial on the same site, Charles Gadsdon's new Imperial was formally opened on Saturday 20 July 1929 by Dr. S.P. Matthews, chairman of Ifield Parish Council.[129] It offered a smart, neo-classical front, a foyer tiled in blue and grey, and an auditorium seating 664. An orchestra of four accompanied the silent films, but talkies arrived almost immediately.

The Imperial was the town's only cinema until the opening of the Embassy in 1938. It served other purposes as well, and in its heyday was one of the leading centres of Crawley life. It provided a venue for important meetings in the town, and was the local meeting hall for the British Legion and the League of Nations Union. The prime minister, Ramsay MacDonald, gave an address here in October 1933 on Hitler and disarmament.

123 *Top.* Another view of the old Imperial pictured in August 1927.

124 *Above.* The devastation is assessed after fire destroyed the old Imperial Picture Theatre on 4 August 1928.

125 *Right.* The new Imperial Cinema which opened in July 1929 just in time for the 'talkies'.

Although primarily used for films, the Imperial cinema was also the scene of live entertainment, notably charity concerts, and public meetings.

It had been built without a balcony. One was added in the late 1920s, shortly before disaster struck. On Saturday 4 August 1928 the building was completely gutted by fire. A policeman discovered the blaze, which had originated at the screen end of the theatre, at 11 p.m. He quickly alerted the fire brigade which prevented the fire spreading to Gadsdon's garage in which was stored 2,000 gallons of petrol.

The damage was estimated at £7,000 and the cinema had to be completely rebuilt.[128]

126 *Above.* The auditorium of Gadsdon's new Imperial Cinema showing the ground floor and circle.

127 *Right.* The foyer and paybox of the Imperial with stairs ascending to the balcony lounge.

When in 1937 it became likely that Crawley would gain a new cinema, the Imperial responded by closing on 19 July for redecoration and alterations, re-opening on Sunday 1 August. However, films still arrived at the Imperial late in the day, with three changes of programme weekly. Matinees were held only on Saturdays. Its seating capacity was now given as 500.

The Embassy, when it opened in August 1938 with earlier access to the new films, proved too much for the Imperial which closed in April 1939.

It became an auction room in the 1940s and 1950s. Then, in 1986, C. Gadsdon Ltd. took back the property and turned the ground floor into a car showroom, inserting a new floor at circle level to create a parts store, reached by a new side entrance.

Although, in 1996, all the original features downstairs have gone, upstairs in the parts area (open to the public) there can be seen many 1929 decorative features on the top of the former proscenium arch, the ceiling and side walls. (In January 1988, plans were approved for Gadsdon's to demolish the property and build a new showroom, offices and four flats, but the scheme has seemingly died.) The name 'Imperial Cinema' can still be seen in the stonework on the front.

1 AUGUST 1938
EMBASSY/ABC/CANNON/MGM/ABC
HIGH STREET

In 1937 interest in building a new cinema in Crawley became apparent as in April an entrepreneur called J.C. Cruttwell was granted permission by the Housing Committee to proceed with a scheme, provided the front elevation was faced with approved bricks and there was only limited use of artificial stone. In August, the large Union Cinemas circuit announced that it had acquired a site for a new Ritz with café. However, Union ran into sudden financial difficulties in October and was taken over by Associated British Cinemas, which let the Crawley scheme drop. This gave the smaller Shipman and King circuit the opportunity to step in.

Their Embassy was built on the site of the *Albany Temperance Hotel* (very likely the same site as the Cruttwell and Union schemes). The entrance was set slightly back from the road with a carriageway for dropping off patrons arriving by car.

128 *Right.* The Embassy, Crawley, on its opening in August 1938.

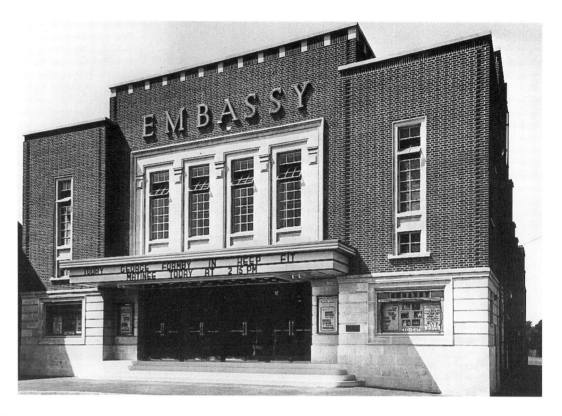

129 *Below.* Auditorium of the Embassy, 1938.

130 *Bottom.* Main foyer, Embassy, 1938.

With 40 cinemas in the south-east of the country, S&K specialised in small country towns and in Sussex had previously built the Regent Crowborough, Pavilion Hailsham and Regent Rye. On past experience, they would have taken over the Imperial to create a local monopoly but they may have felt that Crawley would only support one cinema and remained confident that the Imperial at the other end of the High Street would soon have to close—as, in fact, it did.

The Embassy was a pleasingly modern cinema, the last to be opened by S&K before the Second World War. Designed by a leading cinema architect, Robert Cromie, with 1,014 seats (covered in cherry-red material with arm rests in grey), it was not as streamlined and striking as some of the circuit's cinemas. The auditorium was described at the time as having 'what might be called a simplified classical style'. The most striking feature was the set of 18 square grilles mounted in six rows of three on the ante-proscenium wall on each side of the proscenium arch, painted in gold and picked out by concealed lighting (a similar device was used to more pronounced effect at S&K's Embassies at Esher, Chesham and Waltham Cross). There was more concealed lighting behind the proscenium surround and illuminating the flat centre section of the ceiling from the sides. The side walls were decorated with vertical shaded flutings and had perpendicular light fittings attached. Polished walnut was used around the side exit below the grilles, and also to face the paybox in the main entrance hall.

The Embassy was opened for the first time at 8 p.m. on Monday 1 August 1938 by the chairman of Crawley Council with Ralph Lynn making a personal appearance and saying a few words. The film programme on that first night consisted of the George Formby film *Keep Fit*; a B feature called *Bulldog Drummond Strikes Back*; a Disney cartoon; and the news.

The Embassy's normal policy was to open around 2.15 p.m. on Wednesday, Saturday and Bank Holidays, at 8 p.m. on Sundays, and at 5.30 p.m. on other days. At this time, Crawley was not big enough to support daily matinees. There were no less than four prices for the stalls (6d., 9d., 1s., and 1s. 3d.) and two prices for the circle (1s. 6d. and 2s.). A large free car park was available.

By the 1950s, when the town's population had soared, the cinema gave three performances daily, beginning at 1 p.m. or shortly thereafter, and often changing programme midweek. On Sundays, a revival programme was presented between 3 p.m. and 9 p.m. A children's show was held on Saturdays.

The Shipman and King circuit was acquired by the Grade Organisation which was itself taken over by EMI in 1967. Then, in 1969, EMI also gained control of the huge ABC circuit. The two circuits were run separately for a while but the S&K cinemas were amalgamated with ABC from October 1971.

On 15 December 1979 the Embassy closed for three months to be divided up into three smaller cinemas at a cost of £250,000. New automatic projectors with 'cakestands' (horizontal revolving platters which carry an entire programme in one continuous reel) were installed along with closed-circuit television to monitor projection when the boxes were unattended.

The Embassy re-opened on 20 March 1980 with a full house, turning away a hundred or more would-be patrons. It now seated 331 in Embassy 1, 234 in Embassy 2, and 118 in Embassy 3.

In 1985, it was decided to rename the cinema the ABC and to reintroduce the old

131 Embassy staff dressed up as nurses to promote the showing of the hit film *The Citadel* in 1939. Seen, from left to right, are: May Moon, Miss Bamford, cashier Joan Beard, J. Lewis and Iris Buckman.

triangle logo by which the circuit had been known until the 1960s. However, the triangle sign was only modestly displayed in a small light box in the centre of the frontage. New staff uniforms reminiscent of the 1930s were tried out.

In 1986, the American Cannon company took over the circuit and insensitively applied its name to every cinema, including Crawley's from 28 November of that year.

Then the Cannon name was retired in favour of a new set of three initials, those of MGM, with effect from 18 June 1993—these prestigious letters, accompanied by a roaring lion, having become available when the Cannon circuit fell under the same ownership as the American Metro-Goldwyn-Mayer company. The MGM name was applied only to the best or most profitable cinemas (others remained as Cannons), so the Crawley cinema was clearly identified as a valuable one.

132 1930s splendour. The circle lounge of the Crawley Embassy.

In a further change of ownership, the MGM chain became part of Richard Branson's Virgin empire in July 1995 but, when Virgin decided to concentrate on its modern multiplexes and sell off almost all the older cinemas, this was one of 90 (another being the Cannon Bognor Regis) that were sold on 2 May 1996 to ABC Cinemas, a recently formed company which reintroduced the historic ABC name and triangle logo on its properties, at Crawley during June.

The Crawley cinema should continue to prosper. With bingo next door in the Sussex House office block and the AMF Bowl next to that, it is part of a small entertainment nucleus. But a big cloud on the horizon is the likelihood of a multiplex opening in or near Crawley.

Addenda: Crawley

In the 1910-15 period (and probably earlier) the George Assembly Room was available for hire to film showmen at a cost of two guineas a night, taking up to 400 people at a time.

In 1920, the Victoria Hall opened in the High Street, generously provided for the people of Crawley by John Penfold. Situated close to the Northgate Restaurant, it was an all-purpose hall used for dances, amateur theatricals, variety shows and, from time to time, films.

After the Second World War, there was a huge expansion of population in Crawley, from 9,500 in 1947 to over 80,000 by 1983 as the new town was built from 1951 onwards. This was of great benefit to the Embassy, especially as there was a dearth of alternative leisure facilities (no dance halls or coffee bars). Crawley was even regarded for a while as needing a further cinema—at least by the Rank Organisation which announced in March 1955 that it would be building a new Odeon.

In *Crawley Old Town, New Town* (1983), John Goepel, information officer for the Corporation at the time, recalled:

> Rank came along and said to us, 'I'll build you a cinema'. We, knowing nothing about it, said 'Yes, you can build it at the end of the Boulevard' (where the Town Hall is now). We already had one cinema, where the Embassy still is, and we thought 'We'll have a nice balance, with one cinema at each end of the town'. He said, 'Look, you're nice people, but you don't know anything about cinemas. I'll build mine next to that one. We'll have them both together: people will come out to the cinema, see that mine is the better one, and come to mine'. So Rank signed a lease to build a cinema within three years, which we were very pleased about. After two and a half years, we went back to him and said 'It's getting near the time, what about it?' He said 'People don't build cinemas these days; they close them. Cinemas are closing down every day. But I'll tell you what: I'll build you a bowling alley'. And so he built a bowling alley. No-one in his right mind would have put a cinema into a New Town where there was already an existing cinema.

Undoubtedly, the Rank Organisation did have second thoughts because of the Embassy as the company opened Odeons in 1960 in the new towns of Harlow and Hemel Hempstead where they could operate without any competition. In fact, the bowling alley did not prove a great success for Rank either, although it survives as the AMF Crawley Bowl.

When, in 1990, the Hawth on Hawth Avenue was opened by Crawley Borough Council as a modern theatre and concert hall, film projection facilities were included. In the main theatre (seating 800) films are frequently shown, usually for one day only on the less busy days, combining specialised pictures with revivals of popular ones already shown at the MGM.

Regarding the new era of multiplexes, an attempt was made (and abandoned) to gain planning permission for a 10-screen cinema and superstore at Copthorne, which would have drawn audiences from both Crawley and East Grinstead (this is detailed in the section 'Other Part-time Cinemas and Plans for New Cinemas'). It is known that the Odeon chain have been looking at possible sites in the Crawley area, and it seems almost certain that one of the many circuits busily opening multiplexes will succeed in bringing this new style of cinema to the Crawley area.

EAST GRINSTEAD

1910
WHITEHALL
47 LONDON ROAD

This was a conversion by caterers Letheby and Christopher of the Grosvenor Hall, dating from 1883, to provide for alternative uses as a roller skating rink, as a cinema and as a theatre for local groups. It functioned in all these capacities at different times of the day or days of the week. The Annual Hunt Ball took place here each May.

The growing popularity of the cinema and the competition of the new Cinema de Luxe saw the end of daytime skating in 1913. The floor was raked to provide a better view of the screen, plush fixed seats were installed, and a projection box (with two projectors to enable the show to continue without inter-ruption for reel changes) was erected on columns against the back wall.

The films were accompanied initially by a resident pianist, later by an orchestra of four, and, during the First World War, audiences enjoyed a rich mix of programmes which always included the Pathé Gazette and combined films with variety. They were arranged by manager Frederick C. Maplesden, whose diary for 1915 suggests that business was good, boosted by the soldiers billeted in the area. Maplesden, who would continue as manager into the 1930s, shot his own local newsreels on 35mm during these early years, surviving examples of which are now held by the Huntley Archive and by the South East Film & Video Archive.

Photographs show the entrance dominated by a canopy stretching to the roadside to protect patrons arriving by car from the weather. Interior views show no circle but a row of boxes on the right-hand side of the auditorium. On the stage a backdrop portrayed

133 An early postcard view of the Whitehall, East Grinstead's first cinema.

119

134 *Above.* The Whitehall in 1921, offering a restaurant as well as a cinema, with its distinctive canopy.

135 *Below.* The frontage of the Whitehall in East Grinstead, as it appeared after enlargement and modernisation in 1936.

a beautiful formal garden while to either side of the proscenium were huge classical murals. The decor was complemented by ornate plasterwork and full-sized female statues and by decorative chandeliers suspended from the open ceiling where the exposed girders rather let down the impression of elegance. However, the roof could be opened up to admit fresh air and daylight for the cleaners. In 1915, there is reference to a capacity for 800 people.

The Whitehall was still put to live use from time to time. The local Operatic Society staged its productions there from 1922 until the Second World War started.

The cinema closed in 1936 for the front to be rebuilt in more modern style (architect: F. Edward Jones), no doubt to help it compete with the new Radio Centre (although Letheby and Christopher owned both, as well as the town's other cinema, the Solarius). The new entrance included stairways and vestibule in an art deco style, a large restaurant, ballroom and three shops, the frontage being named Whitehall Parade. The auditorium was left unaltered and the Whitehall re-opened on 16 November 1936. The seating capacity was now 570.

After war was declared, the cinema was frequented by servicemen based in the area, and *Gone with the Wind* played to virtually full houses throughout a three-week run despite increased admission charges.

Live entertainment was still put on. Even after the local repertory society and operatic society stopped, professional companies were still coming in 1940. But then the story of the Whitehall came to an abrupt conclusion with the county's most devastating war-time bombing incident and probably the worst single war-time disaster in a British cinema building.

Showing on the dull, misty Friday of 9 July 1943 was the comedy *I Married a Witch*, starring Veronica Lake and Fredric March, with a Hopalong Cassidy western as the supporting feature. The audience of 184 included many children, some evacuees from London, who had come straight from school. They had seen the news and were watching the western when a familiar notice announcing an air raid was displayed on the screen so that anybody who wished to leave could do so.

East Grinstead had become known as 'Little London' because of the severity of bombing. Generally, cinemas served as a safe haven from bomb blasts and audiences were reluctant to leave them. But they were not immune to a direct hit and the Whitehall may have been more vulnerable with its lack of a proper ceiling and balcony.

Shortly after 5 p.m. a single German Dornier 217 on its way back from a raid over London flew out of the clouds, jettisoned a string of bombs and indiscriminately strafed the ground with its machine-guns. Bullets ricocheted off the front of the cinema. Inside a bomb crashed through the roof of the auditorium and the building collapsed—in the words of one witness, 'like a pack of cards'.[130]

John Parsons was one of many children inside the cinema and 40 years later he recalled (in the *Evening Argus*, 8 July 1983):

> I was thirteen at the time. It was a dirty old day. I was with two or three mates and we had gone to the cinema straight from school. Suddenly the roof just seemed to open up. We scrambled out to the front of the building and there was another bang. Some soldiers from next door held us inside the building because the plane was still about.

The attack killed 108 and injured 235, many of them in the cinema. One third of the dead were children, one third were women, and most of the rest were soldiers from the 1st Canadian Army stationed in Sussex. The fact that the children were mostly in the cheap seats at the front helped to save many of them. In the 1983 newspaper feature, another survivor remembered: 'The back of the Whitehall was just a pile of rubble, although the front was intact. We desperately groped at the bricks to get people out—if you saw a pair of feet, you just pulled. There was a row of Canadian soldiers still in their seats with their eyes open, covered in dust and all dead.'

Although the frontage stood, further along London Road there was a huge gap where other buildings had been destroyed. More properties were hit in the High Street. Besides

136 Interior of the Whitehall with floor cleared for ballroom use.

137 The day after the county's worst wartime incident. On the left of the picture the frontage of the Whitehall remains, supporting ironically an air raid siren, but many were killed when a bomb fell on the cinema in July 1943.

the Whitehall, the bombs that day destroyed or badly damaged Sainsbury's, the *Warwick* public house, a watchmakers, an ironmongers and a furniture store. Only minutes later, anti-aircraft fire brought down the German bomber. It crashed into woods at Bletchingley, Surrey, killing its three crew members.

Post-war building restrictions in favour of housing prevented the cinema being rebuilt, although the licence was renewed at a cost of £1 per year until 10 February 1957 when it was allowed to expire. By this time the restrictions had been lifted but cinema attendances were on the decline and the site was put to other uses. The 1930s frontage survives in 1996—the name 'Whitehall' can still be seen cut into the stonework high up while the wartime disaster is recalled by a plaque erected by the East Grinstead Society on the 20th anniversary. The former cinema entrance is occupied by key cutters Mr. Snob.

c.1913
CINEMA DE LUXE/SOLARIUS
20 LONDON ROAD

The long, narrow Cinema de Luxe was an adaptation of a building which had begun life in 1875 as the Public Hall and most recently been the business premises of the hardware

and furniture company, C.M. Wilson. It was located on the other side of the street from the Whitehall and had a capacity of 425.

Photographs reveal a flight of five marble steps leading from the pavement to an open vestibule protected at night by folding security gates, with a central box office flanked by doors to the stalls and to a small balcony.

The ventilation in the narrow auditorium was so poor that one of its earlier managers, Mr. N. Holdsworth, distributed free paper fans to lady patrons during a summer heatwave. At this time evening performances were continuous from 6.30 p.m. to 10.30 p.m. with daily matinees at 3 p.m. Tickets were priced at 3d., 4d., 6d. and 1s. The early Chaplin comedies proved so popular that a life-size cut-out of the comedian was placed outside the box office with a placard proclaiming 'I'm here today'.

In the early 1920s the Cinema de Luxe was operated by Leo J. Flinn. In the middle of the decade it was owned and managed by V.G. Lovell. By the late 1920s, it had been taken over by A. Freedman through a London company, Freedman and Hauser.

Records dated 2 September 1931 note that the Cinema de Luxe was still licensed but had not been showing films for some time. Freedman may well have faltered at the cost

138 A postcard view of the Cinema de Luxe. 'The Small House With a Big Reputation' read the adverts.

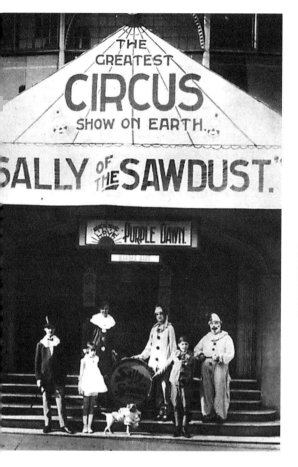

139 *Left.* Elaborate promotion by staff of the Cinema de Luxe of the W.C. Fields film *Sally of the Sawdust* in September 1925.

140 *Above.* Auditorium of the Solarius, East Grinstead.

of installing sound equipment for the new talkies. The cinema eventually re-opened with the inferior Mihaly sound system. In 1933, Freedman made way for Letheby and Christopher, owners of the Whitehall.

At this point, it was completely remodelled and called the Solarius, the name linked to sunburst decorative features over the proscenium arch and on the side walls. The sound was now provided by the leading Western Electric system (as at the Whitehall). Including a small circle, the Solarius seated 390.

Once Letheby and Christopher had opened the Radio Centre in 1936, the Solarius with its low seating capacity became a liability and it closed in 1938. Left unused, it suffered a serious fire early in 1940.

In a recently published book, Tony Hounsome noted that a banner poster advertising the last film screened at the Solarius—*History Is Made at Night*, starring Charles Boyer—could still be seen pasted to the derelict building a decade or more later.[131]

In 1996, the site is occupied by the *East Grinstead Courier* and F.W. Woolworth.

11 APRIL 1936
RADIO CENTRE/CLASSIC
KING STREET AND LITTLE KING STREET

In 1934, William Christopher of Letheby and Christopher started to develop King Street and work began in 1935 on a new 1,012 seat cinema with a streamlined winged frontage and entrance on the corner of King Street and Little King Street, the auditorium side wall running down the side of the latter. It was designed by F. Edward Jones who had been responsible for the new façade to the Whitehall and whose other work outside East Grinstead included the reconstruction of the Picture House (later Gaumont) Dalston, North London, a share in the new 1922 auditorium of the Theatre Royal Drury Lane, and the design of the Madame Tussaud's Cinema at Baker Street (bombed in 1940) and the Regal cinema at West Norwood, South London.

The name of the East Grinstead building and the curved double proscenium arch were suggested by the celebrated Radio City Music Hall in New York. There was a domed roof over the foyer in glass and ferro-concrete. The

141 The Radio Centre, with its magnificent frontage, in the 1930s alongside the even more streamlined Caffyns motor garage. The film being shown was *Dishonour Bright* with the comedian, Tom Walls.

142 Café area of the Radio Centre with well overlooking the main foyer.

circular entrance hall, with glass dome and well, reflected the then fashionable art deco style. Naturally, given the owning company's catering activities, a restaurant was included and the tables were on the first floor around the circular space, giving a view of the ground floor entrance hall. An organ was planned but never installed.

The opening of a modern cinema was a major event in the town's history. On Saturday 11 April 1936, a full house joined baritone

Thorpe Bates in a selection of popular songs before the Gaumont-British News and one or two shorts gave way to the main feature, the Jack Hulbert comedy *Jack of All Trades*.

G.W. Argent recalled (Cinema Theatre Association *Bulletin*, March/April 1989) that the Radio Centre 'boasted its own electricity supply by using two Ruston Hornsby horizontal gas engines with 5-ton flywheels so, even with power cuts, the lights would still shine and the projectors roll.'

In 1941, because of the large number of soldiers based in the area, a special licence was granted to open on Sundays between 3 p.m. and 9 p.m.

Letheby and Christopher sold the Radio Centre to Randolph E. Richards *c*.1948 and it became the sole inland property among the eight theatres on his otherwise coast-based circuit (Eastbourne, Hastings, Brighton, etc.). Letheby and Christopher continued with their catering business elsewhere, which is still operating today. The gas engines at the Radio Centre were replaced with mains' power in the 1950s and the old engine house became a store.

In 1953, the Radio Centre was one of many cinemas that presented the coronation of Queen Elizabeth II in black and white as it happened on large screen television.

When CinemaScope was installed in February 1955 at the Radio Centre, the curved inner proscenium arch had to be removed and the outer one cut away in order to fit the new wide screen. The aerial drama *The High and the Mighty*, starring John Wayne, was the first film shown in the new process.[132]

Along with the rest of the Richards circuit, the Radio Centre was acquired by the Classic chain in 1966 and the cinema renamed the Classic from 29 May of that year. Six years later, it was split up to provide three small Classic cinemas upstairs and a bingo hall on the ground floor. Classic 1 (with 477 seats, based on the former circle) and Classic 2 (94 seats in the old circle lounge/café area) opened on 31 August 1972 and Classic 3, seating 106 in the former stage tower, followed on 15 December 1972. Thus East Grinstead returned to the three choices of film programmes it had had for part of the 1930s.

The film centre was renamed Cannon along with other Classics around 1985/1986 after the circuit was acquired by the Cannon company. At this time, Cannon were paying £10,000 per annum rent on a lease extending 24 years 5 months from 21 January 1982 and subject to five-year reviews (this had been initiated as an arrangement between Classic and an associated property company). On 2 December 1987, Cannon signed an agreement to surrender the property for redevelopment on twelve-months' notice without compensation.

The bingo hall closed down but the cinemas continued for a while. Claiming that they had been running at a substantial loss, Cannon closed the three screens on 4 January 1989, a day earlier than originally announced to avoid a protest demonstration. Among the last films shown was *Who Framed Roger Rabbit?*. The words 'The End' appeared on the display panels provided for film titles below the canopy.

143 The auditorium of the Radio Centre showing the curved proscenium arch before the introduction of CinemaScope.

144 The Radio Centre, East Grinstead, as it looked in its final years as the Cannon. An estate agent's board invites enquiries for the site.

The freehold of the site was sold at auction on 8 March 1989 and the building was demolished in April 1990.

4 AUGUST 1995
ATRIUM CINEMAS
ATRIUM CENTRE
KING STREET

The Town Council was anxious to have cinemas in the town and late in 1989 passed revised plans for a new leisure complex on the site of the Radio Centre now that they included two cinemas. These were rather remotely placed on the top floor, accessible only by lifts or several flights of stairs. In due course, a glaringly modern, glass-fronted £11 million building called the Atrium, out of keeping with its surroundings, arose on the site.

A nightclub named The Base was the first part of the leisure development to open on 12 December 1991 and a bowling alley followed, but the space allocated to two 250-seat cinemas on the upper level remained unused despite reports that they would open in late 1991, then in January 1992, then (after a postponement to deal with soundproofing problems caused by the bowling alley underneath) on 1 July 1992, then (after a delay attributed to receiving specially ordered American seating) around the end of October 1992. By the latter date, an application had been made to convert the entire leisure centre, including the nightclub and bowling alley, to office use. The owners of the development went into administrative receivership in May 1993.

A company called Jollity Ltd. took over in March 1995. Another organisation, Melodybright, then negotiated to acquire the cinema space and in August, after a gap of six years, it was possible once again to have a proper night out at the cinema in East Grinstead. Opening night films at the Atrium Cinemas were *Batman Forever* and *Free Willy 2* while celebrities in attendance included David Jacobs and Debbie Grant but no film stars. Each cinema seats 240 with Dolby stereo and tickets can be purchased in advance on the ground floor of the Atrium.[133]

HASSOCKS

28 November 1938
Studio/Orion
Keymer Road

The Studio was opened by the Fletcher-Barnett Syndicate, whose partners were Walter Fletcher and Charles Barnett. The cinema was identical to their Studio cinema opposite the gates of Elstree Studios in Hertfordshire, which had opened in March 1936, and so this carried the same name. The architect of both was E.B. Parkinson of Huntingdon. The partnership was also behind the Studio at Bletchley, Buckinghamshire.

In 1938 when the cinema was planned, Hassocks, with its Fergusson Estates development, was considered to be a growth town of the future. The site for the new cinema was the gardens of Dale House, which stood in ruins just beyond the end of a line of village shops. Approval of the building application was not without incident as objections were raised that the site had been scheduled for residential purposes, while the Lord's Day Observance Society made representations against proposed Sunday performances. However, on 26 July 1938, plans were passed by the Town Planning Committee.[134]

145 The cinema at Hassocks—originally the Studio, renamed the Orion in 1947.

Construction of the cinema was completed in only 15 weeks, under the supervision of A.P. Belton, of T.J. Braybon and Son, the Brighton builders. This was a fine achievement considering the inclement weather experienced and the need to fill in a small lake and divert a stream running through the centre of the site.

The Studio had a neon-lit frontage of multi-coloured Keymer facing bricks, manufactured two miles or so away in Burgess Hill, and picked out with red dressings. The roof was covered with russet-coloured Trafford tiling to blend with the brickwork, in contrast to the more common grey roof sheeting. The general construction of the building was in cavity brickwork built around a steel frame structure which carried the roof trusses. Tall upright Crittall windows, made to the design of the architect, had an ornamental feature above them carried out in Roman tiles. Entrance steps were finished with biscuit-coloured terrazzo, inlaid with non-slip old-gold carborundum.

Tall glass doors led to a spacious vestibule in green and gold, with lounge and cloak-rooms adjoining. An inner vestibule led to the auditorium, which had a general colour scheme of green and pink. The walls were lined with acoustic boarding worked in panels with V joints. The main ceiling was similarly treated. The auditorium had concealed cornice lighting throughout, with additional lighting niches in the walls. The stage had only footlights, wired in three circuits. There were no battens.

The Studio had two pairs of electrically operated tabs. The screen pair were side opening, rigid-edged festoons, and the main tabs were red velour with satin bands at the base. When the curtains were closed, further satin decorations on the leading edges met to make a tower design. The proscenium surround was carried out in heavily moulded fibrous plaster, and on either side were dummy grilles with concealed lighting.

The stalls seated 651, while the straight balcony held 160, a total of 811. The seating, with Dunlopillo armpads throughout, was in old gold and on the extreme sides of the auditorium there was a line of twin seats. The girls on the staff wore uniforms in rose pink, trimmed light green and gold, and the page wore maroon, also trimmed in light green and gold.

The inaugural film was *The Prisoner of Zenda*, which had opened the prestigious Odeon Leicester Square in London just over a year earlier. Here in Hassocks it was supported by a Disney cartoon, *The Clock Cleaners*, *The March of Time*, and the Gaumont-British News.

The cinema opened daily at 2 p.m. and ran continuously until 10.30 p.m. The original manager, Major Kenneth Johnston, remained at the cinema until the mid-1950s.

The war years were a boom time for cinemas in general and for the Studio Hassocks in particular. Prior to the D-Day landings in 1944, Brighton was one of several South Coast towns to be a prohibited area and Hassocks was the limit of travel southwards for people without a special permit. For some reason, the Studio Hassocks was allowed to show films much earlier than before, concurrent with South London.

146 & 147 The foyer of the Studio as it looked at its opening in 1938.

148 The auditorium of the Studio, Hassocks, in 1938.

149 The auditorium, looking towards the balcony, 1938.

Then the Studio obtained a concurrency booking arrangement with the Perrymount Haywards Heath by which both cinemas were offered the same films on the same dates. The Perrymount was part of the huge ABC chain and it is quite surprising that a small independent circuit should have gained such a favourable arrangement. Although the two cinemas almost always did play the same programme, they

150 The projection room at the Studio, Hassocks, 1938.

received their films very late in the day, three or four months after they first started their general release and even longer after their first showing in the West End. The hit film *The Seventh Veil* played the Lewes Odeon at the end of January 1946 but didn't open in Hassocks until May. The Studio advertised itself as 'the West End Theatre in the Country' but it was certainly not West End in terms of film dates. It was also apt to become flooded in the front stalls area. After a heavy rainstorm, there were two pictures—one on the screen, the other reflected in the water on the floor.

The Fletcher-Barnett Syndicate sold their other cinemas to bigger chains but Hassocks had not grown as expected and this property was not highly sought after. Shortly after the War, the cinema was licensed to Thomas E. Merrals, of T.E.M. Cinemas, based at the Plaza Sittingbourne. In June 1947 it was acquired by E.F. Lyons who earlier bought the Plaza Hastings, Roxy St Leonards, Town Hall Cinema at Midhurst and the Scala Burgess Hill,

creating the Cranfield Cinemas circuit. Shortly after he added the Studio Hassocks, it was announced that matinees would henceforth be held there only on Wednesdays, Saturdays, Sundays and Bank Holidays, while the name was changed to Orion from 9 July onwards. The same name was given to most of the other Cranfield cinemas, including the one at Burgess Hill.

In the 1950s, the Hassocks Orion leaped onto the CinemaScope bandwagon long before the Perrymount and other mid-Sussex cinemas. It advertised the mid-Sussex première of the first CinemaScope film, 20th Century-Fox's *The Robe*, which played from 29 November 1954 for six days, three times daily (but was not shown by the Perrymount). When the Orion opened *The Command*, it advertised itself as 'The only cinema with CinemaScope between London and Brighton' (the same film was shown in a non-'scope version at the Perrymount). The Orion played further Fox CinemaScope films ignored by the Perrymount.

In 1963, the cinema was redecorated for its 25th anniversary but the following year owner E. F. Lyons died and his widow placed the Orion Hassocks on the market. It was being operated by Walter Gay Promotions of Worthing, Gay having been earlier connected with Lyons as manager of the Orion Midhurst when that closed in 1962. A series of Continental films had been booked, including some art house attractions like *Jules and Jim*, and the final programme to play the Orion, on Wednesday 30 September 1964, was a one-day booking of an Italian sex comedy, *Every Night of the Week*, with *Here We Go Again*. The preceding three-day attraction had been a Hollywood comedy *Wives and Lovers* supported by *Striptease Murder*. The previous Thursday, Friday and Saturday it had played the Cliff Richard musical *Wonderful Life* concurrent with the Perrymount.

The asking price for the cinema was £20,000 (apparently the balance of the mortgage due on the property). An offer of £12,000 from independent cinema operator Myles Byrne was refused. The property was sold to a developer and it was demolished in 1968/69, to be replaced by a parade of shops that recalls the cinema, as it is named Orion Parade.

(*This section is based on original research by John Fernee.*)[135]

HAYWARDS HEATH

26 December 1911
Heath Theatre
The Broadway

Haywards Heath's first cinema opened on the Boxing Day Tuesday of 1911 with three separate performances at 3 p.m., 6.45 p.m. and 8.30 p.m.

Plans show this to have been an adaptation of a motor garage owned by Charles W. Wood. The architect for the structural alterations was Alfred Carden of Brighton and his plans, for Graham Cooper of 34 Ship Street, Brighton, were approved by Haywards Heath Urban District Council on 20 November 1911. The work was carried out by Horace Finch, a builder of Perrymount Road, Haywards Heath.[136]

The opening 90-minute programme consisted entirely of short films (full-length features had yet to arrive). Titles included *Lost in the Jungle*, *Views of Finland*, *Preparations for the Durbar*, *The Haywards Heath Fat Stock Show* and *Jane on Strike*, combining the appeal of films shot on exotic locations with a local

THE HEATH THEATRE,
LIMITED,
THE BROADWAY, HAYWARDS HEATH.

THIS THEATRE WILL BE OPENED
to the Public
ON BOXING DAY,
TUESDAY, DECEMBER 26th,
When Performances will be given at 3 p.m., 6.45 p.m.
and 8.30 p.m.
During the remainder of the Week, Performances
will be given each Evening at 6.45 p.m. and 8.30 p.m.,
with MATINEES on WEDNESDAY & SATURDAY,
at 3 p.m.
A First-class Programme of Up-to-date
Pictures will be shewn, and there will be an entire
change of Programme on the Thursday
Evening.
During the whole week Special Engagement of
MEEY AND HUGH,
The Well-known Comedians and Patterers.

Prices of Admission : 1s., 6d., and 3d.

interest item probably filmed by the cinema itself to attract audiences. There was also live variety as part of the show, the first attraction being Meey and Hugh, 'Well-known Comedians and Patterers'.

151 *Mid-Sussex Times* notice of the opening of the Heath Theatre on Boxing Day, 1911.

152 'A first-rate place to shake off dull care.' The Heath Theatre—left of telegraph pole—with the word 'cinema' filling the three windows above the entrance.

youngest handcuff king and jail breaker'; this disciple of the great Houdini brought out the House Full notices. 'A first-rate place in which to shake off dull care' was the verdict of the reporter in the *Mid-Sussex Times*.[137]

Official film of the Delhi Durbar which, only days before, had been shown to the King and Queen in Calcutta, proved so popular in Haywards Heath that extra matinees had to be put on in January 1912. The management announced that cycles would be stored free of charge but the Durbar film attracted 'prominent residents' in their motor cars.[138]

On Monday 22 January 1912 the cup tie between Brighton and Hove Albion and Darlington was screened for the benefit of local football supporters. By now 'star' films, over 1,000ft. long, were being shown, the audience bursting into patriotic applause at key moments of *The Battle of Trafalgar*.[139]

By the end of April 1912, the national Pathé newsreel was being shown with footage of the sinking of the *Titanic* earlier that month. Specially shot local news attractions included coverage of a flower show in Victoria Park which was seen in July 1913. Local news items of this kind were a widespread feature of early cinema programming.

Reports in the *Mid-Sussex Times* for 1915 suggest that comedies were then the major draw, although the local correspondent was not himself so easily impressed, finding in the Keystone Kops comedy *The Great Toe Mystery*, shown in June, that 'there was, as usual, the Keystone hop and rush and pistol firing which many people consider so funny'.[140] Charlie Chaplin, however, merited less grudging praise and in December the reviewer noted that his appearances in *Charlie by the Sea* were greeted with loud cheers by the youthful element in the audience.[141]

The cinema was operated initially by a local company, Heath Theatres Ltd., but by 1915 it came to be associated with a small circuit called Southern Entertainments that was based in Brighton and also operated the Crowborough Picture House and Havant Empire. This was headed by J. Van Koert, who ran the Heath for the rest of its life.

Around 1916, a special bus was advertised which left the Heath at 8.30 p.m. on Wednesdays and Saturdays for Cuckfield to enable its inhabitants to reach home after the first evening show.

153 The telegraph pole again partly obscures this early view of Haywards Heath's first cinema.

The manager was F.J. Pitt. Prices of admission were 3d. and 6d. for the stalls, and 9d. (unreserved) or 1s. (reserved) for the balcony, with reductions for children and servicemen. As some patrons were prepared to pay one shilling, four times as much as those in the cheapest seats, it is clear that here, as elsewhere, the cinema drew audiences of all classes and means. Programmes were changed twice a week and 3 p.m. matinees were confined to Wednesdays and Saturdays only.

The local correspondent of the *Mid-Sussex Times* (26 December 1911) waxed positive about the new cinema's appeal:

Hitherto people in the country have had to go into Brighton for their pleasure, and it is an open secret that the Picture Theatres in that town have for some time past been simply 'coining money' ... With the prospect of increased railway fares at an early date the public in and around Haywards Heath no doubt will be glad to drop into the Heath Theatre when they want a change.

The mixed programmes of filmed dramas, comedies and travelogues were interspersed with touring variety acts. An early visitor was the escapologist Harry Herd'uni, 'the world's

The Heath's only competition in early years came from shows at the Public Hall and these seem to have stopped by the 1920s. By 1932, the Heath was too small (with an apparent seating capacity of 400) to meet the demand for film entertainment (and it may well have proved unsuitable for sound films), so J. Van Koert opened a new, larger cinema that year, the Broadway. He reduced prices at the Heath, which showed single features plus 'full supporting programme' and changed programmes midweek. Both cinemas were licensed to open on Sundays and did very well as the only ones, apart from those in Hove, permitted to show films on that day over a wide area.

Dennis Williams recalls the Heath:

The projection room was at ground level. The rewind room was on the other side of the foyer and, when a part was shown, there was a change-over and someone took the spool out of the bottom spool box, stuck it under his coat, and walked across the foyer to the rewind room, changed the spool, and brought the other one back. Officially, there was a little wooden case in which the spool should be put but—human nature being what it was—nobody bothered with it, so very often if you went to the Heath you'd see the operator crossing the foyer with a spool of inflammable film.[142]

Such was the increasing popularity of films that in 1936 J. Van Koert opened the Perrymount cinema in the same street as the Heath and Broadway. The Perrymount was a larger, more modern replacement for the Heath

which closed on 30 May 1936, the day the new cinema opened. The last three-day programme consisted of *Whipsaw* plus *The Hell Cat*.

The cinema has long been replaced by a more modern building. For many years gas company showrooms were based here. In 1996 the former entrance area is occupied by two businesses: a recruitment agency, Kelly Services, and a convenience store, Down at '59'.

12 September 1932
Broadway
The Broadway, Perrymount Road

Operated by Mid-Sussex Cinemas, a company formed by J. Van Koert with F.S. Youles as a fellow director, the Broadway was built on land that sloped downwards on the west side of Perrymount Road. Such a slope could be an advantage in creating the rake for the stalls floor of a cinema but here the ground fell away so much that it was necessary to descend a flight of stairs (with gardens to each side) to reach the entrance. Although the railway line passed close behind the cinema, there was sufficient room for a car park at the rear.

The joint architects were Peter D. Stonham and S.C. Addison of Eastbourne, whose plans were drawn up in November–December 1931. Stonham was the architect and businessman behind the earlier Picturedromes at Bognor Regis, Chichester, Eastbourne and Worthing.[143]

154 In the foreground the curved frontage of the Broadway cinema, whilst in the distance, behind the inevitable pole, the white gable-ended façade of the Heath Theatre.

with a staircase each side leading to the balcony which seated (according to the plans) 231. The stalls floor accommodated 494, providing a total of 725 seats in all (although 850 was claimed at opening). The seats were upholstered in green while the carpet had a gold and brown pattern. The woodwork was again in teak. The lighting system allowed 27 different blends of colour to play on the proscenium arch.

Rather unusually, this cinema had back projection, which required substantial space behind the screen. Here, the box was situated at the back of a stage 24ft. deep that could be used for vaudeville acts after the screen was moved out of the way. The proscenium width was 20ft. 9ins. On behalf of back projection, the owners pointed out that it offered a clearer image as the beam did not have to pass through cigarette smoke in the auditorium and it was safer because the box with its inflammable film was outside the auditorium. Projectors were adapted to show the film the other way round. For the projectionists it must have been a particularly lonely existence, so distant from the rest of the staff and unable to see anything of the audience.

The Broadway was formally opened on a Monday by Sir William Campion. The show began with a selection from the Haywards Heath Town Band. The main feature was *Goodnight Vienna*, a very popular British musical starring Jack Buchanan, supported by a Laurel and Hardy short *Come Clean*, a travel film *Father Nile*, a Krazy Kat cartoon *Svengarlic*, and British Movietone News. Prices of admission were set at 9d. for the stalls, and 1s. 6d. and 2s. 4d. for the balcony.

When the Perrymount opened, the Broadway was relegated to second place. In late July 1937, both halls were taken over by the large Union Cinemas chain which collapsed only a few weeks later from reckless over-expansion and was rescued by another big circuit, Associated British Cinemas. First 'managed by ABC' (with the circuit's trademark triangle sign displayed on the frontage), then fully acquired along with the rest of the circuit in 1942, the Broadway seems to have shared the flow of new releases fairly equally with the Perrymount as there was little to choose in seating capacity between them and three major national releases were available each week (the ABC, Odeon and Gaumont programmes).

155 *Top.* The Broadway after its acquisition by the Union Cinemas chain in 1937.

156 *Above.* Foyer, the Broadway, Haywards Heath, 1937.

The Broadway had a semi-circular façade finished in rough Snowcrete and floodlit at night, with sets of windows on the first floor displaying a vivid sunburst design. There were solid teak entrance doors with three panes of bevelled glass. The name appeared in chromium-plated letters across the top of the façade. A central paybox and a cigarette and chocolate kiosk were located in the vestibule

However, in 1947, the supply of Hollywood films dried up after the American distributors refused to pay a new import tax demanded by the Board of Trade. Cinemas were forced to show many reissues and audiences declined. The Haywards Heath cinemas were particularly badly affected as the population had come down sharply from the war years when the area had received many evacuees and when travel to Brighton and its entertainments had been restricted.

The film industry warned the government that the continued existence of many cinemas was under threat and, to drive home the point, the Haywards Heath Broadway was closed on Saturday 31 January 1948, after a three-day revival of the Tyrone Power swashbuckler *The Black Swan*, for 'an indefinite period' because of the shortage of films. As there was normally a change of programme mid-week, ABC claimed it had become impossible to find four main features and supporting films each week. This was the only cinema closed by any of the national circuits because of the tax crisis and, while it may very well have been running at a serious loss, its shutdown was at least in part a campaign move.

Following government concessions, new Hollywood films returned and on Monday 25 October 1948 the Broadway re-opened with a three-day run of *The Naked City* plus *Son of Rusty* and British Movietone News. It offered matinees daily but was closed on Sundays. At this time its seating capacity was given as 701.

Then on Saturday 26 January 1952 the Broadway closed again 'until further notice' following a three-day run (concurrent with the Orion Hassocks) of a John Wayne war film *Flying Leathernecks* supported by *Hard, Fast and Beautiful* plus Pathé News. This time the reason given for closure was 'additional fire precautions required by East Sussex Fire Brigade' (Haywards Heath was then part of East Sussex). The Fire Brigade's demands are not specified, so it is difficult to judge whether they played a major part in closing the cinema or whether they were a useful pretext for shedding an unprofitable business. The likely answer is that ABC decided it wasn't worthwhile investing further money in the Broadway to conform to the safety requirements. In any case, the cinema didn't re-open. It was certainly very unusual for an ABC cinema to close down

at this time when the film business generally was in a very healthy state.

The premises were disused until, around 1960, they were acquired by J.W. Upton and Sons and used as a furniture showroom for many years. The building was eventually closed, then demolished in 1987 and replaced by an office block, Rockwood House, occupied in 1996 by the Brown Shipley/Holmwoods Group.

157 *Below.* The Broadway, Haywards Heath. Auditorium from rear stalls.

158 *Bottom.* The Broadway. Auditorium to rear from front stalls, 1937.

30 MAY 1936
PERRYMOUNT
PERRYMOUNT ROAD

Trading as Mid-Sussex Cinemas, J. Van Koert and F.S. Youles built and opened the Perrymount as a larger replacement for the Heath. The plans, announced to the local press at the beginning of December 1933 and approved on 25 June 1934, were the work of architect F.T. Hackman. The builder was John H. Hackman Ltd., the company which had earlier built the Broadway.

The Perrymount name was derived from the street on which it was located, but this did not stop one local paper referring to it in a listings column as the Paramount when it first opened, as if it were the latest addition to the chain of luxury cinemas bearing that name.

The Perrymount development, near the railway station end of the road, included a café-restaurant, dance hall and three lock-up shops. The cinema seated 800 in a stadium arrangement whereby the rear section was stepped. The proscenium arch was curved, like that of the East Grinstead Radio Centre opened a month earlier. There was concealed lighting on the splay walls. Amber floodlights in the ceiling could be used to produce the effect of a rising sun. A full-size stage was claimed with scenery loft and dressing rooms. The curtains were in rich orange while the seats were brick red. In fact, the auditorium was overall very plain, cheap-looking and lacking in atmosphere. Externally, the cinema was unusual in that it had no neon lighting.[144]

The Perrymount opened on a Saturday evening with a British double-bill: *Come Out of the Pantry*, a musical comedy starring Jack Buchanan, and *A Cuckoo in the Nest*, one of the Aldwych farces starring Tom Walls and Ralph Lynn. This programme continued until Wednesday. Prices of admission were 9d., 1s., 1s. 3d., 1s. 6d., and 2s. The Perrymount opened daily at 2.45 p.m. (Sundays from 7.30 p.m.) whereas the Broadway, under the same management, opened at 5.30 p.m. with afternoon shows only on Wednesdays and Saturdays.

The Perrymount café, open from 11 a.m. to 10 p.m. daily (except Sundays), occupied part of the space above the foyer and could seat seventy. The dance hall was also over part of the foyer, extending above adjoining shops. There was a gala dance featuring the Jack Ellis Band on the same night as the cinema opened. Tea dances were later held on Fridays from 3.30 p.m. to 6.30 p.m.

The Perrymount and Broadway were taken over by the Union Cinemas circuit in July 1937. The owners had little choice. Union had just declared its intention to build one of its opulent Ritzes, complete with Compton organ, placing a hoarding announcing this fact on a site at the top end of Broadway near the premises of auctioneers A.L. Mulclure. As long as it gained entry into Haywards Heath, the company didn't care whether it built its own

159 *Below.* The Perrymount, Haywards Heath, after the takeover by the Union Cinemas chain in 1937.

160 *Bottom.* Foyer of the Perrymount in 1937.

cinema and forced the others out of business or whether it took over the existing cinemas instead. However, Union collapsed from over-spending almost immediately and, as described in the history of the Broadway, the circuit came under the management and later full control of the efficiently-run Associated British Cinemas circuit.

The cinema shared in the post-war boom in cinema-going when there were few alternative leisure attractions. Huge queues are recalled in 1947 for *Night and Day*, the Cole Porter biopic starring Cary Grant.

On 1 October 1949, the Perrymount started an ABC Minors Club on Saturday morning for children between the ages of five and fifteen, presided over by 'Uncle Jack' (manager J.B. Hudson). A sing-along to words displayed on the screen preceded the film show of cartoons, short, serial and feature. Minors were encouraged to demonstrate any performing talent on stage.

Other events of this period included a reception for war hero Lieutenant Hett of H.M.S. *Amethyst* on Sunday 12 November 1949. On Christmas Eve, a carol concert and community singing took place on stage, featuring the town band. Talent competitions were also staged on Friday nights with prizes. For the 15th birthday week, the best of these amateurs appeared on stage on Tuesday, Wednesday and Friday evenings while on Thursday evening a Miss Perrymount 1950 beauty competition was held.

In 1955, the proscenium arch lost its curve when it was widened to take a CinemaScope screen. The concealed lighting on the splay walls was dropped. The first film to be shown in the process was the Alan Ladd western *Drum Beat*, starting on 9 May.

The dance hall gained a reputation for bad behaviour (on one occasion, somebody's ear was cut off) and it closed. The café also went, affected by the decline in cinema attendances, especially the drop in older patrons.

Important ABC cinemas were actually called ABC in the 1960s (like the Ritz Horsham) but the Perrymount evidently didn't qualify as it was never renamed. Programmes were now usually shown for a full week and its seating totalled 658. While it was still open, the cinema was sold to a Brighton property development company which proposed to

build offices and raised the possibility of including two small cinemas seating 150-250 in the redevelopment.

The Perrymount closed on Saturday 11 November 1972 after a seven-day run of the Clint Eastwood western *Joe Kidd*, supported by *Subterfuge*. A local action group headed by Mrs. Betty Moon organised a petition, which over 1,000 people signed, aimed at keeping the cinema open.

It stood derelict for many years before being demolished in December 1984. In 1996, its site is the pedestrian entrance and part of the car park of an office block set further back, Sussex House.

161 & **162** The auditorium of the Perrymount, Haywards Heath, 1937.

137

Back Row (left to right): Mrs. E. BRAYSHER, Mrs. L. HARTLEY and Mrs. F. KNAPP (Cleaners).
Centre Row: Mr. T. AYLWIN (3rd Operator), Miss M. NYE and Miss M. WRIGHT (Usherettes), Mrs. LAKER (Waitress), Mrs. R. BARNETT (Usherette), Mrs. B. MORGAN (2nd Cashier) and Mr. D. SMITH (Junior Operator).
Front Row: Mr. D. SMALL (Doorman), Mr. R. HOGG (2nd Operator), Mrs. PIERCE (Cook), Mr. J. B. HUDSON (Manager), Mrs. J. PALMER (Cashier), Mr. F. BOTTING (Chief Operator) and Mr. R. CLEMENTS (Doorman).

2 JULY 1993
THE PLATFORM CINEMA
BURRELL ROAD

The Platform Theatre opened on 17 September 1992 in a spacious warehouse formerly used by a dairy on an industrial estate close to Sainsbury's and the railway station. It offered a variety of live events from classic plays to modern farces, pantomimes and jazz shows. 180 seats were obtained from Glyndebourne Opera House and installed on raised tiers, giving excellent sightlines.

In 1993, a grant of just under £5,000 enabled the Platform to become a part-time cinema as well. The money was used to buy a new screen with adjustable masking for the different screen shapes, plus two old Gaumont Kalee projectors from the closed Tivoli cinema in Eastbourne: one for actually showing the prints, the other to provide spare parts. The Platform Cinema was opened on a Friday at 8 p.m. by actress Greta Scacchi who appeared in the film being shown, Robert Altman's *The Player*, and who came from Haywards Heath. She brought her baby daughter and brother and in her speech recalled the importance of her childhood visits to the Perrymount. Music, free wine and a buffet were also featured on the opening night.

After that, films ranged from mainstream attractions to specialist films, foreign and classics, some shown in a regular Tuesday night season.

Although the Platform was primarily a theatre, it was so well outfitted as a cinema that it provided a proper film-going experience and deserves listing as one of West Sussex's cinemas. Sadly, however, after a cinema presentation of *Richard III* and a theatre revival of *Look Back in Anger*, the Platform closed on 6 July 1996, a victim of declining audiences and lack of funding.

163 Staff of the Perrymount pose for the 15th anniversary brochure, May 1950.

164 The Perrymount, Haywards Heath, decorated for the coronation of Queen Elizabeth II in 1953.

Addenda: Haywards Heath

Before the Heath cinema opened in 1911, the Public Hall was advertised as suitable for cinema showmen to hire at the rate of one pound and five shillings a night. Some films were apparently shown here even after the Heath cinema opened.

Following the closure of the Perrymount, films were presented on some nights of the week at the multi-purpose, flat-floored Clair Hall, close to where the Perrymount had been in Perrymount Road. Even since the opening of the Platform, screen entertainment has continued to be featured at Clair Hall, which can seat 350.

HORSHAM

c.1908
GEM PICTURE THEATRE
ALBION ROAD AND SPRINGFIELD ROAD

This very early and short-lived cinema (almost certainly a conversion of an existing building) was at the corner of Albion Road and Springfield Road, next to the Roman Catholic chapel, which was exactly opposite St John's Church.

Arthur Northcott's *Popular Entertainment in Horsham 1880-1930* collected several vivid reminiscences of attending this primitive hall with its macadam floor, whitewashed brick interior walls, and about eight rows of wooden forms seating in total under 100 people.[145]

Patrons entered straight from the street rather than through a foyer. They chewed peanuts and the shells covered the floor, making a noise underfoot when the audience left. A scented spray was used to improve the atmosphere several times during each performance. The film was projected from behind the screen, which was held in a wooden frame. It was necessary to spray the cloth screen before each show and perhaps during it, apparently to keep it cool and to help the image be seen clearly through the material. There were children's shows on Saturday afternoon for 2d. which included an orange or a sweet at the end.

The Gem was owned by Harold Bingham. A.J. Preedy was the manager in 1910. It was obviously ill-suited for the impending era of feature-length films, and it is thought to have closed in May 1912, superseded by the Central Picture Hall and the Electric.

Later it became Rice's motor showroom, but the area in which it stood has now been redeveloped with the United Reformed Church occupying its place.

13 OCTOBER 1910
CENTRAL PICTURE HALL/WINTER GARDEN
NORTH STREET (CORNER OF LINDEN ROAD)

The Central Picture Hall was the brainchild of E. Anderson and K. James Jarvis, two men from Tonbridge in Kent. The financial backing came from Anderson and C. Green, and it was in Anderson's name that the plans for a hall and cinema were submitted in June 1910. Jarvis was a builder who became the manager of the cinema until 1920 when his wife took over.

The building had a steel framework clad in corrugated iron, and the walls were partly covered in green fire-proof asbestos. The screen on the wall at the street end of the cinema was made of solid asbestos, and the picture size was 12ft. tall by 9ft. wide. As a safety measure to impress the public, there were no less than three exits. Electric fans were placed at each end of the auditorium.

165 The Central Picture Hall, Horsham, the county's first purpose-built cinema, shown in a still from the Cricket Week film of July 1913. The manager, K. James Jarvis, stands by the door.

DIRECTOR

The cinema seated 250 on wooden benches and on a wet Thursday night, 13 October 1910, an invited audience saw a combination of films and variety acts that the *County Times* described as 'a pleasingly varied programme, with fine cinematograph pictures predominating'. The general public was admitted the following day, and there were three evening performances (except Sundays) at 6 p.m., 7.30 p.m. and 9 p.m., with admission at 3d., 4d. or 6d. Shows originally lasted an hour.

By January 1911, the cinema had gone over to continuous shows from 6 p.m. to 10 p.m. daily except Sundays, with matinees on Wednesdays (3 p.m.) and Saturdays (2.30 p.m.). Plans were submitted in March and September 1911 for alterations that increased the seating capacity by 70 and sloped the floor to provide a clearer view of the screen.

Feature-length films had arrived by 1914 when pictures were changed on Mondays and Thursdays but were accompanied all week by a live act, such as Barney O'Reilly, 'A Rael Oirish Comedian', in April 1914.

The war made its presence felt in two ways. The War Tax increased prices to 4d., 5d., 7d. and 11d. in 1916, and programmes now included such films as *The Battle of the Somme*, released by the War Office only weeks after the opening of the campaign in July 1916.

Posters proclaimed the Central Hall as 'The Noted House for Best Pictures in Horsham'[146] but competition from the improved Electric was such that in March 1918 Anderson submitted plans for the reconstruction of the cinema. Jarvis was again responsible for the design and building, the hall closing on 9 August 1919 and re-opening on 23 October that year with 600 seats and a small balcony. The Plans Register in March 1918 refers to the cinema as the Winter Garden although it was still being called the Central Hall in directories in 1930.[147]

The advent of the superior Capitol in 1923 caused problems for both the Central and the Carfax (the former Electric). Both soon fell under the ownership of the Blue Flash Cinema Company which had opened the Capitol.

Sound equipment was installed in the Central in September 1930, nearly a year after the Capitol had first shown talkies. It was around this time that the cinema seems to have become generally known as the Winter Garden. The large Union Cinemas circuit took it over on 14 October 1935, together with the other two Blue Flash cinemas in Horsham.

166 *Right*. Films and variety combined. A wartime poster from February 1915.

167 *Far right*. Another wartime poster, from June 1916.

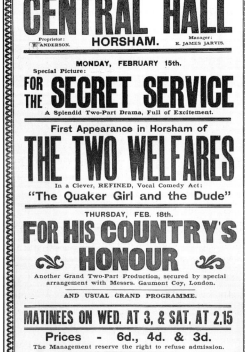

168 Central Picture Hall, Horsham, May 1930, showing the crime story, *The Return of the Rat*.

When Union opened the new Ritz in June 1936, it announced a 'sensational cut' in admission prices here and at the Carfax, with evenings and Saturday matinees priced at 3d., 6d. and 9d., and weekday matinees at 2d. and 3d. The two cinemas were relegated in group advertising to a very inferior position compared with the Ritz and Capitol.

The Winter Garden, Carfax and Capitol all ran into difficulties obtaining a renewal of licence for 1937. The Winter Garden seems to have been closed from 3 January, re-opening on the last day of the month after its licence was renewed on condition that (as at the Capitol) 'the secondary lighting and the matters in connection with the sanitary arrangements are dealt with within three months'.

Both cinemas lacked a system of secondary lighting (to come on if the main lights failed) and nothing had been done to remedy this three months later. On Friday 30 April, the magistrates decided that unless secondary lighting was installed by the following Friday morning, 7 May, the licences of both cinemas would be suspended. A Union Cinemas representative promised that every effort would be made to comply but, while the Capitol was put in order, it was clearly decided that the Winter Garden was not worth the expense and it closed forever on Thursday 6 May 1937. The empty shell of the building remained standing until the late 1960s.[148]

c.OCTOBER 1911
CARFAX ELECTRIC THEATRE/CARFAX
29 CARFAX (AT REAR)

This cinema was originally entered through the alley at the side of the *Stout House* public house and had a small sign suspended over the pavement drawing attention to its obscure location. The plans for the 40ft. long hall and operating box were submitted in June 1911 by the brewers King and Barnes but the cinema was established by two brothers, Philip Charles Bingham and Harry F. Bingham, who were respectively manager and projectionist.[149]

The precise date of opening is not known but Arthur Northcott reproduces in his book an advertisement for a programme showing 26-28 October 1911. In common with its rival, the Central, it began with separate evening performances but soon changed to continuous shows from 6 p.m. to 10 p.m., and it charged the same prices of 3d., 4d. and 6d.[150]

Between 1914 and 1921 plans were submitted on eight occasions by the Bingham brothers for additions and alterations, including in April-September 1914 the addition of a gallery.[151] This raised the capacity to 400.

In 1917, the Binghams acquired Walter Oldershaw's outfitter's shop at 28 Carfax, next to the pub and directly in front of the auditorium, and converted it into an entrance to the cinema. Other improvements were

169 Entrance to the Horsham Electric Theatre at the rear of 29 Carfax, c.1916.

made, the name modified to the Carfax Theatre, and Hilaire Belloc was invited to the re-opening.

The rivalry with the Central was intense. The balcony was enlarged in 1919, prompting the Central to undertake reconstruction to make itself more attractive to the town's picturegoers. But from 1923 both cinemas were outclassed by the new Capitol built by the Blue Flash Cinema Company.

In 1927 the Binghams sold the Carfax to Blue Flash which also took over the Central to own all three of the town's cinemas. It was decided that the Carfax would become the down-market hall with one low price of 6d. for all seats, showing lowbrow comedy, westerns and thrillers. At the Capitol and Central Hall, more sophisticated attractions would be presented and only the front stalls would be available for 6d.

In 1929, the Carfax closed for a week before becoming a live theatre, presenting a season of plays by Frank Buckley's Repertory Company. It was fitted out with an enlarged stage and special lighting, and adjustments were made to the seating. It lasted as a live theatre for less than a year, during which time films were still presented on Sundays. In March 1930, the Carfax became the second Horsham cinema equipped for talkies.

On 14 October 1935, this became part of the Union Cinemas circuit after its take-over of Blue Flash. By the end of 1936, Horsham had its new Ritz and Odeon, the Capitol was still an important cinema, and the Carfax and the Winter Garden were very much also rans, competing with late bookings of pictures at lower prices. When difficulties were encountered in renewing the Carfax's licence, Union simply closed the cinema on 22 January 1937.[152]

The *Stout House* pub still survives in 1996. New shops stand to the other side of the alley which once led to the Carfax auditorium but now leads to the back of the Princes Place shopping centre.

7 November 1923
Capitol
London Road

The Capitol Theatre was designed by C.J. Kay of local architects Godman and Kay for the Blue Flash Cinema Company, to be used both as a cinema and live theatre. The directors of the owning company were officers of the Royal Sussex Regiment and the name Blue Flash derived from the blue shoulder flash of the regiment. The managing director was Captain Rupert Charles Godfrey Middleton M.C., who had created the Blue Flash Association for demobilised men of the 4th Battalion of the Royal Sussex Regiment. In building cinemas, he hoped to employ ex-bandsmen as members of the orchestras that accompanied the silent films. Blue Flash opened the Coliseum at Shoreham in March 1923 and the Capitol followed in November.

The name Capitol came from the great national temple of ancient Rome and Blue Flash believed that it had previously been used as a cinema name only in the centre of New York and in Cardiff. The Horsham building was erected on the site of nos. 5, 7 and 9 London Road, and construction began early in 1923. It had to be set well back from the main road because of 'ancient lights' rights of neighbouring buildings.

The design was Italian in style with red Lombardic roof tiles and an ornate fountain in the large forecourt copied from the Villa Albani in Rome. Up to twenty cars could be parked in the forecourt. The seating capacity was on the low side, around 625—a far cry from the huge seating capacities of the Capitols in New York and Cardiff.

The cinema opened at 2.15 p.m. on Wednesday 7 November 1923 with *Chu Chin Chow*, starring Betty Blythe, and with Frank Watts, a baritone from the London Opera House, who sang in synchronisation with the image on the screen. The following week brought Mary Pickford in *Tess of the Storm Country*. There were continuous evening performances from 5 p.m. to 10 p.m. with matinees on Wednesdays and Saturdays at 2.15 p.m. Prices were 9d. (front stalls), 1s. 3d. (back stalls) and 2s. (grand circle).

The films were projected from behind the screen. It was claimed on behalf of this system that it was quieter (as the noise of the projectors was further away), safer (as any fire caused by the inflammable film would be well outside the auditorium), clearer (as there would be no smoke in the way of the beam) and less stressful on the eyes. However, it needed space behind the screen and was never widely adopted. Here the Simplex projectors had a throw of a considerable distance onto a special screen made of Irish linen, which had to be fairly transparent for the picture to show through to the audience and which needed to be treated and cleaned once a year.

An orchestra of 15 was hired under the leadership of Arthur Samuel Yarnold, and a temporary organ was placed on stage for the opening. The organ built for the theatre by Hill, Norman and Beard was not ready and did not come into operation until May 1924. The console was positioned in the orchestra pit to the right of the stage and the organ blower room was at the rear of the building below the projection room. On Sundays, when films were not shown, the orchestra gave its own regular concerts.[153]

The Capitol was the finest cinema in Horsham, putting on stage shows as well as films, and had a restaurant with outdoor balcony tables for use in summertime. The Blue Flash Company acquired both the Central Hall and Carfax to control all three cinemas in the town, but it is indicative of the Capitol's superiority that in October 1929 it was the first to have sound apparatus installed.

The Union circuit took over the town's three Blue Flash cinemas on 14 October 1935. It seems likely that Blue Flash knew of plans by the Union and Odeon circuits to build modern cinemas in the town, and decided to sell to Union rather than fight the new competition. Union liked to control all the cinemas in a town and may have hoped to scare off Odeon by its move.

Once Union's Ritz and the Odeon had opened, the older Capitol with its smaller seating capacity ranked a weak third. In 1937,

170 The Blue Flash Company's Capitol Theatre, *c.*1931, the inspiration of Captain R.C.G. Middleton M.C. of the Royal Sussex Regiment.

171 *Top.* Foyer of the Capitol, Horsham, *c.*1936.

172 *Middle.* Auditorium of the Capitol from under the circle, *c.*1936.

173 *Bottom.* The Capitol, Horsham. Auditorium to rear, *c.*1936.

Union Cinemas collapsed financially and, along with the Ritz, the Capitol came under the control of a major circuit, Associated British Cinemas, from October. It closed for a while in 1938 for interior modernisation and re-opened with 644 seats.

During the peak years of cinema-going, there were plenty of attractive new films and reissues to keep all three cinemas busy, even though the Capitol often changed programmes on both Mondays and Thursdays. Albert Foster, who joined the staff as a rewind boy in 1943, working from 10 a.m. to 10.30 p.m. for 27s. 6d. per week, recalls that when really popular films with such draws as Tarzan or Roy Rogers were shown, it was by no means uncommon for queues to stretch from the paybox all around the vestibule, then outside along the Roman colonnade and up and down the car park. A second paybox was used when the cinema was really busy, located down a covered passage to the right of the cinema—this admitted patrons to the cheaper seats at the front through the exit to the right of the screen.

Mr. Foster remembers the air of excitement in the projection box as each new programme was checked for bad joins, trailers made up for forthcoming attractions, and new prints waxed to prevent chatter. The same newsreel was shown by both the Ritz and the Capitol and it was the rewind boy's job to shuttle the tin of film back and forth on a bicycle. There was a serious fire at the Capitol on one occasion, caused when the film broke in the aperture gate and caught alight, resulting in one fireman being overcome by the fumes and needing to be rescued.[154]

By 1950 the Capitol had become a more difficult cinema to programme profitably as audiences began to decline and the Ritz took the profitable ABC circuit release. Around March 1951, the rear projection system was removed to the Astoria at Aston, Birmingham, and a conventional projection system installed.

The Capitol abandoned matinees and did not open on Sundays. In 1953, the local

Council began considering purchasing the building for a new civic centre. A deal was reached by which it would be acquired for £11,000 in the autumn of 1954. The cinema was losing so much money by this time that ABC did not wait for the take-over but closed the Capitol on Saturday 21 August. It opened at 5 p.m. that day with a revival double-bill of two British comedies, the smash hit *Doctor in the House* plus a satire about television, *Meet Mr. Lucifer*.

The Council retained chief projectionist Harold Scott as manager and caretaker. The Capitol was made available for hire and re-opened with the Horsham Operatic and Drama Society's production of *The Desert Song* from 4 to 9 October 1954. Other musical productions—*The Pirates of Penzance*, *Tom Jones*—soon followed and the Capitol quickly became well established as a live venue.

Films returned for a while from 1972 when a part-time Regional Film Theatre was started, joining a network organised by the British Film Institute to show pictures of specialised interest. Glenda Jackson appeared at the opening ceremony on Saturday 29 January 1972 which was followed by her film *Sunday Bloody Sunday*, commencing a week's run. Thereafter the RFT was scheduled to operate on Wednesdays, Thursdays and Fridays of alternate weeks with occasional full weeks.

In 1981 the Council began discreet negotiations to sell the Capitol to Marks and Spencer as the site for a new store. There was considerable uproar when the deal was completed and the Capitol closed in January 1983, even though the Ritz had been acquired to become a new arts centre.

13 June 1936
Ritz/ABC/Horsham Arts Centre
North Street

The Ritz was built for National Provincial Cinemas, a subsidiary of Union Cinemas, with Union's regular architects, Verity and Beverley, supervising the work of L.H. Parsons of the local practice Godman and Kay (which had, of course, designed the Capitol). The design incorporated many attractive art deco features in the foyer and lounge, although the auditorium was very plain except for the decorative plasterwork around the proscenium.

On the first night there was a link with the old Blue Flash Cinema Company when its managing director, Major Middleton, introduced Mr. E.T. Neathercoat, C.B.E., J.P., of Holbrook Park, who performed the opening ceremony. They were supported by film star Arthur Riscoe and organist Harold Ramsay, who gave a recital on the cinema's Compton organ (two manual, four rank, with a melotone unit and illuminated rising console). The films shown were a Laurel and Hardy short, a Mickey Mouse cartoon, and the feature comedy *When Knights Were Bold* starring Jack Buchanan.[155]

The Ritz gave Union four cinemas in the town, enabling the company to dictate terms to distributors and hopefully deter further competition. The company rushed construction of the Ritz in six months but its hopes that the Odeon chain would drop its plans were in vain and a new Odeon opened nearly four months after the Ritz.

The Ritz was on the edge of town near the railway station. No exact seating figure is available for its opening but a figure of 1,086 was given later. It was a spacious building and, like the Capitol and Odeon, had a forecourt and café. Its name was mounted on two sky signs (an American device much favoured by Union but rarely employed otherwise in this country).

174 An advertisement for the Capitol from the *West Sussex County Times* of 28 February 1936.

175   *Above left*. The Ritz, Horsham, after being renamed the ABC in February 1967.

176   *Above right*. Interior view of the Ritz in 1984 prior to conversion to the Horsham Arts Centre.

177   *Left*. The full depth of the auditorium of the Ritz before it was subdivided to become the Horsham Arts Centre.

178   *Below left*. The Capitol auditorium of the Horsham Arts Centre retaining the proscenium arch of the Ritz cinema.

179   *Below right*. The new stepped seating and balconies of the Capitol auditorium within the Horsham Arts Centre.

Union Cinemas had over-extended and ran into a financial crisis, falling under the control of Associated British Cinemas in October 1937. The Ritz became the regular outlet for the ABC circuit release and enjoyed many prosperous years with direct access to a good share of the hit films. It opened on every other Sunday in the 1950s, alternating with the Odeon. The organ was occasionally used as an added attraction, being played by Molly Forbes in Christmas week of 1954.

The Ritz was renamed ABC on 20 February 1967 during a two-week run of *My Fair Lady* as part of a policy giving the ABC circuit a clearer brand image.

However, the national decline in cinema attendances made the ABC no longer profitable and in 1975 it was put on a list of properties for gradual disposal. It was acquired by the Council in January 1982 to become the town's new arts centre in place of the Capitol. The Council continued to run it until November 1983.

The building then underwent an elaborate conversion to become the Horsham Arts Centre. The old circle was removed. The front stalls area was converted into a new Capitol Theatre, retaining the original proscenium arch and splay walls with all their rich plasterwork, which has been painted (a little sickeningly) in peach and orange with gold bands, the latter powerfully framing the opening and directing the eye in towards the stage. A suitable valance with three gold bands across it has been added, with concealed lighting reinstated in the coves and to pick out the vertical decorative features. The old side exits have been removed. The seating has been extended backwards, stepped up towards the old circle area with a gallery added as well.

Happily, the Capitol Theatre auditorium is used for some film shows besides a busy programme of live events. The seating is not very comfortable and there is no curtain in front of the screen but otherwise the space is a delight. When it had been the Ritz cinema, only front stalls patrons had really appreciated the detail of the plasterwork decoration, but it is now in close proximity to the entire audience and provides a sumptuous setting.

The area once occupied by the rear stalls has been levelled. To the right, as one enters the building, it now provides an enlarged entrance hall, leading through to the Capitol

Theatre's front stalls and off to a flat-floored studio space added on the right. To the left in the former rear stalls area is found a new full-time cinema reviving the Ritz name and seating 126 on one floor. The seats face towards the front of the building, in the opposite direction to those in the Capitol. The Ritz is entered at the back left, from the extended entrance area.

When the original Ritz closed, it still had art deco trough light fittings suspended from the main foyer ceiling and these have been preserved but moved to the outer foyer. The original staircase to the circle has also been retained, over to the left as one enters, and this now leads to a much enlarged bar and café area which occupies most of the old circle space. Part of the rear auditorium ceiling can still be seen here. This area leads to the new circle and gallery of the Capitol Theatre.

The Horsham Arts Centre is a splendid and ingenious adaptation of an old building that preserves its best features. It sets an example that has been too little emulated elsewhere.

180 An advertisement for the Ritz from the *West Sussex County Times* of 18 October 1936.

7 OCTOBER 1936
ODEON/CLASSIC/MECCA
NORTH STREET

The Odeon was the 26th purpose-built addition to the circuit in 1936, a year which had also seen an Odeon open in Littlehampton. The Horsham Odeon was designed by George Coles, a leading cinema architect who also lived locally, and it displayed considerable flair. Like the Capitol and Ritz, it had a set-back entrance with a forecourt for patrons arriving by car, but here there was a pylon, illuminated from within, carrying a vertical Odeon sign that lit up in neon at night. This drew attention to the cinema from a distance.

The Odeon's entrance hall had a central island paybox and two staircases leading straight up to the circle foyer and café. Standard circuit carpet in a soft rose colour replaced the rubber flooring downstairs and the circuit's distinctively designed ash stands and settees were prominently placed. The walls had thin horizontal bands and with the ceilings gave a modern art deco feeling that extended to the auditorium where bands on the side walls led the eye towards the proscenium arch.

A relatively plain space, the auditorium had two decorative towers set in the splay walls, illuminated from a concealed source and topped by a light fitting. On each side, nearer the screen, there was a clock in the typical

181 *Above left.* The Odeon, Horsham, in its opening year, 1936.

182 *Left.* Entrance hall and paybox, 1936.

183 *Top right.* Auditorium from circle showing main tabs, 1936.

184 *Middle right.* Proscenium arch and splay walls from stalls showing screen tabs, 1936.

185 *Below right.* The circle lounge, Horsham Odeon, 1936.

circuit style with the words 'THE ODEON' replacing some of the numerals on an octagonal-shaped face like the initial letter of the trademark Odeon sign. The stalls seated 766 and the circle 492, giving a total of 1,258, making it Horsham's largest cinema.

The decorative scheme throughout the cinema was grey speckled with blue and gold, and the seating was grey and scarlet. Odeons had a democratic policy by which every seat was the same and only its position dictated the price. The most expensive seats, in the front of the circle, cost 2s. 6d., five times the cheapest at 6d., closest to the screen on the stalls floor.

This Odeon was very expensive to build, costing £33,555 or £27.19 per seat compared with an average of £20 (a similar-sized Odeon which made its bow ten days later at Newport, Isle of Wight, cost only £24,913).

The opening proceedings, on the evening of Wednesday 7 October 1936, took four hours. Crowds lined the Carfax and North Street, and in front of a full house the Rt. Hon. Earl Winterton, M.P., expressed his pleasure in opening the third new Odeon in his constituency (the others being at Worthing and Lancing).

The evening included a programme by the Band of the Scots Guards and a half-hour concert by Jack Payne and his 20-piece band. The opening picture was *Little Lord Fauntleroy*, starring Freddie Bartholomew. The manager, I.A.N. Beadle, formerly at the Odeon Worcester Park, Surrey, was introduced, and a collection was taken for Horsham Hospital.[156]

Union Cinemas attempted to undermine the Odeon by announcing, in virtually a full page spread in the *West Sussex County Times* (2 October 1936), a cut in admission prices at the Ritz, Capitol, Winter Garden and Carfax cinemas.

Three months after the Odeon opened, Saturday morning pictures began at 9.30 a.m. on 9 January 1937 with the Odeon Children's Circle. This offered a Ken Maynard western *Doomed to Die* plus a serial and Mickey Mouse cartoon comedy. Tickets were 3d. and 6d. and every child received a free gift. For regulars, there was a membership card, badge and on birthdays a greetings card and an offer of free admission.[157]

The Odeon played its circuit release quite successfully for many years supplemented by some Gaumont programmes as the Gaumont

186 *Above.* Saturday morning pictures at the Horsham Odeon, advertised in May 1946.

187 *Right.* Advertisement for the Horsham Odeon from the *West Sussex County Times* of 6 September 1946.

circuit had no direct outlet in Horsham. It opened on alternate Sundays for many years, rotating with the Ritz.

When the Capitol closed in August 1954, the Odeon demonstrated its faith in the future of the cinema by announcing the early installation of a new wide screen and the arrival of CinemaScope in November.[158] The wide screen was inaugurated for the week commencing Monday 18 October when a new version of *Romeo and Juliet* was shown. CinemaScope did not arrive until 1955.

However, the continuing decline in attendances eventually made its mark and the Odeon was one of 47 weaker properties disposed of as a going concern by the Rank Organisation to the Classic circuit in December 1967. This changed hands on the ninth of the month when it became the Classic—hardly an appropriate name for a non-classical building showing new films but one reflecting the circuit's origin as a group of repertory cinemas.

As the Classic, the building was divided to provide two small cinemas upstairs which opened on 26 May 1972, releasing the stalls for bingo. Classic 1 seated 310 in the old circle with a new screen installed in front of

it, while Classic 2 seated 110 in the former café area. The bingo club was operated by Mecca which took over the cinemas from Classic on 11 December 1973, calling them Mecca 1 and 2.

Both cinemas were closed on 10 January 1976. The last films shown were *Bite the Bullet* plus *The Omega Man* in Screen 1 and *All Creatures Great and Small* plus *The Beautiful People* in Screen 2. Bingo was not a lasting success and closed, players being offered a bus ride to another Mecca hall. The entire building languished empty and unwanted for a while but had been demolished by the beginning of November 1981. An office block now stands in its place.

Addenda: Horsham

The earliest presentations of animated pictures in Horsham were at the King's Head Assembly Rooms on 25-26 November 1896 and at Horsham Carnival in Springfield Meadow on Bank Holiday Monday 2 August 1897.[159]

LANCING

31 OCTOBER 1933
ODEON/REGAL/ODEON
45/49 PENHILL ROAD

This Odeon has a curious and unflattering place in the history of the celebrated circuit. It became the least important of all the cinemas opened as Odeons and the first to be dropped by the company. It was situated in a side street and made little impression on anyone. And yet it was not a totally undistinguished building.

An Odeon at Lancing does not feature in the list of new cinemas that circuit founder Oscar Deutsch was working on during 1931 and 1932, although the Odeon Worthing does appear. Like the Odeon Kemp Town and Rothbury Portslade, the Lancing cinema seems to have been an opportunity spotted or accepted by Deutsch and his co-directors, F. Stanley Bates and W.G. Elcock, as a low-cost means of enlarging their circuit (the fourth director of the particular company formed to build and own this theatre, R.A. Gates, held the mortgage of £7,500 and was probably the local partner who brought the scheme to Odeon.)

As the Worthing cinema was already in the pipeline, it seems curious that Deutsch should have wanted a second Odeon in the same area. It is true that Lancing, which then had a population of 7,000 (swollen to a degree by visitors in the summer), did not possess a cinema, but the Odeon's location within the town was poor: it would have been hard for visitors to find, built out of the centre along a side road that was mainly residential. There were ordinary houses next door to the cinema and the land it occupied had previously been fields used as a nursery. Lancing did have the carriage works of the Southern Railway, giving a core of workers who would have welcomed a cinema on their doorstep.

188   The Odeon, Lancing, in its opening year, one of the first cinemas in the Oscar Deutsch empire.

189   The auditorium of the Lancing Odeon with its 'atmospheric' decorative scheme, 1933.

151

190 The Odeon in Lancing, photographed *c*.1934, showing its curious location in a residential side street.

Whereas specific architects are associated with other Odeons, company records indicate in the case of Lancing that the architect was 'arranged by builder'. On top of the £7,500 cost of building the cinema, £2,000 was spent on furnishing and equipment with £100 of additional expenses, making a total of £9,600, a fraction of the £40,700 spent on the Worthing Odeon. The company expected to pay £520 per annum in mortgage interest and £300 per annum to redeem the mortgage over 20 years.

While the entrance block is on Penhill Road, the auditorium had to be set some distance behind at right angles, extending across the end of the back gardens of the adjacent houses after leaving space for an outdoor side exit passage. (Although Ingleside Road now runs down the side of the former cinema past the end of the auditorium, there was originally only a path, the road being built after the Second World War to provide access to new housing.)

Externally, the building had nothing in common with the streamlined modern movement buildings (like the Odeon Worthing) for which the chain became famous, other than the distinctive lettering of the Odeon name that became a trademark. The cinema had small Odeon signs mounted on the side edges of the canopy with the letters picked out in neon to show up at night, plus a large Odeon sign at roof level without any neon.

Beneath the canopy, the main entrance doors were set a little back and on the walls to each side were displayed the opening times of the cinema, ticket prices, etc. Above these,

on either side, the Odeon name appeared in a different, blobby, triangular style that could also be seen at the Odeon Lewes.

A refreshment room (not quite a café) seems to have been located over the entrance. The auditorium had 691 seats on a single, sloping floor with an aisle that was off centre, to the left. The decorative scheme in the 'atmospheric' mode (like that at the earlier Weymouth Odeon) was credited to Mrs. Lily Deutsch, wife of Oscar. This attempted to give the audience an impression of sitting outdoors. The side wall dado was painted to look as if it were made of stone while above there were images of blossoming bushes, cypress trees and distant mountains to suggest a southern European landscape. In a true atmospheric cinema this would have been carried out in relief while the ceiling would have been curved to represent the sky—here the flat ceiling was left plain to give an open-air feeling but the effect was spoilt by decorative ventilation grilles (modern radiators set into the 'outdoor' stone walls provided another jarring note). Tiled roofs did project out over the side exits and over the two balconies on either side of the proscenium. The Odeon carpet was in the circuit's art deco style.

The Odeon was opened on a Monday evening by the Rt. Hon. Earl Winterton M.P., supported by the Mayor of Worthing, while the film star Rene Ray added a touch of glamour to the proceedings. Oscar Deutsch was also present. The programme (proceeds in aid of local hospitals) consisted of the feature film *The King's Vacation* plus a Disney Silly Symphony cartoon and the Pathé Gazette newsreel.

The Odeon played films much later than Worthing and seems to have been such a letdown that, from 2 March 1936, it was renamed Regal to disassociate it from the main circuit and the Odeon Worthing.

Licensing records show that 5s. per week was charged for Sunday opening which was also subject to certain conditions. The records also reveal a steady flow of managers, suggesting it was a starting point for managers who went on to better things. Ignatius Morris held the first licence from 3 October 1933 and was followed within a few days of opening by John Stanley Coldrick, to whom the licence was transferred on 7 November. Mr. Coldrick gave way to Edward George

Rhodes from 23 October 1934 who was in turn replaced by John Walker on 15 January 1935. The licence then went to W.J. Gray from 12 March 1935 but he made way for Jessie Cameron Brewer on 27 August 1935. She remained in charge for several years, during which time the cinema became the Regal, lasting until 7 March 1939 when the building was leased to Basil Edward Fortesque, who was then completing construction of the new Luxor cinema in the centre of Lancing. Fortesque must have thought it a good idea to control both cinemas, to obtain better terms from distributors and regulate where films played. However, on 23 March 1940, just two months after the Luxor opened, the Regal was closed. This may have been intended as a temporary measure, a response to staffing difficulties and low attendances, as Fortesque renewed the licence on 11 February 1941.[160]

However, he must have indicated later that year that he no longer wanted to hold on to the Regal, as it was returned to Oscar Deutsch. The Odeon chief found a new lessee in Mrs. Merriman-Langdon, who had taken the Rothbury Portslade off his hands. Fortesque surrendered his licence on 14 October 1941 to a new manager, Louis Carr, and the Regal re-opened two days later, on Thursday 16 October, at which point the Luxor took a a full-page advertisement in the local paper to tout its superior facilities. It seems that Mrs. Merriman-Langdon was persuaded to take the Regal on particularly favourable terms but it still proved too difficult to operate successfully, at least under wartime conditions. Once again it was handed back to Odeon: the circuit resumed control from Sunday 30 August 1942 and kept it going themselves. The name was still Regal but it advertised as 'An Odeon Theatre'.

Then the Odeon name was reinstated from 25 March 1945 and the cinema struggled on, benefiting from the general boom in cinema attendances just after the war. Matinees were soon restricted to Wednesdays and Saturdays in most weeks whereas the Luxor had them daily. The end came after four months of rumours on Saturday 20 January 1952. The manager at closing was William Tull. The last main programmes consisted of a Monday to Wednesday run of the X-certificate Continental comedy *Clochemerle* (plus *A Life*

in Her Hands) and a Thursday onwards booking of the British wartime comedy *Appointment with Venus* (plus *The Man With My Face*). Unlike the Luxor, the Odeon had put on Saturday morning shows for children, and these were now transferred to the surviving cinema.[161]

The day after closure the cinema became the property of the Shipman and King circuit, which was taking over the Luxor and wanted the Odeon shut to reduce competition. And so the Odeon Lancing became the first actual Odeon cinema to close for economic reasons (others had been hit by German bombs), although it was the decision of its new owners not to keep it open. On the following Wednesday, a 'To Let' board appeared, and the building was offered as industrial premises, a controversial move as the area was regarded as residential. Further cinema use was prohibited.

In fact, the Odeon was put to industrial use, initially as a chromium plating works, and became forlorn and run down, a bit of an eye-sore. It was a welding and engineering workshop in 1975. In recent years, it has remained standing, retaining its canopy and somewhat smartened up in appearance. The front part is clearly labelled Regal House, nicely recalling its cinema past, with plumbers' merchants Leamey's of Lancing in occupancy. A video company has set up offices on the first floor. The auditorium has been used by Ingleside Garage with a new roof and wide double doors. There are no vestiges of the old cinema foyer or auditorium to be seen.

191 The Lancing Odeon in its current use, June 1995.

17 January 1940
Luxor
South Street

The Luxor was a local enterprise by a specially formed company, Luxor (Lancing) Ltd., headed by Basil Edward Fortesque. It was situated in a prominent central position, close to the railway. A delay in receiving the large steel girder supporting the circle and a slowdown after the start of the Second World War in September 1939 resulted in the Luxor making a low-key debut several months late on Wednesday 17 January 1940.

The architect was W. Frazer-Granger and it had 998 seats, 800 in the stalls and 198 in the steeply stepped balcony. The entrance was set in a curving parade of shops with a flat-topped tower overhead to carry the name of the cinema. A long, wide passage led directly

192 An impressive full-page advertisement for the new Lancing Luxor in the *Shoreham Herald* of 21 March 1940.

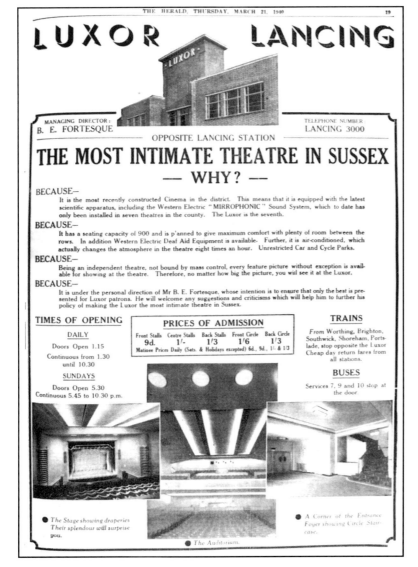

to the auditorium block behind, with stairs to the right for access to the balcony and to the restaurant area over the entrance. The interior decorations were Marblecote sprayed red and gold over cream.

The original intention had been to put sprung maple flooring down for a ballroom but the ship carrying the wood from Canada had been sunk on the way over and the idea was abandoned. There was a car park and space for cycles at the rear.

The Luxor was a very attractive building, far superior to the Odeon, and, as previously described, B.E. Fortesque did for a while operate both cinemas to ensure that the Luxor was not disadvantaged by a cinema belonging to a major circuit. The manager, Mr. Kirk, joined the Luxor from the Regal Petworth.

The opening ceremony was performed by leading aircraftman E. Pearce who before the war had worked on the project as chief assistant to the architect. The feature shown was the Crazy Gang comedy *The Frozen Limits*. The Luxor offered continuous performances from 1.30 p.m. to 10.30 p.m. with a special programme on Sundays commencing at 5.30 p.m., the initial Sunday feature being a revival of the Astaire-Rogers musical *Carefree*. Prices of admission were: dress circle, 1s. 6d.; circle and back stalls, 1s. 3d.; centre stalls, 1s.; front stalls, 9d.[162]

In 1940, a youngster left school at the age of 14 and became the rewind boy at the Luxor. The son of a once prominent film producer, Sydney Samuelson went on to a distinguished career in the cinema world as founder of a leading film services company and more recently head of the British Film Commission. He was appointed a Commander of the Order of the British Empire (CBE) in 1978 and knighted in 1995 for his services to the British film industry. In an interview for this book, he recalled:

My first work was before the cinema opened— to help with what they now call the builder's clean because it was going to have to be highly polished and sparkling and it was covered in cement dust. I can't tell you how grateful I was to have what I thought was such an exciting job. I felt I was already on the second rung of the ladder of a career because there was one chap below me even. You wouldn't think anyone could be below a 14-year-old rewind boy but in those days cinemas had page boys with buttons all the way up their front and there was a page boy at the Luxor. I earned ten shillings a week. That was my starting salary.

The Luxor had the last pair of Ernemann 7 projectors to be imported before the war started. They came from Kiel and were water-cooled, the Rolls Royce of projection. The arc lamps were also Ernemann, and they had Western Electric Mirrophonic sound which was the last word in sound at that time.

The cinema was struggling because Lancing and that whole coast became a defence area during the war—what that meant was that you could live there if you already lived there, you could move out, but you couldn't move in. And we had air raid scares as well. At the beginning, when there was an air raid warning the sirens went off. We were phoned up in the box: 'Close down, air raid warning'. So we used to close down the film, put up the house lights, close the tabs. Mr. Fortesque or his deputy, Mr. Kirk, used to walk on and say, 'I'm terribly sorry, ladies and gentlemen, but there is an air raid alert. If you would like to stay in the cinema, the show will resume but if you wish to leave we will give you a note so that you can come back in and see the rest of the film at another time.' Everybody used to stay and he'd walk off and we would start the show again. And then I think we must have conformed with other cinemas and just put a slide on, over the picture, just saying 'Air raid alert'.

And that happened on a regular basis—I would think it happened three or four times a week. And one time we were showing a film called *Raffles* with David Niven and we lost all power—that was when the power station at Kingston along the coast had been hit, and it was during the day. We used to occasionally see the Luftwaffe flying along not too far above our heads. That was the business of running a cinema in war-time with very, very few people paying. But it never closed. Mr. Kirk was called up. It must have been a relief to Mr. Fortesque as it meant a salary that didn't have to be found.

The chief, Frank Chipperfield, was an autocrat. He'd been pirated from the Plaza Worthing which was the big ABC house, and he got four pounds ten a week (he'd got four pounds at the Plaza). And he hated me, the boy, because he felt that crewing in the projection box was his job and nobody else's and he hadn't appointed me—Mr. Fortesque had.

My first weeks were spent doing nothing but scrubbing and polishing. The projection box and rewind room were scrubbed every day and one other room was also scrubbed, whether it was the battery room, the rectifier room, the projection staff rest room, the switch room. There was one room for every day of the week. If the chief didn't make me cry once a week, he'd failed in his training

programme. It was the done thing—you gave youngsters a hard time. He was such a swine but his standards were very high. There was never a fault in a changeover while he was there—he didn't allow that kind of thing. Although it was so miserable for me because of all the cleaning and polishing, the box was run rather like the bridge of a ship and I've kept to his standards all my life.

The second projectionist left to take a job spray painting camouflage on factory buildings because it obviously paid much better money. The chief had a blazing row with Mr. Fortesque and walked out. And as he had brought the third with him from the Plaza Worthing, a sense of loyalty in the mind of the youth caused him to walk out with his chief. By that time I was, I suppose, about fourteen and a half and, although I had never been allowed officially to even do a changeover, I was allowed to do the rewinding after some weeks and I was never allowed to do anything else. Friday was a good day for me because it was the chief's day off and the second was kind of friendly and he used to let me do changeovers and switch and fade in the non-sync, as it was called—the gramophone record player. And he used to sometimes let me do the lights as the tabs came across. We had a festoon curtain there, so the top lights and the footlights were different colours and the festoon curtains picked up one colour one side and a different colour on the other. What it meant was, for one or one-and-a-half days, I ran that show all on my own without any problem at all. I was called in by Mr. Fortesque and he said, 'I'm going to make you joint third. I'm going to give you a rise to a pound a week.' He brought the chief in from a cinema they also owned around the corner, the Regal. We had a chief and joint thirds and the page boy became the rewind boy. There was no second. Having joint thirds caused him not to have to pay for a second.

The cinema was designed for theatrical use. There was a 36ft. wide proscenium, a stage 20ft. deep, and three dressing rooms. Sydney Samuelson remembers:

193 The auditorium of the Luxor taken from the balcony, 1940.

DIRECTOR

194 The Luxor in Lancing, seen here in later life, as a bingo hall.

A tremendously exciting time came with Dunkirk as suddenly we had thousands of troops who had just managed to get out billeted all around and they used to put on stage shows. Somehow the Forces always had a half-dozen guys who were professional musicians, and a couple of comedians and girls who were dancers. They put on really professional stage shows and suddenly we were in the theatre business putting on variety shows at the Luxor Lancing. There was a tremendous amount of work. We used to do rehearsals at night and up in the box we had a moving spotlight and I thought it was absolutely sensational following an act with a spotlight from the back.

Unfortunately, Samuelson had to leave the Luxor when the family moved to Birmingham where his father had taken a new job.[163]

Looking to the future, there was also provision at the Luxor for the installation of large-screen television, as had been demonstrated at several cinemas in the late 1930s. It was indeed an exceptionally well-equipped cinema for a small town, worthy of a major circuit undertaking.

In 1942, control of the Luxor passed to the London-based H. Bentley circuit, later known as the J.H.L. Associated Company and Bentley Circuit (Management) Company. B.E. Fortesque was the general manager in charge of several cinemas in Essex as well as the Luxor.

Three-day amateur productions by the Lancing Amateur Dramatic Society (later the Lancing Players) were staged several times a year after the War. The Sussex Film Society also held performances on Sunday afternoons in the late 1940s, putting back the start of public performances.

In the early 1950s, the Luxor was advertised for sale in the trade press as a going

concern. As stated in connection with the Odeon, the Shipman and King circuit took over the Luxor on 21 January 1952, buying and closing the Odeon at the same time and transferring its Saturday morning pictures for children to the Luxor. (S&K also operated the Hailsham Pavilion in Sussex and a string of cinemas in country towns.)

The concentration of attendances at one cinema undoubtedly helped the Luxor for many years. In the summer of 1957, it was decided to end stage bookings but the Luxor still had many years as a full-time cinema ahead, finally being sold to a bingo operator in 1965. The last major film presentation was *Lawrence of Arabia*, which ended a five-day (Monday to Friday) run on 25 June. On Saturday 26 June 1965, the X-certificate film *Splendour in the Grass* was revived for adults only with free admission ... a very strange way to close down a cinema.[164]

The new operators had already taken over the Hailsham Pavilion from S&K for bingo and this had led to successful negotiations for the Luxor. It then spent many years as a bingo hall, with the manager moving the screen festoon curtain forward to the proscenium where it was raised and lowered at the beginning and end of bingo sessions, demonstrating a pleasing continuity of showmanship.

In time, bingo lost its appeal and the auditorium was demolished in the early 1980s. A block of flats called Freshbrook Court now stands on the site of the cinema car park while the auditorium area has become parking space for the shop occupying the old foyer, Walter Wall Carpets. Only the front survives.

In 1996, the name Luxor still adorns the tower in front with remnants of neon tubing attached, although one of the finials on top of two rounded brick columns has been broken off. The canopy remains, carrying the name of Walter Wall Carpets which has made very few alterations to the entrance area. The coving and ceiling of the entrance hall are original while cinema carpet covers the stairs leading to the first floor. The former balcony foyer still has the doors to the circle and restaurant, although those to the balcony are bricked up immediately behind, as can be seen through the glass. There is a laylight which lets in natural light during the day and still has one of two orange light bulbs with reflectors that lit up for cinema patrons in the evening ...

FORTHCOMING
CINEMA
ATTRACTIONS

LITTLEHAMPTON

11 MAY 1911
ELECTRIC PICTURE PALACE/
ELECTRIC/REGENT
TERMINUS ROAD

Situated opposite the railway station, this was originally the Terminus Hall Theatre and Skating Rink which had already presented occasional film shows before being launched as the Electric Picture Palace in 1911.

On 28 October 1908, an article appeared in the *Bognor Observer* announcing that George E. Redman intended to run animated pictures every night at the Terminus Hall during the month of November in conjunction with Michael Shanly, who three months earlier had begun showing films on the Pier at Bognor.

In December 1908 the Hall was the venue for a benefit performance in aid of Redman and Harry Joseph who together were described as 'the pioneers of the Animated Pictures at Littlehampton this winter'.[165] Joseph was a prominent figure on the local entertainment scene and next appears on August Bank Holiday 1909 running a Grand Bicycle Gymkhana and Evening Fête on the Sports Field, complete with balloon ascent, parachute jump, fireworks and animated pictures.[166]

Joseph Poole's Myriorama played at the Terminus Hall for a week from Monday 20 September 1909 and included 'the very latest Bioscopic Revelations'. A week later the *Observer* reported that the Hall was to be re-opened as a Grand Picture Palace on Saturday 2 October 1909 with two evening performances daily, at 7 p.m. and 9 p.m., and a matinee on Saturdays.[167]

The lessee and manager then was Wally Rice, who had moved from Kingston to take over the *Terminus Hotel* and Theatre. He combined animated pictures and vaudeville for a short time before adding skating in mid-December 1909. The main fare under Rice seems to have been theatricals and musical concerts, and only occasionally are film shows mentioned in the local newspapers in 1910. In August of that year, Alfred West's pictures depicting *Life in Our Navy and Army* had met with a 'huge success' during Bank Holiday week, and at the end of the month patrons had seen, according to the *Littlehampton Observer* of 31 August, 'some very excellent cinematograph pictures ... including the Johnson-Burns fight and the Brussels fire'.[168]

The regular presentation of films in the town began the following year when the Terminus Hall was re-opened under new

---

The New Electric Picture Palace
(Opposite Railway Station, Littlehampton)
Will OPEN on
THURSDAY NEXT, MAY 11th,
When a high-class, up-to-date Programme of
ANIMATED PICTURES
Will be showing continuously from
6 to 10.30 p.m.
The following Programme will be shown on
Thursday, Friday, and Saturday,
MAY 11th, 12th, and 13th.
The New Gendarme (very laughable).
A Sin Upardonable (interesting Drama).
The Temples of Nikko (beautifully coloured and very interesting).
The Bolted Door (splendid Drama).
Schulby has the Small Pox (very amusing).
Madame Tallim (perfectly coloured).
Tontolini Dreams (a real comicality).

Complete change of Programme twice weekly.
Popular prices: 3d., 6d., and 1s.
Open every Evening from 6 to 10.30 p.m.
Special Children's Matinee Saturdays at 3.
Admission, 1d. and 2d.   Adults, 3d. and 6d.
Manager: Sydney C. Shepherd.
Chief Engineer: D. Holderness.

---

195 Advertisement in the *Littlehampton Observer* on 10 May 1911 announcing the formal opening of the Terminus Hall as a regular Picture Palace.

196 One of the early programmes of short films presented at the Picture Palace in 1911.

THE NEW PICTURE PALACE,
LITTLEHAMPTON.
(Opposite Railway Station).

A High Class and Up-to-date Programme of
ANIMATED PICTURES
shewing continuously from 6 to 10.30 p.m.

Thursday, Friday, and Saturday, May 18th, 19th, and 20th.—Babylas Inherits a Panther (comic) ; Nick Winter and the Money Coiners (comedy drama) ; Rapids of Magdapis (scenic) ; Mystery of Lonely Gulch (drama) ; Foolshead More than Usual (comic) ; Border Ranger (drama) ; Fat Jack and Slim Jim (comic).

Monday, Tuesday, and Wednesday, May 22nd, 23rd, and 24th.—He Who Laughs Last (comedy) ; Youth the Winner (very amusing) ; The Lone Dale Operator (exciting drama) ; Turtle Fishing (very interesting) ; Saragevo (beautifully coloured scenic) ; Kate's Romance (drama) ; The Doctor (pathetic drama).

Popular Prices :—3d., 6d., and 1s. Special Children's Matinee, Saturdays at 3. Admission, 1d. and 2d. Adults 3d. and 6d.
Manager, Sydney C. Shepherd. Chief Engineer, D. Holderness.

management as the Electric Picture Palace. The *Littlehampton Observer* (26 April 1911) welcomed the development:

There is but little doubt that one of the most popular forms of amusement of the present day is the Picture Palace. With their constant variety and change of pictures they have caught on with the public in a wonderful way and have evidently come to stay, and the announcement ... that the Terminus Hall is to be very shortly opened in the capacity of an Electric Picture Palace will be welcomed as adding one more attraction to the amusements of the town.

The latest methods are being used, the power being obtained from a 15-20 horse power engine, which is being installed in an addition to the present building. This engine, driven by gas, will develop a very high current, and the machine will be installed in one of the present dressing rooms under the gallery, which will be bricked in and made perfectly fire proof, and the pictures will be shewn through a small opening in the wall onto a screen at the other end of the room.

The latest form of plaster screen is to be utilised, concentrating the pictures in the clearest possible manner. A great feature will be that pictures of passing events are to be shewn within a day or so of their happening, and local events, if of sufficient importance, will be included in this scheme.

The new Electric Picture Palace was a venture of Charles Letchford Shepherd of

Maxwell Road, Littlehampton, who within fifteen months went on to launch further cinemas at Arundel and at Bridport in Dorset. The announcement of the opening in the *Observer* promised the people of Littlehampton

... a High Class, Up-to-Date Cinematograph Theatre:
Only the Best and Latest Animated Pictures will be shewn. Comedy, Drama, Tragedy, Educational, Trick, Travel, Topical, Comic. The most Wonderful Sights in the World. Constantly Changing. Complete Change of Programme Twice Weekly. Open every evening 6 to 10.30. Continuous Performance! No waiting! The Public may enter at any time and the programme lasts nearly two hours. Popular prices 3d., 6d. and 1s. Special Children's Matinee Saturday at 3. Admission 1d. and 2d. Adults 3d. and 6d.[169]

Shepherd's managing partner, engineer and chief projectionist was his neighbour, Desmond Sidney Holderness, who supervised the installation of the generating plant.

On opening night, Thursday 11 May 1911, a packed house included members of the local Council specially invited by Shepherd. The programme that evening included two dramas, *A Sin Unpardonable* and *The Bolted Door*, supported by a coloured travelogue of Japanese scenes, *The Temples of Nikko*. The reporter for the local paper was impressed by the plaster screen, 'there being a complete absence of the flickering which is so often seen in animated pictures'.[170]

The first local interest films were presented within a fortnight of the opening—including the laying of the foundation stone of the Cottage Hospital by the Duchess of Norfolk on 22 May—and within a year Holderness himself was filming local events for almost immediate screening, early examples including Whitsun holiday scenes, launching of the lifeboat, children's sports and the Hospital Parade.

The Pathé Gazette newsreels were immediately popular. The footage of the coronation of George V and Queen Mary shown early in July 1911 drew crowded houses that included by special invitation inmates of East Preston Union Workhouse.[171] A month later, Shepherd arranged for a change of newsreel twice weekly (presumably rather than once a week) so that major national events could always be seen within two or three days of their happening.[172] Indeed, the following June he screened the Derby on the evening of the

day the race took place—which the *Observer* (12 June 1912) found a remarkable achievement 'considering the limitations of the train service to the town'.

'Star' pictures soon proved their worth at the box office. A film of Charles Dickens' *A Tale of Two Cities* proved a great attraction in September 1911 and such was the demand that year for the pantomime film *Cinderella* at Christmas that morning, afternoon and evening performances had to be scheduled for Boxing Day.[173]

Coloured films also drew packed houses. *The Queen's Necklace*, 'a beautiful hand-coloured historical drama' issued by Pathé Frères, thrilled audiences in February 1912 both at Littlehampton and on Bognor Pier.

Improvements to the equipment were also carried out by Holderness. In January 1912, a modern motor-driven projector was installed to increase the steadiness of the pictures, previously hand-cranked, and emergency power was arranged so that films could still be shown if the engine failed.[174] In May of the same year came 'the celebrated and up-to-date Vivaphone and Pathéphone', an early attempt at synchronised talking and singing pictures that, according to the *Observer* (15 May 1912), went down well with Littlehampton audiences: 'Most accurately timed, the results were received with tremendous enthusiasm, so much so that on Saturday evening two encores were insisted on.'

Another innovation was books of tickets at reduced rates—twelve 1s. tickets for 10s., twelve 6d. tickets for 5s., and twelve 3d. tickets for 2s. 6d.[175]

Packed houses seem to have been the norm and during the Easter holidays in 1912 the hall remained open throughout the afternoon and evening. Shepherd enhanced his reputation at the end of April 1912 by putting on a special benefit performance in aid of the Lord Mayor's Fund for widows and orphans left destitute by the *Titanic* disaster, several local families having been bereaved by the tragedy.[176]

It was soon necessary to increase the seating accommodation of the hall and provide an extra entrance. On 16 September 1912 a new gallery was opened and the *Littlehampton Observer* (18 September 1912) commented:

> The new gallery at the Picture Palace has added greatly to the comfort and convenience of the patrons of the hall. The new seating accommodation is arranged in tiers and nearly a hundred can be accommodated in this portion of the house. Comfortable tip-up seats are provided, and being on a level with the screen a fine direct view of the pictures is obtained ... The singing pictures are heard to even greater advantage than in the body of the hall.

The success of the Electric Palace encouraged the Olympic Syndicate to convert the Olympic Hall in Church Street into a rival cinema in December 1912. However, within a year, the new Olympic Cinema Theatre (subsequently renamed the Empire and Palladium) came under the management of Shepherd and Holderness.

On 11 May 1914, during the third anniversary programme at the Electric in Terminus Road, Holderness presented his senior partner with a barometer on behalf of their employees, now nearly twenty in number. Unfortunately, this high point was soon followed by two setbacks, one serious.

'Fiery Films at Littlehampton. Picture Palace badly damaged. Explosion in Operating Room' headlined the *Observer* (19 August 1914), adding:

> Littlehampton was all excitement about half past eight on Friday night for the Fire Brigade bell was ringing furiously, and a great tongue of flame, and later a dense column of smoke, shot out of the roof of the Electric Picture Palace.

Fire, the great dread of the early picture house proprietors, had struck the Electric on 14 August. A short length of film had been left in the projector, jamming the next film which soon caught light. One of the projectionists, in pouring sand over the burning films, knocked the lantern and a piece of white hot carbon fell on the floor igniting a spool of film. The blaze spread, despite the attention of 25 firemen, gutting the operating room and damaging the roof and screen. No one was injured, even though the staff had difficulty persuading the public to leave.

Four days earlier, Shepherd and Holderness had been refused a licence for Sunday evening performances at the Electric. They offered a petition signed by 343 adult residents supporting the application, but were strongly opposed by the local clergy for seeking to desecrate the Sabbath.

While the building was being repaired, Shepherd and Holderness continued with films at the Empire. The Electric re-opened in a

QUEUE HERE

remarkably short time, on 10 September 1914, when patrons were reassured that should another fire occur it would be confined to the lantern chamber (projection box). This former dressing room was now surrounded by walls 14 inches thick, with a deep concrete floor and an asbestos-lined ceiling.[177]

The re-opening attraction was *The British Army in Peace and War*. Early in the War, Shepherd was complaining of the difficulties it had caused in obtaining films from Europe and through the decline of British film production. When the Hepworth film *The Grip of Ambition* was shown at the Electric at the end of November 1914, the local paper cryptically added: 'a British production, observe'.[178] Shepherd bemoaned the fact that he could no longer be sure of what films would arrive and from early December 1914 advertisements and reports on presentations at the Electric are notable by their absence from the *Littlehampton Observer*.

It is significant that when the licence was renewed on 12 April 1915, it was not in Shepherd's name but in that of Maurice William Mansbridge, who remained a licensee until 1924. Shepherd reappears as licensee in April 1924 but died soon afterwards and the licence was transferred to his widow, Kate, on 3 November 1924. She continued to own and manage the Electric until 1929, her licence including Sundays from September 1925.[179]

197 *Above*. 'Fire at the Electric Palace Littlehampton—the picture screen shattered by force of explosion.' A postcard showing the fire damage on 14 August 1914.

198 *Right*. The Regent, Littlehampton, as a bingo hall in 1973. The entrance was through the doors in the Air Training Corps building to the right. A neon sign with the cinema's name is just visible suspended from the cornice half way along the side wall of the auditorium.

In 1929 she sold the Electric to the proprietors of the town's Palladium, H. Filer and S. Shinebaum. It was renamed the Regent in 1931.

By 1937 both Regent and Palladium were part of H. Filer's South Downs Cinemas chain which also operated properties at Bordon, Lee-on-Solent, Petersfield and Portsmouth. Being the oldest cinema and with only 650 seats, the Regent suffered from the competition posed by the larger Odeon and Palladium as well as from its location, on the edge of the town centre if opposite the railway station.

Almost inevitably, the Regent was the first to close as audiences plummeted and popular films were hard to obtain. It never dropped its afternoon performances and it became noted as the home of horror films, a policy which drew the younger element but paled after a while. In an attempt at economy, it played the same reissue films as the Palladium on Sundays but at different times, prints being bicycled between the two halls.

The Regent closed abruptly on Wednesday 25 May 1960 after a three-day run of a British drama *The Shakedown* supported by *Girl in the Woods*. It had advertised a three-day double bill presentation from the Thursday of *The Flying Fontaines* (the supporting feature at the Odeon Worthing the same week) and *Face of a Fugitive*, but would-be patrons arrived to find the cinema 'Closed until further notice'. A spokesman for South Downs Cinemas told the local paper, 'We are hoping this may be a temporary measure. The cinema has been closed because there is an acute shortage of films, insufficient to go round the three cinemas in Littlehampton. It might well be that the position could be remedied. Business has only been fair for some considerable time.' However, closing a cinema so abruptly in midweek suggests some unexplained crisis.

An alternative use for ailing cinemas had surfaced: bingo. South Downs Cinemas re-opened the property as the Regent Bingo and Social Club in June 1961 for the summer season. By January 1962, it was opening only on Fridays to cater for the reduced population in winter.

Bingo lasted until 1974. Then it became auctioneers' rooms for a while. Subsequently it has turned into Regent House, the premises of the Controlroom Manufacturing Company.

16 December 1912
Olympic Cinema Theatre/ Empire Theatre/Palladium
Church Street

This property began life on 16 March 1910 as the Olympic Hall Rink for roller skating, promoted by the Olympic Hall and Skating Rink Syndicate and built by Linfield and Sons of New Road, Littlehampton. Plans were in hand from the first to introduce a movable stage so that theatrical performances could also be presented during the summer season. Films were another part of the scheme but only infrequently, being presented for the first time for two nights only on Thursday and Friday 26 and 27 May 1910: 'The First Series of Animated Pictures Procurable depicting every incident in the Funeral of the Deeply Lamented King Edward VII'. The *Littlehampton Observer*

199 The Olympic Hall pictured on its opening as a skating rink in March 1910—the year new rinks were also opened at Bognor (Kursaal) and Chichester (Olympia). 'Built in two months' said the local paper.

Olympic Cinema Theatre,
CHURCH STREET, adjoining HIGH ST.,
LITTLEHAMPTON.

Proprietors—Olympic Hall Syndicate.
General Manager—Mr. G. E. Redman.

Opening Date—
MONDAY NEXT, DECEMBER 16th,
At 6 p.m.

Continuous Performance nightly, 6 till 10.30.
Popular Prices—3d., 6d. 9d.
Books of 12 tickets to any part of the house
issued at reduced prices.

Special Children's Matinee each Wednesday and
Saturday at 3.
The Lastest and Most Up-to-date Electric
Pictures, comprising Dramatic, Comic, Cowboy,
Travel, Scientific, and other subjects.

In December 1910, a series of films was shown for a week at the Olympic but it was to be two years before the Syndicate introduced moving pictures on a full-time basis, promising 'The Latest and Most Up-to-date Electric Pictures, comprising Dramatic, Comic, Cowboy, Travel, Scientific, and other subjects'. The hall had been fitted throughout with electricity and offered continuous performances nightly from 6 p.m. to 10.30 p.m. at popular prices of 3d., 6d. and 9d., with children's matinees on Wednesdays and Saturdays.[181]

Now known as the Olympic Cinema Theatre, it was opened on the Monday evening of 16 December 1912, a report appearing in the local newspaper two days later:

The entire building has undergone a complete change. A handsome plush fit-up replaces the usual stage proscenium, and the sheet is draped to fit the picture in a very artistic manner ... A small foyer has been added to the main entrance... Many more tip-up seats have been added, and these are all raised in sections, thereby affording patrons an uninterrupted view.

The opening programme was a strong one, including one of the finest feature films we have witnessed, *The Money Kings* ... The operating was practically noiseless and the picture is one of the steadiest we have seen and is of large dimensions. The music was also very appropriate and good. During the evening the theatre is at intervals sprayed with an antiseptic scent vapour, which is delightfully fragrant.[182]

200 Advertisement in the *Littlehampton Observer* on 11 December 1912 announcing the opening of the Olympic as a full-time cinema.

noted that there were 'crowded houses' for the 'very steady and clear picture' of the funeral in which the faces of the mourners, including the Duke of Norfolk, were 'easily distinguishable'. These images were supplemented by a film of aviators Paulhan and Grahame-White on their London to Manchester flight. There were two houses nightly and special matinees for children.[180]

201 Auditorium and stage of the Olympic, Littlehampton, *c*.1913.

202 The Palladium, Littlehampton, in 1973.

There were two changes of ownership the following year. The Dollar Film Company, a London concern, took over in late March and introduced vaudeville artistes, then six months later the business was bought by Charles L. Shepherd who had opened the Electric Picture Palace in the town in 1911.[183] He closed the Olympic to make a number of improvements, including the installation of a Pathé machine which gave a far steadier picture, and he renamed the building the Empire Picture Theatre when it re-opened on Thursday 2 October 1913 with the drama *The Wanderer Descends*, a comedy called *Tresses and Curls*, and the first episode of a twelve-part Edison serial, *What Happened to Mary*. He also added the bi-weekly Gaumont Gazette to his programmes.[184]

However, Shepherd's reign did not out-last the First World War, and by 1920 there had been yet another change of name, to Palladium. The new licensee was Joseph Marshall, on behalf of Littlehampton Palladium Limited, and his licence included Sunday opening from September 1925.[185]

Marshall was followed by Messrs. H. Filer and S. Shinebaum, who in 1929 also bought the Electric from Kate Shepherd. In the early 1930s, with 890 seats, the Palladium had occasional variety on its 20ft.-deep stage (there

were three dressing rooms). The Palladium and Electric were then operated by H. Filer alone, who made them part of his South Downs Cinemas chain from around 1935. They enjoyed a monopoly until the Odeon arrived in 1936.

The Palladium had a canopy with the name on the front and the word 'cinema' on the side attractively presented in stained glass; but externally it always looked rather like a drill hall with an unornamented frontage. Inside it became very old-fashioned with its long, narrow, barrel-vaulted auditorium and small balcony seating 125.

Nevertheless, the Palladium outlived not only the Electric but the relatively modern Odeon-turned-Classic and eventually became part of a small chain run by Myles Byrne. It then passed to other hands and plans were put forward to convert the building into a multi-purpose leisure centre, turning the stalls floor to a night club, bingo hall and restaurant while extending the balcony slightly to create a 180-seat cinema. There were several objections and an outline application was submitted to replace the building with flats.

The Palladium closed on 28 September 1986 and was sold to a property developer. Demolition followed before the year's end to make way for flats.

23 MAY 1936
ODEON/CLASSIC
HIGH STREET

The only major circuit cinema in Littlehampton was constructed in a central position on the site of The Lodge, which had been an imposing private residence, latterly home of the local branch of the Constable brewing family. It was pulled down in 1930 and the site was later acquired by Oscar Deutsch for another of his Odeon cinemas. The plans by cinema specialist Andrew Mather were submitted on 1 July 1935 and the building was constructed at a cost of £20,792.[186]

The Odeon had a staid exterior in stone with urns mounted on the front edges to either side of a curved recess above the entrance and canopy. This section was flanked by a lower line of shops to each side and vertical Odeon signs were mounted on the sides of the recess, the letters fitting between horizontal grooves. Above the canopy and in front of the recess, an Odeon sign was mounted on a slab which had a frieze in classical idiom. The three Odeon signs were lit up by neon at night while the recess and main sign were flood lit from the top of the canopy. The cinema may have been a scheme inherited from another promoter as it was not designed in the circuit house style

203 The Odeon in Littlehampton, 1936. The shop units are temporarily covered by advertising for the grand opening of the cinema.

like, for example, the Odeon Well Hall, South-East London, which had opened three days earlier and came from the same architect's practice.

At Littlehampton, there was a spacious foyer with a staircase on one side leading up to the balcony which, with 532 seats, unusually had more seats than the stalls. In fact, the balcony scarcely overlapped the stalls, being largely positioned over the foyer, and so the stalls floor area was not that extensive, with only 438 seats, making a total of 970.

The auditorium was plain but pleasant, relying primarily on concealed lighting of the ceiling to illuminate the auditorium during intervals (there were no chandeliers or laylights). The illustration shows the striking screen tabs with which the cinema opened and indicates how far back the screen was set until CinemaScope required it to be brought forward in the 1950s so that the ends of the wide picture could be seen from the side seats. Odeon clocks were mounted over the front side exits and the floors exhibited the circuit design of carpet with its distinctive art deco pattern.

As the most modern and best equipped cinema in town, the Odeon charged more than its two rivals, with the cheapest seats costing 9d. as opposed to 6d. The Odeon and Palladium both had 2s. as their highest price while the Regent went no higher than 1s. 6d., reflecting its lesser status.

With the advantage of strong circuit releases, the Odeon did well enough in the holiday season but had to struggle during the rest of the year. In the 1930s, the town's population was 10,181—very low out of season to support three cinemas with a total of 2,300 seats.

After the Regent had closed, the Odeon and Palladium relied on a town population that was now 16,220 as its immediate source of patronage during the non-holiday months. The film shortage that had killed off the Regent plagued the Odeon and Palladium as in 1963 it was reported that they had played no less than 25 reissue programmes between them. In 1964, the Odeon played big hits like *Lawrence of Arabia*, *A Hard Day's Night* and *Goldfinger* for two weeks apiece.

In December 1967, the Odeon became one of 49 marginal cinemas taken over from the Rank Organisation by Classic Cinemas in

204 The foyer of the Odeon, Littlehampton, in 1936.

205 Auditorium of the Littlehampton Odeon in 1936. Note the way the screen is set well back on the stage behind highly decorative screen tabs.

weekly batches. Classic immediately gave the cinema its own circuit name, placing a small vertical sign in front of the frieze above the canopy. The outline of the letters of the Odeon name remained clearly visible where they had been plucked from higher up on the outer sides of the frontage.

Classic soon introduced bingo on some nights of the week, retaining films on the others. Strip lights were suspended from the ceiling to provide the brighter illumination necessary for seeing the bingo cards.

According to the *Littlehampton Post* (11 May 1974) there had been plans to convert the property into a triple cinema, disco and bingo hall. But the newspaper reported that Victor Freeman, who ran the former Odeon Bognor Regis as the Regal Cinema and the Theatre Royal in Bognor as a bingo hall, was negotiating to take over the Classic. He succeeded and it went straight over to bingo, the last film (*The Belstone Fox*) being shown on Friday 31 May or Saturday 1 June 1974 (sources vary). It opened the following day as the Regal Bingo Club.

Bingo lasted several years, then the building was demolished in 1984 to be replaced by shops.

206 The Odeon in Littlehampton, known as the Classic in 1973.

Addenda: Littlehampton

A recollection exists of a visit at eight years of age to 'the cinematograph' at the Drill Hall in Pier Road in what must have been 1896 or 1897.[187]

A photograph (reproduced in Chapter 4) shows the Old Barn Theatre in the High Street, demolished *c.*1897, with a large notice advertising 'Animated Pictures'.[188]

Harry Joseph, who had started entertaining audiences in Littlehampton in the early 1890s, opened his Kursaal, a combined fun palace and pierrot theatre, in Pier Road near the Arun Mill in 1912, on a site later to be developed by Butlin's. On 17 February 1913 he took out a cinematograph licence for the Kursaal to show films as an adjunct to the theatre, music and dancing. By 1915 the Assembly Rooms and the Pagoda Pavilion were also screening some films.[189]

After the closure of the town's last cinema in 1986, films were not to be seen anywhere publicly until it was decided to introduce them at the Windmill Theatre at the Green in Windmill Road on a part-time basis around the live events. This building started out as a 'shelter hall' in 1912 but by 1927 it had become exclusively a theatre, organised by Charles Dore, the entertainments manager for Littlehampton U.D.C. It was refurbished and renamed the Western Pavilion in 1968 and became the Windmill Theatre in 1973, incorporating a restaurant.

In 1989, the control box was enlarged to take new projection equipment at a cost of around £37,000. Films were to be shown 22 weeks of the year, and the first presentation was the Hollywood comedy *Working Girl* on 5 May. Cinema has now spread to around thirty-two weeks of the year and the seventh anniversary of film shows was celebrated on 5 May 1996 with a special display of quad posters for sale, public visits during the morning to the projection box, and the presentation of three Harrison Ford films (*Indiana Jones and the Last Crusade*, *The Fugitive* and *Clear and Present Danger*) at 1989 prices. As a cinema, the Windmill has 252 seats.

MIDHURST

BY 1910
PUBLIC HALL/ELECTRIC/
CINEMATOGRAPH THEATRE
TOWN HALL CINEMA/ORION
NORTH STREET

The Midhurst Public Hall and Assembly Rooms were built in the Queen Anne style from the designs of William Buck of Horsham and opened in February 1882. A bold and ornate piece of architecture with a distinctive spirelet, it contained a hall 70ft. by 35ft., capable of seating 700, with a platform at the west end.[190]

Although its history of showing films can be traced back to the very birth of cinema in the county, and although it was to remain in cinema use for over half a century, the building would always look like a public hall and retain a flat floor and galleries on three sides.

Miss Maggie Morton, whose company had provided Christmas theatricals in Chichester, Bognor, Midhurst and Petersfield since the early 1890s, brought her pantomime *Blue Beard* to the Public Hall for the two nights of Tuesday 29 and Wednesday 30 December 1896, having played at the Corn Exchange in Chichester over the Christmas period. As part of this

207 An early postcard view of, on the right, the Public Hall in Midhurst, with its spirelet and clock, one of the county's first venues for moving pictures.

167

208 Advertisement for films at the Public Hall from the *Midhurst Times* of 3 October 1913.

Electric Pictures
— AT THE —
PUBLIC HALL, MIDHURST.
☞ CONTINUOUS SHOW.   6.45 to 10.30
TO-NIGHT *(Friday)* and TO-MORROW *(Saturday)*
The Favourite Son
ALSO A GOOD SELECTION OF OTHER FILMS.
October 9th, 10th & 11th
The Lion Hunters
BY GAUMONT.
A Graphic Film showing how a mother was saved from the Lions. Without doubt this is one of the best wild animal films of the year. The story is a thrilling one.
AND OTHER HIGH CLASS FILMS.
PRICES OF ADMISSION: 3d., 6d. and 1/-
MATINEES on SATURDAYS at 2.30 (Children 2d.)

209 The Public Hall, on the far right, pictured in 1921, with posters advertising Fox News and other films.

production, she introduced two crowded houses to the first animated pictures to be seen in Midhurst, a set of shorts comparable to those exciting great interest in London at the Empire, Alhambra and Crystal Palace.[191]

There were at least two exhibitions of living pictures at the Public Hall during 1897—Mr. P.M. Short bringing his Kinematographe for one evening on Wednesday 25 August and Lieutenant Walter Cole showing the Queen's Jubilee Procession on the Animatograph for one night on Tuesday 7 September.

There is little in the local press to suggest that in the next few years film shows were anything other than occasional and irregular entries in the programme of entertainments at the Hall. Indeed, in 1899 there would seem to be no exhibition of films, even though Cole again appeared, with a variety show, in September. The Walford Family Company from Redhill visited Midhurst for one night in August 1902, using three Cinematographs in conjunction to show films of the end of the Boer War and the acclamation of Edward VII and Queen Alexandra. Yet in 1904 there are again no advertisements or reports of visits by cinematograph companies. Single evening productions by London theatrical and vaudeville companies, performances by the local Snowdrop Minstrels and the Midhurst Choral Society, musical concerts and a Christmas pantomime, the occasional Café Chantant, and political meetings formed the basis of entertainments provided at the Public Hall in this period.[192]

However, the building does seem to have become a cinema by 1910, when it was being managed by one C.J. Bowyer.

An advertisement and article in the *Midhurst Times* on 28 March 1913 announced an innovation by the Midhurst Cinema Company:

Pictures at the Public Hall. Moving pictures are quite a craze in almost every town and now Midhurst is possessed of that sort of entertainment. Last evening was the initial show of a series of Gaumont films by the Midhurst Cinema Company. The pictures were highly appreciated by a large audience. They will be shown every Thursday, Friday and Saturday at 6 p.m. and 8.30 p.m., and there will be a matinee at 2.30 on Saturday afternoons, when children will be admitted at the low price of 2d.

The first programme of Gaumont offerings included the western drama *Garrison Triangle*, the 'screaming comedy' *Lucky Lobster*, and 'a trick film', *Roscambole's Gloves*, supported by an 'interesting and instructive' nature film. There was to be a constant change of programme and adults were admitted for 3d., 6d. and 1s.

The style of advertisements changed later in the year when they were headed 'Electric Pictures', anticipating a change in name—for in the *Kelly's Directory* for 1922 the hall is listed as the Midhurst Electric Cinema.

The licensee from 20 September 1923 was James Carson, who lived at The Nook. Under his proprietorship it became known as the Cinematograph Theatre. The licence was transferred on 14 May 1925 to Arthur Augustus Scrase who continued to operate the cinema as the Electric, for many years in partnership with G. Tozer.

Mr. Scrase was obliged to spend heavily on alterations and improvements in 1936 in order to meet the requirements of the County Architect. Even so, half the balcony had to be closed and seating was restricted to 60 in the other half. The total seating capacity was reduced from 550 seats to 450. Other stipulations limited the scope of live performances. Scrase complained to the magistrates about the effect on his business, but to no avail.

On 30 September 1938, the licence was transferred to Harry Percival Evelyn Mears of Wimborne Road, Bournemouth. He operated a small chain of cinemas called Moderne Cinema Properties, based in Bournemouth. It was now known as the Town Hall Cinema and substantial modernisation seems to have occurred as the original 18ft. proscenium width became 35ft., seating was reduced to 380, and a café was now attached. The foyer gained a modern rubberoid floor.

The business was sold to Cranfield Cinemas on 17 August 1943. Plans were immediately submitted for alterations and, despite the war, the building closed for a month to allow the work to be carried out. The old operator's box and the rewinding room were removed, the hall was further modernised, and reseating increased the capacity to 560.

Sunday opening, which had been denied the cinema in the inter-war period, was granted in September 1943 for the duration of the War and as long as troops were quartered in the neighbourhood.

The Town Hall Cinema was renamed the Orion in 1947 when seating had apparently jumped to 750, no doubt in response to the post-war boom in cinema attendances. The cinema also offered a 25ft.-deep stage, two dressing rooms, while the café was now styled a restaurant.

FORTHCOMING CINEMA ATTRACTIONS

210 The Orion, Midhurst, in July 1961, a year before its closure.

In April 1949, Cranfield Cinemas obtained a licence for Sunday films at Midhurst, initially from 2.30 p.m. to 10 p.m. but after 1954 from 2.15 p.m. to 9.45 p.m.

The growth of television ownership eventually took its toll on the number of admissions, and in November 1957 the Secretary of Cranfield Cinemas wrote to the Clerk of the Justices at Midhurst asking for a reduction in the £1 per week charged in respect of Sunday opening 'in view of the big drop in attendances, and the continued falling off in cinema patronage'. He noted that attendances at the Orion in Midhurst for the 10 weeks ending 9 November 1957 had dropped to 10,564 compared with 15,055 for the same period in 1956.[193]

A major attraction could temporarily reverse the trend. In 1958, the Orion played *The Bridge on the River Kwai* to full houses every night, and this would be remembered as its biggest box-office hit, at least of later years.

An advertisement for June 1960 shows the Orion offering continuous daily performances from 4.45 p.m. with prices at 2s., 2s. 9d., 3s. 3d. and 3s. 9d. A Children's Cinema Club was held every Saturday at 1.45 p.m.. The building had by this time been partly painted and fitted with illuminated signs, giving it a more modern image.[194]

However, the cinema was now up for sale at £15,000 to include fittings although in August 1960 Cranfield Cinemas announced: 'News flash! If the increased patronage that we have enjoyed this past three months is maintained—*this theatre will not close.*' But attendances in the winter of 1961-62 were particularly bad and the cinema remained for sale, although the asking price was reduced to £12,000. It was sold to new owners who took over the site on 1 October 1962.

The Orion closed on Saturday 15 September 1962 on the last night of a three-day run of the British comedy *Twice Round the Daffodils* supported by *Candidate for Murder* with one show each evening, doors opening at 6 p.m. The final press advertisement is the nicest the authors have ever seen for such a melancholy occasion: below a heading 'ORION MIDHURST announcing THE END' came the final film programmes and then:

The Cast (Orion Cinema) Manager Walter Gay; Chief Projectionist Terry Lewis; Relief Projectionist Arthur Lane; Cashier Joan Naldrett; 1st Usherette Margaret Lewis; 2nd Usherette Rosemary Evans; Relief Usherette Audrey Edwards; Dear Mrs. Mopp Florence Lewis. We wish you all good health and good fortune. A very warm welcome awaits you from Our Friends at the Rex Haslemere— Savoy Petersfield—Granada Chichester.

This historic building was demolished in 1966 for a supermarket, originally an International store, now Gateway, but in the Spring 1989 issue of the *Midhurst Magazine* (vol. 3, no. 1) Alec Annand recalled the Orion in the early 1950s in an article 'Gas, Flicks and Forge':

Many are those who regret the passing of the Orion Cinema (now Gateways), where so many did their courting under cover of 'the flicks', where as the war-poet Alun Lewis put it, 'Peace was the back seat in the cinema'. To 'Flossie', now a grandmother, who started her first job at fourteen straight from school as an usherette, 18/6 a week was a reasonable wage; she felt quite important in her green and orange uniform, pressed every afternoon (there were no matinees, just two performances, 4 p.m. to 9). Films were shorter then, and changed every three days—except Laurence Olivier in *Henry V*, the sensation of its day. 'Flossie's' pin-up, however, was not Olivier, but a cowboy actor called Ronald Reagan, especially in *Kings Row*; she got Norman, her boy-friend, who worked the film projector, to get her a big photo of Ronald Reagan to hang over her bed. 'I dreamed of no-one else for years: he really was good-looking.' The projector always broke down at least once a fortnight; the audience were then given complimentary tickets and invited to return next day. Music was provided by records played from the projection box. People came in all the time, and often sat through the performance twice. Each Tuesday evening the old men came in from Budgenor Lodge and sat in the side seats on the left. The Orion Cinema provided the only form of night entertainment except for pubs available in Midhurst. How are the mighty fallen: no cinema now in Midhurst, nor in Haslemere, nor in Chichester!

PETWORTH

Born in 1903 at Barnsgate Farm, Byworth—a small hamlet about one mile south-east of Petworth—Tom Stanley Collins is the key figure in the history of cinema in the town. He placed a highly detailed 12-part account of much of his career in the *Bulletin* of The Petworth Society (no. 28, June 1982, to no. 42, December 1985) and the following slightly revised extracts are reproduced with the kind permission of his daughters, Annette and Jeannette Collins, and the editor, Peter Jerrome. They are lengthy but they do give a very rare detailed account of running a small cinema.

Collins began by describing an early obsession with films that led him to start a private cinema with a hand-wound 35mm projector in the cellar of his home. Still a schoolboy, he would provide an hour-long programme on Saturday evenings for which he would charge a halfpenny admission to include a chocolate drop and small glass of weak lemonade.

He recalled:

There was a travelling cinema show once a week at the Swan Assembly Rooms and I made myself known to the owner. His name was [Arthur] Barrett, and [he] travelled around the villages during the week to give one nightly show to each. I told him I would like to help him in any way possible. [...] He told me he wanted somebody to look after the portable generating plant, only somebody a bit more mature than I. This plant was housed and bolted down on the floor of a large Buick van with a canvas roof which

had been used as a Red Cross Ambulance during the 1914/18 War. [...] I told him I knew what a film projector was like as I already owned a small home 35mm model. However, I really convinced him that he should give me a trial and that I would work for the first week with no pay. [...]

My duties were from 7 p.m. to 10 p.m. each evening by keeping the 5hp two stroke engine running at constant speed by a hand-controlled throttle, also to keep the oil drip feed glass container reasonably filled, adjusted so that the engine did not have too little or too much lubrication. [...] I travelled to Pulborough, Storrington, Billingshurst and cycled home after the show each evening. I did not go to Steyning as cycling that distance in the winter months was much too far. I did not know what my wage packet would be until after my first week's work. But as Saturday came I was given fifteen shillings, so my weekly earnings amounted to twenty-five shillings [Collins earned ten shillings a week as a car mechanic during the day], a lot of cash to be able to earn at my age in those

211 Outside the Swan Room Picture Palace at Petworth. Miss Mabel Golds is seated front. The date is before the First World War.

212 Arthur Barrett's travelling cinema in 1920. The van is parked in North Street opposite the *Wheatsheaf* public house. Mr. Barrett (right); the Whitcomb family on the left.

days. Within the next two or three weeks I got used to everything ... there were times I helped to dismantle the projector and stand, also the portable operating box mounted on to the stage in each village hall. This projector was of French design, made by the famous Pathé Frères. This was a small machine with motor attached and ran as sweet and quiet as a grandfather clock. At the rear of the stand under the lamp house was a controlled studded arc resistance with an amp meter attached. The volt meter I had in the van. The lamp house was held in position by a couple of thumbscrews to a fixed focus position. The carbons were of low intensity type. Mr. Barrett informed me this was one of three travelling cinemas in the country operating and making their own electricity.

Collins later went to live with his grandmother in Whetstone, near Finchley, and worked in Pimlico. Every Saturday evening he went to the Grand Hall cinema in Finchley and had soon gained access to the operating box. There he helped out three nights a week and gained some complimentary tickets. When he moved into bed and breakfast accommodation at Wandsworth Common, South London, he obtained an evening job as a rewind boy at the Lavender Hill Pavilion, earning 5s. a week.

He returned to Petworth when his parents agreed to buy him a car so that he could set up a taxi business. At this time the Swan Room in the *Swan Hotel* was being run as the Pictorium cinema on Thursdays, Fridays and Saturdays by Mr. A.N. Pillans and his wife (Arthur Barrett, the previous operator, had only hired the hall on Saturdays). Collins drove the Pillans to and from church on Sundays. One day he was invited in for a cup of coffee by Mr. Pillans.

As we all three sat down, Mr. Pillans broke the silence and his first words to me were, Would I like to take over his cinema concern? I had to ask him again because I couldn't believe what he said to me. They both repeated the question. My hand holding the cup became somewhat unsteady from excitement and it seemed ages to me before I was able to give them an answer. [...] The reason why they wanted to dispose of their cinema enterprise was that Mrs. Pillans, a French lady, wanted to return to Bournemouth as she did not like the country life. We discussed the proposition and the price for the going concern. The Pillans would accept a figure of £250, this price to include a Powers No. 6 projector and 12ft.-13½ft. spools, a lamphouse with arc and the usual resistances, a quantity of red plush tip-up seats, a screen, some curtains, carpets, a Kelvin generating plant, a switchboard and some outside still frames and poster boards. All this together with a short lease based on a quarterly tenancy by Trust Houses Ltd. at the *Swan Hotel*. [*Kelly's Directory* for 1915 shows the 'owners', i.e. landlords, as Home Counties Public House Trust Co. Ltd.]

With his parents' support, Collins bought the cinema operation and was accepted as the new tenant although, as he was under 21 and not old enough to hold a cinema licence, his father stood as proxy for him.

I shall never forget my first opening night. I wanted to do the operating myself to save expense. I started up the Kelvin plant, cutting the arc in, and lacing up the projector for the very first time. It seemed all was in readiness to start the show. Unfortunately, I laced up the projector with the film inside out. It looked perfect on the screen but when the title of the film came on one would have to read it as though you were looking

CINEMA

through a mirror. However, it didn't take me long to find my mistake. The arc control I had little trouble with as I had some experience before, but only having one projector we had to stop to change reels. Fortunately, with a Powers No. 6 machine, the square boxes could take a double reel spliced together which would last approximately twenty minutes. The time taken to replace with another spool of film would be approximately two minutes. Our patrons were quite used to this inconvenience. The two-reel comedies, serials, etc. could be projected non-stop.

Film travellers seemed to call every day. [...] One or two film companies offered complete programmes consisting of cartoon, serial, two-reel comedy and main feature. We did not play a newsreel at this time. A programme lasted for about two and a quarter hours and as it finished just before 10pm this enabled our patrons to catch their buses from the Square.

The films came in transit boxes by train to Pulborough Station and then by branch line to Petworth Station, to be brought up usually in the station bus. There were times when our films arrived late, giving us about five minutes to unpack and spool up. What a scramble this was to get the next reel of film mounted up ready for the projector. [...]

Our weekly programmes consisted of the following. Monday: a free night. Tuesday: a whist drive. Wednesday: a dance comprised of a piano and drums, and sometimes a banjo thrown in. Thursday/Friday/Saturday: the cinema. The seating comprised Bentwood chairs coupled together by battens in lots of five for easy moveability. The better class seats were red tip up ones mounted onto a raised platform. This assembly hall had a seating capacity for about 150 but no standing room was allowed as we only had a centre gangway. The heating was very primitive, by two open-type fireplaces using coal as fuel. Unfortunately, the flickering flames caused some reflection onto the screen, so we changed over to coke, only to find that our patrons were being choked by the fumes. With these fumes mixed with tobacco smoke, it was not a very nice mixture for anyone to sit through for a two-hour period. The small electric fan in the centre of the ceiling did little to improve this situation. We had to think of some other means to heat the place and decided to buy two gas fires and through fitting metal hoods to each fireplace this proved successful. The early patrons always made a quick dash for seats near the warmth.

The screen size was approximately 10ft. by 6ft. with a black surround, but it had no screen tabs. I thought I could add this later on. The operating box outside the building was made of corrugated iron, with a sheet metal

floor, suspended on 12ft. 6in. x 4in. wooden pylons. This enabled us to project through the large window of the hall. In the winter the operators, and I was one of them, just froze and had to wear an overcoat with our hands on the lamp house to try and keep warm for lacing up the machine. In the summer it was none other than a sweat box, so it was going from one extreme to another. [...]

During one weekend [a friend] suggested that we should brighten up a bit by fitting up two large glass electrical fittings the same as one could see for street lighting in the larger towns. After two weekends, we had this fitted up with two 200 watt lamps in each. This was something for the town to see—so different from the old gas burners and fittings sited on every street corner. This lighting was a good advertisement—people would come out at night to see the glare and it really put the cinema on the map. Business started to improve and more local people were becoming cinema-minded, especially with the bigger type of films. I introduced some sound effects, such as rolling peas on a drum to represent rain, shaking a large piece of sheet metal for thunder, letting the air escape from an old lorry car tyre to represent a steam loco, always with a foot pump handy to keep the pressure up, and half a coconut shell tapping on a piece of wood representing horse hoofs at a gallop. All this made such great fun.

During one hot summer morning, the hotel manager wanted to see me in his office. I expected a complaint from him with regard to our engine noise at night, but this was not so. He surprised me by asking if I would be prepared to give up Saturday evening's performance during the summer months on alternate weeks from Easter to mid-September so that he could use the hall for coach parties when required for catering. I told him that a Saturday night was usually my best take, although in summer it was not so good unless wet. The Saturday matinee, of course, would not be affected. He went on to say that I would be paid compensation to cover any losses. I hesitated to give an answer but I could see he was working under instructions from head office, which made things very difficult for me. Having a short lease with a quarterly tenancy, I had a feeling it would be better if I agreed. Fortunately, my programmes were booked on a flat rate so there was no bother with the renters. This arrangement did not last long. I received a letter giving me three months' notice to quit the Hall, so this really put paid to my first cinema project. Not only had I lost my ingoing cash but everything that went with it. The trouble was finding another suitable hall in Petworth.

The Petworth Pictorium cinema closed in 1924.

FORTHCOMING CINEMA ATTRACTIONS

1926
CINEMA HALL/ELECTRIC CINEMA/ PICTUREDROME
POUND STREET

Stanley Collins continued:

So Petworth had no cinema. I was only hoping that one day something would turn up. In the meantime, to keep my hand in, I gave my services by operating at the Midhurst Cinema some six miles away, travelling back and forth on my Norton motor cycle. I was paid my travelling expenses both ways. [...]

It was almost eighteen months to the day before I was able to find a piece of building land, measuring some 30ft. by 70ft., leasehold with a yard in the front to take about eight cars or a lorry or two, situated on the junction of the Chichester and Midhurst roads. This position was not altogether a desirable one but it made a start for something bigger. I made my own plans and presented them to the Council for approval. They were accepted, as most tradesmen in the town wanted a cinema again, to bring back the lost villagers from outlying districts.

The cinema is referred to in the *Midhurst Times* in April 1926 as the Cinema Hall and later as the Electric Cinema but these may not have been real names, just a generic title. However, in the *Midhurst Times* dated 21 January 1927, it is referred to as the Picturedrome in connection with a special showing in two parts of a French production of *Les Misérables*.

Stanley Collins recalled:

This hall was 55ft. long by 22ft. wide leaving a 4 ft. pathway each side of the building for exits. It was constructed of gal-iron corrugated sheeting with sheet asbestos lining, with a wooden framing approx. 12ft. to the eaves and 17ft. to the ridge, built on brick surrounds with 1 in. T and G flooring. It gave seating for 180 people. The ground rent was £25 per annum with a 25 year lease. The operating box was attached to the outside of the building, approximately 6ft. from the ground and, being lined with asbestos plain sheets, it was much warmer than the previous one we had in the Town. A small shed 8ft. by 7ft. housed a 6hp Douglas twin engine direct coupled to a 4 kw dynamo previously used for searchlight work during the later part of World War One. The Powers No. 6 projector, seats, carpets, curtains, came out of store; instead of using ordinary wooden chairs, I was able to buy some plush running seating on iron standards to seat about ten persons for each block.

QUEUE HERE

To heat the hall we installed two large combustion stoves totally enclosed. This saved any trouble with flames flickering. [...] The early patrons made a dash to sit near the stoves and some of them nearly scorched themselves by pulling the running seating as close as possible. There was only the centre gangway and no standing room was allowed. An 18 inch electric ventilation fan I fitted at the back of the hall to draw the foul air and tobacco smoke away, but the trouble I found with this was that it also drew out the warm air. During the summer months I reversed the running of the motor to draw the cool air in, but this arrangement didn't please those sitting at the back on the raised platform who paid 1/10d [9 pence today] to use the plush tip up seats: they complained of the cold air piercing down their necks, so I fitted two oscillating 12 in. fans, one for each side of the hall, with a sliding resistance fitted to the large fan for just ticking over. The screen size was a little larger than our previous one at the Swan Rooms, measuring 12ft. x 7ft. with a black surround with screen tabs, worked either by me or by the usherette.

My younger sister played the piano but I took over some evenings to relieve her when I had extra part-time help with the projection work. [...] We introduced lucky seat numbers taken from the numbers of admission tickets sold and scratched three or more numbers onto a black slide to show on the screen during the interval session. Those holding the lucky numbers were given a complimentary ticket each for a free seat during the following week. Serials kept our patrons together through wet, fog, or ice—they didn't want to miss an episode. I gave them what they wanted, serials such as *Elmo the Mighty*, *The Sacred Flame*, *The Perils of Pauline* and many others to follow on. [...]

I found it was such a tie for my sister Margaret to be playing each night. [...] Advertised in our local paper there was a pianola attachment for sale. This was an instrument that could be fitted over the keyboard of a piano with music rolls propelled and worked by one's feet. I went along to see it and decided at once this was just the thing we wanted. I bought it for £5, together with a number of music rolls: each roll would last about ten minutes or one could extend this time by pedalling a little slower. The only trouble was when rewinding a roll one could hear the noise it made practically all over the hall, so we usually rewound the rolls during the interval. Our patrons didn't mind because they had music by mechanical means with no mistakes which did happen at times with any pianist through tiredness being so near the screen. Certainly the pianola was a godsend as Tom, Dick or Harry could play the thing after a little tuition. All one had to do was to pedal away for two and a half hours.

213 The Picturedrome, Petworth, 1930, showing two American films, *Interference* and *The Case of Lena Smith*, released in the UK in 1929.

By 1930, talking pictures had arrived. Stanley Collins installed sound-on-disc equipment, making his own amplifier. There were problems in synchronising the sound, played from a disc, with the image on the film running separately through the projector.

Improvements were made to the outside appearance of the cinema:

> I had the idea of building a false front to eliminate the front apex of the cinema's pitched roof... I made a large wooden sign about 25ft. by 2ft. long with the words PICTUREDROME painted in red, and also fitted the two large electric glass bowl fittings over the top which we had previously used at the *Swan Hotel*. We [had] also built a small glass canopy over the entrance doors which we replaced with large glass panels to give extra light to our small foyer and fixed a crash barrier in front of the box office made from iron water pipes and cemented this into the floor. This unique contraption, painted in aluminium, saved the front of the flimsy box office from caving in when everybody rushed forward to be first in. All this improvement was accomplished during the summer months, but no planning was ever thought of, still less permission from the Council to do these alterations and additions to the property. With the coming of talkies we decided to run extra performances but only with the bigger films that we were able to book.

When sound-on-disc was discontinued in favour of soundtracks printed alongside the image on the film itself, Collins could only afford the cheap Imperial system, obtained from a small firm in the Midlands:

> This comprised an electric cell mounted inside the drum and connected to a pre-stage amplifier conveniently fixed onto the wall between two projectors. For the showing of sound-on-film we had to mask out the right hand top corner of the screen to eliminate the sound repluses and this reduced the screen width by about one foot. Our equipment now consisted of the following: two Kalee No. 7 projectors, with Kalee type arc lamps, low intensity arcs and Tandem resistances to supply the two arcs and a slide lantern on a stand. As all this equipment was installed in the 10ft. by 8ft. operating box we found it difficult to move around when two persons were working together.

Collins was forced to widen the box by 4ft. Another problem was that hailstones or heavy rain could be heard hitting the gal-iron roof, which had only thin asbestos sheets underneath to form the ceiling. Tarring and sanding the roof helped, but then the tar would melt in hot weather and clog the rainwater gutters.

The cinema was closed on Sundays and Collins knew that he had little chance of being

allowed to open then if he applied for permission. On Saturdays, he rented a large shed in which to store safely the cycles used by many young people who rode in from the outlying villages, charging two pence a time, half of which went to the attendant. Some of the bicycle lamps were borrowed and kept alight to warm up the box-office for the cashier as this was outside the hall.

One day, two of the directors of a cinema circuit based in the Portsmouth area came to Petworth to explore the idea of building a new cinema there. Collins knew that he had to find a site before they did and he arranged to see Lord Leconfield, who owned most of the area. Leconfield offered unsuitable land too far out of town, but Collins spotted a better location while looking from his present cinema at the Midhurst Road opposite. Set on the brow of a

hill, this contained eleven allotments and a house owned by his lordship who agreed to sell the space, 88ft. long by 33ft. wide, for £700, provided that the house was retained for private use. In September 1936, Collins submitted plans (which he 'more or less' drew up himself) to the Council which were approved after several modifications. Next came a 25-year mortgage from a Bognor Regis building society. A builder from Tillington called Boxall was engaged to construct the new cinema.

The Picturedrome closed when the new cinema was ready. In its final years, it had given one performance nightly except for Saturdays when it ran continuously. Seat prices had ranged from 9d. to 1s. 9d. The cinema's site is now occupied by part of the garage at the roundabout where Pound Street meets Midhurst Road.

An Evening at the Cinema

Recollections of the Picturedrome in the twenties and thirties are published in the *Petworth Society Magazine* (No. 84, June 1996).

The memories come crowding in. Free from school on Saturdays, several of us in the afternoon would gather outside the somewhat flimsy box office, clutching our sixpences, the price of admission, with maybe a few extra pennies for sweets or crisps. Films would only be shown if there were sufficient prospective audience, I think the minimum number was twelve. There were rarely too few, and how we enjoyed it—especially the serials, which always left off at a real cliff hanger leaving us all agog until the following Saturday to wonder if the Hero, having been firmly tied down in the path of an oncoming train, would be rescued in time, or the Heroine, lost in the jungle, would be found before the prowling leopard reached her! Such excitement! The only sound was the piano, played by a competent pianist, on whom depended the entire success of the atmosphere.

Suiting the melodies to the dramas being enacted on the screen, they would be soft, smooth and romantic for tender scenes, rapid crescendo for moments of intense excitement, or solemn crashing chords for those of fear and danger! It was really very clever. I, being taught the piano at that time, hoped I would be able to model my playing on the performance of that maestro!

Films were shown every evening, the main feature being changed at mid-week. My mother and I would go together, usually once a week. Seats then cost (in pre-decimal currency) ninepence, one shilling and threepence, or one shilling and ninepence. We would have to wrap up warmly in winter, for the heating was minimal, our feet would get stone cold, but we would not have missed it for anything.

There was a heightened sense of anticipation—an almost magical air of mystery and romance about those old silent films, and when the 'Talkies' first arrived, the audiences were handed a paper on leaving the cinema and asked to 'vote' for their preference, by ticking either the silent or talking space indicated. I remember thinking that talking would spoil it all, and marked my paper accordingly. However, voices won! How could they not? Since which time, sophisticated sound has reached astonishing and deafening levels. Even the youngest of us will not be here, but one wonders what the next one hundred years have in store!

Then, sometime in the early thirties, our new 'proper' cinema was built near the bottom of the Midhurst road. It was real luxury compared to the former somewhat makeshift one, and was enjoyed by all for years. It is alas, no more, TV took over, and it eventually became the Youth Centre and swimming pool.

Marjorie Alix

6 May 1937
Regal
Midhurst Road

Stanley Collins has described the later stages of construction:

We were now in the first week of April 1937 and had to decide soon on our first opening date. This was not an easy thing to do, because there were so many little things still to be finished, such as the fixing of the outside display cabinets, installing the ticket machine, electric lamp fittings for the foyer and the underside of the canopy, front entrance door mats with wells to take them, lino tiles for the lobby and cloaks. The large illuminated hall clock I made and installed myself using the wall for numerals to be mounted on. The hands I made from very thin aluminium. A number of willing helpers came to our aid to break up barrel loads of brickbats, large stones, and every bit of rubble we could find to make a car park. We had only the use of a hand roller.

We seemed to have covered everything except to find a name for our new hall. So after some family discussions we decided to call it The Regal being in remembrance of their Majesties' Coronation. The large red metal neon sign was proudly erected 25ft. high on the front elevation, making it an imposing symbol for many to admire and see.

All we had to do now was to fix a firm date for the opening night. We made it May 6th and had only now to allow for the advertising. I made a number of double crown poster boards and fixed them up around the town with a certain number for the outside villages. I eventually wrote to RKO Radio Pictures Ltd., informing them of my opening date and saying that the proceeds of the night's takings would be devoted to the repair of St Mary's Church organ. They were quite willing to supply me with a suitable and complete programme, and enclosed a list for me to choose from. I was fortunate enough to acquire the film *Swing Time* with Fred Astaire and Ginger Rogers. The rest of the programme was made up with a Pathé Pictorial, comedy, cartoon, for a two-hour programme, all with no charge. I soon got to work again with fifty colour double crown posters and a four page programme.

The head gardener of Petworth House (and later television gardening expert) Fred Streeter carried out, at Lady Leconfield's request, the planting of flowering shrubs and fruit trees to each side of the cinema's borders. A floral arrangement for the stage on the opening Thursday evening was also arranged by Streeter.

Lady Leconfield addressed the opening night audience, declaring that it was 'great fun' to open a cinema but admitting, 'I rarely go to see a film other than those I have taken myself in many different parts of the world'. However, she hoped that everyone in the district would patronise 'the flicks' at the Regal. Although much of the audience consisted of invited guests, some seats had been sold to the public and £20 was raised for the organ repair fund. Many had to be turned away.

214 *Below.* The Regal, Petworth, in its opening year, a photograph taken by George Garland in November 1937.

215 *Bottom.* The Regal, again displaying some imaginative advertising, at a Christmas showing of *Snow White*, December 1938.

216 The stage and auditorium of the Regal, Petworth, in May 1942. Earlier in the year, in Warships Week, lectures were held here, and a propaganda cinema van toured the district, to raise funds for a Motor Torpedo Boat.

Stanley Collins described the Regal's later years in writing but unfortunately the appearance of his reminiscences in the *Bulletin* of the Petworth Society was terminated at this point. Mr. Collins has since died and efforts to trace the remaining material have proved unsuccessful.

The car park could take around seventy cars. Collins himself lived in the house on the site. From other sources, it is possible to add that the Regal had a 24ft. proscenium opening, Kalee sound system, 400 seats with a raised tier at the back but no balcony, and originally charged from 6d. to 2s. for full-price admission.

At a later stage, a café or restaurant was attached to the right of the building (as faced) and was still being advertised at the end of 1960. A new 'wide vision screen' had been installed by the end of 1954 and CinemaScope followed. The programme was usually changed midweek (a hit film would play a whole week) and there were matinees on Saturdays only.

Still owned and operated by Stanley Collins, the Regal closed on Sunday 29 April 1962 with an unspecified one-day revival booking. The last week of new main features had consisted of the comedy *No, My Darling Daughter* from Monday to Wednesday, and the John Mills war drama *The Valiant* from Thursday to Saturday, with the usual matinee on the Saturday. Collins referred to insufficient support, the fact that Petworth had not been allowed to grow, and the way that people had become more mobile (and therefore apt to go to other cinemas). He signed a contract on Thursday 24 April selling the entire site, including his house, with the cinema being converted to a youth community centre. He expected to settle in Swanage where he hoped to build a cinema and concert hall. The former Regal still operates as a youth centre run by the Sylvia Beaufoy Trust.

SELSEY

1913
SELSEY HALL/CINEMA/PAVILION
HIGH STREET

The new Selsey Hall was built on the site of an old thatched house by a local resident, Henry W. Hocking. The architect was Harold A. Woodington of Jermyn Street.[195] A 21-year lease of the building was taken by Thomas Sidney Jones of Brent Road, Plumstead, and on 26 July 1913 he applied to Chichester County Petty Sessions for a cinematograph licence for the hall.

Superintendent Ellis, Deputy Chief Constable of West Sussex County Constabulary, opposed the application on the grounds that the staircase leading to the balcony, only 2ft. 7ins. wide, was extremely dangerous. A decision was deferred so that the magistrates could make their own inspection. Meeting on 9 August 1913, they granted a licence on the understanding that no more than forty people should be allowed in the balcony.[196]

The front of the hall was unpretentious with a single double-door entrance, although the Register of Licences shows that there were

217 An early view of the Cinema Hall, Selsey, from a postcard, *c*.1914.

179

218 The frontage of the Selsey Cinema renamed the Pavilion in 1924.

219 A photograph showing the damage to the Selsey Pavilion after the fire in August 1926.

three other exits. The dimensions of the hall were 40ft. by 60ft. It had a flat wooden block floor and was lit by electricity and gas.[197]

The Selsey Hall was used for various functions, including live shows and dinners, but seems to have operated primarily as a cinema, using 350 fold-away chairs. It was described as the Cinema Hall when in October 1914 it was used for a series of variety entertainments to promote recruiting. Two months later, Captain Carey of the Royal Sussex Regiment made an appeal for recruits for 'Lowther's Lambs' during a film programme.

Jones was succeeded as manager of the hall on 24 July 1915 by John Frederick Baron of Sandy Mount, Manor Road, Selsey. Throughout the First World War, it continued to be used for concerts, plays, variety shows and lectures as well as cinema, and indeed was the venue for a Peace Dinner on 3 September 1919.[198]

By 1922 *Kelly's Directory* reveals that the building, as the Selsey Cinema, was under the management of Messrs. Chrippes and Cleere. Two years later the proprietors were Frederick William Phipps, a local estate agent, and Bertie Woodland, from the Isle of Wight, who renamed their venue the Pavilion. It was used for concerts by the Selsey Minstrels and the local Musical Society. Good class vaudeville

shows were often featured and the Russian Ballet Company performed at the Pavilion in September 1925.

A cutting suggests that at this time cinema performances were largely confined to the winter months and the Pavilion had become an all-year-round entertainment centre for residents and visitors alike.[199]

In July 1926, Phipps applied for permission to give cinema shows on Sundays, to put Selsey on a par with Bognor, which had had them for quite a time, and Littlehampton, which had more recently succeeded after a prolonged duel against religious interests. Phipps claimed that this would be appreciated by a village where the population had grown by 1,500 in recent years and reached 5,000 during the season. The application was backed by Police Superintendent Brett who argued that Sunday cinema kept young people off the streets. Perhaps this swayed the magistrates, who granted the licence, at least for the summer season.[200]

Disaster struck, however, after a Friday night dance on 20 August 1926 when a carelessly discarded cigarette set fire to some seating, eventually causing £2,000 worth of damage to the roof, the front of the building and the manager's office. The stage (12ft. deep with a proscenium width of 20ft.) and the two dressing rooms escaped, but the building had to be closed for the remainder of the season.[201]

The Selsey Horticultural Society held its annual show here in the early 1930s and the Selsey Follies were a frequent stage attraction between the wars. A. Balfour Johnson was the proprietor in the mid-1930s when it had 260 seats and used the obscure Morrison sound system. Sophie Tucker, who visited Selsey for a holiday each year, usually put on a show for which the top admission price ran as high as 7s. 6d.

220 Selsey Pavilion auditorium after the fire in August 1926.

221 A war-time programme for the Pavilion, Selsey, April 1941.

THURSDAY, April 24th.
Duggie Wakefield and Paddy Brown in
SPY FOR A DAY
Also SOME LIKE IT HOT

SUNDAY, April 27th.
Hugh Williams and Greta Gynt in
DARK EYES OF LONDON
Also GIRL FROM RIO

MONDAY, April 28th.
Jean Parker and James Dunn in
SON OF THE NAVY
Also I TAKE THIS OATH

THURSDAY, May 1st.
Bing Crosby and Dorothy Lamour in
ROAD TO SINGAPORE
Also EMERGENCY SQUAD

SUNDAY, May 4th.
Allan Jones and Walter Connolly in
GREAT VICTOR HERBERT
SHORTS

PAVILION
Selsey.
TELEPHONE—309.

PROGRAMME
for APRIL, 1941.

POPULAR PRICES.
PLEASE KEEP THIS PROGRAMME
:: FOR REFERENCE ::

NOTE CHANGE OF
OPENING TIMES.
Evening Performance 6-15 p.m.
Saturday Matinee 1-45 p.m.

222 A later view of the Selsey Pavilion, with altered entrance, from a colour postcard post-marked 1958.

Kelly's Directory names H.C. Wills-Rust as the lessee of the Pavilion in 1938. Films were still shown during the Second World War despite the high incidence of air raids on Selsey, evidence of the popularity of cinema as a refuge from a harsh reality. An advertisement for the last week of May 1941 shows three changes of film per week with evening performances at 6.15 p.m. and Saturday matinees at 1.45 p.m., Boris Karloff and Marjorie Reynolds opening the week in *Mr. Wong in Chinatown*.[202]

In the post-war years the Pavilion (by now fitted with the better British Acoustic sound system) had a succession of operators—Kinetours, P.J. Lintott, Rodney Hesse and, finally, Jack Tupper.[203] From the late 1950s films were shown only in the summer months

and the Pavilion was shut during the rest of the year except for special events and the local Christmas pantomime show. Film programmes changed midweek during the height of summer, three times a week at the beginning and end of the season. Films were several months old by the time they reached Selsey but they continued to be a holiday attraction until the autumn of 1964 when the season concluded with a two-day booking of the Disney family film *Summer Magic* on Friday 18 and Saturday 19 September.

The building survives in 1996, adjacent to the *Crown* public house, looking much the same as it ever did on the outside. But it is no longer in entertainment use, having become the premises of W.K. Thomas & Co. Ltd., a business handling disposable catering supplies.

SHOREHAM

c.28 FEBRUARY 1910
WINTON'S HALL/STAR THEATRE/
STAR ELECTRIC PICTURE PALACE/
STAR/COURT KINEMA
CHURCH STREET

This tiny early cinema was the first permanent venue for animated pictures in Shoreham. It began life as a Congregational Church of the Countess of Huntingdon's Connexion, which was established in 1800 in Church Street, or Star Lane as it was sometimes known. When a new chapel was built in Buckingham Road in 1908 the original building was used as a lecture and concert hall by William Edward Winton, a High Street printer, whose claim to fame is as the creator and organiser of the August carnival in Shoreham.

The old chapel was now called Winton's Hall and it was in this name that the magistrates at Shoreham Petty Sessions granted a cinematograph licence to Mr. Winton on 28 February 1910. This was conditional on the public being denied access to the tiny balcony. It was still known as Winton's Hall on 13 July 1914 when a 12-month cinema licence was granted to Arthur Hodgins, who had evidently succeeded the printer. Later in the year on 12 October, however, it was as the Star Theatre that Hodgins successfully applied for an alteration in the Sunday opening hours from 8-10 p.m. to 6.30-9 p.m.[204]

In 1915 the cinema is listed in *Kelly's Directory of Sussex* as the Star Electric Picture Palace.

In 1922, the Star was operated by Matthews, Holder and Co. with W.G. Holder as the resident manager. It is remembered by a local resident of the period, Peter Loftus, as being 'rather like a doll's house' with its miniature balcony. There were three changes of programme weekly and prices of admission ran from 5d. to 1s. 3d. Around 1923 its name was changed and it is referred to in the Petty Sessions Agenda Books as the Court Kinema from 1924.

223 Shoreham's first picture house, on left, shown in an early local newsreel.

224 The old Court Kinema, Shoreham, on left, now a Co-Op storage building.

183

Its licence was renewed in the name of Frederick Beecham on 22 March 1926 but it had closed by the following year, probably unable to withstand the competition offered by the Duke of York's and Coliseum.[205]

It later reverted to use as a chapel and then became a warehouse for the Co-Operative store in the High Street, in which usage it remains.

c. June 1911
Bijou Electric Empire/Bijou/
Duke of York's
High Street

Built largely of wood with a corrugated iron roof and an earth floor, this seems to have been 'The Garage' in the High Street for which, according to the Agenda Book for Shoreham Petty Sessions, a six-day cinematograph licence was granted on 19 June 1911 to Messrs. Cooke and Tulk. It is likely that the latter partner was in fact Arthur Turk who appears in the 1913 *Kelly's Directory of Sussex* as lessee of a cinematograph theatre in the High Street.[206]

By 1914, the cinema was called the Bijou Electric Empire for it appears under that name in the *Shoreham and District Blue Book* of 1914-15. It was evidently operating on a seven-day licence by then because, on 5 October 1914, the Justices approved an alteration in its Sunday hours from 8-10 p.m. to 6.30-9 p.m., causing the rival Star Theatre a week later to make an identical application, also approved.[207]

In his book on *Bungalow Town*, published in 1985, N.E.B. Wolters recalled that in its early days the Shoreham film studio used the Bijou to view the rushes of its films. 'The cinema had been converted from a boat-building shed. It was lined with match boarding, decorated with painted scenes surrounded by laurels in an oval shape. Cheaper seats were simply forms and those paying slightly more had forms with carpet tacked over.'

Reminiscences in *Memories of Shoreham* (Shoreham Society, 1994) place the Bijou behind the old shipyard, next door to a fish shop. When it rained, the noise on the iron roof drowned out the musical efforts of the lady pianist.

Fred and Audrey Wells remembered, 'The front row was tuppence, the middle row eightpence, and the back row was a shilling. If you went into the front row, you had to buy a bag of peanuts and throw the shells on to the wet floor to soak up the mud.' The earth floor was no doubt replaced in later years.

Kelly's Directory for 1925 indicates that it was then managed by L.E. Lacroix. The Petty Sessions Agenda Book shows that from the preceding year it had been somewhat grandly renamed the Duke of York's Cinema—in fact, because it had come under the same ownership as the Duke of York's in Brighton, i.e. Sussex Picturedromes. This company purchased the freehold in September 1929 and then sold it in April 1930 to E.R. Suter, who owned a yacht-building yard nearby. Mr. Suter promptly leased it to a local resident, A.B. Chipper.[208]

Only a few months after the blaze at the cinema in nearby Southwick, it was the turn of the Duke of York's to catch fire. In the early hours of Wednesday 5 August 1931, it was completely destroyed by a blaze so fierce that it threatened to spread to other properties in the vicinity (in fact, E.R. Suter's yacht-building yard was slightly damaged). The loss was estimated at £3,000. All the furnishings and the gas engine used for generating electricity were ruined. Only the main wall to the front of the building remained standing. The fire was probably fuelled by 17,000ft. of inflammable nitrate film believed to have been in the building at the time.

In a 1992 interview with John Grover on behalf of the Shoreham Society, Bert Taylor recalled working at the cinema:

> I left it just a few weeks before the fire. I was working as a general dog's body and as second operator. In those days the old talkies were on records, so when you went from one reel to another one you had three people in the operating box. There was one on each projector and one on the switchboard at the back. That used to be the guv'nor, he used to be there. The operator himself was on the new machine and I was on the one that was going to shut down. There were all the different marks at the end of a reel, the signs that it was finished. As soon as he saw the sign, he used to say 'Over' and I used to shut mine off, and he started his up so there was no stoppage. The guv'nor at the back just turned the switch. The power there was all generated by an old gas engine at the back, more or less in Suter's yard. You had to tug on the big wheel to get that started up.
>
> Then three times a week I had to go to Shoreham station to pick up the films. I used

to take the Thursday to Saturday films to the station on Sunday morning and pick up the films for the Sunday evening performance. And I used to repeat that on Monday morning for Monday to Wednesday's performances. We used to have a newsreel, then a comedy and the main film. At interval time, I used to go round with the chocolates. Then I was also the bill poster. I went round on my bike in Shoreham and to Bramber, Beeding and Steyning. I had to take the glue and a long brush. I got fed up one day. I thought, 'I can't go all round there', so I just threw the posters in a hedge. But somebody found them, because I got ticked off about it.

Another job was to sweep up first thing in the morning. Do you know where all the rubbish used to go? In the river. We used to walk all the way down to the end there and tip it over the side. If the tide was going out, it wasn't so bad.

I wasn't there all that long, because the people next door, Edmondson's, ran a fish shop. They wanted a lad there, and I was getting a bit fed up with the cinema, so many hours there and only seven and six pence a week. So I got a start there, at about twice as much.[209]

1920
COLISEUM THEATRE
NEW ROAD

The Coliseum Theatre was built during the First World War at a low price as a garrison theatre with flytower for the troops who were stationed around Brighton.

In 1920, it became a cinema. The proprietor was M.J.H. Browne and the resident manageress was Queenie Millard. There was one show nightly with three changes weekly, and prices ranged from 5d. to 1s. 10d., seven pence higher than at the Star. With a population of 5,737 in 1922, Shoreham had no less than three cinemas but of course the film-making in the area would have heightened interest.

The Coliseum was either taken over or re-opened on 5 March 1923 by the Blue Flash Cinema Company, a business created by former officers of the 4th Battalion of the Royal Sussex Regiment and named after the regiment's distinguishing insignia. That same year, the Company built and opened the Capitol at Horsham, with a view to employing many of the Regiment's demobilised servicemen who needed work, especially former bandsmen who could accompany the silent films of the period. The Coliseum and Capitol functioned as both live theatres and cinemas with rear projection

equipment set up at the back of the stage to show the films.

The Coliseum had a proscenium width of 28ft., a 30ft.-deep stage and eight dressing rooms. An augmented orchestra of six performed when films were being shown. According to Peter Loftus, 'It had a lot of period atmosphere and its name lent it grandeur'.

In 1925, Florence Tyrell took out theatrical, music and dancing licences as well as the cinematograph licence for the Coliseum.[210]

In *Memories of Shoreham*, Henry Perham recalled growing up in the town in the 1920s:

> No Saturday in Winter was complete without a visit to the pictures. Mostly the Colosseum [sic] or 'Colly' to see silent films of course, all accompanied at an appropriate moment by yells from the youthful audience, such as 'Look behind yer, mister!' Although further from Old Shoreham than the Duke of York's, the 'Colly' was favoured because at irregular intervals you sometimes were given a free orange or a bag of sweets. However, the more knowing of us on those occasions went up into 'the gods', simply because if you were downstairs every now and again you might be assaulted by either a hail of orange peel or empty sweet bags and their less popular contents.

Cynthia Bacon, in her contribution to *Memories of Shoreham*, considered the Coliseum to be the lesser of the two cinemas during her childhood and remembers it being known as 'the flea pit'.

By 1930, the proprietor of the cinema was Hugh Riley, by 1933 the Sussex Theatres Company. At this time it was still offering films and variety acts. On 19 February 1935, it was licensed to Frederick John Freeman, already licensee of the town's recently opened Norfolk cinema, indicating both were under the same control. Louis Halpern succeeded Freeman as the licensee of both cinemas from 17 November 1936 to well into the war years, during which period the owning company of both properties was a small enterprise called United British Cinemas (London) Ltd. and the Coliseum seated 808.[211]

With the difficulties of war-time evacuation and coastal travel restrictions, the owners may have decided to concentrate on their other cinema and the Coliseum closed on 12 July 1941.

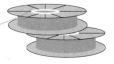

CINEMA

Another possible reason for closure was suggested by local resident Tony Turner (quoted from an undated newspaper clipping):

My mother, then Miss Dorrie Smith, used to go and play the piano for the silent pictures. When we went, the picture would often break, or the talking would go. People would cry out, 'Put another shilling in the meter!' As far as I can remember, they shut it down as a cinema because one of the projectionists got badly burned or electrocuted.

The building was eventually taken over for light engineering by Deri Engineers and Mr. Turner worked in the machine shop where the old stalls seating had been. The area under the stage was used to test equipment. The company used the building until the early 1960s when an American firm took over and moved operations to Burgess Hill.

The former Coliseum was demolished and its site, on Brighton Road at the corner of Eastern Avenue, is now occupied by part of the Adur Civic Centre.

27 MARCH 1933
NORFOLK/RITZ
NORFOLK BRIDGE, VICTORIA ROAD

This cinema, with 700 seats on one floor, is recollected by Cynthia Bacon in *Memories of Shoreham* as 'the greatest centre for us young people', referring back to her childhood when she much preferred it to the Coliseum. However, it is dismissed by Peter Loftus as 'a building of no interest'. Sir Sydney Samuelson concurs: 'It was a very, very basic cinema. It was very shabby and of very poor construction. It must have been put up very cheaply.' Dennis Williams goes further: 'It was a dismal cinema. Certain cinemas have a depressing effect on you.' A poor epitaph for its architect, Arthur

225 The Norfolk Cinema, Shoreham, flying the flag, probably in its opening year, 1933.

Singleton! An obscure 'All British' sound system, Kamm, was installed, which probably added to the unfavourable impression while it lasted.

Licensing records suggest that the Norfolk opened under the management of Frederick J. Freeman, who also became the licensee of the Coliseum from 19 February 1935. By 1937, this was operated, like the Coliseum, by United British Cinemas (London) Ltd. and had new Gaumont-British sound apparatus. Both cinemas were licensed to Louis Halpern. Matinees were offered on Mondays, Wednesdays and Saturdays and, as at the Coliseum, prices ranged from 6d. to 1s. 6d.[212]

By the mid-1940s, however, the Norfolk was owned by a local company and booked by M. Overmass, who ran two cinemas at Andover, Hampshire. It underwent a change of name to Ritz with effect from Sunday 2 November 1947.

The seating capacity came down to 526 in the wide screen era. In the 1960s, the Ritz felt the pinch of falling attendances and introduced bingo on Tuesdays and Fridays from Friday 4 October 1963. Bingo then seems to have been cut back to Fridays only. However, films finished on Saturday 25 January 1964 after a two-day (Thursday and Saturday) booking of *Carry On Cabby* supported by *The Partner* after it had been decided to concentrate on bingo five nights a week from 29 January, staying closed on Mondays and Tuesdays.

This did so poorly that films returned from Sunday 8 March 1964 for five days of the week, the Ritz closing on Tuesdays and carrying on with bingo on Fridays. The first two film attractions, *From Russia with Love* and *Tom Jones*, were smash hits of the preceding year and did well. The owners later attributed this to 'curiosity value' over the return of films when interest rapidly died away, forcing the Ritz to close permanently as a cinema on Saturday 9 May 1964 after the five-day run of *The Pink Panther*. Demonstrating the declining interest in cinema-going, manager F. McCalla told the *Shoreham Herald* (8 May 1964) that average Thursday night audiences at the Ritz had fallen from 450 in 1956 to about 50 in 1964.

Arrangements had been made for the Ritz to be taken over by Bunny Sisling of Hove for another stab at bingo. The new operator had run bingo at the Southwick Social Club and it was played at the Ritz for several years. But the building was demolished in the 1970s and its site is now occupied by Bellamy's Garage.

SOUTHWICK

LATE MARCH 1924
PICTURE HOUSE/PLAZA/NEW KINEMA
ALBION STREET

A barn-like building dwarfed by the Methodist Church next door, the former stable and depot (for a horse tramway which ran for a short while between Shoreham and Hove) was converted into a very basic, low cost cinema called the Picture House. The Agenda Books for Shoreham Petty Sessions first refer to the Picture House on 24 March 1924 when George Sheffield applied successfully for a cinematograph licence. Earlier volumes covering the period June 1919–August 1923 do not appear to have survived, so it is possible that there was a previous application on behalf of the cinema. It can be presumed to have opened as soon as the licence was granted.

There were a number of transfers of licence over the next few months before Alfred Barnett took over later in 1924 and he it was who renewed the licence on 23 March 1925.[213]

226 The tall façade of the Methodist Church dominates this aerial view of Southwick in the 1920s. Adjacent, left, are the flat-roofed premises of Highams the printers, and then comes the cinema.

The building had two dressing rooms and a 10ft.-deep stage. Frederick John Freeman, in whose name the licence was renewed on 22 March 1926, took out a theatrical licence in 1928 and offered variety as well as films. Freeman was also behind the cinema at Burgess Hill.[214]

In 1928, the Agenda Books refer to the building as the Plaza, a rather inappropriate name, according to Dennis Williams, 'as it was far from being luxurious'. At this time it had 340 seats.[215]

It was now operated by Percy Victor Reynolds who also owned the Picturedrome Portslade a mile or so away and had operated the cinema at Burgess Hill before Freeman. Williams recalls Reynolds:

He was a very elegant man. I heard that at one time in his early days he had been on the stage. I could believe it, he looked that kind of chap. He was beautifully spoken and every night he always wore evening dress at the cinema, which was very unusual for that type of cinema.

Fire broke out in the early hours of Monday 15 December 1930. The stage and many seats were badly burned and the Panatrope equipment destroyed. It took three hours to get the flames under control and the cost of damage was estimated at £1,000.

Dennis Williams declared (*Cinema Theatre Association Bulletin*, May/June 1992):

Apparently the insurance cover was sufficient to cover the rebuilding of the cinema, although the new building was little better than its predecessor, and was furnished and equipped with secondhand seating and fittings. The only new equipment was a BTH sound system—the old Plaza had never shown sound films.

The building re-opened on 6 April 1931, now called the New Kinema, and Reynolds sold it to John Ephraim Greaves during the following year. Dennis Williams surmises that this was to help raise the finance to rebuild the Picturedrome Portslade as the Pavilion.

Having visited it as a child in the '30s, Sir Sydney Samuelson remembers the New Kinema now as 'a terrible fleapit'.

With 461 seats (no balcony) and prices ranging from 6d. to 1s. 3d. in 1939, the New Kinema stayed in business. Dennis Williams visited it in 1942:

I recall that the cinema was very run down and dilapidated, extremely cold and draughty, and the screen lighting was so poor that if anyone struck a match the picture faded from the screen!

He adds:

The only improvement that ever took place in the cinema's lifetime was the replacement of the incredibly old Ross front shutter projectors by Kalee 12s. The arcs were equally ancient Gaumont low intensity models which may have survived from the Plaza days. The power supply was DC mains and the arc power supply was from a two-unit motor generator by Brooks Electric Motors of Huddersfield.

'Very dark and dingy' was the recent comment of another patron who knew it well.

In 1946, a fire broke out in the projection room and spread to the rewind room, destroying all the film in the building. However, the auditorium was hardly if at all affected and the cinema was back in business within four weeks.

Then, on Wednesday 24 March 1948, the New Kinema was gutted by a fire which broke out soon after the audience had left at the end of the evening performance at 9.50 p.m. The main feature, completing a three-day run, was MGM's Technicolored *The Romance of Rosy Ridge*, which featured a fire in one of its more spectacular sequences. The blaze at the New Kinema was discovered by a policeman at 10.30 p.m. and brought under control in half an hour, but the asbestos roof collapsed and the auditorium was gutted.[216]

Southwick Council eventually bought the site and adjoining shops, then cleared the entire area to create an open space and recreational area.

Addenda: Southwick

From 1910 for a few years, the Town Hall, with a capacity of 250, was offered for hire to film exhibitors.

WORTHING

1906
WINTER HALL
PORTLAND ROAD,
CORNER OF MONTAGUE STREET

Worthing holds a special place in the history of cinema in West Sussex as the first town in which films were shown to a paying audience (see Addenda to this section) and it is also the first town in West Sussex to have gained a full-time cinema building.

This came about when Michael W. Shanly of Hampstead, the 'Deckchair King' who owned the deckchair concession in Worthing, Bognor and many other resorts and who would also run early cinemas in Bognor and Littlehampton, acquired the Winter Hall. Formerly the Congregational Chapel built in 1842, it was no longer needed after the congregation moved to a new church in Shelley Road in 1903. The old building was renamed the Winter Hall and became a place of entertainment. 'Shanly's Animated Pictures' were established here in 1906 and the building became known as 'Shanly's Cinema'.

The capacity was 600 and an advertisement shows that it was open daily from 2.30 p.m. to 10.30 p.m. In his *The Dream Palaces of Worthing*, Fred T.P. Windsor includes a 1908 advertisement for singing and talking pictures at the Winter Hall via the 'Cinematophone', one of many attempts to add the missing dimension of sound. Another advertisement shows that there were two three-day programmes per week, with no Sunday performance, and that tickets were 1s., 9d., 6d. and 3d., with reduced prices for children (3d. and 2d.) and 'special prices' for soldiers and sailors. The titles listed include dramas, westerns, romances and official war films, while there was a full live variety programme

included. By 1921, Shanly was screening serials and local news footage.[217]

In a column on early Worthing picture houses (*Worthing Herald*, 10 February 1956), 'Galleryite' remembered:

> The Winter Hall, like the St James's Hall [see later], had a gallery or balcony on three sides of the building, the screen being on the fourth side, of course. Here were the cheapest seats, which cost fourpence, if I remember rightly, the 'posh' seats being on the ground floor at prices of eightpence and a shilling. Side seats in the balcony were not at all popular as they gave a distorted view of the screen, and they were usually occupied only at crowded houses on bank holidays and Saturday nights. The operating box at the Winter Hall was at the back of the balcony, with seats built around it.

227 The old Congregational Chapel in 1903 shortly before becoming the first full-time cinema in West Sussex.

189

228 *Left.* An early picture of the interior of Worthing's first cinema.

229 *Above.* St James's Hall, a chapel converted into a theatre and music hall, turned to cinema in 1908.

230 *Below.* A cinema sign, on the left, marks the site of St James's Hall in this postcard view, postmarked 1917.

Regular patrons when passing the front of the box bobbed their heads to avoid the rays of the projector but casual visitors were unaware of this and walked boldly past, thus showing an enormous shadow of a head on the screen. Occasionally a lady with a large hat and feathers to match would dither in front and completely black out the screen and then there were shouts of 'Sit down!' from the audience. [...]

There was a curious seating arrangement at the Winter Hall on the ground floor. The best seats (covered with white antimacassars) were at the front, and the cheaper seats at the back, as in 'live' theatres. I have never heard of this system in other cinemas. I saw many of the early Chaplin films at this cinema; 'Westerns' were also popular and sometimes two films dealing with the American Civil War were shown in the same programme.

Films continued to be presented by Shanly until October 1923 when the competition became too fierce and the cinema was forced to close. Messrs. Boots now occupy the site.

1908
ST JAMES'S HALL
MONTAGUE STREET

The second venue for films in Worthing was very near the first and also a converted chapel—in this case, the Worthing Tabernacle of 1839. Renamed St James's Hall in 1908, it played a mixed diet of concerts, variety shows and films, and claimed in a cinematograph trade annual two years later to be 'specially fitted for pictures'. At this time it was leased by a Mr. Scott and Mr. J.W. Mansfield, with the latter as manager, and seems to have become a full-time cinema. The capacity was stated to be 500.

The St James's Hall was recalled as a cinema from 1914 or later by 'Galleryite' in the *Worthing Herald* (10 February 1956):

There was a small stage with a grand piano which supplied accompaniment to the films, and Mr. Mansfield sometimes played his cello in the interval. At other times Mr. Jack Andrews (tenor) sang 'I'll sing thee songs of Araby' and similar popular ballads of the period. It was a comfortable hall, though small by modern standards, but some excellent films were shown there including many of the early Hepworth films, featuring Henry Edwards, Chrissie White, Alma Taylor, Violet Hopson, Stewart Rome, and many others now remembered only by 'old-timers' like myself.

J.W. Mansfield continued to operate the Hall but by the early 1920s films were only shown occasionally. For several summers, it featured live entertainment from Philip Ritte's Concert Party (a company that included a young comedian called Arthur Askey) but it closed down completely in the mid-1920s. The building became a music shop, then an electrical shop. It is now occupied by Horne's, the outfitters.

[PRE OCTOBER] 1911
CINEMA ELITE
GRATWICKE ROAD

The roller skating rink called the Elite was converted into the Cinema Elite with modern tip-up seats. It was managed by B.R. Stent. Programmes were changed on Wednesdays and Saturdays and its admission prices of 2d., 4d. and 6d. in 1911 were substantially lower than those at the Winter Hall or the Electric (see below).[218] It made the strange boast that 'All our pictures are shown natural size'—could this have been an ingenious excuse for a small screen image?

The Cinema Elite was operated by Messrs. Whitten, Hopkins and Gibbs in conjunction with the Elite Rink Company. However, it lasted only until 1915 before closing down. Latterly, the site has been occupied by a car spares company.

7 OCTOBER 1911
ELECTRIC THEATRE
THE KURSAAL, MARINE PARADE

The Electric Theatre was on the first floor of the Kursaal (which was retitled the Dome in 1914 when its German name became unacceptable). The Kursaal, pronounced 'koorsahl', originated in Germany as a building for the use of visitors at a health resort or watering place. It became the name attached to leisure complexes. (Other Kursaals on the South Coast were at Bexhill, opened in 1896, and at Bognor, opened in 1910—both now gone.)

The Worthing Kursaal was the brainchild of Carl Adolf Seebold, a German-Swiss born in 1873 who settled in Worthing in 1904 and would become the town's leading impresario, taking over the New Theatre Royal on arrival and eventually owning three cinemas (the Dome, the Picturedrome and the Rivoli). He

purchased Bedford House in 1908 and erected the Kursaal on the front part of the lawn while turning the rear into pleasure gardens. It was designed by Theophilus Arthur Allen, a London architect who had been educated at Lancing College.[219]

The Kursaal was conceived as an all-round entertainment complex and opened in three stages, beginning in June 1910 with the gardens, used for pierrot shows and concert parties. Then came the Coronation Hall (used for roller skating, concerts and meetings), opened on Easter Saturday 15 April 1911. Finally, the cinema above, the Kursaal Electric Theatre, made its bow a few months later, on Saturday 7 October 1911, operating continuously daily (except Sunday) from 3 p.m. to 10.45 p.m. with a change of films every Monday and Thursday. Prices of admission were 3d., 6d. and 9d. The seating was initially of movable chairs but comfortable tip-up seats were soon installed. A piano accompaniment was provided by a player who was, in the customary manner, screened from public view.

Among the inaugural pictures were a Vitagraph film called *The Convict's Pet* and a Lion film *A Bolt from the Blue*. Within a few weeks of opening, a second projector was installed, doing away with the waiting between the short films while spools were changed (this was before feature-length films came in). Films shown later in 1911 included one on the electrification of the Brighton Railway from Victoria to Crystal Palace and, on 20 December, what the *Worthing Gazette* called 'a superb representation of the Niagara Falls'.[220]

When the Coronation Hall was turned into the Dome Cinema in 1921, the Electric Theatre became a dance hall or ballroom, re-opening in October as the King's Hall Ballroom.

Then, from 1960, it has been a bingo hall which has been operated for nearly thirty years by brothers Robert and Attilio Miele. There have been suggestions that it might become a cinema again, to provide a second screen at the Dome.

231 An early view of the Kursaal, Worthing, completed in 1911, a magnificent Edwardian entertainment complex, with gardens, skating rink, electric theatre, billiards, ballroom and restaurant.

The Kursaal, Worthing.

29 July 1914
Picturedrome/
New Connaught Theatre/
Connaught Theatre
Chapel Road/Union Place

This purpose-built cinema opened with 860 tip-up seats (plus four boxes) on one floor. Built on the site of Stanmer Lodge at the corner of Chapel Road and Union Place, it was the enterprise of a specially formed company headed by Eastbourne-based architect Peter D. Stonham with Worthing building materials agent E.J. Baldwin and Worthing builder W.W. Sandell (of Frank Sandell & Son) among others involved.

The better seats (priced 6d., 9d. and 1s.) were reached through an entrance built across vacant space from Chapel Road. The boxes, to seat four, were priced at 5s. The cheapest seats (at 3d.) were entered from Union Place through doors that led to the left of the screen.

Crowds lined the streets for the opening, performed by the Mayoress, and a packed house admired the cream decor and rose-coloured furnishings. The first manager was C.W. Woolgar. There was a change of films every Monday and Thursday, but no screenings on Sunday. An afternoon performance took place at 3 p.m. and evening shows were from 6.15 p.m. to 10.30 p.m. Within two years, continuous performances from 3 p.m. to 11 p.m. had been introduced.

In November 1914 a new manager, F.H. Turner, arrived from the successful Cinema de Luxe at Bexhill. Audiences remained strong during the war, encouraged by discounted books of tickets and long-running cliffhanger serials. A new advertising slogan was adopted: 'The Finest Kinema on the South Coast'.[221]

The empty space on Chapel Road was filled in by a new development completed in 1917—the Connaught Buildings, which enclosed the entrance to the Picturedrome with shops to either side and a public hall above. The Connaught Hall was used for dances, whist drives, concerts and dramatic productions.

The Picturedrome needed to be completely redecorated and reseated in June 1919. Within eighteen months, Stonham had not only added new Picturedromes at Bognor, Chichester and Eastbourne but also taken over the Connaught Hall and adjoining Kandy's

Café to form an entertainment complex centred around the Worthing cinema.

Audiences fell after the war and the cost of film hire rose. Then in 1921 the Dome Cinema opened and engaged in an elaborate advertising contest with the Picturedrome over which site had the best choice of films, the best ventilation, the most luxurious accommodation, the best orchestra, etc.

Worse was to follow in 1924 when C.A. Seebold, who operated the Dome, also opened his new Rivoli cinema nearby. The Picturedrome could not compete with this more luxurious, more up-to-date and larger rival, and suffered heavy losses. Under general manager Leonard King it still opened every weekday from 3 p.m. to 10.30 p.m. and on Sundays from 6 p.m. to 9 p.m. Then in 1926, with mounting debts, it fell under the

232 The auditorium of the Picturedrome in Worthing, after the redecoration in 1919, with the roof representing a balustrade and star-spangled sky.

233 Mobile advertising for the Picturedrome. A Tilling-Stevens bus of Worthing Motor Services Ltd. after rebuilding at the Chalk Pits Museum, Amberley, in 1992.

DIRECTOR

management and (shortly afterwards) owner-ship of Mr. Seebold, who then ran all three cinemas in Worthing.

All were wired for sound when the talkies arrived but soon it was Seebold's turn to suffer from unwelcome competition when it became clear in 1933 that modern cinemas were to appear in Worthing. Seebold's first response was to fight on by closing the Picturedrome in May of that year for extensive improvements (to the design of local architect Arthur T.W. Goldsmith). It re-opened on 31 July with Cicely Courtneidge in *The Soldiers of the Queen*, boasting a new stage and proscenium arch, redecorated auditorium and new screen.

Unfortunately for Seebold, the modernisation failed to keep audiences from flocking to the new Plaza and Odeon or preferring the older Rivoli and Dome, especially when the appeal of the films at the Picturedrome dropped because it was now last in line. But happily a solution was to hand. A repertory company in the neighbouring Connaught Hall, now called the Connaught Theatre, was doing turnaway business and the Picturedrome closed on 16 June 1935, after a Sunday one-day presentation of the Joe E. Brown comedy *The Circus Clown* plus *There Goes Susie*, so that the theatre company could take over the larger auditorium.

The building re-opened a little over three months later, converted into the New Connaught Theatre, presenting live shows only, with a new frontage and entrance on

Union Place that was as distinctly brash and modern as the exterior of the Odeon. Its ribbon windows turning the far corners, its tiled frontage in black and cream faience and its art deco signage made the New Connaught look every inch a 1930s cinema rather than a theatre. The old entrance on Chapel Road was no longer needed and became a shop. Historian John Willmer makes the interesting claim that this was the first purpose-built cinema to be turned into a live theatre.

Soon becoming simply the Connaught Theatre, the building has had a troubled history, closing for a period in 1966 from lack of audiences, being taken over by Worthing Council, and closing again in 1986 for a while.

Regrettably, the tiles on the front of the Connaught were stripped in the mid-1980s and not replaced: since that date it has looked very plain externally. A completely modern auditorium has now been built within the old one: the original ceiling dome still survives above the current ceiling.

When in 1986 the Dome became the town's only cinema, the Connaught installed projection equipment and began presenting films in the spring of 1987 while continuing primarily with live theatre. The first motion picture to be shown on the site for 52 years was *A Chorus Line* on 2 March 1987. Films have continued to be shown here (with 514 seats available) and have also been introduced in the former Connaught Hall (see later).

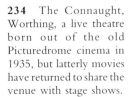

234 The Connaught, Worthing, a live theatre born out of the old Picturedrome cinema in 1935, but latterly movies have returned to share the venue with stage shows.

235 The Kursaal was renamed the Dome in 1914, and seven years later its Coronation Hall was converted into the Dome cinema.

18 July 1921
Dome Cinema
Marine Parade

The Dome Cinema was a conversion at a cost of £8,000 of the downstairs, flat-floored Coronation Hall (opened in 1911 and previously used for roller skating, concerts and meetings). The plain hall, with its exposed roof girders, was transformed with the introduction of decorative plasterwork, quality oak panelling, a ceiling with large domes, and expensive light fittings. The windows were panelled over, the floor given a slope (or rake), and 950 modern tip-up seats were installed. The side galleries were retained and boxes were introduced at the back. The stage, on which an orchestra had played in one direction to roller skaters and in the other (through open doors in the rear wall) to crowds in the pleasure gardens, was now occupied by a cinema screen.

The Dome Cinema replaced the much smaller upstairs Electric Theatre, reflecting the increased demand for film entertainment on the sea front. It has been suggested that the Electric's projection box may have been retained to serve the new cinema with the projectors being repositioned.

The change was implemented by the owner of the complex, C.A. Seebold. The first feature to be shown on the opening Monday night was *Pollyanna*, starring a top favourite of the day, Mary Pickford, and it was accompanied by a six-piece orchestra. A refreshment room and a cloakroom were located alongside the foyer.

The Dome began by offering continuous performances from 3 p.m. to 10.30 p.m. with a separate Sunday show from 6 p.m. to 9 p.m., changing its programme on Mondays and Thursdays. In 1924 (along with the rival Picturedrome) it participated in a British Film Week, taking up the Prince of Wales' rallying cry to show only British films by screening a romantic tale, *The Starlit Garden*, and Fred Karno's sketch, *Early Birds*.[222]

Directly facing the sea and close to the Pier, the Dome was always in a strong position to attract holiday-makers in the season, although less well placed for trade during the rest of the year.

When, from the mid-1930s onwards, the town had the Rivoli, Plaza and Odeon, all much larger, the Dome was often forced to play a weak combination of second-run films, circuit releases shunned by the other cinemas, and off-circuit programmes of lesser new 'product', usually for six-day runs with separate Sunday shows. Its excellent location saw it through, together with lower prices than some of the opposition, especially for its cheapest seats.

236 The paybox and category board of the Dome, Worthing, *c.*1980.

playing such hit films as *Jaws*, which ran for many weeks.

The conspicuous frontage of the Dome on Marine Parade had suffered over the years. There was the loss in the 1950s of the cupola on the prominent octagonal dome, while flagpoles, an ornamental guardrail and a canopy for the balcony also disappeared at some point, spoiling its appearance.

The foyer and auditorium, however, have retained most of their ornate decoration. For film use, the galleries along the side walls are unneeded, the rake is not generous, and the ceiling is rather low (as in many modern cinemas), but all this can be forgiven for the rich sense of period the auditorium evokes.

Back in the 1960s, the area around and including the Dome—the Old Warwick Quarter, the town's historical centre for fishing—was selected by Worthing Borough Council for comprehensive redevelopment. The cinema (now seating 737) was purchased by the Council in 1969. The Council then let the cinema, but only on three-year leases subject to renewal, and this of course made it pointless for managements to spend any substantial amounts of money to improve the facilities. There were some advantages, as the cinema retained many features like its original mahogany paybox and old-fashioned category board above it which might have been swept away in any thorough attempt to modernise the building.

When the future of the Dome came under threat, the Worthing Society began a campaign to save it from demolition, seeking listed building status. Around this period, two art nouveau bronze figures forming electroliers, which were mounted on the marble columns flanking the steps to the auditorium in the main foyer, vanished.

By this time, the Odeon had been demolished and the Dome had become the only cinema in town (although the Connaught Theatre began part-time showings of films). The Council rejected a proposal for a longer five-year lease and only approved another three-year renewal.

The Dome gained a certain fame (or notoriety) when several scenes in the acclaimed 1987 film *Wish You Were Here* were shot at the cinema, showing both the interior and exterior. Set in the early 1950s in an unnamed coastal town, the story did not reflect too well on the cinema as its fictional projectionist (played by

In the spring of 1949, two years before his death, C.A. Seebold leased the Dome and Rivoli to a new company formed to take them over, Rivoli and Dome (Worthing) Ltd. The Dome advertised regularly as 'One of the Warmest Theatres on the South Coast', having the advantage of a much smaller and more compact auditorium than most of its rivals. CinemaScope was fitted in 1954, requiring a new proscenium arch to be installed in front of the old one (which remains in place to this day). The number of seats was reduced slightly from 875 to 851 by the removal of the rows closest to the new wide screen.

After the Rivoli was destroyed in a fire in 1960, the Dome benefited because the somewhat better films booked for the Rivoli were transferred to its screen from 31 January. The Dome had been opening at 4 p.m. and now returned to an earlier start at 1 p.m. But even the absence of the Rivoli did not help much as by this time almost all the best general releases were being taken by the Plaza and Odeon. The Dome responded with separate performances of special presentations: in the summer of 1960, *Gigi* ran from 3 to 30 July, *South Pacific* followed from 31 July to 27 August, then *Solomon and Sheba* played for two weeks, returning for a further fortnight. *El Cid* was the attraction of the summer season in 1962.

When this 'roadshow' era was ending, the Dome had the good fortune to inherit the ABC circuit release from the Plaza after that closed in 1968. This resulted in the Dome

Tom Bell) was a randy middle-aged character who seduces a teenager (Emily Lloyd), brings her to his room inside the actual dome, and makes her pregnant. (The rooms in the tower had once housed two billiard tables.) *Wish You Were Here* had a première presentation in late 1987 at the Dome which helped to spotlight the building's clouded future.

The Council informed the lessee, Stephen Wischhusen, that his lease would not be renewed when it expired in June 1988. In the event, the lease was renewed—but for just one year. Redevelopment was then to take place, conditional on a small cinema being included in the replacement building. Wischhusen had expressed interest, given a longer tenure, in renovating the Dome's interior as well as installing new seats and more modern projection equipment. The cinema, now seating 650, was attracting audiences of over 200,000 a year, a creditable figure.

The threat of closure prompted a public meeting attended by over 600 people and the formation of the 'Save the Dome' campaign. 30,000 signatures appeared on a petition demanding the preservation of the cinema through a long lease that would enable it to be improved. Possibly inspired by events at the Odeon (described later), the Council had a structural survey carried out which apparently painted a gloomy picture—but this was disputed by an independent survey which found the building to be in a better state.

New attempts were made to have the Dome complex listed for its historic significance as an early, multiple-use leisure centre that had been essentially unaltered, but these, not for the first time, were rejected by the Department of the Environment. The campaign, ably spearheaded by local resident Robin King, attracted the support of the Cinema Theatre Association, the Twentieth Century Society (then the Thirties Society), the Civic Trust and the Georgian Group (the Victorian Society later became involved). These efforts were finally rewarded when, in May 1989, the Dome was listed grade II.

Along with the recession, this helped to scotch the redevelopment scheme that Worthing Council had been exploring with the Burton Property Group under which, as a feeble concession to the public uproar, the frontage would have been retained and a new auditorium built at right angles to the present one.

The Council would still only allow Wischhusen a year's lease but he began restoration work on the auditorium, having some of the seats reupholstered. Externally, in 1990, a section of the cornice crashed onto the pavement, narrowly missing a cyclist and damaging the columns of the building.

Now the Council seemed intent on selling the freehold and allowing the Dome to be converted into another use such as a sports club, bowling alley or nightclub, drawing on the fact that the auditorium had not originally been used as a cinema, blithely ignoring the alterations of 1921 which had transformed its appearance.

237 & **238** The ornate splendour of Worthing's Dome auditorium in 1991.

239 The Dome in Worthing, still a cinema, June 1995, undergoing repairs while the 'Save the Dome' campaign fought on.

FORTHCOMING CINEMA ATTRACTIONS

conservationists made plans to raise a further £35,000 to replace decorative features that had been lost. The following year, repairs to the dome itself began and on 8 February the builders were putting in new steel beams when concrete supports suddenly moved. There were fears that the tower could collapse and the cinema (as well as the bingo hall upstairs) was forced to close. Police cordoned off the area and buses were diverted. However, the all-clear was given and the cinema was able to re-open the following day. In April, a new 8ft. high fibreglass cupola, costing £5,000, and a 9ft. flagpole reappeared. The ornamental guard rails at the base of the dome were promised when a further £4,000 had been raised. Pleased with attendances at the Dome, Robins Cinemas were interested in adding two further small cinemas to either side of the entrance to overcome the difficulties of operating just one screen and to spread the overheads.

Then, in September, the Council claimed that a further £390,000 needed to be spent on the cinema, on top of the sum, reported at between £300,000 and £350,000, it had paid out already. Rather than incur further costs, it decided to sell the freehold or, if no reasonable offers were received, to hand the building over to the Dome Preservation Trust. This charity announced plans to spend £4 million on the Dome, adding three further cinemas and a film museum. However, its proposals were dependent on funding from the Millennium Commission. The Council accepted a bid, apparently worth £1 million, from a leisure operator wanting to turn the Dome into a nightclub. The Council indicated that the Dome would also be available for banqueting, conferences and fashion shows through the proposed new owners, who hoped to provide a cinema elsewhere in the complex.

The full Council finally voted to retain the freehold and accepted the case for keeping the Dome Cinema. Unfortunately, Stephen Wischhusen's tenancy had collapsed and the cinema struggled on a week-to-week basis under temporary managers and Council supervision while a new operator was selected. There were several applications and the Council chose the prominent independent chain, Robins Cinemas (then operators of the two-screen Robins at Burgess Hill), giving them initially a six-month lease while long-term considerations were sorted out.

No sooner had Robins arrived than the wiring was condemned during a routine inspection and the Dome closed on Thursday 25 March 1993 even though its certificate was current to the end of April. Estimates for rewiring went as high as £100,000 and for a moment the Dome seemed doomed, but with some timely assistance by Seeboard sufficient rewiring was carried out at a cost of £26,550, paid by the Council, to enable the cinema to re-open. Robins waited for a hit film to bring back the Dome, choosing *Indecent Proposal*, which played from 14 May 1993. In July 1993, *Jurassic Park* was shown to a full house at a charity screening to raise funds for the Dome Preservation Trust, the organisation now most directly involved in safeguarding the building.

In 1994, the Council decided to spend £225,000 on restoring the Dome, while

Robins Cinemas continue to operate the Dome under a six-month lease ending on 7 November 1996 while plans are drawn up for alterations to adapt it for nightclub use and permission is sought to carry them out. At the very least, the proposed new uses, such as banqueting, suggest that the sloping floor would be replaced by a flat one.

The battle is not yet over. On 18 July 1996, the Dome celebrated its 75th anniversary as a cinema, and there are many hoping that it will go on to celebrate its centenary.

10 MARCH 1924
RIVOLI
CHAPEL ROAD,
JUNCTION WITH NORTH STREET

Worthing's first big cinema, the Rivoli, was designed by Burdwood and Mitchell of Baker Street, London, for local entrepreneur C.A. Seebold. Adjacent shops formed Rivoli Parade. It was built at a cost of over £75,000 on the site of Worthing Lodge, which had most recently been a doctor's home and surgery.

The Rivoli seated 1,680 in stalls and balcony, and there were six boxes on the ground floor. A two-manual pipe organ with 16 speaking stops was supplied by Jardine's of Manchester and there was an orchestra of 11 to accompany the silent films in the evenings. Like several other cinemas of the period, the Rivoli had a sliding roof that was opened for fresh air on fine evenings. At first-floor level there was a large tea room formed round a well overlooking the spacious entrance vestibule. The opening attraction was the Douglas Fairbanks version of *Robin Hood*.[223]

In 1929 the Rivoli showed the first talking film in Worthing, *The Singing Fool* starring Al Jolson.

Seebold ran all three of the town's cinemas with mid-week changes of programme until the Plaza and Odeon arrived, and continued to operate the Rivoli and Dome until 1949 when both were leased to a new company formed for the purpose. At this time, seating at the Rivoli was quoted as 1,696, suggesting that a few more seats may have been squeezed in to cope with demand in the immediate post-war boom years.

By virtue of its size, the Rivoli remained a leading cinema along with the Plaza and Odeon, and, in the absence of a Gaumont cinema in the town, often was able to show that circuit's weekly release programmes. Its prices were for many years the same as the Odeon's and its seating was reduced only slightly to 1,656 in the mid-1950s. However, from 1959, in a reorganisation of the Odeon and Gaumont releases into a superior weekly Rank release and an inferior National programme, the Rivoli lost out to the Odeon.

On Sunday 17 January 1960, the Rivoli started a seven-day run of the British comedy

The Navy Lark supported by *The Oregon Trail*. New prices had just been introduced as 'a rearrangement', increasing the stalls to 2s. and 3s., the circle to 3s. 6d. and 4s., but patrons were assured that the Rivoli was 'still cheaper than elsewhere'. Shortly after 6 a.m. on the morning of Tuesday 19 January 1960, two policemen noted smoke coming out of one of the exits at the rear of the cinema. Nearly seventy firemen fought the blaze that was raging inside, but three quarters of an hour later the roof collapsed and the auditorium was gutted. It was the worst fire in the town for 10 years.[224]

The lessees of the Rivoli transferred future bookings to the Dome from the end of January, beginning with a revival of *The King and I*. Mrs. Seebold, the widow and heir of C.A. Seebold (she had been his secretary for many

240 The Italianate frontage of the much-loved Rivoli seen here at its opening in 1924.

241 The auditorium of the Rivoli, Worthing, in 1924.

years and knew the business well), decided against rebuilding the cinema. However, the Rivoli's commanding frontage survived for many years although the ball on top was removed in early 1965 when the foyer was converted to become sales and auction rooms for Fox and Sons from March of that year. The surviving end wall of the auditorium was demolished to open up the former stalls floor for vehicle access, providing parking space for 60 cars. Above were the exposed girders that had once supported the balcony.

The Rivoli's Italianate frontage remained as a local landmark until it was finally demolished, along with the adjacent shops, on 29 April 1984 to allow Chapel Road to be widened.

14 December 1933
Plaza
Rowlands Road
(corner of Eriswell Road)

Erected on the site of an amusement park, the Plaza was the first of three super cinemas announced in late 1932 actually to be built and opened—the others were the Odeon and an unrealised cinema designed for Lou Morris by architect Robert Cromie to suggest a streamlined showboat in grey and white.

Although Kay Bros. were the promoters when work started in December 1932 and the cinema was to be called the Hippodrome, it

emerged a year later as the Plaza under the control of Lou Morris who had abandoned his Cromie scheme in favour of this one.

The architect was Harry Weston. The façade was rather plain and ponderous, but the convex central feature was neatly emphasised in neon at night. The cinema had 2,005 seats in stalls and circle, making it the largest ever to operate in West Sussex. It was equipped with a stage 30ft. deep, suitable for full stage shows. The proscenium was 45ft. wide. There was a ten-rank Compton organ, which had an amazing illuminated glass surround that covered it entirely and changed colour to match the music. In addition, the Plaza boasted a café restaurant, a separate ballroom, covered queueing space at the side of the building, and a free car park.

The interior design was by Mollo and Egan who provided an underwater theme with King Neptune and his court being featured in the decorations. (Harry Weston later designed the Gaumont Chichester which had another underwater decorative scheme.) The screen tabs had the look of an aquarium and the house curtains sported large bubbles. When the house lights came up, rays of sunlight pierced the ceiling like the surface of a pool. The decor was rose and pale gold, the carpets were mottled green, and the seating was also in green. The Plaza claimed to be the first cinema in Worthing with a full air conditioning system.[225]

The Mayor of Worthing, Alderman H. Duffield J.P., presided at the opening ceremony. The big attraction on screen was *The Song You Gave Me*, starring Bebe Daniels and Victor Varconi, supported by two cartoons and the Gaumont news. The organ was played for the first three days by Tommy Dando (who came for the occasion from a Lou Morris cinema in Rotherham). Continuous performances were offered from 1.30 p.m. to 10.45 p.m. Monday to Saturday, and from 5.30 p.m. to 10.30 p.m. on Sundays. Prices ranged from 9d. to 2s. 6d.

Lou Morris was a promoter who made a practice of opening cinemas and quickly selling them at a profit. C.A. Seebold, who owned the other three cinemas in the town, was anxious to acquire the Plaza. In 1934, Morris contracted to sell it to Seebold for £60,000 (£20,000 for the shares, £40,000 for the mortgage) and accepted Seebold's deposit of £2,000. However, Morris then sold the shares for only £17,000 to a Mr. Weston—seemingly not the architect of the building (who did become a cinema owner) but rather 'an Odeon nominee', as described in one trade paper report, since it was the Odeon circuit that took over the property. Seebold successfully sued for breach of contract and claimed damages of £7,600, on the grounds that, had he acquired the Plaza, he would have been able to book films for his other three cinemas in the town on far more favourable terms than with the Plaza as a rival enterprise. In November 1936, the Official Referee awarded Seebold damages of £3,000, plus costs.

The Odeon circuit had its own new cinema in the town but seems to have acquired the Plaza because it feared the power that Seebold would exercise if he controlled all the other cinemas in Worthing. However, Odeon then leased the Plaza to the big national chain, Associated British Cinemas, from 5 February 1936. ABC had its own fixed weekly release and would not be competing against the Odeon for titles.

For more than thirty years, the Plaza functioned as an ABC circuit release outlet, showing in the 1940s and 1950s primarily the productions of Warner Bros., MGM and its own Associated British pictures.

During the Second World War, the Plaza had a narrow escape (recalled in Rob Blann's 'Remember When' column in the *West Sussex*

Gazette, 15 December 1994). While a full house was engrossed in MGM's Spencer Tracy war drama *The Seventh Cross* on Sunday 17 December 1944, a real war drama was enacted when a crippled, fully loaded Lancaster bomber just managed to avoid the cinema and crashed on the beach at low tide, catching fire and exploding. Only one of the crew was still on board (his body was found in the wreckage) and he was heralded in the local press as 'The Man Who Saved Worthing'.

The difficulty of running such a large cinema out of season with attendances generally

242 The Plaza in Worthing was the county's largest cinema, shown here in its opening year, 1933.

243 The auditorium of the Worthing Plaza, with the Compton organ, and the underwater decor, 1933.

244 Looking across the auditorium of the Worthing Plaza, 1933.   **245** The foyer of the Worthing Plaza, in its opening year, 1933.

on the decline, combined with an awareness of the large number of older people in the town who were likely to support bingo, caused ABC to shut the Plaza as a cinema on Wednesday 11 December 1968. The last films to be shown were the comedy *The Bliss of Mrs. Blossom* with Shirley MacLaine and Richard Attenborough supported by a bank raid story, *The Violent Four*.[226]

The Plaza re-opened for the eyes-down brigade in January 1969 with Bobby Pagan at the organ. People were queueing long before the doors opened at 7 p.m. and the building filled to capacity with 1,700 players. (The organ was removed in 1970 and shipped to the Western Division of the Organ Society of Australia at Melville, near Perth.)

After ABC sold its bingo interests, the club was operated by the Star company. Later, the local Red Lion group took over, only to be acquired by Granada in 1985. Since then, Gala have succeeded Granada and given the building their name. Along the way, a false ceiling has been inserted, extending forwards from the underside of the old balcony to reduce the capacity of the building, creating a more intimate atmosphere and saving on heating costs. The upper half of the original auditorium, including the entire circle area, has remained abandoned and disused.

24 MARCH 1934
ODEON
LIVERPOOL GARDENS

The Odeon was a landmark in British cinema architecture when it opened, as was recognised by its listing as a significant building. Its destruction, which deprived Worthing of a valuable amenity (not adequately replaced to this day) and of one of its very best 20th-century buildings, is a sorry episode in the history of the town.

Oscar Deutsch set about planning an Odeon circuit in December 1931, each of the theatres he built to belong to a separate company. He first registered a company to open an Odeon in Weymouth, then in November 1932 registered Odeon (Worthing) Ltd. along with similar companies for schemes at Canterbury and Worcester Park. The Odeon Worthing took some time to complete and became the ninth addition to the new circuit, following the Odeons at Weymouth, Kingston-on-Thames, Canterbury, South Harrow and Lancing in 1933, and Worcester Park, Tolworth and Kemp Town in 1934.

Most of the early buildings were undistinguished architecturally but the Odeon South Harrow introduced the streamlined look and the use of cream-yellow faience tiles that

246 'Oscar Deutsch Entertains Our Nation.' During the 1930s Deutsch created an empire of 300 cinemas. Architecturally, Worthing was one of the most outstanding examples, shown here in 1934.

247 The auditorium of the Odeon, Worthing, in its opening year, with Compton organ on lift.

became an essential feature of the now celebrated Odeon style. Through the skill of architects Whinney, Son and Austen Hall, the Odeon Worthing made commanding use of an island site and introduced the tower feature that would become another Odeon characteristic. An Odeon sign and an Odeon clock were mounted on the flat-topped tower, which was lit from within at night. There was a rounded, flat-roofed two-storey wing extending forward as well as a lower, curving extension over the entrance. A canopy extended around the two curving sections and down one side of the building as a protection for queues. Areas of cream-yellow faience tiles carried thin projecting bands of jade green at the top edge and above and below the line of windows. The main auditorium block was in contrasting brick.

The Odeon had 1,531 seats—1,076 on the stalls floor and 455 in the balcony. The site was leased for 99 years at £1,250 per annum, the building cost was £32,500, there were £6,000 worth of furnishings and equipment and £2,200 of expenses, adding up to £40,700. Rent, mortgage interest and redemption amounted to approximately £80 per week. Though only half the claimed cost of the Plaza (which may have included the purchase of a freehold), this was very expensive compared to most other new Odeons, more than twice the cost of the Odeons at Lewes and Bognor Regis which opened later in 1934 but these, of course, were much smaller, seating under 1,000.

As a matter of general policy, Odeons avoided cafés or organs but exceptions were made, particularly at seaside locations and to compete with a rival cinema that offered them. These circumstances applied to Worthing (the Plaza had both café and organ, the Rivoli had an organ), and the Worthing Odeon prominently advertised its café on both the tower and the extension in which it was to be found.

The Odeon name was set in mosaic across the floor in front of the pay box, an unusual feature also seen at the later Odeon Well Hall in south-east London. The organ was a Compton of three manuals, six ranks plus solo cello, with a specially designed illuminated 'jelly mould' surround to the console which was on a centrally placed lift in front of the proscenium arch (the instrument was first played by Henry Wingfield). The auditorium was rather plain, apart from the bright carpet in Odeon circuit pattern, the illuminated grillework above the front side exits in the stalls and a huge central fitting in the middle of the ceiling which cast out indirect light from concentric, descending bands. There were also two plaques in bas relief immediately above the stalls front exits next to Odeon clocks.

The gala opening was attended by the M.P. for Worthing, Earl Winterton, and Oscar Deutsch. The manager was E.C. Colman, a cousin of the film star Ronald Colman. The opening night picture was a British comedy, *Aunt Sally*, starring Cicely Courtneidge.[227] As Robert Elleray notes in his book, *Worthing—Aspects of Change*, the arrival of the Odeon and the Plaza just before it had almost doubled the total of cinema seats in Worthing, with a population of 45,000, to around 6,500.[228]

Competition was fierce and large advertisements in the local papers were not uncommon. In the *Shoreham Herald* (8 July 1938), the Odeon manager, now G. Stevens, took out a half-page advertisement for the Polynesian epic *The Hurricane*, starring Jon Hall and Dorothy Lamour as native lovers, and as a further inducement offered 20 'Marama' dolls (named after the character played by Lamour), which performed a clockwork hula dance, as competition prizes for the best amateur reviews of the film.

Sir Sydney Samuelson's reminiscences of working at the Luxor Lancing are extensively featured elsewhere, and he also offered these memories of the Odeon:

The Odeon Worthing was the Rolls Royce. It was a strange building because it was wider than it was long—I suppose that was the site they had available and they had to do their best with it. It was definitely the luxury house of the area even though the Plaza had an organ just like the Odeon did (in my youth I always thought a cinema which had an organ was top flight). When *Snow White and the Seven Dwarfs* came out, it was a sensation—the first full-length cartoon, and it was a wonderful film. We never went to the cinema as kids—too expensive. *Snow White* was so special, my mother decided that she was not going to have her four children as the only

248 Bruce Denham (Danny Jones) at the organ of the Worthing Odeon.

249 *Right.* Advertisement for the Odeon, Worthing, from the *Shoreham Herald*, 6 June 1941.

250 *Below.* The Odeon in Worthing as it looked *c.*1974.

children of the school who had not seen *Snow White and the Seven Dwarfs*, and hang the expense—so on her Wednesday afternoon closing [she ran a shop] we went down the road and got on the bus to Worthing and we went up for this great event, to see *Snow White and the Seven Dwarfs*. And my mother said, 'One and four halves', and the girl in the box-office said, 'No half price for *Snow White*.' It was the difference between us being able to go and not go, and we didn't go. We went up the road to the Plaza and we saw Robert Taylor and Wallace Beery in *Stand Up and Fight*, Jane Withers in *Always in Trouble*, and the newsreel. I remember that so vividly—my mother's anger![229]

The Odeon functioned successfully for 40 years as a single-screen cinema, showing pre-releases concurrent with the West End of London during the holiday season. The last resident organist was Danny Jones, who used the stage name of Bruce Denham. The organ was removed in 1962 and broken down. On 6 July 1964, a new restaurant concept called the Corrola was launched on two floors. However, by the early 1970s, catering was leased to outside operators and there was a steak house based here.

In late March 1974, work started to convert the Odeon into a three-screen centre at a cost of £70,000 by the simple means of enclosing the area under the circle and dividing that down the middle into two small cinemas, each seating 120, with a new shared projection box at the back. The circle, seating 450, functioned as the largest cinema, Screen One, using the original screen, and from upstairs the cinema had not altered except for a slight extension of the mini-cinemas beyond the circle front and an empty front stalls area.[230]

Launched as the three-screen Odeon Film Centre on 6 June 1974 with *Papillon* in Screen One, *Sleeper* in Screen Two and a revival of *The Guns of Navarone* in Screen Three, the cinema gained a new lease of life that carried it into the 1980s. By this time the central light fitting in the auditorium was no longer in use. Externally, the clock had been taken off the side of the tower and the Odeon name no longer appeared at the top while the main neon sign above the entrance had been replaced by a smaller, modern sign in which the letters of the cinema name were in separate boxes that lit up inside.

At the lowest point in UK cinema admissions, in 1984, the Odeon was sold to a group of property developers during the autumn. But the cinema continued operating until the new owners were ready to proceed with their scheme. Although it had become 'uneconomic', Odeon's interest in keeping it functioning for as long as possible indicates that it was still trading profitably. In fact, the Odeon carried on for another two years, closing on 27 September 1986. The final films were *Aliens* in Screen One, *A Letter to Brezhnev* and *My Beautiful Laundrette* in Screen Two, and *FX Murder by Illusion* in Screen Three.

In the spring of 1987, English Heritage accepted the closed Odeon building for listing. Understandably upset at this last-minute threat to their scheme, the new owners of the property arranged a structural survey. Some-what surprisingly, this found that the tower and upper part of the façade were dangerous. Permission was therefore granted for the Odeon to be pulled down despite its listed status. The hair-dressing salon that was occupying the former café area remained open to the last possible minute, even when wooden panels were erected around the rest of the building in mid-September. The Odeon

was demolished by the end of the year and the site redeveloped as part of a shopping mall and offices. We shall not see its like again.

3 JUNE 1995
RITZ
UNION PLACE

The former Connaught Hall, opened on 7 October 1916, had been used for the 28 years before 1995 for building scenery and holding rehearsals for the Connaught Theatre adjoining. It retained its proscenium arch and elaborate Edwardian decor. A decision was taken to re-open the space as a multi-purpose venue with a separate entrance on Union Place, initially using it as a cinema, a low cost means of getting started and generating income for further restoration. Alternative comedy and fringe drama were among the other activities in mind. £30,000 was spent to provide basic cinema facilities, including 220 seats, and the first film shown was *Nell* on 3 June 1995. The aim is to achieve full refurbishment to its original Edwardian splendour by 1999.

Addenda: Worthing

The Pier Pavilion at Worthing holds a special place in the history of cinema in West Sussex. The reconstructed Pier was opened on 1 July 1889 and included a Pavilion at the seaward end. It was a popular venue for concerts during the season and in the week beginning 31 August 1896 staged Lieutenant Walter Cole's presentation of 'electric animated photographs'. This is the first known occasion in the county on which films were shown to a paying audience. The Pavilion had a seating capacity of 450 and continued to be put to occasional cinema use before the First World War. This Pavilion was destroyed by fire in September 1933, but meanwhile a new Pier Pavilion had been opened at the shore end in 1926 and this, refurbished in 1980-81, remains today.

The Theatre Royal is also associated with early cinema in Worthing. The original Georgian building of that name, situated in Ann Street, had ceased to function as a theatre in 1855, but retained a recognisable theatre front and was not demolished until 1970. Two of the earliest travelling exhibitors of animated pictures are advertised in the *Worthing Gazette* as visiting the Theatre Royal in 1896—John D. Ablett bringing Paul's Theatrograph on 27-28 November and Baruch Blaker his Cinematoscope on 11-12 December. It is possible that the old theatre had been brought back into use or that the shows occurred in the New Assembly Rooms on the west side of Bath Place. This latter building had hosted Joseph Poole's Myriorama in April 1896, and was to be converted a year later into a handsome 1,000-seat theatre and renamed the New Theatre Royal.[231]

The New Theatre Royal primarily staged live shows but also screened some films. Launched by F.E. Ovenden, it was run by the eminent local impresario C.A. Seebold from 1904 to 1922. Among the films seen here: newsreels during the First World War at intervals in the stage shows; presentations of special attractions like D.W. Griffith's *The Birth of a Nation* in 1917 and *Intolerance* in 1918; films on Sundays while it ran as a live theatre. It closed in 1929 and the

251 Exterior of the New Theatre Royal, Worthing, with notices announcing the proposed new Astoria cinema, *c.*1930.

following year an announcement was made that the building would be reconstructed to become an Astoria cinema, part of the new circuit being forged by veteran exhibitor E.E. Lyons under the name of National Provincial Astorias Ltd. of Astoria House, 82 Shaftesbury Avenue, London. The first of the Astorias was at Brighton where Lyons had for many years operated the Academy before selling it to Gaumont-British.

A board was erected above the canopy of the recently closed theatre advising 'Worthing's Astoria—The modern talkie theatre will be erected on this site—Tea rooms and lounges—Accommodation for 2000 persons'. The Astoria was to extend from an entrance on Bath Place through to Montague Gardens. The fly tower and stage area would have abutted the rear of F.W. Woolworth's 3d. and 6d. store.

Work finally began on reconstructing the theatre *c.*1934 and went on for 15 weeks, during which time the old auditorium was gutted. The project was then halted and never resumed. A combination of factors was responsible. The Plaza and Odeon had opened and the Astoria would have faced problems in obtaining important first-run films. Existing Astorias at Brighton and Purley were in financial difficulties, largely as a result of booking problems. And E.E. Lyons died on 9 August 1934. The building was completely demolished and a new Woolworth's occupied the site.

The records of the Gaumont-British company indicate that it held a site at West Worthing but no further details have come to light.

In November 1951, plans were announced to open an American-style drive-in cinema, to be designed by leading architect George Coles, but, like many other schemes for open-air cinemas, this never saw the light of day.

However, in 1996, the celebration of the Centenary of Cinema saw Homefield Park temporarily turned into a drive-in cinema, the first of its type in West Sussex, with an audience capacity of 1,600 (400 cars). The films shown, on 30-31 August, were *Jurassic Park* and the James Bond movie *GoldenEye*, with car radios used to obtain the soundtrack and the image projected onto a screen measuring 20m x 10m.

OTHER PART-TIME CINEMAS AND PLANS FOR NEW CINEMAS

This is a round-up of the film showings in smaller towns and villages of West Sussex and the unfulfilled plans for new cinemas (outside the towns featured earlier) that have come to light.

BALCOMBE

Erected by public subscription and opened in 1902, the Working Men's Club and Institute was subsequently rebuilt as a memorial to the men who gave their lives in the First World War. A brick and tile building regarded locally as one of the most impressive village halls in the country, it was named the Victory Hall and opened by Lord Denman of Balcombe Place on 10 November 1923. With a capacity of about 300, it was showing films once a week on Saturdays in the early 1930s, charging 5d. to 1s. 3d. The earliest films shown were silent as Bill Paine remembered them being accompanied by a man playing the piano.[232]

Minutes of the Hall Committee show that it was booked to Mr. E. Carter on 4 August 1939 for one month, at a fee of one guinea for 'cinema performing' on condition that there was a responsible person in charge as well as an operator. Mr. Carter continued to present films, as a further entry on 11 March 1940 offered him a reduction in the fee for his film show on Tuesday 5 March as a measles epidemic had cut the attendance.

Although the Committee felt that film shows were an asset to the village, it expressed doubts on 6 May 1940 about their future because of poor attendances. For the remainder of the war, it was the regular dances which attracted big numbers, being particularly popular with the Forces stationed nearby.

Cinema shows resumed after the war. Stuart Davis was quoted a fee of £2 per night for a four-week contract on 22 February 1946. In May members were expressing concern at the behaviour of children at the shows. In November, the cinema was running at a loss and by 19 December the programme had been suspended. However, there are references in the Committee Minutes to cinema performances in the hall in 1948 and 1949.[233]

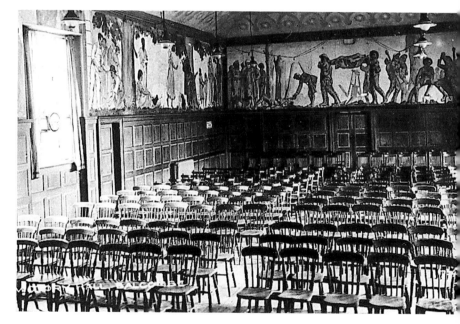

252 An interior view of the Victory Hall at Balcombe. Projection was through a small opening, covered up in this photograph, above the stretcher in the First World War frieze.

BILLINGSHURST

Arthur Barrett ran films here every Tuesday in the early 1920s, apparently calling his operation the Electric Cinema. He charged 4d. to 1s. 10d. Film shows continued at what was called the Village Hall Cinema but this was reported closed in 1927.

COPTHORNE

In September 1995, a planning application was made for a site just off the M23 at this small village between Crawley and East Grinstead. It was for a Homeworld complex which would have consisted of a ten-screen cinema with 2,250 seats and £20 million superstore/retail warehouse, plus parking for 1,300 cars. Co-Operative Retail Services were behind the scheme which faced strong opposition from Council planning advisers and was reported to have been withdrawn in February 1996 on legal advice.

CUCKFIELD

The Queen's Hall in the High Street was built to commemorate Queen Victoria's Diamond Jubilee in 1897 on a site given by Captain Charles Warden Sergison. It replaced the *Talbot Hotel* as the principal meeting place in the town for lectures, dances and concerts. The Blue Flash Cinema Company of Horsham set up a cinema in the Queen's Hall on Thursdays in the early 1920s, charging from 3d. to 2s. 4d. The hall had a capacity of 200.

EAST PRESTON

The Register of Cinematograph Licences granted by the Magistrates of Arundel Petty Sessional Division shows that a 12-month licence was granted to Arthur Harold Jeffries for the Young Men's Christian Association Hut at East Preston on 19 November 1923.[234] Jeffries, of South Norris, East Preston, was secretary of the local Y.M.C.A. Also used for local dramatic productions, the Hut had been given by Reginald Warren of Preston Place who before his death in 1911 had also donated the village cricket ground.[235]

The Register begins in April 1921 so it can be safely assumed that no licence had been granted in the two years before 1923. It is not clear when cinema ended as the surviving Register finishes in 1928 with films still showing at what was now called the Red Triangle Institute. Jeffries had remained as licensee until 1926, being succeeded by Edward R. Peaty who renewed the licence on 1 October 1928 for another 12 months.

The building continued to serve the parish well—providing accommodation for the library from 1949.

EAST WITTERING

Two proposals emerged at the end of 1934 to provide East Wittering with its own permanent cinema. One was submitted by London estate agents Clifton, German and Company in November for a cinema and entertainment hall to be called the Kursaal in Longlands Road. Designed by E. Brian Tyler of East Street, Chichester, the plans show a hall of 120ft. by 40ft. with stage, three dressing rooms and foyer, the cost to be nearly £5,000. The scheme was rejected by Chichester R.D.C.

253 The Church Hall at East Wittering was the main venue for Bill Floyd's mobile cinema in 1947-55.

on 21 December 1934 on the grounds that the cinema would be detrimental to a purely residential area.[236]

The second proposal was submitted by Mrs. Florence Mercy Wyatt of Meadowscroft on 18 December 1934. This was for the Wittering Cinema, to be built in Stocks Lane. The plans were informally approved on 15 January 1935 but that was the end of it.[237]

Films did come, however, to East Wittering after the Second World War when local resident W.J. Floyd set up a mobile cinema and made the Church Hall in East Wittering his principal venue. Originally known as the Parish Room, the hall was built around 1890 and extended in 1924. It was used for entertainments and even for a time as a school.

Bill Floyd, now aged 92, still lives in East Wittering and recalls setting up his travelling film show in 1947. While in the R.A.F. he had watched mobile film units at work and after demobilisation he purchased a Gaumont-British 16mm projector and hired films from such distributors as Warner Bros. and MGM.

His first main feature at East Wittering was *A Canterbury Tale*, and his presentations usually included a Pathé Gazette newsreel and a serial. A programme for August 1948 shows that he was then giving performances at 5.45 p.m. and 8 p.m. every Tuesday, including each week an episode of *Adventures of Tarzan*. Admission was 1s. 9d. for adults and 1s. for children.

The capacity of the hall was about 200 but Floyd remembers it was full only once, for *A Queen Is Crowned*, the Technicolor film of the coronation in 1953. Normally, there were fifty to sixty children at the early performance and perhaps thirty adults at the 8 p.m. show. Advertising was through posters displayed in the village and by printed programmes.

Monday became the regular night for East Wittering and on the other nights of the week Floyd would visit other village halls in the area. He was not allowed to show films within three miles of a 35mm cinema but eventually his village circuit included West Wittering, Birdham, Slindon, Yapton, Walberton, Eastergate, Eartham ('where seventeen or eighteen people was a full house'), Harting, and, in Hampshire, Horndean and Hambledon. These would have just one evening performance.

Floyd moved his equipment, including an 8ft. by 6ft. screen, in a Vauxhall station wagon, and his wife collected the money. His itinerary was extended to holiday camps— Newbeach at Earnley, Gibsons and Pontins at Bracklesham—and there he would also give children's matinees. He was also required to provide continuous performances rather than break to change reels, so he traded in his Gaumont projector for two De Brie 16mm projectors.

The village film shows continued until 1955 when they succumbed to the competition of television, but Floyd's work for the holiday camps went on into the 1960s. He was still providing a full season of film shows at Newbeach, from May to September in 1963, more than sixty years after the first travelling showmen had arrived in the county.[238]

The hall at East Wittering was demolished to make way for the St Anne's sheltered flatlets scheme, and a new Village Hall was opened in November 1976. After the closure of Chichester's last cinema, the Granada, there were for a time one-day presentations of films under the name Cinema One on Thursdays in the Village Hall.

EASTERGATE

The Arundel County Bench Minute Book reveals that the Rev. William Dennis Yoward, rector of the parish of St George, Eastergate, was granted a 12-month cinematograph licence at the County Bench on 14 November 1910 for the Parish Hall. He also took a six-month theatrical licence. The licences were renewed annually until October 1914 when they seem to have lapsed.[239] Built in 1908 at a cost of £2,000, the Parish Hall was considered the finest rural hall in Sussex. It was used for concerts and meetings, and could accommodate 450 people. Yoward was one of the benefactors and a progressive figure as, apart from embracing the cinema, he also owned the first motor car in the area.

HENFIELD

Films were being shown regularly at the Assembly Rooms in the High Street from 1924 or earlier. A red-brick building of three bays, it had been built by a private company in 1886 and was bought by the parish council in 1920. It had been used for stage shows and public meetings and had even housed German

254 A programme for Kinetours, a travelling cinema company which visited several villages in the county, 1944.

Kinetours Ltd.

VILLAGE CINEMAS

PRESENT

CINEMA SHOWS

at times and places detailed below.

Monday & Thurs. **STORRINGTON VILLAGE HALL.**

2 DISTINCT SHOWS AT 5.30 & 8.15 P.M.

Tues & Fridays **ASSEMBLY ROOMS HENFIELD.**

CONTINUOUS SHOW 6 TO 10.15 P.M

Wed. & Sats. **PULBOROUGH VILLAGE HALL.**

CONTINUOUS SHOW 6 TO 10.15 P.M.

Admission : 1/- and 1/9

Monday, Nov. 27th, for three days.
Anton Walbrook, Roger Livesy and Deborah Kerr in

THE LIFE & DEATH OF COLONEL BLIMP

THREE GREAT STARS IN A DELIGHTFUL STORY

Owing to extreme length of this grand film, the first show will commence at 5.30 p.m.

FILMED IN GLORIOUS TECHNICOLOR

A Great Film Week at your Village Cinema

Thursday, Nov. 30th, for three days.
YOUR FAVOURITE SONGSTRESS
Deanna Durbin in

HIS BUTLERS' SISTER

WITH
Franchot Tone and Pat O'Brien

PRICE ONE PENNY.

For the convenience of our patrons in Pulborough and District, there will be a matinee performance at 2.30 each Saturday until further notice.

---

prisoners of war before Joseph Johnson, its clerk, took out a cinematograph licence on 1 September 1924.

There may well have been previous licences but the records for 1919-23 have not survived. Subsequent Petty Sessions records, Agenda Books and Licence Registers, suggest that after 1924 the Assembly Rooms continued to be licensed for films for most of the inter-war period. A Licence Register for 1933 to 1942 shows that a new licence was granted to Joseph Johnson to commence 7 February 1933 for a year, prohibiting Sunday shows. This was seemingly not renewed on expiry, but a further licence was issued to Johnson starting 16 October 1934 and then renewed in his name every February until Percy J. Dewdney became the new licensee for the year commencing 14 February 1939, remaining so until February 1942 or later.[240]

In the late 1930s Henfield provided the venue for travelling shows presented by Kinetours Ltd. Based in Hove, this company was then visiting four West Sussex villages on a regular basis to set up a cinema on particular nights of the week. Henfield was its stopping place on Mondays, but it also served Pulborough, Steyning and Storrington, sub-sequently adding Slindon to its schedule.

Films continued during the Second World War and a programme for November 1944 reveals that by then Kinetours were presenting two different shows per week at the Assembly Rooms on Tuesday and Friday evenings (continuous from 6 p.m. to 10.15 p.m.). Admission was 1s. and 1s. 9d. The programme contains a mixed bag of films featuring such stars as Bing Crosby, Tommy Handley, Dorothy Lamour, Randolph Scott, Deanna Durbin and Alan Ladd.[241]

The Assembly Rooms was sold in 1974 and later converted to shops. The proceeds went towards the cost of a new £110,000 Village Hall opened in November of that year with an auditorium capable of seating 300.[242]

HURSTPIERPOINT

The Drill Hall Cinema was established during the period of 'silent' film production in the hall off the High Street, hidden from view behind a cottage. This was operated in the early 1920s on Mondays, Tuesdays, Thursdays and Saturdays by the Blue Flash Company of

Horsham, which offered two different programmes each week. The hall held 280 and seats were priced from 3d. to 2s. 4d. One of the pianists was Maurice Heathorn, later well-known locally as a sign painter. The building still stands as a nursery school.

Around 1929, the Chinese Gardens Cinema was opened in Western Road. This was attached to the *Chinese Gardens Hotel* and Pleasure Grounds that had opened on a five-and-a-half acre site in 1843. Once part of this former leisure complex, the *Pierpoint* public house survived until the mid-1990s. The cinema was first based in a blue tent (on what was latterly the site of the *Pierpoint*'s car park), and then in the nearest of the two halls alongside the public house, remaining in use as a reception hall until the entire site was replaced by houses. In the 1930s, a sign suspended from the end of the building carried the word 'Cinema'. Like the rest of the complex, the cinema had no Chinese trimmings despite its exotic name. Films seem to have been shown on certain nights of the week until the end of the 1940s. The equipment was brought by van and one local resident recalls the noise of the projector at the back of the hall and the chairs being of the movable variety, enabling the hall to be used for other functions.

PULBOROUGH

In 1910, the Corn Exchange (capacity: 250) was listed in a film trade annual as available for showing films. It was a popular venue for concerts, theatricals and penny readings. At the time it belonged to the *Swan Hotel* and still held a weekly market for corn. With the *Swan*, it was pulled down in 1958 to make way for the new *Swan Hotel* and shops.

By 1923, a part-time cinema was established on Wednesdays by Arthur Barrett, who also went to Billingshurst on Tuesdays, Storrington on Fridays and Steyning on Saturdays, and had earlier shown films in Petworth. Competition arrived in Pulborough in 1922 when the Blue Flash Company started the Swan Cinema on Mondays, charging 3d. to 2s. 4d., with a seating capacity of 150. This was presumably based in the Corn Exchange rather than another part of the *Swan Hotel*.

A single visiting cinema was operating here *c*.1929 to *c*.1936. Later in the decade and during the Second World War, the town was visited regularly by Kinetours Ltd. of Hove which presented film shows every Tuesday. However, a programme for November 1944 reveals that the company was at that time visiting Pulborough on two evenings a week —Wednesdays and Saturdays—and was

255 The Chinese Gardens at Hurstpierpoint. Films were shown in the hall with the pitched roof and chimney. A 'cinema' sign has been mounted on the end.

256 The Village Hall at Pulborough promoting the wartime epic, *In Which We Serve*, in 1944. The cinema was a great morale-booster, and in Britain weekly audiences averaged 25-30 million (half the population).

offering continuous performances from 6 p.m. to 10.15 p.m., with matinees on the Saturday at 2.30 p.m. Shows included the British Paramount newsreel. The manager at this time was Mr. C. Bowyer. The venue was the Village Hall in Lower Street which had been built in 1931-32, and admission cost 1s. and 1s. 9d. Noel Coward's morale-raising war drama *In Which We Serve* attracted packed audiences to the patriotically be-flagged hall.[243]

Here as elsewhere the rise of television put paid to the travelling village cinemas and there is no mention of film shows among the many activities at the Village Hall listed in the excellent W. I. Scrapbook of 1958.[244]

SLINDON

This was a later addition to the weekly schedule of the Kinetour travelling cinema operation, being visited on Wednesdays by the end of the Second World War.

STEYNING

The Public Hall in the High Street was built in 1886 at a cost of £2,200 by the Steyning Public Hall and Assembly Rooms Company. It was used for public functions and theatricals, and contained billiard and reading rooms. The secretary, Douglas Wood, was the licensee.

In 1910, the Public Hall was offering Shanly's Animated Pictures. (Michael W. Shanly operated early cinemas in Bognor, Littlehampton, Worthing and elsewhere outside West Sussex.) One source gives the cinema capacity as 300, but *Kelly's Directory of Sussex* (1909) suggests 400.

The secretary in the early 1920s was John Arthur Cornwell, and in the Petty Sessions Agenda Books it is in his name that the annual cinematograph licences were granted. By this time the building is being called the Town Hall.[245]

In 1922, the Blue Flash Company of Horsham put on different shows at the Town Hall on Wednesdays and Fridays with seats for 200 priced from 3d. to 2s. 4d. On Saturdays, Arthur Barrett arrived with his show, charging 4d. to 1s. 10d.

The Town Hall continued to be licensed for cinematograph purposes in the 1930s under the name of its secretary, Walter William Rapley, who was succeeded by Charles Bateman from 11 February 1941.[246]

In the late 1930s, Kinetours, the company based in Hove, visited Steyning on Thursdays to present film shows which continued until at least 1945.[247]

STORRINGTON

The Village Hall at Storrington was hired out to travelling cinema operators from the early 1920s. Built in 1894 on land in West Street donated by the Rector, it served a variety of purposes with its stage hired out for concerts and theatrical entertainments and its facilities including a library and billiard room.

By 1922, according to the *Kinematograph Year Book*, there was a choice of travelling cinemas on Fridays. Arthur Barrett offered one show, charging 4d. to 1s. 10d. (In *Storrington in Living Memory*, Joan Ham reproduces a photograph of the Village Hall showing the sign 'Picture Theatre' over the entrance. This dates from the mid-1920s and includes Arthur Barrett standing in a group outside the building.)[248] The rival show was that of the Blue Flash Company of Horsham which set up the Village Hall Cinema, pricing admission from 3d. to 2s. 4d., with seats for 200. However, it is unlikely that this competition continued for long. The Agenda Books for Shoreham Petty Sessions are missing for 1919-23 but when the series resumes Harold Gordon Beckett appears on 24 March 1924 applying for a cinematograph licence for the Village Hall. This was renewed annually until 26 March 1928 (in the name of D.E. Beckett) after which the Agenda Books are again unavailable.[249]

Ron Ham has gathered some recollections of early cinema in the Village Hall from long-time residents of Storrington:

A screen, about 10ft. by 8ft., was installed on the Village Hall stage and the projector was in a 'box' near the entrance of the hall. In the early days a pianist accompanied the silent films and the audience had to wait between reels while one was removed and the next one was loaded and the projector laced up. Each reel ran for about 20 minutes and the crowd would start barracking if the change took too long. Many feature films were three or four reelers, so at least two breaks in the film's continuity were required for this operation.

One said that, as a lad, he rewound the films on a hand re-winder after each one was shown and in addition it was his job to creep up to the stage to tell the pianist to play faster or slower, whichever the subject matter on the next reel demanded. One lady said 'I could not go to the pictures unless my brother took me' and added that it cost threepence or sixpence to go in.[250]

257 Storrington Village Hall in the mid-1920s. Arthur Barrett is third left and the sign for his 'Picture Theatre' is visible over the entrance.

FORTHCOMING CINEMA ATTRACTIONS

Later in the 1930s and early 1940s, films were presented by Ronald Vine, who owned a wireless and electrical shop in the Square. (He was co-licensee of the Village Hall with Daisy Mary Ellis from 7 February 1933—or earlier—to 13 November 1934 when Jacob Behr took over. No issue of a licence was recorded for 1935-36, then one was issued to Alan James Wood Morrison on 27 October 1936 and renewed annually to 12 February 1941.)[251]

A true cine enthusiast, Vine showed films at children's parties in their homes and for public entertainment in a number of nearby village halls. He hired cartoons and feature films on various gauges—9.5mm, 16mm, 35mm—to suit the occasion.

Ron Ham, his nephew, still retains the carbon arc unit that was used as the light source for his 35mm projector in halls where strong illumination was required for a long 'throw' between the projection box and the screen. In places where there was no electricity, the arc, projector and lighting were powered by a petrol-electric generator mounted in the back of a lorry parked outside the venue.

In her book, Joan Ham records the night when Ron Vine slipped away, leaving two re-wind boys in charge, and returned to find that a slip in the mechanism had clawed a row of jagged holes along the middle of an entire reel of film. He spent hours ironing the film flat again before returning it to the distributor. A happy-go-lucky character, he was undaunted by most situations, even when his lorry and generator burst into flames.[252]

The Hove-based Kinetours company was also active in presenting films here, hiring the Village Hall on Fridays from the late 1930s for many years. During the Second World War attendances were boosted by the hundreds of Canadian soldiers based in camps in and around the village. In return, they allowed many locals to visit their own temporary cinemas behind the wire.

The billiard room at the hall was an A.R.P. post and Joan Ham records that the Wardens, when 'on call', would watch the films in reverse from behind the screen on the stage.

People remember the travelling cinema coming on Friday nights but a Kinetours schedule for November 1944 reveals that it was then presenting two separate programmes a week in Storrington, on Mondays and Thursdays, each with two shows at 5.30 p.m. and 8.15 p.m. In the final week of that month, locals could watch two 1943 productions: the British film *The Life and Death of Colonel Blimp* and then the Deanna Durbin musical comedy *His Butler's Sister*. Admission was 1s. and 1s. 9d.[253]

The village cinema is fondly remembered as much for being a social occasion as a source of entertainment. Today the Village Hall is still used for local events and evidence of the long disused projection box can be seen, ingloriously, in the ladies' toilet.

WEST HOATHLY

In 1946 as cinema attendances shot up nationally, Granada, a leading cinema circuit, decided to branch out into 16mm temporary screenings. It formed Century Mobile Cinemas, planning to set up seven units that would tour Surrey and Sussex. The first of these started operations at West Hoathly on 28 October 1946.

Each of the cinemas used two B.T.-H. projectors and offered two performances on a fixed night or nights of the week, charging 1s. 9d. for adults (children 1s. and 1s. 3d.), using an 8ft. 6in. Turner screen. No other locations have come to light, although plans were made for screenings at Liphook in Hampshire. This venture did not last long.

Appendix 1

FILMS OF CECIL HEPWORTH SHOT IN BOGNOR, 1907-08

The following short films, made by Cecil Hepworth and Lewin Fitzhamon, are listed as having been shot in Bognor (see Chapter 2).

As other films made in this period by the same company are listed without locations, it is possible that if they survive they might, on close scrutiny, also be attributed to Bognor. Equally, other titles, not listed but referred to in recollections, might indicate that more films were made in Bognor than those listed below.

August 1907

A Sailor's Lass. CHASE. Cast: Dolly Lupone, Lewin Fitzhamon.

Simpkin's Saturday Off (200ft.). CHASE. Cast: Thurston Harris.

A Seaside Girl (325ft.). CHASE. Cast: May Clark, Frank Wilson, Thurston Harris.

September 1907

A Tramp's Dream of Wealth (425ft.). COMEDY. Cast: Thurston Harris, Gertie Potter.

Dumb Sagacity (450ft.). ANIMAL RESCUE. Cast: Gertie Potter.

October 1907

A Letter in the Sand (200ft.). CHASE. Cast: Dolly Lupone, Thurston Harris.

The Artful Lovers (300ft.). COMEDY. Cast: Thurston Harris, May Clark, Dolly Lupone, Frank Wilson.

November 1907

Dying of Thirst (175ft.). ADVENTURE.

The Heavenly Twins (350ft.). COMEDY. Cast: Thurston Harris, Gertie Potter.

Persevering Edwin (400ft.). COMEDY. Cast: May Clark, Thurston Harris.

September 1908

A Thoughtless Beauty (400ft.). COMEDY. Cast: Gertie Potter. Retitled *Forced to Consent* (275ft.).

A Fascinating Game (250ft.). COMEDY. Cast: Gertie Potter.

An Unfortunate Bathe (275ft.). COMEDY. Cast: Gertie Potter.

October 1908

The Schoolboys' Revolt (250ft.). COMEDY. Cast: Bertie Potter, Gertie Potter.

The Nursemaid's Dream (450ft.). TRICK. Cast: Gertie Potter.

Source: *British Film Catalogue*. Denis Gifford (David and Charles, 1986).

Appendix 2

FEATURE FILM-MAKING AT THE SHOREHAM STUDIO

This list is of all the known productions made at Shoreham, 1919-23.

THE PROGRESS FILM COMPANY

1919

Sweet and Twenty   Director: Sidney Morgan. Cast: Joan Morgan, Langhorne Burton, Arthur Lennard.

Lady Noggs   Director: Sidney Morgan. Cast: Joan Morgan.

A Black Sheep Director: Sidney Morgan. Cast: Arthur Lennard.

The Scarlet Wooing Director: Sidney Morgan. Cast: Joan Morgan.

1920

Little Dorrit Director: Sidney Morgan. Cast: Lady Tree, Joan Morgan, Langhorne Burton.

Two Little Wooden Shoes Director: Sidney Morgan. Cast: Joan Morgan, Langhorne Burton.

The Woman of the Iron Bracelets Director: Sidney Morgan.

The Children of Gideon Director: Sidney Morgan. Cast: Joan Morgan, Arthur Lennard, Langhorne Burton.

By Berwyn Banks Director: Sidney Morgan. Cast: Arthur Lennard, Langhorne Burton.

A Man's Shadow Director: Sidney Morgan. Cast: Arthur Lennard, Langhorne Burton.

1921

Moth and Rust Director: Sidney Morgan. Cast: Sybil Thorndike, Langhorne Burton.

The Mayor of Casterbridge Director: Sidney Morgan. Cast: Fred Groves, Mavis Clare, Pauline Peters, Warwick Ward.

A Lowland Cinderella Director: Sidney Morgan. Cast: Joan Morgan.

1922

The Lilac Sunbonnet Director: Sidney Morgan. Cast: Joan Morgan, Arthur Lennard, Warwick Ward.

Fires of Innocence Director: Sidney Morgan. Cast: Joan Morgan, Arthur Lennard.

Rogues of the Turf Director: Wilfred Noy. Cast: Fred Groves.

Little Miss Nobody Director: Wilfred Noy.

WALTER WEST PRODUCTIONS

1923

Was She Justified Director: Walter West. Cast: Florence Turner.

Hornet's Nest Director: Walter West. Cast: Florence Turner.

Appendix 3

The rural charm and seaside vitality of West Sussex, plus its special attractions such as Arundel Castle, the Bluebell Railway, Gatwick Airport, Goodwood, Parham House and Petworth Park, have made the county a popular location for feature films. This list is based largely on *West Sussex on the Silver Screen*, a booklet published by West Sussex County Council in 1996, and grateful thanks are extended to its compiler, Martin O'Neill, and to all who contributed information. The list is not definitive—it excludes the Shoreham films which are listed in Appendix 2—and additional information would be welcomed by the authors of this book.

The films are listed chronologically, according to the year of their first showing, and alphabetically within individual years.

1913

King Charles. Wilfred Noy (Director). P.G. Ebbutt (Principal Star). Based on novel by Harrison Ainsworth (*Ovingdean Grange*). Subject: HISTORY. Scenes filmed in Steyning, notably Church Street.

1921

Tansy. Cecil Hepworth (D). Alma Taylor (S). Novel by Tickner Edwardes. ROMANCE. Downs around Burpham.

1922

The Wheels of Chance. Harold M. Shaw (D). George K. Arthur (S). Novel by H.G. Wells. COMEDY. Chichester, including Priory Road.

1930

Rookery Nook. Tom Walls (D). Ralph Lynn (S). Play by Ben Travers. COMEDY. Steyning.

1933

The Man from Toronto. Sinclair Hill (D). Jessie Matthews (S). Play by Douglas Murray. COMEDY. Amberley.

The Song of the Plough. John Baxter (D). Stewart Rome (S). DRAMA. Downs.

Up to the Neck. Jack Raymond (D). Ralph Lynn (S). COMEDY. Bognor.

1947

Black Narcissus. Michael Powell, Emeric Pressburger (D). Deborah Kerr (S). Novel by Rumer Godden. DRAMA, India. Leonardslee Gardens, near Horsham.

1948

Esther Waters. Ian Dalrymple, Peter Proud (D). Kathleen Ryan (S). Novel by George Moore. DRAMA, 1873-85. Mentions Shoreham and Goodwood, features shots of the Downs.

1951

Mr. Drake's Duck. Val Guest (D). Douglas Fairbanks Jnr. (S). Radio play by Ian Messiter. COMEDY. Filmed mostly in Steyning, notably in the old market behind the station and at Northover Farm.

1954

One Good Turn. John Paddy Carstairs (D). Norman Wisdom (S). COMEDY. Crawley High Street.

1957

Hell Drivers. C. Raker Endfield (D). Stanley Baker (S). CRIME. Ford Airfield.

1958

Battle of the V.1. Vernon Sewell (D). Michael Rennie (S). Book by Bernard Newman (*They Saved London*). WAR. Shoreham Harbour and Old Salts Farm, Lancing.

1961

Don't Bother to Knock. Cyril Frankel (D). Richard Todd (S). Novel by Clifford Hanley. COMEDY. West Wittering.

The Innocents. Jack Clayton (D). Deborah Kerr (S). Story by Henry James (*The Turn of the Screw*). FANTASY. Bluebell Railway.

1962

A Prize of Arms. Cliff Owen (D). Stanley Baker (S). CRIME. Arundel and along A27 in Angmering/Poling area.

The Punch and Judy Man. Jeremy Summers (D). Tony Hancock (S). COMEDY. Bognor Regis.

Waltz of the Toreadors. John Guillermin (D). Peter Sellers (S). Play by Jean Anouilh. COMEDY. Bluebell Railway and Parham Park.

1964

A Hard Day's Night. Richard Lester (D). 'The Beatles' (S). MUSICAL. Gatwick Airport.

1966

The Deadly Affair. Sidney Lumet (D). James Mason (S). Novel by John le Carré (*Call for the Dead*). CRIME. Gatwick Airport.

Khartoum. Basil Dearden (D). Charlton Heston (S). HISTORY. Bluebell Railway.

1967

Up the Junction. Peter Collinson (D). Suzy Kendall (S). Book by Nell Dunn. DRAMA. Worthing seafront.

1970

The Birthday Party. William Friedkin (D). Robert Shaw (S). Play by Harold Pinter. DRAMA. Worthing, notably Chapel Road, South Street and seafront.

The Man Who Had Power Over Women. John Krish (D). Rod Taylor (S). Novel by Gordon Williams. DRAMA. Gatwick Airport.

The Railway Children. Lionel Jeffries (D). Dinah Sheridan (S). Novel by E. Nesbit. CHILDREN, 1905. Disused railway, now Downs Link Way, a bridleway running between Steyning and Rudgwick.

1971

Mary Queen of Scots. Charles Jarrott (D). Vanessa Redgrave (S). HISTORY. Parham House.

1972

Savage Messiah. Ken Russell (D). Dorothy Tutin (S). Novel by H.S. Ede. DRAMA, 1910. Bluebell Railway and Arundel Wildfowl and Wetlands Centre.

1973

Adolf Hitler—My Part in his Downfall. Norman Cohen (D). Jim Dale (S). Book by Spike Milligan. COMEDY. Bluebell Railway.

1974

Mahler. Ken Russell (D). Robert Powell (S). MUSICAL. Bluebell Railway.

The Black Windmill. Don Siegel (D). Michael Caine (S). Novel by Clive Egleton (*Seven Days to a Killing*). CRIME. The windmill is 'Jack', the black tower mill at Clayton.

1975

Barry Lyndon. Stanley Kubrick (D). Ryan O'Neal (S). Novel by Thackeray (*The Memoirs of Barry Lyndon*). ADVENTURE, 1770. Wedding filmed at Petworth House Chapel.

Lisztomania. Ken Russell (D). Roger Daltrey (S). MUSICAL. Bluebell Railway.

Tommy. Ken Russell (D). Ann-Margret (S). Opera by Pete Townshend. MUSICAL. Bluebell Railway.

1978

Silver Bears. Ivan Passer (D). Michael Caine (S). Novel by Paul Erdman. CRIME. Petworth House.

1979

Dracula. John Badham (D). Frank Langella (S). Novel by Bram Stoker. HORROR, 1913. Bluebell Railway.

1981

Tess. Roman Polanski (D). Nastassja Kinski (S). Novel by Thomas Hardy (*Tess of the d'Urbervilles*). DRAMA, period. Bluebell Railway.

1985

Dance with a Stranger. Mike Newell (D). Miranda Richardson (S). CRIME, 1953. Goodwood and Worthing beach.

A Room with a View. James Ivory (D). Maggie Smith (S). Novel by E.M. Forster. COMEDY/DRAMA, begins 1907. Bluebell Railway.

A View to a Kill. John Glen (D). Roger Moore (S). James Bond film. CRIME. Amberley Chalk Pits and Chichester Harbour.

1987

Wish You Were Here. David Leland (D). Emily Lloyd (S). ROMANCE/DRAMA, 1950's. Worthing and Bognor Regis. Rustington Village Hall.

1988

Tree of Hands. Giles Foster (D). Helen Shaver (S). Novel by Ruth Rendell. THRILLER. Gatwick Airport.

1991

The Power of One. John Avildsen (D). Stephen Dorff (S). DRAMA, South Africa, 1930's. Christ's Hospital, Horsham.

Where Angels Fear to Tread. Charles Sturridge (D). Helena Bonham Carter (S). Novel by E.M. Forster. DRAMA, Edwardian. Bluebell Railway, Horsted Keynes end.

1992

Blue Ice. Russell Mulcahy (D). Michael Caine (S). CRIME. Gatwick Airport.

Wild West. David Attwood (D). Naveen Andrews (S). DRAMA. Gatwick Airport.

1993

The Young Americans. Danny Cannon (D). Harvey Keitel (S). CRIME. Gatwick Airport.

1994

Black Beauty. Caroline Thompson (D). Sean Bean (S). Novel by Anna Sewell. DRAMA. Bluebell Railway and Horsted Keynes station.

The Madness of King George. Nicholas Hytner (D). Nigel Hawthorne (S). HISTORY. Arundel Castle.

1995

Haunted. Lewis Gilbert (D). Aidan Quinn (S). Novel by James Herbert. DRAMA, early 1900's. Parham House. Christ's Hospital, Horsham.

Appendix 4

PRINCIPAL CINEMAS IN WEST SUSSEX

The following is a list of the buildings regularly used for cinematograph shows together with their opening dates.

Arundel	Electric Palace	Queen Street	22 Jul 1912	Church Hall
	Arun	Queen Street	9 Jan 1939	Purpose-built
Bognor	Pier Pavilion	Bognor Pier	1 Aug 1908	Pavilion
	Olympian Gardens	Esplanade	14 Nov 1910	Concert Hall
	Pier Picture Palace	Bognor Pier	3 Jun 1911	Purpose-built
	Kursaal/Theatre Royal	Belmont Street	Jun 1911	Purpose-built
	Pier Theatre/ Pier Cinema	Bognor Pier	10 Sep 1911	Theatre
	Picturedrome/ Cannon/ABC	Canada Grove	5 Jun 1919	Assembly Rooms
	Odeon/Regal	London Road	14 Jul 1934	Purpose-built
	Odeon 1 & 2	Butlin's	26 Apr 1994	Purpose-built
Burgess Hill	The Cinema/ Scala	Cyprus Road	c.1913	Purpose-built
	Scala/Orion	Cyprus Road	3 Dec 1928	Purpose-built
Chichester	Poole's/Exchange/ Granada	East Street	May 1910	Corn Exchange
	Olympia Electric Theatre	Northgate	1 May 1911	Purpose-built
	Picturedrome/ Plaza/Odeon	South Street	26 Jul 1920	Purpose-built
	Gaumont	Eastgate	20 Sep 1937	Purpose-built
	New Park Film Centre	New Park Road	1982	Former school
Crawley	'The Tin Hut'	East Park	pre-1911	–
	Imperial Picture Theatre	Brighton Road	1911	Purpose-built
	Victoria Picture Theatre	High Street	pre-1914	–
	Imperial Cinema	Brighton Road	20 Jul 1929	Purpose-built
	Embassy/Cannon /ABC	High Street	1 Aug 1938	Purpose-built
East Grinstead	Whitehall	London Road	1910	Grosvenor Hall
	Cinema de Luxe/ Solarius	London Road	c.1913	Public Hall
	Radio Centre/ Classic	King Street	11 Apr 1936	Purpose-built
	Atrium Cinemas	King Street	4 Aug 1995	Purpose-built
Hassocks	Studio/Orion	Keymer Road	28 Nov 1938	Purpose-built

Haywards Heath	Heath Theatre	Broadway	26 Dec 1911	Garage
	Broadway	Broadway	12 Sep 1932	Purpose-built
	Perrymount	Perrymount Road	30 May 1936	Purpose-built
	The Platform Cinema	Burrell Road	2 Jul 1993	Theatre
Horsham	Gem Picture Theatre	Albion Road	c.1908	Conversion
	Central Picture Hall/Winter Garden	North Street	13 Oct 1910	Purpose-built
	Carfax Electric Theatre	Carfax	c.Oct 1911	Purpose-built
	Capitol	London Road	7 Nov 1923	Purpose-built
	Ritz/ABC/ Arts Centre	North Street	13 Jun 1936	Purpose-built
	Odeon/Classic/ Mecca	North Street	7 Oct 1936	Purpose-built
Lancing	Odeon/Regal/ Odeon	Penhill Road	31 Oct 1933	Purpose-built
	Luxor	South Street	17 Jan 1940	Purpose-built
Littlehampton	Electric Picture Palace/Regent	Terminus Road	11 May 1911	Terminus Hall
	Olympic/Empire/ Palladium	Church Street	16 Dec 1912	Olympic Hall
	Odeon/Classic	High Street	23 May 1936	Purpose-built
Midhurst	Electric Cinema/ Orion	North Street	1910	Public Hall
Petworth	Pictorium	Market Square	pre-1914	Swan Assembly Rooms
	Picturedrome	Pound Street	1926	Purpose-built
	Regal	Midhurst Road	6 May 1937	Purpose-built
Selsey	Selsey Cinema/ Pavilion	High Street	1913	Selsey Hall
Shoreham	Winton's Hall/ Star/Court Kinema	Church Street	28 Feb 1910	Church
	Bijou Electric/ Duke of York's	High Street	c. Jun 1911	'Garage'
	Coliseum	New Road	1920	Theatre
	Norfolk/Ritz	Victoria Road	27 Mar 1933	Purpose-built
Southwick	Picture House/ Plaza/ New Kinema	Albion Street	24 Mar 1924	Depot and stable
Worthing	Winter Hall	Portland Road	1906	Chapel
	St James's Hall	Montague Street	1908	Chapel
	Cinema Elite	Gratwicke Road	1911	Skating Rink
	Kursaal Electric Theatre	Marine Parade	7 Oct 1911	Purpose-built
	Picturedrome/ Connaught	Union Place	29 Jul 1914	Purpose-built
	Dome Cinema	Marine Parade	18 Jul 1921	Coronation Hall
	Rivoli	Chapel Road	10 Mar 1924	Purpose-built
	Plaza	Rowlands Road	14 Dec 1933	Purpose-built
	Odeon	Liverpool Gardens	24 Mar 1934	Purpose-built
	Ritz	Union Place	3 June 1995	Connaught Hall

Appendix 5

SOUTH EAST FILM & VIDEO ARCHIVE
collecting and preserving a century of moving images

Since 1895 'moving pictures' have been made in the South East of England. This rich history includes documentaries, newsreels, advertisements, features, television programmes, artists' films and videotapes and 'home movies'. Much of this heritage has already been destroyed. What remains has until now been largely inaccessible and forgotten.

We have already lost forever most of the film made in the silent period (c.1891-1929). The National Film & Television Archive in London estimates that only 17 per cent of all pre-1929 British work has survived. The destruction of this history took place because many believed that these early films had no commercial value with the coming of sound. This tragedy took place before the first film archives came into existence in the 1930s and long before the arrival of the first regional film archives in Britain in the 1970s.

Not only do we have a lost history, but the films which have survived are also in danger. Film is a very fragile medium. It is easily torn and scratched through repeated use and all films on film stock manufactured up to the 1950s are now chemically unstable and therefore in a state of natural decomposition. Nitrate film, the medium for most professional film production from the 1890s to 1951, is highly inflammable and can self-combust. Old films made on 16mm and 9.5mm are beginning to shrink and will not survive without proper archival care. Early colour stock is now fading. And we should have no confidence in the long-term preservation of film on videotape as we do not yet know its lifespan.

The South East Film & Video Archive (SEFVA) was established in 1992. The function of this regional film and video archive is to locate, collect, preserve and promote films and videotapes made in the four counties of Surrey, Kent, East Sussex and West Sussex. SEFVA is committed to establishing and maintaining a public collection of moving images, addressing the particular problems of nitrate film, developing SEFVA Study Centres across the region and promoting the Archive through projects with record offices, museums, schools, libraries, societies and businesses. Our collection is housed at our Conservation Centre at the West Sussex Record Office in Chichester and our office is located at the University of Brighton.

The SEFVA Collection now stands at around 400 items. This material has come from record offices, museums and private collections across the region. It includes newsreels, corporate documentaries, feature films from the Progress Film Company of Shoreham (1919-1921) and promotional material produced for the Royal Sussex Regiment between the 1920s and 1950s. We are building a 20th-century moving image history of this region.

SEFVA exists because of the support it receives from the University of Brighton, the County Councils of Surrey, Kent, East Sussex and West Sussex, the Borough Councils of Brighton and Hove, Hove Museum & Art Gallery, South East Arts and the British Film Institute.

SEFVA is searching for moving images which show any aspects of life and work in the South East. Items may be either donated or deposited for long-term loan or lent for copying. The Archive will respect the wishes of all donors and observe all copyright. The Archive can be contacted through the West Sussex Record Office at County Hall, Chichester. (tel: 01243-533911).

Footnotes

Chapter One

1. *Worthing Gazette*, 26 August 1896.
2. *Cinema and Technology: Image, Sound, Colour*. Steve Neale (Macmillan, 1985).

Chapter Two

1. See *The Rise of the Cinema in Great Britain*. J. Barnes (Bishopsgate Press, 1983). John Barnes is the great historian of Victorian Cinema and all studies of this field rely on his scholarship.
2. *Edison's Invention of the Kineto-Phonograph*. W.K.L. Dickson and Antonia Dickson. *The Century*, June 1894.
3. *Optical Magic Lantern Journal*, Vol.9 No.108, May 1898, pp.198-199, as quoted in *The Pioneers of the British Film*, J. Barnes (Bishopsgate Press, 1988).
4. *Came the Dawn. Memories of a Film Pioneer*. Cecil M. Hepworth (Phoenix House).
5. Chichester Institute of Higher Education. Gerard Young Collection, GY5005.
6. *Bognor Post*, 20 January 1951.
7. *Bognor Post*, 5 December 1959.
8. *Bognor Post*, 12 December 1959.
9. *Bognor Post*, 19 December 1959.
10. *Bognor Observer*, 24 July 1907; 8 July 1908; 14 July 1909.
11. *British Film Catalogue*. Denis Gifford (David and Charles, 1986).
12. *Bognor Post*, 29 April 1961; 7 December 1963; 16 May 1964.
13. *Littlehampton Observer*, 31 May 1911; 5 June 1912.
14. *Littlehampton Observer*, 12 June 1912.
15. *Littlehampton Observer*, 3 July 1912.
16. *Littlehampton Observer*, 14, 21 August 1912.
17. *Littlehampton Observer*, 16 October 1912.
18. *Littlehampton Observer*, 8 May, 27 November 1912.
19. *Littlehampton Observer*, 25 December 1912; 17 June 1914.
20. *Three Pennyworth of Dark*. Tony Hounsome (East Grinstead Town Museum, 1995).
21. *Popular Entertainment in Horsham 1880-1930*. Arthur Northcott (Mrs. Joan E. Northcott, 1988).
22. *Filming the Boer War*. J. Barnes (Bishopsgate Press, 1992). *Will Evans, the Musical Eccentric*, is in the collection of the National Film & Television Archive.
23. *The Bioscope*, 1 October 1914.
24. *Bungalow Town—Theatre and Film Colony*. N.E.B. Wolters (Shoreham, 1985).
25. *The Bioscope*, 1 July 1915.
26. A copy of the original plan is in the collection of Shoreham Library. Copies of the indentures are with the South East Film & Video Archive.
27. *The Bioscope*, 21 October 1918.
28. *Bungalow Town*, above.
29. From the interview with Stanley Mumford conducted by N.E.B. Wolters. Photocopy, South East Film & Video Archive.
30. *Bungalow Town*, above.
31. *The Bioscope*, 2 September 1920.
32. *The Bioscope*, 8 December 1921.
33. *Bungalow Town*, above.
34. Letter from Dennis Bird to the South East Film & Video Archive, 13 June 1995.

Chapter Three

1. *Pathéscope Monthly*, August-September 1931.
2. From an interview with Cecil Cramp, recorded by Alan Readman for the West Sussex Record Office, 27 June 1995.
3. *Bognor Post*, 10 February 1934.
4. *Bognor Post*, 24 February 1934.
5. *Bognor Post*, 10 March 1934; *Bognor Observer*, 7 March 1934; *Pathéscope Monthly*, August-September 1934.
6. From an interview with Vera Worthington, recorded by Alan Readman for the West Sussex Record Office, 5 September 1995.
7. *Bognor Observer*, 13 February 1935.
8. *Bognor Post*, 10 November 1934; *Bognor Observer*, 21 November 1934.
9. *Bognor Post*, 10 November 1934; *Bognor Observer*, 24 October, 14, 21 November 1934; *Amateur Cine World*, Vol. I No. 9, December 1934.
10. *Amateur Cine World*, Vol. II No. 4, July 1935.
11. *Bognor Observer*, 30 January, 6, 13, 20 February 1935.
12. *Amateur Cine World*, Vol. II No.6, September 1935; *Bognor Observer*, 21 August 1935.
13. *Bognor Observer*, 1 May 1935.
14. *Bognor Observer*, 11 March 1936.
15. *Amateur Cine World*, Vol. II No.5, August 1935.
16. *Amateur Cine World*, Vol. III No. 1, April 1936; Vol. III No. 3, June 1936; *Bognor Observer*, 11, 25 March 1936.
17. *Bognor Observer*, 20 February 1935; 18 March 1936.
18. *Bognor Observer*, 6, 20 May 1936.
19. *Bognor Observer*, 17, 24 June, 8, 15, 22 July 1936.
20. *Bognor Observer*, 22 July 1936; *Sight and Sound*, Vol. 5 No. 20, Winter 1936.
21. *Bognor Observer*, 17 March 1937.
22. *Bognor Post*, 13 March 1937; *Bognor Observer*, 17 March 1937; *Sight and Sound*, Vol. 6 No. 21, Spring 1937.
23. *Amateur Cine World*, Vol. IV No.4, July 1937; Vol. IV No. 6, September 1937; Vol. IV No. 11, February 1938.
24. *Bognor Post*, 26 March 1938; *West Sussex Gazette*, 24 March 1938; *Bognor Observer*, 23 March 1938.
25. *Amateur Cine World*, Vol. IV No. 11, February 1938.
26. *Amateur Cine World*, Vol. VI No. 1, April 1939.
27. *Amateur Cine World*, Vol. VI No. 1, April 1939.
28. *Bognor Post*, 23 November 1946.
29. *Sight and Sound*, Vol. 3 No. 12, Winter 1934-35, Vol. 3 No. 13 Spring 1935; *Chichester Observer*, 30 January, 6 February 1935; *Bognor Post*, 15 January 1938; *Yesterday Magazine*, No. 2, June 1988.
30. *Sight and Sound*, Vol. 4, No. 14, Summer 1935; *Chichester Observer*, 27 March 1935.
31. *Chichester Observer*, 29 May, 23 October, 6 November 1935.
32. *Chichester Observer*, 17 July, 23 October 1935.
33. *Chichester Observer*, 22 January 1936.

34. *Chichester Observer*, 17 July 1935; 4 March 1936.
35. *Sight and Sound*, Vol. 5 No. 18, Summer 1936; *Chichester Observer*, 18 March 1936.
36. *Chichester Observer*, 25 November 1936.
37. *Amateur Cine World*, Vol. II No. 5, August 1935.
38. *Lancing and Shoreham Times*, 25 October 1935.
39. *Lancing and Shoreham Times*, 1, 29 November 1935; *Amateur Cine World*, Vol. II No. 12, March 1936.
40. *Amateur Cine World*, Vol. III No. 2, May 1936.
41. *Lancing and Shoreham Times*, 1, 29 November 1935; 10 January 1936; *Amateur Cine World*, Vol. II No. 11, February 1936; Vol. II No. 12, March 1936.
42. *Lancing and Shoreham Times*, 25 October 1935; 17 January 1936; *Bognor Observer*, 29 January 1936.
43. *Shoreham, Lancing and District Times*, 3 July, 18 September 1936.
44. *Shoreham, Lancing and District Times*, 11 January 1936.
45. *Amateur Cine World*, Vol. V No. 2, May 1938.
46. *Littlehampton Post*, 2 April 1938.
47. *Littlehampton Post*, 16 April 1938; *Amateur Cine World*, Vol. V No. 3, June 1938.
48. WSRO, Cinema Reminiscences. Letter, 5 October 1995.
49. *Chichester Observer*, 27 June 1985.
50. WSRO, Cinema Reminiscences. Interview, 29 September 1995.
51. WSRO, Acc. 9317.
52. WSRO, Acc. 9813.
53. WSRO, Cinema Reminiscences. Letter, 5 October 1995.
54. WSRO, Cinema Reminiscences. Interview with Keith Baker, 11 April 1996.
55. *The Post*, 10 April 1986.
56. WSRO, Cinema Reminiscences. Interview, 11 May 1996.
57. WSRO, Cinema Reminiscences. Interview with Hugh Hale, 11 April 1996.

Chapter Four
1. *Worthing Gazette*, 26 August 1896.
2. Worthing Reference Library, Snewin Year Books.
3. *Worthing Gazette*, 25 November 1896.
4. *Worthing Gazette*, 2 December 1896.
5. *Worthing Gazette*, 9 December 1896.
6. *Worthing Gazette*, 16 December 1896.
7. *Edwardian Worthing. Eventful Era in a Lifeboat Town.* Rob Blann (Blann, 1991). See also the section on W.K.L. Dickson at Worthing in Chapter 2.
8. *West Sussex County Times*, 21 November 1896.
9. *West Sussex County Times*, 9 October 1897.
10. *West Sussex County Times*, 7 August 1897.
11. *West Sussex County Times*, 24 July 1897.
12. *West Sussex County Times*, 9 October 1897.
13. *West Sussex Gazette*, 24 December 1896.
14. *Chichester Observer*, 22 December 1897.
15. *The British Cinema.* Article by Marie Seton in *Sight and Sound*, Vol. 6, No. 21, Spring 1937.
16. *Chichester Observer*, 3 December 1987.
17. WSRO, Graylingwell Mss. AN/4; ZA/2/1.
18. WSRO, Graylingwell Ms. MJ/2/5.
19. See the section on Hepworth in Chapter 2.
20. WSRO, Graylingwell Mss. ZC/1-3.
21. WSRO, Graylingwell Mss. MJ/8/3-4.
22. *Chichester Observer*, 16 November 1898.
23. *Chichester Observer*, 8 February 1899.
24. *Chichester Observer*, 8 December 1897.
25. *Chichester Observer*, 26 July, 16 August 1899.
26. *Chichester Observer*, 5 September 1906.
27. *Bognor Post*, 20 January 1951.
28. *West Sussex Gazette*, 24 December 1896; 7 January 1897.
29. *Midhurst Times*, 27 August 1897.
30. *Midhurst Times*, 3 September 1897.

31. WSRO MP 461.
32. *Bognor Observer*, 9 October 1907.
33. *Cathedrals of the Movies. A History of British Cinemas and their Audiences.* David Atwell (Architectural Press, 1980); *Islington's Cinemas & Film Studios.* Chris Draper (London Borough of Islington).

Chapter Five
Much of the text for this chapter is based on information consolidated by Allen Eyles from various sources over a period of thirty years. Some details (such as the figures for building and outfitting Odeons) come from internal records given to him (or copied by him), others from conversations with managers and executives over the years.

1. *Littlehampton Observer*, 12 June 1912.
2. WSRO, Arundel Petty Sessions, Licensing Minute Book, 1877-1915.
3. WSRO, Arundel Petty Sessions, Licensing Minute Book, 1877-1915.
4. *Littlehampton Observer*, 9 September 1914.
5. WSRO, Arundel Petty Sessions, Register of Cinematograph Licences, 1921-28.
6. WSRO, BO/AR16/1/190.
7. *West Sussex Gazette*, 18 August 1938.
8. *West Sussex Gazette*, 12 January 1939.
9. *Bognor Post*, 7 November 1964.
10. *Bognor Observer*, 18 April 1957; *Bognor Post*, 7 November 1964.
11. WSRO, Add. Ms. 21,171.
12. WSRO, Add. Ms. 21,107.
13. *Bognor Observer*, 7 April, 12 May, 7 July 1909.
14. *Bognor Observer*, 12, 19 May, 23 June, 11, 25 August 1909.
15. *Bognor Observer*, 4 August 1909; WSRO, Add. Ms. 21,171; *Bognor Post*, 13 March 1965.
16. *Bognor Observer*, 21 November 1909.
17. *Bognor Observer*, 20 July 1910.
18. *Bognor Post*, 13 March 1965.
19. WSRO, Add. Ms. 21,108.
20. *Bognor Observer*, 15 June 1910.
21. WSRO, Chichester Petty Sessions, Cinema Licence Register, 1910-19.
22. WSRO, Add. Ms. 21,108.
23. *Bognor Observer*, 31 May 1911.
24. *Bognor Observer*, 14 June 1911; WSRO, Add. Ms. 21,108.
25. *Bognor Observer*, 7, 14 June, 19 July, 30 August 1911.
26. *Bognor Observer*, 13 September 1911.
27. *Bognor Observer*, 11 October 1911.
28. *Bognor Observer*, 17 April, 30 October, 27 November 1912.
29. *Bognor Observer*, 28 February, 30 October, 20 November 1912.
30. *A History of Bognor Regis.* Gerard Young (Phillimore, 1983).
31. *Bognor Observer*, 17, 31 May 1911; 5 September 1975.
32. WSRO, Chichester Petty Sessions, Cinema Licence Register, 1910-19.
33. *Bognor Observer*, 13 November 1912.
34. *Bognor Observer*, 9 April 1913.
35. *Bognor Observer*, 13 September, 1 November 1941.
36. *Bognor Observer*, 1 February, 10 May 1947; 5 September 1975.
37. *Bognor Post*, 1 July 1961.
38. WSRO, Chichester Petty Sessions, Cinema Licence Register, 1910-19; *Bognor Observer*, 13 September 1911.
39. *Bognor Observer*, 3 July 1912.
40. *Bognor Observer*, 30 October, 6, 13 November 1912.
41. *Bognor Observer*, 16 June 1969.
42. WSRO, Add. Ms. 21,179.
43. *Bognor Post*, 14 June 1969.
44. *Bognor Observer*, 18 September 1929.
45. *A Scene from the Paradise Rocks.* Unpublished memoirs of a Bognor childhood by Michael Alford.
46. *Bognor Observer*, 11 January 1969.
47. *Chichester Observer*, 8 December 1897.
48. *Bognor Observer*, 18, 25 September 1901; 22 March 1957.
49. *Bognor Observer*, 2 September 1908.
50. *Bognor Observer*, 17, 24 November 1909.
51. *Bognor Observer*, 9 October 1907; 3 May 1911.

52. *Bognor Observer*, 9 August 1911.

53. WSRO, Chichester Petty Sessions, Cinema Licence Register, 1910-19.

54. *Bognor Observer*, 14 February 1912.

55. WSRO, UD/BR16/1/1047; *Bognor Observer*, 19 March 1919.

56. *Bognor Observer*, 4 June 1919.

57. *Bognor Observer*, 19 March 1919; *Chichester Post*, 3 July 1926.

58. *Christmas at the Pictures*. Barbara Ovstedal. *Country Life*, 5 December 1968.

59. *Bognor Post*, 22 May 1971.

60. *Bognor Post*, 18 May 1968. Memories of Mrs. Eve White.

61. *Christmas at the Pictures*, above.

62. *Bognor Observer*, 30 April 1954; 7 September 1979.

63. *Bognor Post*, 21 April 1962.

64. *Bognor Post*, 7 June 1969.

65. *Bognor Post*, 2 July, 6 August 1983.

66. *Bognor Post*, 17 December 1983; 25 August 1984.

67. *Bognor Observer*, 18 July 1934.

68. *Bognor Observer*, 11 July 1934.

69. *Bognor Observer*, 10 September, 17 December 1954.

70. *Bognor Post*, 9 November 1963.

71. *Bognor Observer*, 24 June 1936.

72. *Bognor Observer*, 14 October 1993.

73. *Cinema is great survivor*. John Milbank, *Bognor Observer*, 28 September 1995.

74. WSRO, UD/BH35/3.

75. WSRO, UD/BH16/2/519.

76. Information condensed from *The Cinema at Burgess Hill*, in *Picture House*, No. 14/15, Spring 1990, and follow-up letter in No.16, pp.35-36, by John Fernee. Material used with the author's permission.

77. WSRO, Add. Mss. 5294, 5295.

78. *Chichester Observer*, 23 December 1896.

79. *Chichester Observer*, 27 October 1897.

80. *Chichester Observer*, 25 October 1899.

81. *Chichester Observer*, 13 February, 10 April 1901.

82. *Chichester Observer*, 11 September 1907.

83. *Chichester Observer*, 26 February 1908.

84. *Chichester Observer*, 13 May 1908.

85. Recounted in *The Early Days of Cinema in the City of Chichester*. Dr. Barbara Stewart Ely, *Chichester History*, No. 11, 1995.

86. WSRO, Chichester Petty Sessions, Cinema Licence Register, 1910-19.

87. *Chichester Observer*, 11, 18 January, 1 March 1911.

88. *Bognor Observer*, 1 June 1910; *Chichester Observer*, 18 January 1911.

89. *The Early Days of Cinema in the City of Chichester*, above.

90. *Chichester Observer*, 10 May 1911.

91. *Chichester Observer*, 11, 25 October 1911.

92. Letter from Bernard L. Mayer, *Chichester Observer*, 10 April 1964.

93. *The Early Days of Cinema in the City of Chichester*, above.

94. *Chichester Observer*, 28 April 1915; 25 October 1916.

95. WSRO, Cinema Reminiscences. Letter dated, 9 March 1995.

96. WSRO, Cinema Reminiscences. Letter dated, 11 January 1996.

97. *Chichester Observer*, 14 August 1929.

98. WSRO, Cinema Reminiscences. Letter dated, 11 January 1996.

99. *Chichester Observer*, 20 November 1948.

100. *Chichester Observer*, 15 August 1980.

101. WSRO, Chichester Petty Sessions, Cinema Licence Register, 1910-19.

102. *Chichester Observer*, 26 April, 3 May 1911; *West Sussex Gazette*, 4 May 1911.

103. *Chichester Observer*, 3 May 1911.

104. *Entertainment Yesterday and Today in Chichester*. Russell Burstow, *Chichester History*, Vol. III No.2, 1988.

105. *Chichester Observer*, 26 April 1911.

106. *Chichester Observer*, 24 May 1911.

107. *Chichester Observer*, 24 April 1912.

108. *Chichester Observer*, 8, 15 May 1912.

109. *Chichester Observer*, 22 May, 5 June 1912.

110. *Chichester Observer*, 3 February 1915.

111. WSRO, Cinema Reminiscences. Holden Ms. 26.

112. *Chichester Observer*, 8 February 1922.

113. *Chichester Observer*, 7 July 1920; 10 April 1967; *West Sussex Gazette*, 29 July 1920.

114. WSRO, Cinema Reminiscences. Letter dated, 11 January 1996.

115. *Bognor Observer*, 18 September 1929.

116. *Entertainment Yesterday and Today in Chichester*, above.

117. *Chichester Observer*, 23 December 1936.

118. WSRO, Cinema Reminiscences. Letter dated, 11 January 1996.

119. *Chichester Observer*, 22, 29 January 1960.

120. *Chichester Observer*, 7 October 1936.

121. *Chichester Observer*, 22 September 1937.

122. *Chichester Observer*, 7, 14 October 1960.

123. *Chichester Observer*, 6 June 1961; Chichester City Archives C32.

124. A fuller account of the rôle of film societies in Chichester is included in Chapter 3.

125. An account of the early screening of films at Graylingwell is included in Chapter 4.

126. Information on the early cinema history of Crawley has kindly been provided by Michael Goldsmith, author of *Around Crawley in Old Photographs* (Alan Sutton, 1991).

127. *Crawley and District in Old Picture Postcards*. Michael Goldsmith (Zalt Bommel, 1991).

128. *West Sussex Gazette*, 9 August 1928.

129. *West Sussex Gazette*, 25 July 1929.

130. WSRO, Add. Mss. 47,871-47,881; 48,391.

131. *Three Pennyworth of Dark*. Tony Hounsome (East Grinstead Town Museum, 1995).

132. *East Grinstead Courier*, 18 February 1955.

133. A fuller history of East Grinstead cinemas is contained in *Three Pennyworth of Dark*, and the authors are grateful to Tony Hounsome for permission to make use of his material in this section.

134. WSRO, RD/CU16/2/3280.

135. Much of this section is condensed from research by John Fernee and used with his permission.

136. WSRO, UD/CU16/2/91.

137. *Mid-Sussex Times*, 2 January 1912.

138. *Mid-Sussex Times*, 16 January 1912.

139. *Mid-Sussex Times*, 23, 30 January 1912.

140. *Mid-Sussex Times*, 15 June 1915.

141. *Mid-Sussex Times*, 28 December 1915.

142. *ex. inf.* Dennis Williams.

143. WSRO, UD/CU16/2/730, 734.

144. WSRO, UD/CU16/2/838.

145. *Popular Entertainment in Horsham 1880-1930*. Arthur Northcott (Mrs. Joan E. Northcott, 1988).

146. Horsham Museum Mss. Cinema Posters. Series C718-761.

147. WSRO MF 704.

148. *West Sussex County Times*, 7 May 1937.

149. WSRO MF 704.

150. *Popular Entertainment in Horsham 1880-1930*, above.

151. WSRO MF 704.

152. *West Sussex County Times*, 29 January 1937.

153. *Popular Entertainment in Horsham 1880-1930*, above.

154. WSRO, Cinema Reminiscences. Account of Albert Foster, 1943-51.

155. *West Sussex County Times*, 19 June 1936.

156. *West Sussex County Times*, 9 October 1936.

157. *West Sussex County Times*, 8 January 1937.

158. *West Sussex County Times*, 27 August 1954.

159. See Chapter 4 on Travelling Film Showmen for a fuller account of Horsham's early cinema history. Readers are also referred to Arthur Northcott's excellent booklet noted above.

160. WSRO, Steyning Petty Sessions, Register of Cinema Licences, 1934-42.

161. *Shoreham Herald*, 11, 25 January 1952.

162. *Shoreham Herald*, 19 January 1940.

163. A fuller version of this interview with Sir Sydney Samuelson is to be found in *Picture House*, the magazine of The Cinema Theatre Association, issue no. 21, Summer 1996.

164. *Shoreham Herald*, 25 June 1965.

165. *Bognor Observer*, 16 December 1908.

166. *Bognor Observer*, 28 July 1909.
167. *Bognor Observer*, 22, 29 September 1909.
168. *Littlehampton Observer*, 10, 31 August 1910.
169. *Littlehampton Observer*, 26 April 1911.
170. *Littlehampton Observer*, 17 May 1911.
171. *Littlehampton Observer*, 5 July 1911.
172. *Littlehampton Observer*, 30 August 1911.
173. *Littlehampton Observer*, 6 September, 13, 27 December 1911.
174. *Littlehampton Observer*, 24 January, 25 February 1912.
175. *Littlehampton Observer*, 13 March 1912.
176. *Littlehampton Observer*, 10, 24 April 1912.
177. *Littlehampton Observer*, 9 September 1914.
178. *Littlehampton Observer*, 25 November 1914.
179. WSRO, Arundel Petty Sessions, Licensing Minute Book, 1877-1915; Register of Cinematograph Licences, 1921-28.
180. *Littlehampton Observer*, 25 May, 1 June 1910.
181. *Littlehampton Observer*, 7 December 1910; 11 December 1912.
182. *Littlehampton Observer*, 18 December 1912.
183. *Littlehampton Observer*, 2 April 1913.
184. *Littlehampton Observer*, 1, 8 October 1913.
185. WSRO, Arundel Petty Sessions, Register of Cinematograph Licences, 1921-28.
186. WSRO, UD/LH16/2/356.
187. WSRO MP 461.
188. WSRO PH 262-264.
189. WSRO, Arundel Petty Sessions, Licensing Minute Book, 1877-1915.
190. Midhurst Town Guide, 1915.
191. *West Sussex Gazette*, 7 January 1897.
192. See Chapter 4 on Travelling Film Showmen for a fuller account of Midhurst's early cinema history.
193. WSRO, Midhurst Petty Sessions, Cinema file.
194. *Midhurst Then and Now*. Vic and Barbara Mitchell (Middleton Press, 1983).
195. Information from plans in the possession of Mr. and Mrs. J.A. Tupper of Selsey.
196. *Chichester Observer*, 30 July, 13 August 1913.
197. WSRO, Chichester Petty Sessions, Cinema Licence Register, 1910-19.
198. WSRO MP 111.
199. WSRO MP 113.
200. *Chichester Observer*, 7, 21 July 1926.
201. WSRO MP 113; *Chichester Observer*, 25 August 1926.
202. Cinema programmes in the possession of Mr. and Mrs. J.A. Tupper.
203. Born in 1902, Jack Tupper continues to live in Selsey with his wife Mollie, the daughter of F.W. Phipps. Having provided the piano accompaniment at Poole's and the Picturedrome in Chichester, he ran a garage and a dance band for some years, before taking over the proprietorship of the Selsey Pavilion in the early 1950s. WSRO, Cinema Reminiscences. Interview, 3 May 1996.
204. WSRO, Add. Mss. 7274, 7276.
205. WSRO, Add. Mss. 7271, 7272.
206. WSRO, Add. Ms. 7275.
207. WSRO, Add. Ms. 7276.
208. WSRO, Add. Ms. 7279.
209. *Memories of Shoreham* (Shoreham Society, 1994).
210. WSRO, Add. Ms. 7271.
211. WSRO, Steyning Petty Sessions, Register of Cinema Licences, 1934-42.
212. WSRO, Steyning Petty Sessions, Register of Cinema Licences, 1934-42.
213. WSRO, Add. Mss. 7271, 7279.
214. WSRO, Add. Ms. 7271.
215. WSRO, Add. Ms. 7272.
216. *Shoreham Herald*, 26 March 1948.
217. *The Dream Palaces of Worthing*. Fred T.P. Windsor (Mercia Cinema Society Publications, 1986).
218. *Worthing. A Pictorial History*. D. Robert Elleray (Phillimore, 1977).
219. Architectural and historical description of the Kursaal. R.A. King, Worthing Society, January 1989. (Worthing Reference Library).
220. *Worthing Gazette*, 1 March, 11 October, 20 December 1911.
221. *The Finest Kinema on the South Coast. The story of the Picturedrome Worthing*. John Willmer (New Connaught Theatre, 1994). This publication has enabled a much more accurate summary of the cinema's history to be presented, and is recommended as a source of further information and illustrations.
222. *The Dream Palaces of Worthing*, above.
223. *The Dream Palaces of Worthing*, above.
224. *Worthing Herald*, 22 January 1960.
225. *The Plaza, Worthing. Souvenir Programme of Grand Opening*.
226. *Shoreham Herald*, 6 December 1968.
227. *The Dream Palaces of Worthing*, above.
228. *Worthing. Aspects of Change*. D. Robert Elleray (Phillimore, 1985).
229. See footnote 163.
230. *Shoreham Herald*, 31 May 1974.
231. A fuller account of the early screening of films in Worthing is included in Chapter 4.
232. *Balcombe. The story of a Sussex village*. Leslie Fairweather (Balcombe Parish Council, 1981).
233. Minute Book in possession of Mrs. Chris Marks of Balcombe.
234. WSRO, Arundel Petty Sessions, Register of Cinematograph Licences, 1921-28.
235. WSRO, Add. Ms. 46,663.
236. WSRO, RD/CH16/1/4501.
237. WSRO, RD/CH16/1/4561; Chichester Petty Sessions, Cinema Papers.
238. WSRO, Cinema Reminiscences. Interview, 14 March 1996.
239. WSRO, Arundel Petty Sessions, Licensing Minute Book, 1877-1915.
240. WSRO, Steyning Petty Sessions, Register of Cinema Licences, 1934-42; Add.Mss. 7271-7279.
241. WSRO, Add. Ms. 29,528.
242. *Victoria County History of Sussex*, Vol. VI Pt III; *West Sussex Gazette*, 21 November 1974.
243. WSRO, Add. Ms. 29,528; MP 140; Garland N23,991.
244. WSRO MP 140.
245. WSRO, Add. Ms. 7279.
246. WSRO, Steyning Petty Sessions, Register of Cinema Licences, 1934-42.
247. WSRO, Add. Ms. 29,528.
248. *Storrington in Living Memory*. Joan Ham (Phillimore, 1982).
249. WSRO, Add. Mss. 7279, 7272.
250. WSRO, Cinema Reminiscences. *Some Memories of the Cinema in Storrington*. Ron Ham. (Unpublished, 1995).
251. WSRO, Steyning Petty Sessions, Register of Cinema Licences, 1934-42.
252. *Storrington in Living Memory*, above.
253. WSRO, Add. Ms. 29,528.

Index

compiled by Ann Hudson

Note: The index covers the main text and Appendices 1, 2, 3 and 5. Page references in italics indicate illustrations; major coverage is indicated by bold type.

EMI, 117
Empire Strikes Back, The, 102
Emsworth, 51, 52
Entering the Water, 5-6
Epsom, 111
Esher, 116
Esther Waters, 219
Evans, Joe, 15
Evans, Rosemary, 170
Evans, Will, 15, *16*
Eventographe, 53, 94
Evergreen, 105
Evershed–Martin, Leslie, 38
Every Night of the Week, 130

Face of a Fugitive, 161
Fairbanks, Douglas, senior, 62, 199
Falconer, David Henry, 102
Fascinating Game, A, 67, 217
Felix the Cat, 105
Fellick, David, 9
Fellick, G., 9
Felpham, 10, 27, 53
Ferring, 39, 40-1
Field, ____, 12
Filer, H., 161, 163
film sizes, 5, 23, 24, 44
film societies and cine clubs, amateur, 25-44
    post-war, 41-4
Finch, Horace, 131
Fire at Sea, 9, 10
Fire Brigade Call, The, 49, 51, 78
fires in cinemas, 57, 67
    Chichester, 104
    Crawley, 114
    Horsham, 144
    Littlehampton, 57, 159
    Selsey, 181
    Shoreham, 184
    Southwick, 188
    Worthing, 199
Fires of Innocence, 218
Fischer, Margarita, 80
Fitzhamon, Lewin, 8, 10, 217
Flavin, Frank, 12
Fleming, James, 79
Fletcher, Walter, 127, 130
Fletcher-Barnett Syndicate, 127, 130
Flight of the White Heron, 82
Flinn, Leo J., 122
Flint, W. Howard, 113
Floyd, B., 12
Floyd, W.J. (Bill), 211
Flude, ____ (wife of Claude), 66, 69, 75
Flude, Claude H.:
    at Pier Pavilion, 65, 66, 67-8
    at Pier Picture Palace, 69, 71
    at Pier Theatre, 75, 77, 81
Flying Fontaines, The, 161
Flying Leathernecks, 135
Flynn, Errol, 105

Following in Father's Footsteps, 12
Forbes, Molly, 147
Forced to Consent, 217
Ford, airfield, 33, 220
Ford, Harrison, 166
Formby, George, 117
Fortesque, Basil Edward, 82, 153, 154, 155, 156
Foster, Albert, 144
Foster and Paulin, Messrs., 39
Four Horsemen of the Apocalypse, The, 75
Fox Movietone Follies of 1929, 99
Fraser, Alan, 29, 33
Frazer-Granger, W., 154
Free Willy 2, 126
Freedman, A., 122-3
Freedman, Bill and Ben, 91
Freedman and Hauser, firm of, 122
Freeman, Frederick John, 88, 185, 186, 188
Freeman, Victor, 73, 166
Friese-Greene, William, 4
From Russia with Love, 186
Frozen Limits, The, 154
Fugitive, The, 166
Fuller, Loie, 47
FX Murder by Illusion, 207

Gadsdon, Charles, 113, 114
Gala (bingo company), 203
Gandhi, Mahatma, 36
Gardener, George Henry, 40
Garland, George, *177*
Garrison Triangle, 169
Gates, R.A., 151
Gatwick Airport, 220, 221, 222
Gaumont Film Company (later Gaumont-British):
    cinemas, 108, 208; Chichester, 59, 101, **108-12**
    circuit release, 85, 134, 149-50, 199
    films, 7, 163, 168-9
Gaumont-British Picture Corporation (GBPC), 108, 110
Gay, Walter, 130, 170
Gaynor, Janet, 62
G.B.-Kalee company, 89
GBPC *see* Gaumont-British Picture Corporation
Geils, John Douglas, 80-1, *80*
George V, King, film of convalescence in Bognor, 26, *35*, 36
German expressionism, 31
Gibbs, ____, 191
Gibson, Roger, 42
Gielgud, Sir John, 72
Gigi, 196
Glitter, Gary, 73
Glue, Bill, 44
Glynne, Mary, 25
Godiva Cinemas (Coventry), 72

Godman and Kay, 142, 145
Goepel, John, 118
GoldenEye, 208
Goldfinger, 165
Golds, Mabel, *171*
Goldsmith, Arthur T.W., 194
Goldsmith, G.A. ('Topsy'), 88
Goldsmith, Michael, 41, 43
Gompertz, Frederick, 108
Gone with the Wind, 121
Goodacre, R.P., 51
Goodnight Vienna, 134
Goodwood, 30, 39, 94, 104, 219, 221
Gorleston-on-Sea, 62
Gosport, 53
Grade Organisation, 117
Granada, 59, 100, 111, 203, 216
    Chichester, 100-2, 111
Grandma's Reading Glass, 4
Grant, Cary, 137
Grant, Debbie, 126
Graves, George, 15
Gray, W.J., 153
Great Toe Mystery, The, 132
Greaves, John Ephraim, 188
Green, C., 139
Greenshields, Archie, 98, 99-100, 105, 106
Grieves, Jeff, 91
Griffith, D.W., 207
Grinstead, East *see* East Grinstead
Grip of Ambition, The, 160
Group 9.5, 25, 44
Groves, Fred, 20, 218
Guermonprez, Harry ('Gomey'), 26, 29, *30,* 32, 34, 35, 40
    and *Cross Currents,* 28, 29
    newsreels, 26, 36
Guermonprez, Henry Leopold Foster, 26
Guile, ____, 12
Guinea Pig, The, 100
Guns of Navarone, The, 206

Hackman, F.T., 136
Hackman, John H., Ltd., 136
Hague, Henri, 111
Hailsham, 116, 156
Hale, Hugh, 44
Hall, Austen *see* Whinney, Son and Austen Hall
Hall, G.S., 98
Hall, Jon, 205
Halpern, Louis, 185, 186
Ham, Ron and Joan, 215, 216
Hambledon, 211
Hampton, John, 87
Hancock, W. and S., 49
Handley, Tommy, 72, 212
Hard Day's Night, A, 165, 220
Hardy, Oliver *see* Laurel and Hardy
Hardy, Thomas, 20
Harlow, 118

Filming *The Man from Toronto* in Amberley, 1932